Two Seasons In The Bubble

Two Seasons
In The Bubble

Living and Coaching Basketball in Bulgaria

By Andrew W. Jones 2/20/13

Lily —
What a thrill to have you reading my
book! Getting to know you as a student
and an athlete has been a great treat

Granny Apple Publishing LLC

for me — and no doubt about it, I
could've used your toughness and grit on
my Bulgarian team! I hope you enjoy
the book. HA3APA8E!
                          — Jones

Granny Apple Publishing, LLC, Sarasota, Florida 34241

GRANNY
APPLE
PUBLISHING

Cover design by Cal Sharp, Caligraphics
A complete list of reference sources begins on page 457.

Cataloging-in-Publication Data

Jones, Andrew W.
Two seasons in the bubble: living and coaching basketball in bulgaria / by Andrew W.
Jones
Granny Apple Publishing LLC advance trade pbk. Ed.
Includes bibliographical references.
Library of Congress Control Number: 2012954815
ISBN: 0985184485
EAN-13: 978-0-9851844-8-3
1. Autobiography 2. Sports

PRINTED IN THE UNITED STATES OF AMERICA

DEDICATION

To Skup:
You helped me through all these adventures
before they ever became a book.

CONTENTS

Dedication v

Author's Note ix

Prologue xi

SEASON ONE

I Open Gym 1

II The Learning Curve 7

III Tryouts 13

IV Modern Bulgaria 21

V An American Education 29

VI Shaking My Head 49

VII Bulgaria in Motion 61

VIII Commie Central 79

IX Cheater Cheater 93

X A Corrupt Christmas 121

XI Tom Robinson Visits Bulgaria 137

XII Thank God You're Not Bulgarian 149

XIII The Jewish Question 173

XIV Things Fall Apart 195

XV Success—That is All 209

SEASON TWO

XVI	A New Start	225
XVII	A Bunch of Strays	235
XVIII	The Cold War	255
XIX	The Turkish Toilet Turning Point	269
XX	Tough Guys	283
XXI	Character Counts	309
XXII	A Bloody Mess	331
XXIII	Bucharest Blues	341
XXIV	Second Class Citizens	359
XXV	Change Matters	387
XXVI	Taking Charge	401
XXVII	The Spanish Showdown	417
XXVIII	Lachoni's	437
	Epilogue	451
	Works Cited	457

AUTHOR'S NOTE

This book describes the author's experience while living in Bulgaria. Most names have been changed in order to protect people's privacy. The names of public and historical figures have not been changed.

PROLOGUE

On Tuesday, August 21, 2007, I was dropped off at O'Hare Airport in Chicago and got ready to board a LOT flight that would take me to Warsaw, Poland. From Warsaw, I would catch my connecting flight, and embark on a two-hour jaunt to Sofia, Bulgaria. This represented the first step in a journey that most people around me didn't seem to understand.

Five months earlier, when I'd announced that I would be leaving Chicago, leaving the place where my parents lived, leaving an apartment I shared with my brother, and taking a huge pay cut, there were few people who saw the logic in my decision. In fact, there were few people who even had any idea where or what Bulgaria was. As a result, after the initial shock of my decision wore off, I'd routinely receive well-wishes such as, "I hope you have fun in Bolivia," or "Enjoy Budapest," or my personal favorite, "Are you really going to Botswana?"

When skeptics—and everyone had at least a healthy dose of skepticism about my moving to Bulgaria for two years—asked me to explain my rationale, the ensuing explanation never fully satisfied anyone. I'd explain how I'd always loved to travel, and that was part of my motivation. I'd explain that, as a high school English teacher, I'd been teaching world literature classes and always telling my students they needed to broaden their horizons and understand the greater world around them. This advice sounded like something I shouldn't just say, but act upon, too. I'd also explain that I wasn't sure I was ready to become a tenured teacher and work at the same school for the next 30 years. But none of these reasons sufficed to completely explain what I was doing—at least in the eyes of friends and family, a few who thought I'd lost my mind. So, after about the twelfth time I was approached by someone who met me with a sour look and a scrunched-up face, saying, "Why are you moving to Bulgaria?" I finally found the most fitting answer:

"Why not?"

I knew I was leaving a great English teaching job and a fantastic basketball coaching job, too. I loved living in Chicago, and had no strong desire to leave. But at the same time, I was 27 years old and curious about the rest of the world. I was single, with no set plan for life, and eager to deviate from the road most traveled. And in the end, there weren't many answers to the question "Why not?" that were powerful enough to deter me. So I went to an international teaching fair and interviewed with schools from all over the globe—from China to Namibia to Aruba to Germany. But none of these interviews, and the job offers that eventually came with some of them, seemed as enticing as the offer I received from the American College of Sofia in Bulgaria. They wanted me to teach high school English and be their boys' varsity basketball coach. And when I was given this offer, I had no answer to the question, "Why not?" I was heading to Bulgaria.

When I accepted the job in Sofia, I knew next to nothing about Bulgaria. I could locate it on a map and that was about it. So I certainly did not head to Bulgaria with any grand project in mind, and writing a book about my experiences there was nowhere on my radar. The grand project, as I saw it, was moving to Bulgaria. Anything and everything that came next would qualify as a very distant second.

In the run-up to my departure, though, a colleague continued to insist that I should write a blog about my day-to-day experiences. At first, I chafed at this idea. I knew very little about blogs and assumed this would take a form similar to the mass emails I had received every once in a while from friends who would travel abroad and want to go on and on about the details of their trips. To me these had always seemed a little too self-serving and far too impersonal.

But my colleague kept hassling me. "A blog is different," he would say. "It will give you the opportunity to be a writer, and write about your experiences for those who will be interested in reading them." He knew nothing about Bulgaria, and promised me that barely anyone else in the States did either. No one, he kept telling me, ever moved to Bulgaria. I had to see this as an opportunity to start writing.

With a little more nudging, I was sold. And once I arrived in

Bulgaria and felt like my world was being flipped upside down on a daily basis, the blog became one of the favorite parts of my day. As I toured Sofia, my new home, and began to meet Bulgarian colleagues and students, I realized that every moment seemed to be a new opportunity to create a blog post about life in Bulgaria. I started blogging about seemingly everything—from an innocuous trip to the grocery store gone awry to the first days of basketball open gym. I still had no intention of my blog being anything more than a blog.

But the more I became immersed in my Bulgarian experience, the more I realized that I was probably in the middle of the most incredible time of my life. I had many experiences where I actually had no idea what was going on. And I started to feel that maybe this entire experience was turning into much more than I had ever bargained for.

During my time in Bulgaria, I'd already become an avid reader of all things Bulgarian—or at least as many things as I could find that were written in English. Reading the *Sofia Echo* was already a part of my daily routine, and the online English translation of the Bulgarian daily newspaper provided a constant flood of information about life in Bulgaria. My historical research was already partly complete through my readings while living there, and then it became even more thorough in preparing to write this book. I relied heavily on three different texts to provide different insights to life in Bulgaria. The historian R.J. Crampton's dense and lengthy study on Bulgaria proved invaluable as it laid the framework for Bulgarian history. Kapka Kassabova's memoir, *Street Without a Name*, provided first-hand accounts of life during the Cold War, and it turned out that the nameless street Kassabova grew up on was less than a mile from where I would make my home in Sofia. Finally, Robert Kaplan's combination of historical study and travelogue *Balkan Ghosts* was the text I was able to relate to the most. He studied the Balkans through the eyes of a traveling foreigner trying to make sense of what this area was like today as a result of where each country had come from.

But more than anything, the book relies on details I wrote in my blog—especially the exact quotes I wouldn't have otherwise been able to remember. Most of the direct quotes in this memoir are the exact remembrances I wrote down on the day the events occurred.

And as I started to write the book, I realized more and more just how signficantly Bulgaria had affected me—not only as a writer—but also as a person.

SEASON ONE

Chapter I
Open Gym

Pavel was the first one to come up to me.

And I really needed someone to come up to me.

What I was watching was supposed to be basketball. It was supposed to be the first day of open gym, and the unofficial first day of the 2007-2008 basketball season. But you certainly could've fooled me.

Passes were hurled behind the back to no one in particular, then flung one-handed overhand like errant birds desperately flailing, and in some cases, believe it or not, the passes were launched with no hands at all.

Offense consisted of who was actually willing to run all the way down the floor and yell loud enough for the ball. Even if this happened, your best bet at getting the ball was just jumping in the air amidst the scrum to retrieve one of the aforementioned passes–or even better, a shot that rocketed off the backboard.

Dribbling? Well, dribbling alternately looked like two different versions of football: 1) the American version of just rumbling down the court with the ball, and 2) the European version with feet playing a prominent role. There wasn't a whole lot of the proper version of basketball dribbling.

In lieu of dribbling the ball, I can't say there was a whole lot of sharing the ball either–or anything that remotely resembled a sense of team or teamwork. Yelling was frequently heard with each missed shot or errant pass. Hands were flung in the air in despair and frustration. Swear words were common, and encouragement was rare. All I had to do was watch two or three possessions and I could pick out a very consistent theme: "It's not my fault! It's yours! And I'm going to yell at you about it!"

And finally, there was defense.

Actually, there wasn't defense. The majority of the players hovered around half court ready to leap high and kick low to either deflect a pass or deflect a human body. But no matter if these attempts were successful or not, most players didn't plan to cross half court to play any more defense.

This was the varsity team.

This was my varsity team.

As I sat in a broken-down wooden chair at half court trying to keep my head up and out of my hands, I focused on keeping my eyes on the floor in front of me, but my vision wandered. *Where was I? What kind of gym was this?* An ominous white inflatable bubble roof loomed over my head, and with every new clank on the rims, the backboards and basket stanchions would shake. There was a net on one end of the court—but just one end of the court. The wooden floor could've reminded me of an old-school parquet, but instead it just looked dirty and slippery. The setting was befitting of the level of play.

For all these reasons, I really needed someone to come talk to me. Someone—anyone.

Pavel was not tall, but stocky. He had short, buzzed hair like so many of the other boys out on the floor. He happened to be one of the few who were hustling, but his version of running wasn't so much running as it was lumbering. He looked like he might hurt someone every time he got the ball or every time a ball carrier—yes, a ball carrier—came near him. Nothing about him made me think of a basketball player, but that seemed to fit with the afternoon in general.

"Coach, Coach," he said as he jogged over to me. "I'm so happy you're here, Coach."

As he extended his hand to me, I knew the appropriate response in this situation, yet somehow it seemed rather hollow coming out of my mouth: "I'm really happy to be here, too."

"My name is Pavel, and I'm really happy you're here."

His smile made me feel even guiltier. Did I have to tell him again how happy I was to be here? This was Sofia, Bulgaria—the American

College of Sofia—and all the images being played out in front of me didn't seem to add up to any semblance of happiness. Pavel continued smiling enthusiastically, and the guilt that I didn't share his enthusiasm continued to well up inside me.

"You know, Coach," he saved me by continuing, "I'm so excited you're here. I'm so excited we have a real coach now. Last year, we didn't really even have practice. The coach just stopped caring. He didn't even want to run practice when he was here."

I hated that I immediately felt a strong bond with the previous coach. What Pavel was saying should've sounded appalling, but as I watched a kid go up to try to dunk and come nowhere near the rim, violently chucking the ball off the wooden backboard, it made a whole lot of sense.

"Last year's coach just quit coming to practice halfway through the year. It wasn't even like we had a team anymore. This year—now this year, just look...."

That was the problem; I was looking. In the middle of an offensive possession, a shaggy, long-haired kid who was wearing loafers expressed his disgust at not getting passed the ball. He loudly bellowed in Bulgarian, thrusting his arms toward the bubble roof, and then immediately trudged off the court and walked straight out of the gym. He didn't say goodbye to anyone, and no one tried to convince him to stay.

"Well, Pavel," I responded, "I love basketball and I love coaching basketball. I won't quit halfway through the year. I think we have a chance to have a great year."

These seemed like the right things to say, but I was aware that saying them out loud just served the function of trying to convince myself what I was saying might possibly, just maybe, have a minute chance of being true.

"I love basketball, too, Coach, and I'm really looking forward to you coaching us. I can tell already that things are going to be different. I really want to work hard. And I promise you, I'm going to work my hardest for this team."

"Well, Pavel," I said, feeling this time that the exact truth was finally coming out of my mouth, "we're certainly going to need your hardest work. We're going to need your best effort."

"You'll get it, Coach. You'll get it, I promise."

I smiled at Pavel. His enthusiasm was easily the best part of the afternoon.

"We've got open gym again tomorrow, right?" he asked.

I paused as I looked out at the court. A kid in jeans and a Slayer t-shirt had just taken a three-point left-handed hook shot. It didn't hit the rim.

"Yes, Pavel. Yes, we have open gym tomorrow."

I really hoped I didn't sigh too audibly when I said that.

At 5:00, open gym ended and I gathered the "team," a rag-tag group of 20-plus boys, and thanked them for their enthusiasm and effort for the first day of open gym. I told them that as a team, we would improve and achieve success by working hard and working together. Today was the first step in this process. I looked forward to seeing them again tomorrow as we continued to get in shape for the season.

When I told them all to put their hands in the middle together as one, this prompted a lot of awkward facial expressions.

"But why? Why would we do that?" someone finally piped up.

"Because we're a team," I responded. "It's what we do together as a team."

The response seemed logical enough so the group of boys leaned in with their arms.

"So what do we say, Coach?" came the next question from the crowd.

"Team," I again responded right away.

"But why?"

This question seemed to resonate with far too many in the crowd, but thankfully I didn't need to respond. A few others in the group remembered the logic from my previous answer and filled in the blanks for the rest.

"One, two, three," I hollered.

"TEAM!" came the response.

While the kids seemed confused by me and this concept of team, that was nothing compared to the confusion I was feeling. It hadn't taken me long to realize that whatever kind of team this was, it wasn't normal to me. Whatever kind of gym we were playing in, it wasn't like anything I'd ever played or coached in before. Whatever kind of basketball I'd just witnessed, it wasn't like anything I'd ever seen before. They certainly weren't the only ones who needed to be convinced of the unity and success of this team. The convincing needed to start with the coach—a shell-shocked coach who was only starting to get an idea of what he was getting into.

TWO SEASONS IN THE BUBBLE

So I walked out of the gym as dusk was about to fall. It was cold. The gray sky foreshadowed rain that was certain to fall. To my right loomed a half-finished brick building–a desolate one that looked like it was half-finished 30 years ago. To my left was a giant concrete slab that purported to house hundreds of people. It was a drab row house that had stood the test of time—and architectural ugliness. I considered the ramshackle nature of this building and couldn't help but link it to the roughshod version of basketball I'd just witnessed. I'd always felt so much pride in the way my basketball teams played the game, but I was now leaving the gym with emotions far closer to bewilderment and despair than pride. My mind was loaded with doubts and searching for answers–searching for solutions to what looked like a problem that was well beyond anything I could handle. I gazed all around me at a world that couldn't have been more unfamiliar, and I felt resigned to the fact that I was walking to my new house and trying to look forward to my new life. At that moment, I tried to listen to my conscience; my best judgment was telling me to walk away.

But there was no walking away.

I was 5,000 miles away from home with nowhere in particular to walk to.

Chapter II
The Learning Curve

Throughout the first 27 years of my life, I don't know if I ever knew anything about Bulgaria. When the notion of going to Bulgaria first entered my consciousness, I tried really hard to remember when I'd ever even heard of anything related to the country. I came up with nothing.

Thankfully–for my own guilty conscience–I wasn't alone. Even within Europe, which would have far more reason to be concerned about Bulgaria than the U.S., Eastern European historian R.J. Crampton reported on this continent's general ignorance of Bulgaria. He noted that "during the second half of the twentieth century, Bulgaria was probably the least known of all the East European states. Even Albania, under the egregious leadership of Enver Hoxha, seemed to receive more media coverage."

Reading this definitely rang a bell in my head, but the bell had nothing to do with Bulgaria. As a kid growing up in the 1980s, I remember my parents telling me about Albania, telling me that that it was the most restrictive and sealed off country in the world. Albania was not a place we would ever visit.

But as far as I could remember, my geographically-inclined parents had never said a word to me about Bulgaria. My history teachers–who I hope were geographically-inclined–had also never said anything about

Bulgaria.

I guess that left it up to me to discover on my own.

But it wasn't like Bulgarians hadn't discovered my country, the United States. Census data showed that as many as 250,000 Bulgarians currently were living in the United States, and Chicago is one of the cities with the highest Bulgarian populations. But though I'd resided in Chicago for the majority of my life, I'd never met a Bulgarian. I'd met plenty of Poles, Ukrainians, Serbs, Russians and Greeks—all from the same Eastern European region—but never a Bulgarian.

One of the most famous Bulgarians—at least as far as Bulgarians are concerned—was the 19th century freedom fighter Vasil Levski. He spoke of the same affliction that I was starting to feel about Bulgaria—barely knowing the country even existed. Levski, as he dared his countrymen to join him to overthrow the Ottoman rule in Bulgaria, boldly stated, "Either we live up to our times, or they will destroy us."

History shows that Bulgaria eventually did release itself from the Ottoman grip and was not destroyed. But in the more than half-century following Bulgaria's first modern independence in 1878, it was difficult to find the bright spots that made Bulgaria stand out to a Westerner looking at its history. In fact, you'd be hard pressed to find a Bulgarian who could point to the bright spots that had occurred historically since 1878.

Bulgaria's independence from Ottoman rule was a welcomed sight all over the world, not just in Bulgaria. The near 500 years of Ottoman oppression of Bulgaria left Bulgaria without much of an identity, and perhaps without much of a history at all. Nevil Forbes, a Bulgarian historian, describes the Turkish domination of Bulgaria this way: "From 1393 until 1877 Bulgaria may truthfully be said to have had no history." And if that wasn't bad enough, he felt the need to elaborate on the Turkish effect on the Bulgarian nation by saying that during these five centuries, "Bulgaria was simply annihilated."

With a history like this, nearly everyone had to be cheering for better times for Bulgaria. Throughout Europe, and especially in England, there were politicians and humanitarians championing the Bulgarian freedom cause. Conveniently, the Russians weren't big fans of the Ottoman Empire, and this led to the Russo-Turkish War of 1877-78. Bulgarian revolutionaries correctly saw this as their chance, and fought bravely to free their country. Many young men, like Vasil Levski, lost their lives fighting the previously indomitable force that was the Ottoman Empire. With a statement that makes it impossible not to like him, Levski declared to the Bulgarian people his undying devotion to the cause: "If I win, so do the people. If I lose, I lose only myself." Levski's words turned out to be prophetic, as he was hanged in Sofia by the Turks, but soon after his country did win. The Russians prevailed over the Turks in the Russo-Turkish War and Bulgaria was free.

But this freedom didn't come with the spoils Bulgaria had expected. While Bulgarians were both shocked and thrilled to have their independence, they had no idea what to do with it. Bulgaria was elated to have its freedom, but this resulted mostly because of Russia's help. During their struggle for freedom, the behavioral precedent had already been set by Bulgaria's neighbors: they were not interested in helping Bulgaria. At no point during the Russo-Turkish war did neighboring countries like Serbia or Greece intervene to join the fight, even though they had vested interests in defeating the Turks, too. Serbia and Greece's shunning of Bulgaria at the end of the 19th century would foreshadow bigger tragedies that carried well into the 20th century.

Following the Russo-Turkish war, Bulgaria's immediate fate was decided at the Congress of Berlin in 1878, a meeting that contained exactly zero Bulgarian representatives. This European congress, following the precedent that had already been set, found it more strategically valuable to appease Bulgaria's neighbors than Bulgaria. And seeing that Bulgaria had mostly relied on foreign aid to gain independence and did not even have a representative at the Congress, you can see how they were easily cast aside by the Western European powers that were making the decisions. As a result, while Bulgaria expected to begin its new nationhood with the lands it had held 500 years before, their new country was much smaller than expected. It did not contain several key parts of what was the Bulgarian Kingdom half a millennium in the past. In particular, the new Bulgarian state did not include Macedonia, or as most Bulgarians viewed it, "Western Bulgaria."

This slight from the European powers enraged Bulgarians. All throughout Europe, it appeared that Bulgarians had friends who were cheering for their emancipation. But these friends mostly just cheered; they didn't play an active role, and didn't care too much once the fighting was over. As a result, the Bulgarian kingdom of old was carved up. In *Street Without a Name*, a memoir about growing up in Bulgaria during the Cold War, Kapka Kassabova sadly signifies that Bulgaria's battle for independence was the moment "where Bulgaria passed from being an Ottoman backwater to being an independent backwater."

Without Macedonia, Bulgarians felt as if part of their homeland, part of their identity, had been taken away from them. They would spend the first half of the 20th century fighting for this identity, and the results were disastrous. Bulgaria eagerly joined the First Balkan War 1912 with the hopes of gaining back Macedonian territories. This time with the help of the Greeks and Serbians they were victorious in this war against the Ottomans, but then they were struck with a fate similar to what had befallen them 35 years previous. Serbia and Greece negotiated a deal without them and left them empty-handed in regards to territories in Macedonia, their main goal of the entire war. Their pride insulted once again, Bulgaria was becoming a bitter country, one that wasn't going down without a fight—another fight.

Less than a year after the end of the First Balkan War, Bulgaria declared war on Greece and Serbia in the hopes of regaining Macedonia. This decision, and this short and brutal war "proved to be a national catastrophe," as R.J. Crampton describes it. Bulgaria was defeated soundly by Greece and Serbia, and just to pour salt in the wounds, Romania joined the fight to take northern Bulgarian territories, and Turkey joined the fight to take eastern Bulgarian territories.

Its pride stung and its people desolate, Bulgaria was not the kind of country to give in, give up or learn from its mistakes. Unfortunately, these mistakes continued throughout the first half of the 20th century. In both World Wars, Bulgaria aligned itself with the side that was most likely to return its lost territory. In both cases, this was the German side. And in both cases, Bulgaria—via Germany—lost, becoming one of the very few European countries (other than Germany) to lose both World Wars. The losses of both Balkan Wars and both World Wars left Bulgaria without many friends, and certainly without much territory or prosperity. Robert Kaplan in *Balkan Ghosts* captures the essence of Bulgaria after all these disasters by writing, "What emerged in the second half of the twentieth century was a smoldering and dismembered ghost of a nation."

Everything I was now learning about Bulgaria made me wonder why I'd never learned any of this information before. But the more and more I read about how Bulgaria had been conveniently tossed aside by its neighbors and the rest of Europe, it seemed to make sense that Bulgaria hadn't entered my narrow American world view. Bulgaria—sometimes by its own hand, and sometimes the result of others' doing—was a completely isolated country. But what I was now learning about this isolation was certainly grabbing my attention. The history of Bulgaria told me this was a proud country that was battling for its identity. It was a country that had been conquered, freed, alienated, betrayed and defeated—over and over again. Bulgarian history was full of moments that could've been glorious and maybe should've been glorious—but moments of glory were few and far between. The Bulgarian identity had been at stake throughout its history, and this was before Soviet Communism ruled the country for some 50 years.

As I read more and more about Bulgarian history, I started to think that maybe it wasn't just the history of a country that I was learning. Maybe these struggles for identity weren't things that were solely part of the past. I sensed they were about to become part of my future.

Chapter III
Tryouts

Nikolai was built like a compact refrigerator, and when he smiled, both his teeth and his bald head seemed to gleam simultaneously. We lingered together at half court of the American College of Sofia's bubble dome gym talking about basketball. I'd only known Nikolai, the girls' varsity basketball coach, for a couple months, but I already viewed him as one of my strongest allies. Not only was Nikolai the girls' varsity basketball coach, he was also one of the longest tenured Bulgarians to work at my school. And perhaps most importantly for me, he spoke some of the best English of any Bulgarian I knew. Since we split the gym after school, we had both been trading stories about our tryouts. But I could tell he had something else on his mind. He looked pensive and slightly nervous, and in turn, this had the same effect on me.

"Well, you say your brother is coming to visit at Christmas, yes?"

"Yes, he's coming at Christmas," I responded.

"Well, would it be possible—do you think he could—is there any way you could have him buy some basketball nets and bring them to us?"

I tried not to laugh—my first American instinct—because this really was an important and serious Bulgarian issue.

"Sure, that's no problem, Nikolai," I told him, "I'll have him pick up a bunch of nets and bring them."

"Oh that would be so wonderful," he was instantly pleased. "You know, you just can't find basketball nets anywhere in this country."

As he mentioned the nets, I couldn't help but look down to one end of the floor where our "best" net was dangling precariously by only a few remaining threads. I had been gazing off into the distance aimlessly as we talked, but now realized that Nikolai's vision had been focused solely on the sad state of our nets. While it could have sounded ridiculous to imagine that the solution to our net problem was coming from the United States at Christmas, I'd been shopping with Nikolai and knew why he was so excited for my brother's visit. To the best of both of our knowledge, there was nowhere in Sofia, Bulgaria's capital city of two million people, where we could find basketball nets. The previous weekend we'd gone shopping together for basketballs and hit the jackpot when we found a sports store that sold rubber-ish indoor/outdoor basketballs that gave the appearance of actually being leather. My first thought was, *No way, we're not buying these*. But all it took was one look at Nikolai's elated countenance and I realized that I, too, should be excited about these basketballs. So we spent 100 *leva* (about 70 US dollars) on three basketballs – and that was the entirety of our allotted basketball budget for the year.

When we'd sat down to talk about the upcoming season, I'd hoped to put in requests for uniforms, but with 100 *leva*, we weren't going to get much. And when I thought of requests for "new uniforms," it wasn't simply that our old uniforms were all in bad shape—our old uniforms took absurd to whole new levels. As I sorted through the large gym bag of team apparel, I was able to take stock of what we had:

7 white American College of Sofia uniforms (*not a bad start*)

4 purple American College of Sofia uniforms (*two had numbers taped on the back*)

6 Dallas Mavericks 1994 uniforms (*are you kidding me?*)

5 Philadelphia 76ers 2001 uniforms (*OK, you're not kidding me*)

Just by looking at the numbers of this sorry stock of uniforms, it was obvious there was no way for our team to properly suit up. I saw this as a big problem—but clearly the previous coach, school administration, and rest of Bulgaria did not. But getting past the numbers, Dallas Mavericks uniforms? Philadelphia 76ers? This was Bulgaria. What in the world was going on?

Despite any reasonable objections I had—and trust me, I was trying to be reasonable—these were our *varsity* uniforms for the year, and our three new rubber-ish basketballs were apparently a boon as we started the season. Nets courtesy of my brother from the States were just icing on the cake.

In looking at the major shortage of basketball-related supplies, I have to admit that I was a little baffled. After a few months in Bulgaria, I was certainly used to things being different, and I'd grown accustomed to chiding myself for ever saying, "You know in America, things aren't like this...." I usually resorted to just thinking this, but tried not to utter it out loud. In terms of basketball, though, the sport wasn't unheard of in Bulgaria. Kids played basketball; there were parks and playgrounds with basketball hoops, and many of my players routinely talked to me about the NBA and how they'd once seen a highlight of Dwyane Wade dunking over Amare Stoudemire. But while basketball did have a presence in the country, all the hoops I saw outside at the parks were very similar: they didn't have nets. The bent and broken rims looked like they could use some repair as well, but I wasn't about to mention this to Nikolai.

In fact, our gym was one of the nicest gyms in the country–at least that's what I'd been told. The gym was, as previously mentioned, an inflatable bubble dome–think Metrodome-size divided by 100–on the north end of the campus built in the 1990s. It contained two almost-full length basketball courts that had volleyball lines within them as well. The wood floors were nothing worth writing home about, but one of the things that made this one of the nicest gyms in Bulgaria was that none of the floorboards were dislodged; we celebrated because they were all actually in place. Incredibly, two of the hoops had glass backboards, but unfortunately, one of the hoops with a glass backboard was raised at least 6 inches above 10 feet, and the rim had a slight upward tilt. If we wanted to play a real, 94-foot game, it was possible to move two of the hoops to play the length of the bubble. Whenever this was mentioned, my players immediately became excited–until I told them they'd have to be the ones to move the hoops.

The bubble was held up by an electric generator and there was only one precarious entrance, a slim revolving door that you had to push pretty hard to get moving. Your prize for getting it moving was having your now-pressurized ears pop immediately upon entering from the outside. During practices and games, I became familiar with the hum of the generator as it kept the bubble inflated. It also became commonplace for practices to be interrupted by what sounded like a Turkish air raid whenever it started raining. The bubble's thin roof floated about 30 feet above our heads. Falling rain hitting this roof created such a racket that there wasn't much of a chance for anyone to hear anyone else talking—or shouting. It was the pounding of the rain versus the pounding of the basketballs. When giant snow chunks would slide their way off the bubble and crash onto the ground, I'd have visions of paratroopers crash-landing hastily in preparation for an attack.

But all these concerns based on noises soon faded once I got used to them. The real problem with the bubble would come if the generator ever failed or was shut off. This mechanism ran 24 hours a day and was solely responsible for keeping the roof of the gym stable. This issue came to the forefront one afternoon during a volleyball game when the generator stopped working. Around 75 people were inside the gym for a volleyball tournament—the Bulgarian fire marshal stated that maximum capacity for the bubble was 40 people—when the generator stopped, and the bubble ominously and quickly started deflating. With only one exit—an exit with a revolving door that didn't move quickly—there was a panicked evacuation as the roof started descending. As the last of the volleyballers and fans were evacuated, thankfully, another coach was able to fix the generator and start working on re-inflating the bubble.

Well, at least we thought he fixed it.

As it turns out, all he did was turn the bubble's generator back on. It had been switched off by the school's head of maintenance, a parting gift for the school (and 75 terrified people) as he'd been fired earlier in the day for his overall laziness and unwillingness to work. After he switched off the generator, he undoubtedly established energy and urgency from all people involved, exactly the qualities that I suppose would have saved his job in the first place.

Perhaps the most alarming part of the whole episode was that the school's deputy director (a Bulgarian) had told me how concerned she was about firing the head of maintenance because she worried what kind of vengeful action he would take the day he was fired. I thought this sounded ridiculous, but it turned out that she was exactly right.

Ridiculous was certainly becoming the norm in Bulgaria, I was learning on a daily basis.

And there was no doubt about this ridiculousness when basketball tryouts started. After having each of the kids sign in on an attendance sheet, I wondered why I'd even bothered. A quick look at some of the last names made me realize that a quick look wasn't going to do me any good. In fact, a much longer look probably wouldn't do me any good either.

Lesichkov?

Radovanov?

Preshlyanov?

Mladenov?

Tsvetanov?

Raszolkov?

Menkov?

I tried to be positive. I tried to tell myself I could pronounce these names. At least they all ended in *–ov.*

But then there were more.

Kristurski?

Boyadzhiev?

Farandzha?

Kuradjiev?

From watching the open gyms and the beginning of tryouts, I tried to calm myself down and lower my basketball expectations in the hope of maintaining sanity. But looking at these names wasn't helping my nerves one bit. As I looked out at a scrum of 35 boys playing what appeared to be basketball, I looked down at my clipboard with the list of names and felt rather helpless. We had a long, long way to go, and I knew that well before I looked at the list of unpronounceable names. Now I was stuck wondering if there was any help coming from anywhere–with either the names or the basketball.

The American head coach from last year was long gone, and it appeared he'd checked out halfway through the last season. The American assistant coach from last year made it very clear to me; he had no interest in being any kind of coach this year. It was difficult for me to take this as a positive omen.

"*Duuuddde,*" he said to me in his very Californian drawl, "just forget about it. All the best players graduated, and we weren't even any good last year. *Duuuddde,* just forget about it; you're not going to be any good."

"I see what you're saying," I tried a patient response. "But I'm not worried right now about how good we're going to be. I'm just wondering if you could help me out with some of the names for the first few days."

"*Duuuddde,*" he started, and I became more and more worried that someone also allowed him to be an English teacher. "I didn't know any of their names last year. There's no way I could help you out this year!"

He laughed.

I tried to.

But it just didn't seem very funny.

At this point, I knew I was alone–alone with a tenuous roof over my head and a group of boys with various versions of –ov in their names. To me, they all blended into one. And while this was true for their names, it was also quite obvious that there wasn't a whole lot of blending happening on the basketball court either. During our initial drills, our team resembled a nine-year-old soccer team playing bunch ball. They might as well have been kicking the ball, too, because traditional basketball passing wasn't working.

I wanted to be enthusiastic.

But I just felt lost.

"So Coach," a player–I didn't even bother trying with his name–came up to me to disrupt my spell, "I see that we have tryouts four days this week."

"Yes, we do."

I didn't have much else to offer here.

"Well, I'd like to come to at least two or three of the tryouts."

I'd like to come to at least two or three of the tryouts?

"I'm not sure what you mean," I responded, hoping that some clarification would somehow make this better.

"Well, I want you to see how committed I am to the team. I really want to play basketball this year, so I'm willing to get to at least two of the tryouts, maybe even three."

It wasn't getting better.

"Well, I'm certainly looking for players who have commitment, but to me commitment means being here every day."

To start the tryout, I'd given a speech about hard work and commitment. Now I was starting to wonder if the definitions of those terms might not have translated cross-culturally.

The player looked at me dumbfounded.

I couldn't believe he was dumbfounded, so I looked right back at him dumbfounded.

"Wait, you're saying I have to come to all four tryouts?"

Not only was I unsure of how to answer this question, I wasn't sure that I even wanted to answer the question to begin with. I gazed out at the basketball court hoping for a pleasant respite from a conversation that I couldn't believe was happening. Instead my eyes fixated on a different kind of respite: two players–one in jean shorts, the other in cargo shorts–were off to the side with one of our brand new rubber balls bumping the ball back and forth to each other as if it were a volleyball. I was only left to hope these two would ask if they had to come all four days. That answer would be easy.

"Look, you don't have to come to any of the tryouts. It's completely voluntary and you can come or not come whenever you want."

This seemed to brighten his spirits.

"Okay, that's great, really great. I'll definitely come to two tryouts, maybe even three. I want you to see how committed I am."

I had little doubt I was going to see this, but I was pretty sure we were going to see "committed" in different ways. Maybe committed didn't translate so well into Bulgarian, I thought. He jogged off toward the court satisfied, and I tried not to hang my head in defeat. Now I had to go over and talk to the volleyball stars about the exact nature of "basketball" tryouts.

As I strolled over in their direction trying to remain calm, it occurred to me that maybe I should have my brother pick up some volleyball nets to bring at Christmas, too.

Chapter IV
Modern Bulgaria

The first half of the 20th century was not kind to Bulgaria. This had become obvious fairly early in my study of the country's history. No matter which geographical direction Bulgaria turned, they looked to another nation that had betrayed them. In *Balkan Ghosts*, a title very fitting when considering the tragedies associated with Bulgarian history, Robert Kaplan notes that Bulgaria became a "bitter and irrational nation in the first half of the twentieth century. Bulgarians hated everybody: Serbs, Greeks, Romanians, Turks." Reading this, I at least took solace in the fact that America was too far away to have formed a strong relationship with Bulgaria.

As best as they could, though, Bulgarians still clung with hope to their own ideas of what their country was, even if Bulgaria itself was an idea that had been conveniently discarded by the rest of Europe. Even if their energy could only be put toward hating their enemies, Bulgaria was a country that wasn't going to let the past just slip away. If nothing else, Bulgarians were determined not to forget.

So when Russia occupied Bulgaria at the end of World War II, most Bulgarians hadn't forgotten the role that Russia had played in their country's history: Russia was the country's liberator, their savior from 500 years of Turkish oppression. While the rest of Europe cringed and squirmed to release itself from the grip of the Soviet Union, Bulgaria considered itself happy to be in the hands of Mother Russia. This was the one—and perhaps only—country that Bulgaria truly considered to be its ally.

As Bulgaria forcefully followed the Soviet communist model, the country soon settled into a half century of restrictive and oppressive totalitarian rule. While countries like Hungary and Czechoslovakia were already mustering resistance forces against the Soviet influence, Bulgaria was far more content to have an ally, even if it was a dominant and all-encompassing ally like the Soviet Union.

Soon Bulgarian schools because Russified and fully steeped in propaganda. A common slogan for a beginner's math class sounded like this: *What is two plus two? Answer: three, but with the help of the Soviet Union, four.* Bulgaria's first communist leader, Georgi Dimitrov, was so entranced by Mother Russia that he hyperbolized the relationship between Russia and Bulgaria to new heights by saying that, "... for Bulgarian people, friendship with the Soviet Union is just as necessary for life as the air and sun is for every living creature."

While Bulgaria—or at least Bulgarian communist party leaders—was beaming with pride over its association with Russia, other Eastern European countries did not see Russia's influence on their countries in this same maternal and loving way. In 1956, Hungarians, incensed by the country's Soviet-imposed policies, protested and revolted for more than two weeks. While the protesters were able to topple the Hungarian puppet government, once they approached the Soviet Union for a withdrawal of forces from their country, the Soviets decided to squash the revolution. In the end, more than 2,500 Hungarians were killed. The Iron Curtain had officially, and brutally, fallen on Hungary. They would remain under Soviet control until the Berlin Wall fell.

In 1968, Prague (Czechoslovakia) enjoyed a revolutionary spring as their leader Alexander Dubcek loosened communism's grip on society, enacting liberal changes as part of the ideal he called "socialism with a human face." The Prague Spring sprung hope all throughout Eastern Europe as writers, musicians, artists, and just normal citizens all felt empowered to have freedoms previously unheard of during communist times. But once the Soviet Union fully grasped what was happening in Czechoslovakia, they left little doubt about their feelings about the freedoms the people were now enjoying. On an August night, 200,000 troops and 2,000 tanks entered Czechoslovakia. Within two days, the Prague Spring and all the reforms that came with it were over. Over 100 Czechs were dead, and Dubcek was forced to recant all his earlier decrees. Czechoslovakia, humbled and oppressed, would also be mired under Soviet control until the Berlin Wall fell.

All the while, though, Bulgaria–a country whose living conditions were the same if not worse than those in Hungary and Czechoslovakia–had no inklings of any kind of uprising. In fact, their position toward the Soviet Union–a force condemned by many throughout the world–could not have been more opposite. While Hungarians and Czechs were dying to have a chance at freedom, Bulgaria's longtime communist dictator, Todor Zhivkov, proposed to Nikita Khrushchev that Bulgaria give up its sovereignty–something that the rest of Eastern Europe was fighting for–and become part of the Soviet Union. After all, Zhivkov stated publicly, "Bulgaria and the Soviet Union would 'act as a single body, breathing with the same lungs and nourished by the same bloodstream.'"

While Khrushchev eventually turned down Zhivkov's proposal, it was comments like these that earned Zhivkov the official honor of Hero of the Soviet Union in 1977. Whether the Bulgarian people saw him as heroic or not is a different issue, but he had the backing of Mother Russia. The Bulgarian dissident writer, Georgi Markov, a Bulgarian who escaped Bulgaria during the Cold War, wrote that Zhivkov was so utterly devoted to the Soviet Union that he "served the Soviet Union more ardently than the Soviet leaders themselves did."

Seeing that so many people in so many countries throughout Eastern Europe were begging, pleading and even dying for the chance to have freedom, it's difficult to grasp why Bulgaria was so unflinchingly loyal to the Soviet Union. Countries all around them were revolting against Soviet oppression, and Romania, their Eastern bloc neighbor to the north, had already completely split with the Soviet Union. Every Cold War conversation I was ever privy to as a child growing up during the 1980s rotated around the hope that any of these countries cut off from the world by Soviet domination could somehow gain freedom. And maybe that's why as a kid I was at least familiar with Eastern bloc countries like Hungary, Czechoslovakia and Romania.

But Bulgaria? It was a dark mystery–and probably not just to a little boy who was growing up in the West. It was hard for any Western citizen to understand exactly what was going on in Bulgaria, one of the few Eastern bloc countries that openly supported the Soviet Union and its policies that Westerners saw as restrictive and unjust.

Considering the relationship between Bulgaria and the Soviet Union, it's even more confounding when you read Mikhail Gorbachev's take on Bulgaria in general. It's clear from his comments–and comments from many others both inside and outside Bulgaria–that if Bulgaria was profiting from their association with the USSR, the profits were still marginal. They were gaining raw materials through shipments from Russia, but these always came at a cost, and a cost that most Bulgarians couldn't usually afford. In his memoirs, referring to a relatively impoverished Bulgaria, Gorbachev wrote that "Bulgaria was a country which had lived beyond its means for a long time." Though the 'means' he refers to didn't exactly make Bulgaria a prosperous nation, some would argue that Bulgaria's relationship with the Soviet Union did keep the country afloat economically. Still, though, to my Western eyes and ears, the closeness of this relationship between Bulgaria and the Soviet Union was still not easily grasped.

Georgi Markov, in his writing about his native country while living in England, tried to help the West understand Bulgaria by explaining the plight of a Bulgarian: "We are subjected to the impact of far more factors and forces than the Western citizen can imagine. While the citizen in the West is constantly striving to acquire ever more, our main instinct is to preserve what we have."

Markov wrote this in his book called *The Truth That Killed*. And sure enough, his version of the truth did get him killed. In one of the rare times that Bulgaria ever made international news, Markov was infamously murdered in London in 1978 when an assassin stuck him in the leg with a poison-tipped umbrella. Markov assumed this had merely been an accident, not an assassination, and never knew what happened. Unfortunately he had been injected with a lethal dose of ricin and was dead three days later. His writing–and perhaps his desire to "acquire ever more" by living in the West–had led to his death.

His explanation of Bulgarians, though, seems to make a lot of sense when you take a look at Bulgarian history. At least it certainly made sense to me when I started to think about all the times that Bulgaria had simply tried to reclaim what they felt was theirs–and this mostly meant Macedonia. The numerous wars they'd fought to regain Macedonia didn't necessarily represent a desire to acquire more, but just a desire to have what they felt belonged to them. Each of these attempts proved to be more and more futile, and more and more disastrous. Each of these new wars ended with them increasing the hatred between an old enemy (Turkey) and kindling feelings of hate for new enemies (Serbia, Greece, Romania). As the world moved into a prolonged Cold War, Bulgaria, unlike its Eastern European neighbors, was in no mood to revolt. Bulgaria was still licking its wounds from the first half of the century.

This reflection on Bulgaria's past made me wonder if my time in Bulgaria would have similar disastrous results for me. Moving to a country that had been such a strong supporter of the Soviet Union would certainly qualify as breaking out of the very American bubble I'd spent my entire life living in. It was hard for me to put any kind of face to what my time in Bulgaria was going to be like. If this had really been the country that had promoted "socialism with a human face," at least I would feel like I could relate to that. But in reality, this was the country that had stood by Russia as it did all it could to stomp down the human element.

During the Cold War, Bulgaria had been about as isolated as isolated gets. All the positive rhetoric that flowed between Sofia and Moscow did not lead to some idealized form of communist living conditions. Bulgaria's urban city centers were inundated with row house, block-style apartment buildings. And honestly, blocks were a far more fitting description than apartment buildings. If a normal citizen wanted to buy a car, waiting 10 years was not out of the ordinary. If a normal citizen wanted to leave the country, well, that usually didn't happen for normal citizens. And with grocery store items constantly in short supply and communication with the outside world extremely limited, I realized that the American bubble I felt I lived in was nothing compared to the bubble Cold War Bulgarians were forced to live in. In her memoir about growing up in Cold War Bulgaria, Kapka Kassabova sardonically points out that Bulgarians "were living inside George Orwell's *1984* but we didn't know it because it was on the list of banned books."

In the same breath, it also seemed that Bulgaria was relatively banned from the education of a Westerner. Whether this was because Bulgaria's pro-Russian stance had offended the West or just that Bulgaria was irrelevant to the West, we'll never know exactly. But as the Cold War and Soviet dominion ended, Bulgaria's next act also put it in a category all by itself. While Vaclav Havel led the Velvet Revolution to bring democracy to Czechoslovakia, the Singing Revolution led to emancipation for the Baltic States, and the ruthless Romanian dictator Nicolae Ceausescu was executed on Christmas Day to bring freedom to Romania, Bulgaria held its first post-communist elections in 1990. And the result of these elections? The Bulgarian people elected the moderate wing of the Bulgarian Socialist Party – more or less the same communists. Commenting on election results that flew in the face of all the rejoicing for freedom and democracy happening all throughout Eastern Europe, historian R.J. Crampton noted that, "Once again, there seemed little consciousness of the fact that government appointments were being decided by a party body.... It was to be some years before Bulgarians and foreign observers were convinced that the change of nomenclature meant a change in nature."

In the 17 years of Bulgaria's post-Soviet freedom before I arrived in Sofia in the late summer of 2007, even though Bulgaria had started freedom in 1990 with communists, a 'change in nature' had finally occurred, albeit slowly and not fully. That's why, as I arrived in Bulgaria, it was considered to be one of Europe's poorest countries. In the grand scheme of a grand continent, both economically and politically, Bulgaria was an afterthought.

More and more, though, Bulgaria was trying to erase this stigma and was starting to creep its way toward the West. More and more, Bulgaria was allying itself with prosperous Europe by becoming a member of the EU on January 1, 2007, and distancing itself from its longtime ally and idol, Russia. But unlike other Eastern bloc countries that immediately looked to put their stamp on their own freedom, Bulgaria was in no hurry to do this. Change might have been coming, but change was just crawling along.

I suppose that's why my first glimpse of Sofia was so startling. The plane landed mid-afternoon on a beautiful sunny August day, and my initial impression was bewilderment. Everyone on the plane was raucously clapping, celebrating, I guessed, the fact that the plane had landed. I wondered if it was rare for a plane to land successfully—especially on a clear, sunny day—but tried to keep these thoughts to myself. After all, the fact that the plane had landed with what I deemed to be an absurd amount of clapping was far better than the other alternative as I was about to take my first steps in a brand new life.

Leaving the airport, I was eager to get my first glimpse of Sofia, my first glimpse of Bulgaria. With it being such a beautiful August afternoon, I was eager to see my new home in all its splendor. But with each new block that we passed, all I saw were blocks—gray communist row house blocks. One after another, they all looked the same—and they all looked dreary.

At this point I realized that everything I'd read about communist architecture and its stunning propensity to make ominous structures ubiquitous was true. To my left were crumbling concrete row houses. Some had graffiti spray-painted on the walls. Many had the glint of broken glass shards in the grass. To my right were more dilapidated concrete row houses. Some had garbage piled haphazardly in the makeshift courtyards. Dogs were eating the garbage.

The only solace I could convince my mind to focus on was the fact that I knew we were on the outskirts of town. I told myself I shouldn't expect much from the outside of a city. When you're blown away by the beauty of a city, it's usually the heart of the city you're talking about. So I leaned forward and asked the Bulgarian driver, Igor, who had proven already to speak passable English, where downtown Sofia was.

"Ahh, downtown—*tsentar grad*—it is that way," he said as he pointed diagonally to his right.

I looked in that direction, but it didn't look any different. There was just another monstrous row house sporting an even darker shade of gray. If downtown was a ray of light off in the distance, I couldn't see past the gray immensity of the row houses.

I started thinking about Soviet math, poisoned umbrellas and Orwell's *1984*. Now that I was seeing Sofia firsthand, all the Bulgarian history I'd been reading didn't seem all that historical. And it was at this point that I started to think that maybe I shouldn't spend too much time in Bulgaria looking for a ray of light.

Chapter V
An American Education

As the basketball season was getting underway, I felt I had no choice but to be optimistic. In my six years of coaching in the United States, I'd known no other way to approach the season. But the realistic side of me was really worried. Looking out at the floor, I noticed two kids were wearing jean shorts. One had on a 1993 Charlotte Hornets' Larry Johnson jersey. In the States, I would've called this a vintage fashion trend, but in Bulgaria, I knew none of my players were even aware of the fact that the jersey was 15 years old. I tried to count how many of my players were actually wearing high-topped basketball shoes, but when I couldn't get past four, I stopped counting, afraid of how depressed I'd get. My team's problems, though, were far greater than simply their attire: the majority of my team moved awkwardly, stumbled while dribbling, traveled frequently, and stood very little chance of making left-handed layups. The majority of my team looked like a bunch of guys who'd just started learning how to play basketball a year or two ago. Unfortunately, that's because the majority of my team had started to learn how to play basketball a year or two ago.

This was a team that was supposed to compete in both national and international competitions—something I couldn't fathom because I didn't know what the competition would be like. But it was also something I couldn't fathom because it was near impossible for me to look at the layup lines and think that these 15 kids could compete at any level in basketball.

And while Pavel, the first player to come talk to me during the first open gym, was holding true to his promise to work his hardest, that kind of effort wasn't representative of the majority of the other 14 guys who had made the team. Even though I was now living in an EU country that supposedly had shed the restraints of communism, evidence of the communist influence was everywhere. During my first few months I'd been reminded by many Bulgarians about the age-old communist workers' remark regarding work ethic: They pretend to pay us and we pretend to work.

As I watched my players go through a layup line, Dimov, a point guard I was told had the most talent on the team, flung a haphazard and lazy attempt at a left-handed layup up toward the backboard. The ball bounded sideways toward the opposite corner of the court. Dimov's head sunk and he immediately stopped running, perched himself under the hoop and let out a primal howl that included several Bulgarian swear words. His diatribe released, he then slowly meandered to the end of the rebounding line after two more players nearly ran into him. In all regards, Dimov wasn't pretending. He wasn't pretending to run, and he wasn't pretending to be irate and irrational following the relatively insignificant act of missing a layup in practice.

I wasn't sure exactly what to address: the profanity-laced tirade simply because he'd missed a layup, or the fact that following missing a layup, he couldn't summon the energy to jog back to the rebounding line. Perhaps more alarming than anything he'd done was the collective reaction of his teammates: none of them seemed to bat an eyelash at his behavior. If one of them missed a left-handed layup, I was worried, each could potentially have the same violent and counterproductive reaction. And as I watched more and more left-handed layups catapulting off various parts of the backboard and rim, I knew that I didn't need to see any more of this.

"Okay, guys," I hollered out after blowing my whistle. "Bring it in here."

I watched as those who had managed to make their layups and those who hadn't sauntered over in my direction in the exact same jean-short style.

"The first thing," I began, even though half the team still hadn't managed to make their way over to me, "is that no matter what happens out on floor at practice, I expect you to work your hardest. I expect you to run."

Some Bulgarian eyes met mine and indicated comprehension, but most didn't. This expectation wasn't familiar.

"What that means," I continued, "is that during our entire hour and a half practice, I expect you to give every ounce of effort you have. At no point will it be acceptable for you to walk during a drill."

I saw Dimov's eyes furrow down toward the floor with these comments.

"If we're going to get better as a basketball team, and if you're going to get better as a player, we're all going to have to work hard. I will give you everything I've got as your coach, and I will expect nothing less from you as a player and as a person. If you're not working your hardest, then don't expect to play in a game. And honestly, if you're not working your hardest, I don't want you in this gym. You're not going to learn anything by giving a 50-percent effort."

I could sense my own anger building as if I'd just missed a left-handed layup, and the tone of my voice ascended several notches.

"And I don't care how many times you make a mistake or your teammates make a mistake. There's no use yelling about it. Whether you're yelling at yourself or yelling at others, this doesn't do any good. You're going to miss shots. You're going to make bad passes. It's going to happen. And if every time that happens you get furious and start pouting, we're never going to be any good. You've got to hold your head high and be ready for the next play."

It was clear to my players that I wasn't exactly happy, and as a result, most of their heads were down. I was hoping that as I talked about holding their heads high that they would get the message and start looking up at me. Most, though, still stared at the cracked wooden floor.

"Are there any questions about this? Do you understand what I'm saying?"

The tenuous silence worried me. Based on what little experience I'd already had—from attending two or three tryouts to bumping volleyballs—I knew there were probably many questions related to what I'd just said. But no questions were forthcoming, and I was relieved not to have to give another answer that seemed so obvious to me it was painful.

"Coach," Pesho, the athletic but basketball-awkward 6'4" center offered, "we understand. We will work hard. That's why we're here. And we'll try to stop yelling. We get it."

That represented a step in the right direction, a step I sensed that we desperately needed. At least one player indicated that he understood. But I wasn't certain that would automatically transfer to the rest of the team, even though he used the pronoun "we." But at this point, I was willing to take any small victory I could. And with that, I set the team up near the baseline for our next drill, a drill I hoped would set the tone for the season.

"What you're going to do," I explained, "is start at one edge of the lane line. When I blow the whistle, you're going to slide to other lane line, and then slide back." I demonstrated the sliding, hoping this wasn't something out of their realm. "Once you get back to where you started, then you're going to close out as if there's a shooter on the left wing. That means you sprint–SPRINT!–to the left wing and close out. When you close out on the shooter, your feet better be moving, and your hands better be up," and again, I demonstrated this. "Now, when I yell 'BALL!' that's when you turn around and look to the basket. At that point, you're going to imagine that a ball is loose in the middle of the lane, and it's your job to get to it first."

I turned to look at my team, and could see the confusion in their eyes. I knew they understood my English, but I saw they were far from understanding my point.

"So what do you think is the quickest way to get to a loose ball on the floor?" I asked them.

Silence was the most immediate answer. It seemed that my mention of "quickest" had completely thrown them off-balance more than the left-handed layups attempts had.

"Well, I think," the shooting guard Menkov spoke up, "you should probably dive on the floor for the ball."

This was exactly the answer I was looking for. But that doesn't mean it was the popular answer amongst his teammates. Several of them immediately shot Menkov a look as if to say, "What? Are you crazy?"

"Menkov," I beamed, "is exactly right. When I call 'BALL!' you need to turn and get on the floor as quickly as possible. The ball is on the ground, and I want to see how important it is to you. So you dive on the floor right away."

"*Ne modje, ne modje,*" were the groans I heard from several team members.

While I was taking Bulgarian lessons twice a week to attempt to gain some semblance of understanding of a language that looked like hieroglyphics and sounded like a Russian invasion, I didn't need Bulgarian lessons to teach me what *ne modje* meant. From day one in Bulgaria, I'd heard *ne modje* all the time, so much so that I thought it might be the national motto. If I asked for my cold cafeteria lunch to be heated up in the microwave? *Ne modje*. If I asked the school's maintenance men to put a shower curtain in my on-campus house so I didn't flood the bathroom taking a shower? *Ne modje*. If I asked a taxi to take me to the center of town during rush hour? *Ne modje*.

Ne modje translates to, "It is not possible."

And all too often in Bulgaria, a land that was supposedly reaching new horizons as it reached to the West, anything new, remotely inconvenient or challenging was met with *ne modje*. Now it had taken up residence on the basketball practice floor.

"But Coach," this time confusion had completely taken over Dimov, "you can't really be serious. You want us to dive on the floor? Dive on this floor?"

"Yes, Dimov," I answered right away. "I want you to dive on this floor—or any floor for that matter."

With that, I dove on the floor for the imaginary ball. I was determined to model toughness, tenacity and perseverance, but it took all the energy I could muster not to look affected by my crash landing on the splintered-wood floor. Landing roughly in the middle of the lane gave me new definitions to the term hardship. When I'd run this drill with American basketball teams, the floor would be shiny and smooth. Diving on it would sometimes result in a majestic slip-and-slide plunge— that while not entirely comfortable—would at worst only result in a minor floor burn. As I launched myself onto wooden planks that seemed one thud away from being dislodged, my entire body not only felt the burn, but also the bruising. This floor—or probably any Bulgarian floor, it seemed—was not made for diving.

But as far as my team was concerned, this couldn't be an issue. With our talent deficiencies, we were going to have to learn toughness, and learn it quick.

So the drill started. The first few rotations—three players at a time— were shaky, and that was probably an understatement. No one really wanted to dive on this floor. But as Menkov lined up for the third rotation, his head was up and the determination of his steely eyes was firing right back at me. When I yelled for them to go, he was off like a pistol. He crossed both lane lines, sprinted to the wing, and when he heard 'BALL!' he soared across the lane, crashing on the floor a good full second before anyone else. He popped right up and sprinted back toward his teammates.

Far more shocked than they were by Dimov's outburst after missing a layup, Menkov's teammates weren't sure if they should high-five him or check his temperature to see if he'd lost his mind. Without a doubt, though, I knew exactly how I felt, and I knew exactly how to react.

"Wow, that was awesome! Menkov, that was incredible! Did you guys see that? Did you guys see that?"

Some of his teammates acknowledged this and started to smile. Others still seemed too baffled by the entire episode—starting with the fact that I was having them do this drill with no basketballs when all they were interested in was shooting—to know how to react. But I could sense that maybe this was catching on.

"Show me someone who can do it better than Menkov just did! Show me someone who cares even more than he does!"

With that, Pavel, who I already knew cared plenty, hustled to the lane line. So did Vasilev—or Vassy—the undersized backup power forward who took his place behind Pavel. The third to sprint to the lane line was Stefan, a lanky sophomore guard who his teammates dubbed *Nadenitza*, because his still-growing lanky body took the odd shape of *nadenitza*, the Bulgarian word for sausage.

I grinned at the three of them as they waited for my whistle. This time, it wasn't just one set of eyes that looked back at me with determination. There were three sets of eyes—eyes that might not have completely understood what they were doing—but eyes that wanted to take part in it.

With the whistle the three of them were off. With the whistle, the squeaking and tapping of their sneakers was loud. And with the call of 'BALL!' all three of them dive-bombed their bodies down onto the floor. In getting up to finish the drill, each popped up quickly with a smile on their respective faces. Their teammates, starting to catch on, cheered. Three more players hurried to the starting line and all looked me in the eye.

With this, in my eyes, basketball season had really begun.

While basketball season began in earnest in late October, my Bulgarian experience had been in full swing for quite some time. And while each new experience on the basketball floor had the potential to floor me, I was getting more and more accustomed to all things Bulgarian. Most of those things started with the place I spent the majority of my time: The American College of Sofia.

Hearing the name "American College" conjured up images of all things familiar and Western that I had associated myself with my entire life. But it didn't take long for me to realize that, while American in name, this was very much a Bulgarian school. Upon being picked up at the airport, Igor, the school's driver, raved in broken English that, "The College is best school in Bulgaria. And you must see how beautiful is our campus. It is very nice, very nice—better than anywhere else in my country."

As the school van rumbled past row houses along potholed roads to campus, we made our way through a dilapidated rusty gate monitored by armed guards. Soon after this, I was presented with the nicest school campus in Bulgaria. The grass was about a foot high, and appeared not to have been mowed all summer long. Our van was being chased by stray dogs that were barking and snapping at the spinning of the van's wheels. As their volume increased, more dogs appeared from the high grass and weeds to join the furious commotion. Trying to distract myself from the rage of the dogs, I noticed some outdoor basketball hoops. Of course there were no nets, and all of them had rims in various states of bending and rusting. With all of these images in front of me, my first impression didn't have much to do with school and education. Igor's words about the "beautiful" campus kept reverberating in my mind. I knew he wasn't joking about this being "better than anywhere else" in his country, and all this had done now was make me worried.

With my first glimpse of the school, I realized right away that there was going to be a steep learning curve. And while the physical appearance of the nicest campus in Bulgaria was alarming, the biggest aspects of culture shock wouldn't be based on aesthetics. Nearly all of the 700 students who attended this American College grades eight through twelve high school were Bulgarian. There was a smattering of international kids—somewhere around 30—from various countries around the world including Australia, Albania, India and Belgium. But nowhere amongst this smattering was there an American.

My students and my basketball players came from all walks of Bulgarian life; some were affluent by Bulgarian standards, some were part of the very small Bulgarian middle-class, and some were poor. Just to give their kids the chance to get an American College education, parents from around the country would send their children to Sofia. In some cases these children stayed with a relative in Sofia. In other perplexing, though not uncommon, cases students as young as 16 rented tiny apartments to live on their own. Entrance to this "most prestigious school in all of Bulgaria" was entirely dependent on an exam these students had taken in 7th grade with the hope of attending high school at the American College. Unlike so many things in a corruption-ridden country, money was not a factor; only your entrance exam score mattered. Getting in and succeeding was no small feat. With the Bulgarian public school system leaving far more to desire than the worst of any urban area in the U.S., getting into a reputable school like the American College quite possibly could represent one the greatest accomplishments in a young Bulgarian's life. The College would teach you to speak English—a rarity in Bulgaria that would open doors for you on the rest of the continent—and give you a quality education that was recognized internationally. With these new skills and credibility, the goal for most of these young Bulgarians was consistent and simple: graduate from the American College and go to university somewhere else.

Anywhere else.

Unfortunately, the Bulgarian university system—while better than the Bulgarian public high school system—wasn't highly reputable in Europe either. If students planned to live their lives in Bulgaria, there was nothing wrong with a degree from a Bulgarian university. But very few American College students planned to live their lives in Bulgaria. As they would routinely—and sadly—tell me, "The rest of Europe sees us as the toilet of the continent. We have to get out if we're going to have a chance at a better life."

Comments like these that I heard frequently in the first few months of my life in Bulgaria always struck me as shocking and sad—mostly because they were the types of comments I would expect to hear during the Cold War when Bulgaria was literally isolated from the rest of the continent. But this was 2007, and Bulgaria had entered the EU. I naively thought that represented a much more level playing field for Bulgarians. Obviously, my students didn't see it this way. They viewed the 2007 version of isolation different from what had occurred in the past, but not that differently. And while many of them displayed pride for their country, I was hard-pressed to find even one who indicated his or her life after high school would be spent in Bulgaria. When I'd ask how many of my students or basketball players thought they would use their university degrees from other countries to help them live a happy and successful life in Bulgaria, the response almost became predictable:

"I'd love to come back," I was told by a female 12th grade student, "but what's the point? You can try as hard as you want to change things here, but things don't change. My parents have already tried, I've already tried. It's hopeless. I have to leave."

Not knowing entirely how valid these sentiments were, I felt I had little choice but to accept them since I heard them so frequently. For all the times I'd hear *ne modje* in Bulgarian, these types of comments in English seemed to seamlessly introduce *ne modje* into my language. So many things in Bulgaria, my students and players would tell me, just weren't possible. And the more I learned about the country from its residents, the more their attitudes were backed up by research. A 2010 article in the British weekly publication *The Economist* gave scientific data to support what I'd hear every day from my students and basketball players. *The Economist's* article about "the geography of happiness" looked at the general happiness of people in the world related to their level of income. Their report had findings on countries all over the world, but saved its report for Bulgaria for the last sentence of the article. The study morosely reported that "the saddest place in the world, relative to its income per person, is Bulgaria."

When I introduced the concept of a pre-season distance running program, the reaction I received made me think I'd just declared to my players that more Bulgarian territory had been taken away by the Turks and the Greeks.

"Wait a minute, Coach," came the first alarmed response, "you expect us to run at least three kilometers twice a week after school? That is not possible."

"It's definitely possible," I tried to be eager with my response, "and it will make you a better basketball player."

For the first team run in the pre-season–an *optional* pre-season– there were 17 kids. To give them time to get acclimated to the running program, we started with one mile, a loop around the College campus. I ran with the players in an attempt to show them that this really *was possible*. As the pre-season running ended for the day, I felt invigorated both by the run, and the fact that all 17 of them managed to finish. When the run was completed, I congratulated them on their effort and talked about how this was going to make each and every one of them better basketball players. As a result, we'd have a mentally and physically stronger team. Feeling good about what we'd accomplished, I told them we'd meet again on Wednesday after school.

On Wednesday, only five kids showed up. For the other kids, I'd learned pretty quickly that a run after school wasn't possible—*ne modje* —or at least not possible within their realm.

And for some of these potential basketball players, I started to understand why they didn't see giving their best effort in basketball was possible. Simply saying that some of my players were accustomed to laziness was the easy answer—and it was also the correct answer in some circumstances. But there was also more to it than that.

Living in Bulgaria and going to the American College of Sofia was not anything that I would describe as the "normal" high school experience. These Bulgarian students needed this high school degree far more than any American student I'd ever encountered had needed one. While playing basketball sounded like fun, that was mostly the extent of it. They felt that basketball should be fun in the intramural sense, not in the "we're going to run twice a week in the pre-season" sense. High school was their ticket out of the country, and for many of them, it was hard to be too concerned with an extra-curricular activity. Playing a sport would be done solely for fun and for the benefit of adding it to a college application, but it would rarely, if ever, fit into the bigger picture or bigger reason for why they were attending the school. It didn't take me long to see how much of a challenge this was going to present for me.

Thankfully, though, the five kids who did regularly show up for pre-season running were forming a foundation for what I hoped would be a team that saw the value of hard work in all aspects of life.

Ilian Menkov was an 11th grader who came from a family that was part of the Bulgarian middle class, a class that would be considered very low by European standards. As the student council president, he was popular and considered a leader by his peers. His father worked for Bulgarian National Tobacco, an industry that had been nationalized, but was under more and more financial pressure since R.J. Reynolds brought his American tobacco corporation to Eastern Europe. As it stood, the national tobacco industry was hanging on, but most people—including Menkov—would say that it was only a matter of time before the nationalized tobacco industry would be overtaken by the American capitalist company. Menkov would speak openly and honestly about his desire to get a scholarship to leave for university, but he didn't speak about that as much as he spoke about his love for basketball.

"I know that people say we aren't supposed to be any good, Coach," he told me during one of our first team runs, "but I don't believe that. I think we can be great."

While I couldn't realistically match his "great" expectations, it was nice to have what I was starting to realize was a very non-Bulgarian attitude on the team.

Alexander Karlov also had a very non-Bulgarian attitude. I'd never heard him utter the phrase *ne modje*. He was constantly smiling and talking, two traits that were generally taboo for Bulgarian men. Sasho— as he was known—was also 6'4", something that excited me tremendously. But then I watched all 6'4" of him play basketball. He lumbered, stomped and did just about everything in slow motion. Sasho was not a good basketball player. But he'd show up twice a week ready to run, and be ready to ask me a question right away:

"What you think of this Holden Caulfield, Coach? We're reading his book in grade 10 English class, and it's just so interesting. Sometimes I really think I relate to him."

As his other team members looked at him derisively, I started to understand why Sasho could relate to Holden. His grades were not good, and his mother was constantly worried that he might not be able to graduate from the school. But Sasho didn't seem too concerned. He was more focused on finishing the three-kilometer run every Monday and Wednesday afternoon. And for that, I was thrilled.

I had little doubt that Pavel would also be a regular at the pre-season runs. He'd told me that he'd be there as much as possible, but that he also had to help his mother take care of his little brother. His dad was busy trying to start a sports apparel business—a rarity in Bulgaria—and wasn't home very often. Pavel's family lived in a row house block apartment not far from school, and his grades were also barely good enough to keep him at the school. He hoped to one day be able to help his dad with the fledgling family business, and his case was uncommon at the school—a student who didn't even appear to have the finances or grades to leave the country. While Pavel had a long, long way to go in terms of basketball performance, it was clear that he loved to play—and loved to play hard.

Anton Vasilev—or Vassy, as he was called—admitted to me the first time he came to pre-season running that he'd never really played basketball before.

"I came to some practices last year," he told me, "but they weren't really practices. I'm not sure what we were doing. But now some of the guys this year have said that you're going to have practices, and you're making people run. Actually, most of the guys I talked to don't really like either of those things. But I think it sounds cool. So I think I want to play basketball."

I knew right away that I wouldn't be able to convince Vassy to play; he'd have to want to do it. As a 16-year-old 11th grader, he was living on his own in a Sofia apartment. He was a good student who wanted desperately to go to school somewhere else in Europe, and a scholarship was the only way that was going to happen. Basketball had nothing to do with that equation, but he thought the idea of working hard sounded cool. Vassy became a regular at the pre-season runs.

Finally, Stefan Nikolov–dubbed *Nadenitza*–needed no convincing of the value of pre-season running. As a 9th grader the previous year, he'd been told repeatedly that he wasn't big enough, wasn't quick enough, and couldn't shoot well enough to ever see the floor. Many of these criticisms were right on, but all of them failed to take into account his heart and determination. Both of Stefan's parents were doctors–an occupation in the West that indicated prestige–and that meant that while he came from a highly-educated background, his family was not well off. Medical professionals in Bulgaria, while many of them were highly-skilled, were not paid like doctors in the West. The most common phrase I'd hear from my Bulgarian doctor was, "I don't know if I can continue being a doctor in this country. The only way I can make a decent living as a doctor is by going abroad."

While Stefan's parents worked long hours in Sofia a surprisingly low salary, Stefan already had his sights on using his American College education to go abroad. But one of the problems with that was that Stefan had no idea what abroad even meant. He, like many of my students and players, had never even been out of the country. He'd never even been on an airplane.

But he loved running, and as we started our pre-season workouts, it was Stefan who led the way with me on every team run.

It was these five who gave me hope–and not only hope for the basketball season, but hope for Bulgaria in general. I'd begun to notice that there was plenty of negativity surrounding, well, far too much in Bulgaria. But these five who were regulars for the "optional" runs twice a week were determined to be positive. They believed in what we were doing.

But the problem was that these were only five players. And of the five, Menkov was the only one who actually had basketball talent. The other four, while I could already sense I was going to love coaching them, were going to require tons and tons of coaching. Calling their talent raw would be an understatement. Simply saying they had talent might not even be true.

The real talent—if you could even call it that—wasn't showing up for the pre-season runs. Martin Dimov, whose father came to pick him up from school in a Mercedes with tinted windows, couldn't be bothered by after school running. "All I need to do," he'd tell me, "is dribble the ball. I don't need to run before season."

Peter Lachev—or Pesho—the 6'4" athlete who I targeted as our starting center, continued to try to plead his case regarding not coming to the workouts: "Coach, I used to play professional basketball," he would tell me, referring to playing for a club team, "and we never ran. That's not how we do things here. This is Bulgaria, not America. I don't need to run." In Pesho's case, he'd say all of this with a well-meaning charm, a well-meaning charm that I sensed worked on many, but to me, his reliance on charm was more alarming than comforting. I knew that Pesho's parents, who were both part of high-society Bulgaria, were in the process of getting divorced, and I could sense that he was used to playing one off the other to get what he wanted. In this case, he wasn't exactly sure how to play me, but one thing was certain: he didn't want to run.

Ivan Ivanov—whose name is the American equivalent of Johnny Johnson—was constantly being hounded by his mother to improve his grades. And, like many 16-year-olds that I was used to in the States, the last thing Ivan was concerned about was his grades. Like the families of several of his teammates, his was not wealthy, and unfortunately, Ivan wasn't sure if he'd be able to leave the country. As a result, he saw less reason to working hard in school because he wasn't the naturally gifted student that so many of his classmates were. His lack of work ethic in school resulted in his mother forbidding him from playing basketball until he got his grades up. Ivan was 6'2", a natural athlete with plenty of talent, but he'd played very little basketball in his life. Throughout the fall he continued to tell me, "Coach, it's the one thing I love. I love basketball. But my mom's really angry. I can't come to the running."

Finally, the one player I'd picked originally as actually having some talent and basketball potential was Konstantin—he went by Kosio—Dimitrov. During the first days of open gym and tryouts, I was convinced that I would never let anyone on the team shoot from farther than 15-feet from the rim; we just didn't stand a chance to make a jump shot. Kosio was the exception. At 6'1", he had a smooth-looking jump shot and was able to handle the ball, and even dribble a little bit with his left hand. Upon first meeting him, I was just as surprised by his fluency in English; he was one of the few players who didn't frequently use the Borat-like phrase *nice, very nice* with alarming frequency. Kosio, as far as I could tell, was smooth on the basketball floor, and a smooth talker, too. But I also sensed his smoothness had been used far too often to his own benefit in the past. Kosio did not see the need to come to the running workouts, and when I expressed my displeasure about this, he finally started showing up–but always with an excuse. "Coach, I can't run today," he'd tell me in perfect and almost unaccented English, "my knee/ankle/groin hurts." The first time it happened, I took note of it, but didn't respond much. By the time he'd come up with his third different injury, I asked some of the few remaining about Kosio and his endless supply of excuses. "Coach," they told me, "that's just Kosio. He doesn't want to run, and he probably never will run."

These were four players I hoped to count on during the season, and I had some reason to believe that they'd become regular attendees of practice once the season started. But the 12th grade talent–and I'd been told there was some–was an entirely different story.

"Coach, I don't think the 12th graders are going to play," Menkov seemed nervous to tell me. "They might show up sometimes, but they've heard that you're having us run a lot ... and, uh, well, they don't want to run. I don't know if any of them will play."

Hearing that the entire 12th grade didn't want to run and didn't want to work hard was a bit stunning, but again, I was beginning to get used to this in Bulgaria. It did, however, leave me to ponder my intrusion into Bulgarian culture and my insistence that practices be filled with running and hard work. While I wanted my players to adapt to my style, I wondered if I should be adapting to their Bulgarian style more. But what I'd learned so far about their Bulgarian style was that it was really easy to not have real practices, and always more convenient–and much more fun–to not have to work hard on the basketball court.

No matter how much I pondered the current state of affairs, all I was left with was five players with minimal talent who I knew would work hard, and a whole bunch of question marks. These were question marks, I decided, that I would only be able to figure out with more time. For now, though, I wasn't going to change course. So I accepted Menkov's news with the understanding that we probably wouldn't have any senior leadership. More and more, I realized that the leadership was going to have to come solely from me. And seeing that the things I believed in most were incredibly foreign to the majority of my basketball players, I was coming to the realization that my role as a leader was placing me on an island, an American island in the heart of Eastern Europe. I guess that's why I wasn't too surprised when the beginning of actual team practices in the late fall resembled chaos far more than order.

"Get your butt down! Get your butt down! You can't play defense standing up! Defense is played with your feet, not your hands!"

I felt like I'd said this at least 400 times in the first week of practice. And I still felt like I was going to be saying it 400 times more.

No matter what I said, it seemed at least half the team would lounge their way through the defensive drills. Those who weren't lounging just didn't seem to have even the first idea how to play defense. Some were trying hard, but it was clear they'd never been asked to do anything like this before in any practice: slide back and forth as if a dribbler were in front of them.

Even when we'd run offensive drills, there'd been dissention based on my rules. During a continuous layup drill, when I declared the team had to make 40 layups in two minutes, they were shocked when I made them run when they only made 28.

"But Coach!" Pesho hollered. "I didn't miss my layups. He did! And he did!" Pesho proceeded to point out several of the offenders.

"It doesn't matter who missed the layups," I thundered in response. "We're a team. If the team doesn't make enough layups, then we run. We're all in this together."

Judging by the muttering in Bulgarian that followed my proclamation, I could tell that my thoughts on *team* and *running* were not popular. Perhaps they were unheard of, I thought.

After the second day of defensive-slide drills that were followed by–God forbid–box-out drills, I was worried that I might be facing a team mutiny. They'd been willing to dive on the floor on the first day, but probably only because they were willing to do anything once. The eagerness I saw during the previous day's drill was mostly gone.

"Coach, you are crazy," Pesho offered up in accented English. "This box-out drill I do not understand. I mean, I understand–but how you make us do this? For every rebound, you put ball on floor. Every rebound, you want me on floor. How can I do this?"

I knew that Pesho intended only to speak for Pesho, but as I saw other eyes waiting for my response, I was worried about how many others he might be speaking for as well.

"Pesho, you don't have to like what we're doing," I responded briskly, "and you also don't even have to be here. But if you want to get better as a player, you're going to have to trust me and start working hard."

The answer seemed to satisfy Pesho for the moment as the next time I blew the whistle, he was the first one on the ground for the ball. He looked up at me with a huge grin, clearly proud of this accomplishment.

"See Coach, see Coach," he motioned to me holding the ball in his hands. "I can do it. I did what you wanted. Now we start playing offense?"

With this, I just blew the whistle again to start the next rotation of the box-out drill.

On the first day of practice, I got the sense the team was willing to feel me out and try to understand what this was all about. On the second day, though, whether it was Pesho's good-natured questioning or others who were more critical, I didn't know if they liked the feeling they were getting.

"Coach, I think we need to talk," Dimov approached me in a friendly manner–far too friendly in my opinion. "Here in Bulgaria, everyone plays zone defense. You know, like 2-3, 3-2, that kind of zone. You have this in America? Well anyway, it seems to me that all these drills are based on us playing man-to-man defense. Here in Bulgaria, we don't play man-to-man defense."

With this latest salvo fired away by my increasingly talkative team, I decided to address the entire team.

"I want to let you know that we're not going to play zone defense in practice today."

Gasp.

"I also want to let you know that we're not going to play zone defense tomorrow or the next day–or the day after that."

More gasps.

"So if you're starting to understand what I'm saying, we're not ever going to play zone defense. We're going to play man-to-man defense, and if you think it's hard, good. It should be hard. Playing man-to-man defense is difficult and that's why people don't like doing it. Playing zone defense is easier and that's why you love it. But if we're ever going to be good, we're going to have to learn to play man-to-man defense. That's the end of the story, and you don't need to ask me about zone anymore."

44

I think they may have been all gasped out at this point, but I felt like it was my time to start gasping. All I'd been doing for what seemed like the entirety of my basketball life in Bulgaria had been defending everything we were doing. The island I inhabited was getting smaller and smaller and it seemed the only boats in the vicinity were rowing the other way.

As we finished practice for the day, I had the team run sprints based on their ability to make or miss free throws. With each new free throw that clanked off the rim or backboard—and the backboard shouldn't ever be used for a free throw—a collective groan was uttered from the group of 15 boys. Kosio's groaning had already led him to sit out in the bleachers, this time claiming that he'd hurt his shoulder and couldn't run. Numerous other misses were accompanied right away by someone howling out, "But Coach, it *eeesn't* fair. Please don't make us run any more. It *eeesn't* fair."

As a free throw was finally made and practice mercifully ended, "It *eesn't* fair" was stuck firmly in my mind. I wondered how fair this entire arrangement was to both coach and players. I wondered about the next day's practice, and the next after that, and the entire season. Would every day be not fair just like this one?

I knew there were good things that had happened in the first few days of practice. I knew that there had been progress made, no matter how slow. But these positive thoughts eluded me as practice finished on the second day. My head was riddled with images of behind-the-back passes that sailed five feet wide of their target; Bulgarian swear words after missing layups; two-handed chest passes that looked more like cannonballs being dropped out of cannons, and finally, the endless protesting of any drill that involved running.

I started asking myself how long it was going to take before the drills we were running would actually look like drills instead of Bulgarian chaos. I started asking myself when running would become a given, and not something I'd have to plead with half the team to do regularly. While my players wanted to settle back into their old, familiar and comfortable habits, I knew this was exactly what I wanted, too. I was yearning for the familiarity and comfort of what I was used to: coaching basketball to hard-working American players who had played basketball their entire lives. Every year I'd ever coached represented a new kind of challenge, but after two days of Bulgarian practice—and two days of constantly challenging my new team—I started to think about what was in front of me. Was I up to this challenge?

As I headed out of the bubble for the night, a slight autumn drizzle was misting away outside. The either half-finished or half-gutted–I couldn't really tell–row house that loomed over the bubble seemed to loom even more than usual as it was shrouded in the mist. I looked around at my surroundings to try to find some sense of comfort, but there wasn't much to be found. I couldn't see much through the mist, and as I'd made my way outside, I now started to hear the savage yelping of the stray dogs that prowled campus. Walking back toward the school, I was happy to run into a human face, any human face.

Nikolai, happy to be headed home for the night, greeted with me a smile. I should've had this same feeling, but my mind was already swamped with thoughts of how to run some semblance of a practice tomorrow.

"Andy," Nikolai started, "you have a very interesting practice. Very interesting, indeed."

I couldn't tell what Bulgarian form of *interesting* he was referring to, but I braced myself for another body blow.

"I watched some of your practice today, and I was–how do you say?–amazed."

"Amazed, Nikolai? What do you mean?"

"I know these boys well. I have seen them grow up in this school, and I've seen them play before. But I've never, never seen them work like how you make them work."

I didn't know what to say, so I just let him keep going.

"These boys, they don't have much training to work hard. But I've never seen them work like what I saw these last two days. This is wonderful for them. I can't believe you are doing what you are doing."

As I still wasn't responding, Nikolai looked at me confused–and then worried that perhaps he'd made a mistake speaking English. I was too flabbergasted overall to come up with a quick and coherent response. The communist workers' motto kept ringing in my head: *They pretend to pay us and we pretend to work.* Was Nikolai pretending to see something wonderful?

"Well, thanks, Nikolai," I told him sheepishly. "We have a long, long way to go, but all I really want them to do is work hard."

"Andy, I can see they will learn how to work hard. I was so happy seeing them working at practice today. It was absolutely wonderful to see."

With that, Nikolai and I parted ways. He was elated with the glimpses he saw from practice, while I walked home in the mist feeling defeated and frustrated after only two days. I tried to use his words as vindication, but all I could think of was how difficult and deflating so many moments of the last practice had been. Our vantage points were clearly different, and I tried to appreciate this. I'd moved to Bulgaria to start to understand and appreciate different viewpoints. But as I walked up the driveway to my Bulgarian home, the mist gathered strength and turned into a full-fledged rain shower. I was wet and cold. And not too far off in the distance, the stray dogs continued barking.

Chapter VI
Shaking My Head

To have any understanding of Bulgaria, you have to know that it is a place steeped in tradition. And to an American with little knowledge of Bulgaria's culture, it's hard not to arrive in the country and see many of these traditions as oddities–oddities that certainly take some getting used to.

First and foremost, I learned how difficult it was to grasp the two most important–and usually simple–expressions in any language, yes and no. Learning the words–*da* and *ne*–wasn't the problem though; it was the corresponding body language that goes with these words.

In Bulgaria, unlike pretty much everywhere else in the world (Sri Lanka is the only other exception), when you want to say "yes," you shake your head from side to side. This headshake for yes usually takes on a bobble-head doll-like quality, but it's definitely a head shake no matter how you describe it. And every time I saw the headshake as I arrived in Bulgaria, I immediately assumed this meant "no." Even though I had been told over and over again that a shake of the head indicated assent, it was nearly impossible to shake 27 years of instinctively viewing a headshake as "no". Even more difficult, I soon discovered, was the fact that nodding your head up and down meant "no". Once again, in these situations, instinct would kick in and I'd feel a sense of satisfaction when I asked a question in Bulgarian and received a nod of the head. Here's a typical example:

"Excuse me," I'd say in Bulgarian at the bus station, "are there any tickets available for the bus to Veliko Turnovo (the medieval capital of Bulgaria)?"

The swift and immediate response from the bus ticket agent was several nods of the head. My reaction was happiness—first that I'd correctly asked in Bulgarian and second that the answer was yes. But that was only half true; the answer wasn't yes. I'd find that out quickly.

"Why are you still standing here?" was barked in Bulgarian in my direction moments later. "I already told you we don't have tickets!"

Dejected on many counts, I'd turn my head in cross-cultural disappointment and walk away. Had I asked the same question and observed the ticket agent shaking his head, I probably would've walked away with the same feeling, assuming he'd said no.

There was rarely a day in the beginning of my time in Bulgaria where this yes/no issue didn't rear its confusing and alternately shaking and nodding head. The youth of Bulgaria represented a bright glimmer of hope for a foreigner, as they realized that they were different than the rest of world and were trying to change to adapt. As a result, some of my high school English students and basketball players had molded to the rest-of-the-world practice of nodding for yes and shaking for no. In theory, this should've provided a rare and welcome form of comfort for someone like me. But it typically didn't work out this way.

"Now," I'd ask my team at practice," do you understand how to run this drill?"

Half the players would shake their heads, and half would nod. Best friends standing next to each other would do the opposite. I'd be utterly confused.

"So what does that mean?" I'd holler. "You're shaking your head yes, or nodding your head yes ... or what? Do you understand or not?"

My players would start looking at each other, each trying to remember if he had shaken his head or nodded. Whatever each had done had been instinctive; it's not something to think about, but just something that happens.

"Okay then, we're going to have to do this verbally. No more head gestures. Do you understand the drill or not? *Razbireteli?*"

There were a series of *yeses* and *das*. I couldn't help but note that even as they verbalized this response, half the players shook their heads and the other half nodded. Getting used to whatever game of charades we were playing here was going to take a lot of practice and a lot of patience, that was for sure.

And this only mirrored the rest of my adaptation to the quirky traditions of Bulgarian culture. After I got my first Bulgarian haircut–I gave instructions to the barber with a series of scissor-clipping gestures–I was "warmly" greeted by my students the next day as they, one by one, came up to the front of the room and slapped me on the back of my head.

"Happy new haircut!" they'd gleefully utter, and then the next slap would be forthcoming.

Seeing the look of confusion on my face, they'd ask, "Wait a minute, in America when people get haircuts, isn't it tradition to slap this person on the back of the head?"

"No," I responded, "in America we don't have any traditions that involve slapping people on the back of their heads."

"Oh, well, here in Bulgaria, we like to celebrate haircuts with a good slap. It's nice, very nice," was the unintentionally Borat-sounding response.

Yes, I thought, *nothing like a good slap to really know you're in the middle of a celebration.*

Throughout its history, Bulgaria had already received its fair share of slaps, so I figured the least I could do was stand up in the front of the classroom and take this form of abuse. The slapping continued every time I got a haircut.

But there were other times when I didn't think any form of abuse would be necessary–specifically, Bulgarian parties. Bulgarians believe, I soon learned, that jackets, purses and backpacks should never be placed on the floor–at a party, in an office, classroom or wherever. The superstitious result of placing one of these items on the floor of a living room, bedroom or classroom would be the loss of all of your money. This was no joke. Early on in my Bulgarian tenure, Bulgarian colleagues freaked out at a staff party when their coats were taken from their spot on a bed and placed on the floor. Seriously offended, they refused to stay at the party until their coats and purses had been removed from the floor and placed safely on top of something, anything. My students were also visibly nervous and upset when I asked them during their first quiz on Orwell's *1984*, the most fitting book I could think to teach first, to place their backpacks on the floor. To avoid a coup d'etat, we ended up agreeing that they could use a common table to place all of their backpacks. Crisis averted, they moved onto the quiz with hopes they'd retain whatever Bulgarian *leva* they currently lay claim to.

The only thing I could claim about my knowledge of Bulgarian traditions was that—once again—I had a lot to learn before I was going to be able to make any sense of my new home. My direct priorities were to teach English and coach basketball, but in no time at all, I could see how these things would take a backseat to all my other cultural learning. Still, though, I was determined to establish a successful model of Bulgarian basketball no matter how many times my players shook their heads to say yes, slapped me on the back of the head, or flipped out when their backpacks sat on the floor.

As much as Bulgarian cultural traditions were interesting, many times to the point of ridiculousness, the tradition behind Bulgarian sport seemed most pressing as I looked at my basketball team. So many things that I thought would be normally accepted—mostly because they were normally accepted in the United States—were anything but with my new Bulgarian team. Concepts like teamwork—sometimes things as simple as not yelling at each other—hard work, hustle, fair play and the importance of having a strong and ethical character were all foreign concepts to them, just like I was the foreigner trying to grasp concepts related to their country. When I'd tell them that hard work would pay off, or that we were going to learn to play the right way, the looks on their faces would indicate great confusion. And as I started to look into Bulgarian sport in general, I started to understand much more where the confusion was coming from.

As a small country with a population of less than eight million people, Bulgaria would never be a prohibitive favorite on the stage of world sports. But, I learned, throughout its sporting history, Bulgaria has had some glorious moments. The greatest moment in recent Bulgarian history, without a doubt, came as a result of Bulgaria's "Golden Generation" of soccer players. In 1994, they shocked the world by defeating reigning champion Germany in the round of eight in the World Cup to advance to the semifinals. Even though Bulgaria lost to Italy 2-1 in its next game (and then the third-place game to Sweden), Bulgarians still celebrated their entrance onto the world soccer stage. Their star, Hristo Stoichkov, who would later go on to play for FC Barcelona, would win the Golden Boot as the tournament's top scorer.

Any routine internet search about Bulgarian athletics will most immediately lead you to this glorious moment in 1994. This wasn't the first time that Bulgaria had tasted glory on the world stage either. During the '80s and '90s, Bulgarian weightlifters dominated the world stage, but the eventual headlines about their dominance dealt much more with scandal than glory. In the 1988 Seoul Olympics, two different Bulgarian weightlifters were stripped of gold medals after testing positive for banned substances. Unfortunately, this only foreshadowed more doping trouble for the next two decades. During the 2000 Sydney Olympics, three more Bulgarian weightlifters—a gold medal-winner and bronze medal-winner—tested positive for banned substances. This led to condemnation from around the world, especially from the International Olympic Committee which decried the weightlifters' actions as "stupid." As a result, the entire Bulgarian team was kicked out of the Olympics; some were sent home without even having a chance to—fairly or unfairly—compete. The entire team was then suspended for 12 months from international competition. Reading about these incidents gave me some insight as to why my players chafed every time I said we were going to learn to play basketball the right way by putting in an honest effort.

And as much as you'd think these embarrassing international incidents regarding the Bulgarian weightlifting team would have led to a new approach to the sport, this wasn't the case either. With international eyes on Bulgaria concerned that cheating would arise again, before the Beijing Olympics 11–*11!*–Bulgarian weightlifters tested positive for banned substances and were subsequently prohibited from traveling to Beijing to compete. Not placing the scandal solely on the broad, steroid-inflated shoulders of the weightlifters, a Bulgarian cyclist and marksman were both also disqualified for doping. One team that did qualify for Beijing was the Bulgarian volleyball team. With a strong showing in the previous World Championships, there was hope that maybe the Bulgarians could earn a medal in Beijing in volleyball. But these hopes were dashed rather quickly as the team failed to perform on the biggest stage. Watching an American broadcast of this Bulgarian Olympic volleyball game, I couldn't help but cringe when the commentators correctly identified the team's biggest problem: themselves. The U.S. commentators continued to point out that the Bulgarian team was spending so much time yelling at each other that it was distracting them from their shared goal of winning a volleyball game. In my basketball practices, sometimes the shared goal was simply making the pass that led to a layup, and all too often that would be interrupted by yelling amongst teammates.

It was doping incidents and stories of cacophony amongst teammates that would cause many Bulgarians to bemoan the fact that their country only made international news when something went wrong–sometimes horribly and unethically wrong. It was also stories like these that helped me understand why none of my players considered playing man-to-man defense an option. Man-to-man defense required more work and much more cooperation between teammates. As they'd been shown all too often by Bulgarian sporting "heroes," the shortcuts were too appealing. And even when these Bulgarian stars were rebuffed internationally, this didn't seem to stop the vicious cycle in Bulgaria.

During the last decade, though, unfortunately the tarnished cycle of Bulgarian athletic mishaps was becoming more and more glaring with each new year. The Bulgarian ice dancing team of Maxim Staviski and Albena Denkova won back-to-back World Championships in 2006-2007, earning them the admiration of Bulgarians and people around the world. But by the time I arrived in Bulgaria, there was little talk of Staviski's ice dancing prowess, and much more discussion of what had happened on the night of August 5, 2007 on a dark road on the Bulgarian Black Sea coast.

Driving his Hummer at speeds in the neighborhood of 100km/hr, Staviski crashed into oncoming traffic, plowing into a compact Honda. The driver, 24-year-old Petar Petrov, was killed, and his 18-year- old fiancée sustained injuries that still have her in a coma today. Staviski's blood alcohol level was .11, well over the legal limit. As an American arriving in Bulgaria to hear this tragic news, it was disheartening to hear about yet another Bulgarian sporting star going down the wrong path. But the events of August fifth weren't nearly as disheartening as the result of the impending legal case: Staviski was given a suspended sentence, paid off the families of the injured and dead, and spent no time in jail.

I was appalled, and sought for answers from any Bulgarian I could find. How could this be justice? How could the legal system look the other way on an act as destructive as this? Something had to be done because I failed to see how this could pass as justice in any country, especially an EU country.

"*Ne modje,*" I was told over and over again by Bulgarian colleagues. "This is Bulgaria; this is the way it is here."

With a fatalistic shrug of the shoulders, the matter was considered closed.

This fatalism was also echoed in Bulgaria's most recent approach to soccer, the country's favorite sport, on the world stage. While 1994 represented the height of Bulgarian soccer prominence, it was all downhill from there. After qualifying for the 1998 World Cup, they did not advance past the group stage, and that was their last appearance in the World Cup. The Euro Cup soccer tournament has not been much kinder to Bulgaria either. The last time they qualified for this tournament—it's held every four years, two years before or after the World Cup—was 2004, and in that tournament, they promptly lost all three games, including an embarrassing 5-0 loss to Sweden.

When I first arrived in Bulgaria, I was eager to attend a soccer match, and knew that Bulgaria stood in third place in their Euro 2008 qualifying group, still very much alive for a spot in the Euro Cup. The first home game that fall pitted them against Romania, a bitter rival, and also the team that was currently in second place. The week before the game, I anxiously approached nearly every Bulgarian I worked with and asked them about getting tickets for Saturday's big game. The response was nearly always the same:

"Why are you going to bother going to the game? If you want to go, fine, but don't worry about getting tickets. There won't be anyone there."

Won't be anyone there? I couldn't believe what I was hearing. With only a few games remaining in qualifying, if Bulgaria could defeat Romania and win their next two games against lesser opponents after that, they'd most likely qualify. Hope was still very much alive, at least in my eyes.

But the Bulgarians I talked to couldn't have been more right. That cold November night, I attended the Romania-Bulgaria game with about 10,000 other people. Less than one-third of the stadium's seats were filled even though the tickets were eight *leva* (about five U.S. dollars). Sure enough, though, Bulgaria pulled out a spirited 1-0 victory to keep Euro 2008 hopes alive.

But maybe those were just my hopes. With the rest of the soccer-crazed country only sort-of watching, Bulgaria didn't win another game. I was surprised, but no one else I talked to was. The soccer team had fulfilled the prophecy so many had held for so long: they weren't going to win.

This, I was discovering, was the number one prophecy held by Bulgarians regarding sport, and the number one sentiment already held by my basketball team: they weren't going to win. I started to realize more and more why they were rebelling against my hard-working tactics. It would be easy to say that they simply didn't want to work—and this was an issue for some—but laziness didn't cover the deep psychological nature of their inferiority complexes. Just like Bulgarians huddling in front of a television on Saturday night to watch a soccer game, my basketball players made their way into practice far too often with a similar attitude: they were going to lose. So really, what was the point?

Bulgaria still retained a passion for soccer, but most of this passion remained below the surface. Their national team struggled on the world stage, and while there was great support for club teams within Bulgaria, the dominant soccer story soon after I arrived in Bulgaria was the fate of CSKA Sofia, the most popular team in Bulgaria. (The CSKA brand originated in Moscow.) After winning the Bulgarian league and earning an automatic berth in the biggest tournament in Europe, the UEFA Champions League, CSKA was ejected from the tournament before it even started. They were kicked out because of a failure to pay their bills—mainly heating, telephone and electric bills. Their debts and lack of concern over these debts became so egregious that UEFA, the soccer federation that rules all of Europe, took notice and booted them out of the league, denying them any chance of making their mark on the European stage.

As I searched through the annals of Bulgarian sport, I tried to find figures I could use to motivate and perhaps inspire my basketball players. But too often, the athletes who had gained fame in Bulgaria had lost it so quickly for various tragic reasons. The lone remaining hope for the country in terms of international glory was Bulgaria's superstar soccer striker, Dimitar Berbatov. When I arrived in Bulgaria, he was in the process of making a transfer to Manchester United, arguably the most famous and reputable soccer team in the entire world. After so many years of Bulgarian futility on the world stage, Berbatov finally represented a sense of pride that Bulgarians longed to have in their athletes and their country. But while Berbatov achieved success with Manchester United, this didn't translate to success for the Bulgarian national team in their competitions for the Euro and World Cups. Increasingly, Berbatov received more and more blame for not leading the national team to qualify for international tournaments. And increasingly, he became more and more frustrated with the burden and criticisms that were placed upon his shoulders.

But these frustrations couldn't even come close to what eventually caused Bulgaria's brightest athletic star to quit the national team and leave the country. During a return to Bulgaria for an international qualifier in late 2009, Berbatov allegedly was faced with quite an ordeal. Here's how the story—which was widely circulated, though never completely confirmed—goes: Berbatov was threatened by the Bulgarian mafia, and told that his family would be kidnapped. If he didn't pay the gang 500,000 British pounds, he, his wife and his child would be kidnapped. Left with little choice, Berbatov and his family fled the country after striking a deal with the mafia. When police tried to talk to him and intervene, he refused to cooperate believing that police and members of the Ministry of Justice were also in on the kidnapping plot. Berbatov paid the kidnappers to allow him to leave the country safely, and soon after that, he quit the national team, opting to focus on his life and career in England.

While my basketball players would criticize Berbatov for his lack of patriotism and commitment to his country, I found it difficult to blame him too much. It's not like the kidnapping scare in 2010 was the first time this had happened to him either. As an up-and-coming 18-year-old star in the Bulgarian leagues in 1999, Berbatov was kidnapped by the boss of a rival team and held for ransom. The incident in 2010 was the second time he'd looked kidnappers straight in the eye, and this man was the most highly regarded and acclaimed athlete in the entire country.

Becoming involved in sports in Bulgaria seemed to come with the inherent risks of danger. Soccer represents the biggest athletic business model in Bulgaria, and unfortunately, Berbatov's kidnapping encounters weren't the only ones associated with Bulgarian soccer. In the summer of 2008, Angel Bonchev, the president of Litex Lovech (a city in northern Bulgaria) soccer club, was kidnapped by a mafia gang and held hostage for 50 days. (The length of his captivity with no successful intervention by the Bulgarian police lends credence to why Berbatov thought he was best off not cooperating with the police and just leaving the country.) When Bonchev's wife was able to broker a ransom deal to free her husband, she went to deliver the money and was then kidnapped herself. Her husband was found soon after this stumbling in the streets, heavily drugged. Upon further inspection, Bonchev had had two of his fingers severed, and when he recovered from the heavy doping his kidnappers inflicted upon him, he then had to figure out a way to get his wife back from the kidnappers. Eventually, after a 157,000 Euro ransom payment, his wife was released. Soon after this, advertisements were abound in the Sofia newspapers for a brand-new and very necessary service: kidnapping insurance.

So as I looked for ways to understand and then motivate my players to become the best basketball players they could be, I found myself distracted by what I worried was a more pressing issue: should I consider purchasing kidnapping insurance?

In the end, I didn't, and decided that researching Bulgarian soccer was only furthering my own sense about doom regarding my basketball team. Finally, with what I felt was the last straw, I sought information about Bulgaria as a basketball country. To my relief, the information I gathered had nothing to do with cheating, nothing to do with drunk driving, and nothing to do with kidnapping. The information I gleaned was straightforward, basic and all pointed to the same fact: Bulgaria was terrible at basketball.

While Bulgaria did have its own professional basketball league, it wasn't doing much to cultivate basketball talent in the country. The last time Bulgaria qualified for the Olympics in basketball was 1964. In EuroBasket competition, at least Bulgaria had managed to qualify several times in the past two decades. But qualification was about as far as they got. Twice—in 1991 and 1993—they finished dead last in the competition. Their best finish was seventh place in 1989, but only eight teams competed that year.

The one highlight of Bulgarian basketball history I was able to find was the story of Georgi Glouchkov. A 6'8" power forward from Tryavna, a town in the center of the country known for its textile industry, Glouchkov was considered the second best big man in Europe, behind Arvydas Sabonis, the 7'2" center from Lithuania who would later go on to play for the Portland Trailblazers in the 1990s. After a sparkling year in Bulgaria where he averaged 23 points and 19 rebounds per game, Glouchkov drew the attention of the NBA. The Phoenix Suns selected him with the 148th pick in the 1985 NBA draft. Upon arriving in America, Glouchkov became the first Eastern bloc player to ever play in the NBA.

I was heartened reading this story and even amused to find out that American basketball fans had given Glouchkov the moniker of "Balkan Banger" during his first season with the Suns. His transition to both America and American basketball, though, was not an easy one. Not surprisingly, growing up in the Soviet sphere of influence meant that Glouchkov didn't speak a word of English. He had great difficulty understanding anything his coaches said. Still, Glouchkov was able to become a regular role player, one who averaged about five points and three rebounds a game. In the middle of the season, the Suns were excited about Glouchkov's potential, and had him pegged as a regular in their rotation for years to come. But as the season wore on, Glouchkov's weight ballooned at a dramatic pace. No one knew the exact reason for this extremely uncommon weight gain for a player, especially during the season, but some speculated it was due to Glouchkov's love of American fast food and candy, American staples that weren't available in Bulgaria. But there was also a more troubling report that Glouchkov's weight issues stemmed from his experimentation with steroids, a theory that couldn't be considered far-fetched considering the recent history of Bulgarian sport.

When Glouchkov reported back to the Suns for his second season, he somehow managed to lose weight at a pace that was even more dramatic than the pace of his earlier weight gain. After blimping out during his first season, Glouchkov reported to summer camp the following year 25 pounds less than the weight he reported the year previous. With his loss of strength needed to battle physical NBA players, Glouchkov made it through the Suns summer camp, but was sent home by Suns at the end of the summer. The Suns never had explanations for any of his weight fluctuations, and it didn't seem to them to matter all that much. Glouchkov lasted one season in the NBA and was never heard of in American basketball circles after that.

At this point, I brought an end to my research of Bulgarian sport. While I was gaining an understanding of some of the traditions behind athletics in my new country, I found it hard to see how this understanding was going to help me improve the quality of the product I was seeing on the basketball floor every day in practice. One story, one fact, and one scandal after another, I'd learned all about sports in Bulgaria, and the optimist in me started to think that maybe what I was seeing on the basketball practice floor really wasn't all that bad. But that was the optimist in me. The realist in me couldn't stop taking in all this information and do nothing but shake my head over and over.

But I should've known that shaking my head out of frustration wouldn't help much. In Bulgaria, by shaking my head, all I was doing was saying "yes."

Chapter VII
Bulgaria in Motion

I sat in the stands watching the girls' basketball game trying not to let my nerves show as our first game of the year was only about half an hour away. My players were excited and antsy, and I was doing my best to keep them calmed down. But it didn't take long for me to lose focus on my team and worry about what was happening on the floor during the girls' game.

After the third consecutive hard foul–one had been called by the referee, two hadn't–the shoving match ensued between the two biggest girls on either team. With the first push of the scrum, Dimov and Vassy jumped out of their seats on the bleachers ready to hurl their venom into the mix. I immediately grabbed Vassy's shoulder and yanked him back down to reality. In the meantime, though, not much was being done about the rising tension on the basketball floor between our girls' team and the Sofia school who had come to play us. With the bubble dome of the gym providing acoustics for the Bulgarian swear words I was now becoming more and more familiar with, hostility between the two girls' teams continued to rise.

I first looked to the referee to see if he planned to calm things down, but he looked uninterested. Then I looked to the two coaches to see which one of them was going to call a timeout before things got really ugly. But both coaches looked even angrier than their players.

They had no intention of stopping this; in fact, their red faces and waving arms looked ready to join the battle.

With this, I made an executive decision to take my team outside and talk to them to make sure they were focused on our game, not the brouhaha that was bubbling inside. While I was baffled at the lack of sportsmanship I was seeing in front of me, I sensed that my players saw nothing wrong; the swearing, posturing and shoving were all expected parts of Bulgarian basketball.

"Now I want you to remember," I finally had their attention once we left the bubble, "that we're here to play basketball tonight. We're not here to fight, we're not here to argue, and we're not here to play dirty."

I paused in the hope of seeing my players shake/nod their heads in agreement. Several of them weren't eager to acquiesce; it took a while before they realized I was waiting for their acknowledgment.

"The most important thing for us tonight is to play our hardest and play our best basketball. If our game gets physical, dirty and inappropriate like this game right now, then we're going to have problems. If you're one of the people who are causing this to happen, you're going to be sitting on the bench."

Looking at my players, I could sense that this might be the most deflating pre-game speech ever. But watching the girls' game, I found myself less and less concerned with how we were going to play, and more and more concerned that the game would turn into a brawl.

Thankfully, my team got the message. Once the game started, their focus was strictly on basketball. And while our form of basketball was still error-filled and pretty ugly from a coach's standpoint, it was nothing like our opponents'.

The other school, it turned out, had no interest in waging a physical battle like their girls' team. In most cases, they seemed to have no interest in even hanging onto the basketball. They were dressed in a variety of t-shirts, and I sensed that the most important player was the one wearing the Marlboro t-shirt, not easy to find in Bulgaria. We gave them our mesh practice jerseys and they were thrilled to all be wearing something similar. I got the impression this had never happened to them as a team before.

While I lamented the fact that my players had only been playing basketball for a year or two, the opponents appeared to have only started playing basketball the previous Tuesday. Upon receiving passes, they typically flung the ball in the direction of the hoop, but their attempts were so misguided that it was difficult to tell whether these were passes or shots. When they launched from 26 feet, slinging the ball side-armed like a discus, I sincerely hoped these were passes, not shots. No matter what they were, this team was making us look like world-beaters.

We started the game on a 48-0 run.

My team was overjoyed.

Perhaps for the first time, I could see broad smiles on the faces of all my players—those on the floor and those on the bench. In huddles during timeouts, players were all ears. Pesho didn't complain, Dimov didn't have any ill-timed suggestions, Kosio actually seemed capable of running up and down the floor, and Menkov and Stefan looked determined as ever. This was basketball. This was fun. This was what they were here for.

The game ended with in a 62-4 score, and my players celebrated like they'd just made the NCAA tournament. I had to admit that while the team we played was the single worst team I'd ever seen, it was nice to have a drama-free afternoon of basketball. After all the coaxing, prodding, demanding and yelling, this game was free of any form of stress. Maybe, I thought, we weren't going to be too bad after all? If the competition was this poor, then maybe I was being too hard on my team.

In my postgame speech, I tried to focus on what we needed to do to improve. This was only one game, and we had a long way to go. We were certain to see better opponents in the future, and this game wouldn't mean much when we looked back on this season. I tried to put things in perspective, and would realize much later how prophetic I was.

"We're going to continue to play games against better competition, and it's not going to come easy. Winning and being successful isn't easy, and that means we have to come to practice tomorrow ready to work even harder."

I sensed, though, that this speech was falling on ears that were only basking in the glory of a 62-4 victory. So I cut the speech short and let them go for the night. But I soon found out that the night–a Wednesday–was just beginning for them. Boyan, a 10th grade bench player, eagerly came up to me moments later.

"Coach," he beamed, "a bunch of us guys are going to go out for drinks to celebrate the victory. We'd love it if you would come with us."

Once again, I had no idea how to respond. On the one hand, I could sense that maybe with this victory, the team was actually starting to respond to my coaching. But on the other hand, it was Wednesday night and Boyan in particular was only 15 years old. Not only were they going out drinking to celebrate the victory–a massive taboo for an American basketball player–but they were so unashamed of this that they wanted to invite their coach.

I had no choice but to laugh at the absurdity of the situation.

"Thanks, Boyan," I told him, "I appreciate the offer, but I think I'm going to head home."

With that, I walked out of the gym as a winner in basketball, but that didn't make me any less confused about what was going on in my life.

Confusion, though, was nothing new to either my basketball team or me. The following day at practice, my players entered a spirited debate over the location of our next game, the first game of tournament to be held the upcoming Saturday.

"Location TBA, I've been to that school in Sofia. It's near the city center, isn't it?" Pesho declared for all to hear in English, a sure sign that he must've been confident in what he was saying.

"No, it's not," Stefan quickly replied. "Location TBA is in Lozonets, an entirely different neighborhood. I know that school, man! You don't know what you're talking about."

"No way," Dimov howled, "TBA is in Mladost. It's right around the corner."

With this latest salvo, voices continued to clang around me in various forms of English with some Bulgarian swear words mixed in as well. While I was now certain that none of my players understood the acronym "TBA," I was quickly coming to an understanding that it didn't take much for them to find reason to disagree and argue.

"Guys, you need to stop arguing," I jumped in, hoping to stem the tide that I'd caused by handing out a paper schedule. "TBA means 'To Be Announced.'"

This was met with a quick, and much needed moment of silence. At least this argument, I figured, ended with no one being right. It took little time for the arguing to ensue once again, though, as this time Pesho, Stefan, Dimov and half of the rest of the team argued over who was dumber. To be honest, I felt like the dumb one for putting an American acronym on the schedule.

"When I wrote the schedule," I told them, "I didn't know where the game was going to be played so I wrote 'TBA.' To be honest, I still don't know where the game is going to be played. I just know we'll be playing in the Third of March tournament this Saturday at 10 a.m."

"Uh-oh," Menkov was the first to respond and several heads nodded along with him.

"What is 'uh-oh', Menkov? 'Uh-oh' to the Third of March tournament? 'Uh-oh' to Saturday morning?"

"No, coach, it isn't either of those. I just have a feeling I know where we're going to be playing."

"Well," I responded with what I quickly realized was a very American confidence and lack of concern, "it shouldn't matter where we play on Saturday morning. It only matters how we play."

With this, I expected agreement from my players, especially since they'd been noticeably excited since winning their first game. But my comment didn't seem to make much of a difference. The majority of the team seemed to side with Menkov about wherever we were going on Saturday morning. Maybe the gym wasn't going to be the greatest, but how bad could it be, really?

I deemed that it made no sense to worry about Saturday's conditions, so we started practice and worked on our latest—and most glaring—issue: motion offense.

As a coach, I'd always been a fervent believer of motion offense because it gives players freedom to make decisions away from the ball, make cuts to the hoop and screen for each other to get open. When I first introduced the idea of a motion offense to my Bulgarian team, they seemed to agree with me on all fronts.

"Coach," Pavel told me right away, "we've never been allowed to run an offense like this. The only offenses we ever learned were ones where we had to follow rules; I was only allowed to play my role in my spot and go nowhere else."

Now inured to the ways of Bulgaria, Pavel's descriptions of previous offenses immediately struck me as perfectly communist: no freedom, play your role and don't ask any questions. I was happy he was acknowledging a brand new era of freedom on the basketball courts of Sofia, unlike the boxed-in isolation I surmised he felt every day living in his communist block row house apartment.

"I think this motion offense is going to be great. I love the freedom. I can do whatever I want."

With Pavel's last statement, I tried to iterate to the entire team that "motion" didn't necessarily mean "do whatever you want." But I soon saw that this was the exact definition they understood.

As we started doing basic five-on-zero offensive drills, my players took to the idea of "motion" right away. They flew all around the court. Menkov sprinted from the top of the key to the corner, while Pavel started at one wing and made a beeline for the opposite wing. Stefan, eager to show off his fitness after all the pre-season running, ran circles around the two of them. Pesho and Ivan occupied the posts, and actually didn't move much. But that's because they were terrified to move; one step in either direction would most likely result in a collision with one of their three teammates who were setting Bulgarian records for speed in the half court.

With all this movement of players, the ball was being volleyed around in rapid-fire fashion. An outsider—perhaps a naïve basketball outsider—might've thought this was a Harlem Globetrotters practice with the ball being thrown and caught at all different angles. But from my vantage point, this was just absurdity on the basketball floor. The types of passes that were being made would never work with a defense on the floor, and when at least three guys were sprinting at the same time on offense, no one was ever going to be particularly open.

I tried to stop the drill time after time to slow them down, and talk about *good* motion, not just *motion for the sake of motion*. But this was falling on deaf freedom-loving ears. Without a defense to slow his barreling progress, Pavel professed his love for the new motion offense.

"Coach, I just love how I can do whatever I want in this offense. It's a feeling of freedom I've never had before."

I tried not to consider his comment on any other plane than the literal, but as I agonized over what I was watching—something akin to a scattered invasion of Macedonia—I tried to take solace in the fact that at least this feeling of freedom was something they liked. Realistically speaking, though, I started to wonder if I would need to install a more communist-styled offense.

Nevertheless, we devoted a good chunk of practice trying to work on the fundamentals of the motion offense. Once a defense was put in place, I was pleasantly surprised by the success of the offense. Some of the beeline sprints to the basket were actually working. Some of the out-of-control sprints across the lane actually resulted in open shots. The defense was actually having trouble guarding this motion offense.

But any signs of success with this new offense were also the direct result of something I didn't particularly want to admit: our defense was terrible.

As we huddled up at the end of the practice, I told the team that I would find out the exact location of 'TBA' for Saturday's tournament game. I talked to them about remembering the fundamental principles of motion offense, and for a change, there was optimism in the air. Players left practice with enthusiasm, and I sensed an eagerness that I'd previously worried didn't exist. Dimov gave me a high-five as he left the gym. Pesho first launched a half-court shot that was nowhere near the target, but then gave me a fist pound and said, "Coach, this was good practice. Good practice."

I couldn't help but feel the contagious nature of their enthusiasm. I'd be hard-pressed to say it was *good practice* like Pesho had said, but I was willing to accept any form of Bulgarian enthusiasm, a characteristic that wasn't always easy to come by.

Menkov was the one, though, who broke the mood on his way out of the gym. He reminded me of the fatalistic—and perhaps realistic—nature of Bulgaria and Bulgarians.

"Coach," he said solemnly, "I like this new motion offense. I think it will be good for us. But I don't know if you understand where we'll be playing on Saturday. On Saturday, I don't think there's going to be much chance for motion the place we're going."

"I'm not sure I understand what you're saying, Menkov," I responded.

"Well," he half-grimaced, "I think you'll see what I mean on Saturday."

With a combination of a foreigner's naivete and excitement, I still approached Saturday with enthusiasm. Though the early December temperatures had dipped near freezing, I was fired up for our first road game. Nikolai had finally notified me of the school's actual location—just a little outside the city's center—and I woke early on Saturday morning eager to see what a Bulgarian basketball tournament was all about.

As I headed out of campus, I began to notice the effects that winter was having on Sofia. We'd already had our first snowfall, but that had since melted, froze into ice, melted again, and now settled into an unattractive and slippery mud. I had celebrated the first snowfall, but then cursed it when it turned to ice; Sofia did not use salt for their walkways. As a result, my first Sofia ice adventures ended with a bruised tailbone from one fall, and a sore wrist from another tumble. Now that the winter temperatures had crept above freezing on this Saturday, I realized that maybe the ice was better than the mud. My walk to the bus stop with a bag of basketballs was perhaps more treacherous in the mud than the ice. And, when I slipped and careened toward the muddy ground, a much dirtier fate awaited. The non-salted icy sidewalks represented the pain of Bulgaria. The thawed muddy sidewalks represented the soiling of Bulgaria.

As I result, I skated my way to the dilapidated bus stop early Saturday morning to prepare to meet my team for the game. Unlike my previous American experiences, there was no team bus to take us to the game. My players–with the exception of a few who were driven to the game–were all doing the same thing I was: sliding along in the mud to go catch a public bus for the game.

The bus stop looked like it was built in 1962, and that's probably because it was built in 1962. The graffiti on the aluminum planks looked like it might've been around since 1962, but at least it was colorful. In reds, greens, blues and yellows, Bulgarian swear words were littered all over the small bus stop wind shelter. As I looked around me, these were the only colors to be seen.

I walked by a restaurant which had what appeared to be a tin roof, right across the street from the bus stop. Above its name, there was a giant sign in all capital letters that said, "HOBO!" I couldn't help but laugh at the notion of a restaurant advertising itself with a word like "HOBO," but this would only appear odd to a Westerner. In the Cyrillic language the letter "H" is the Latin equivalent of "N," and the letter "B" is the Latin equivalent of "V." So in Bulgarian, the restaurant was advertising itself as "NOVO" which translated to "new." From my vantage point, though, as I slip-slided in the ice-mud, this new restaurant appeared to be enticing homeless people to come dine.

Other than the HOBO restaurant, there wasn't much difference between my other viewing options. To my left, right, front and back were Soviet-era communist blocks. Each wore a different depressing shade of gray, and the outside of each building showed off different states of disrepair. The grass courtyards–calling them courtyards is giving them more credit than they deserve–had turned to mud, like the rest of Sofia, from the melted snow and ice. As I looked around for color in this world, my choice was pretty simple: gray communist block or brown mud.

Thankfully, the Sofia 76 city bus showed up to bring new color to my world. The bus had been, at one point, white and orange, but now wore stains of time and wear. It now sported brown where it had been white, and another shade of brown where it had once been orange. As I stepped onto the bus, I couldn't help but notice that the safety instructions on the windows were all written in French. Like nearly every 76 bus I'd taken, the bus came from a foreign country—a foreign country that didn't want this bus anymore. Sofia's public transit system was operated at a very low cost because they accepted donations from Western Europe; the buses France and Germany refused to put into service any more made their way to Sofia to provide top-of-the-line transportation.

On this Saturday morning, I was able to enjoy the relative emptiness of the bus and the city streets. With streets that were designed by the Soviets to hold no more than 50,000 cars, the fact that at least 10 times that many Sofia residents now owned cars caused massive traffic jams every day. It could take more than 30 minutes just to cover the two-kilometer straightaway outside the college. And the fact that many Sofia residents still didn't have cars meant that most rides on the 76 were guaranteed to be packed, slow moving and worst of all, foul smelling. Just the week before, I'd ridden the bus home at night and got a whole new set of bruises when a drunken hobo—an actual hobo, not the Bulgarian word for "new"—decided to lie on the floor of the packed bus with his bottle of booze, and start flailing his legs, kicking at anyone and anything that got near him. Showing my lack of Bulgarian preparedness, I was one of the last people to shove myself out of the way. He caught me in the shin twice while drunkenly slurring his speech, screaming that he needed money. As sad as he was, the looks on the rest of the bus riders saddened me even more: none of them seemed to have a reaction to this. It was clear they'd seen it many times before.

But this Saturday morning, I wasn't faced with any of these issues, and as a result, I was brimming with optimism. My team was 1-0 and about to play in the Third of March tournament—a tournament that ended on the third of March, but started in December—against a school named after Stefan Stambolov. Stambolov was a Bulgarian prime minister at the end of the 19th century and a Bulgarian nationalist hero. He was considered one of the "Founders of Modern Bulgaria," a modern Bulgaria that was passing me by as the 30-plus year-old bus rumbled along Sofia's downtown streets. Like too many Bulgarian heroes, it seems, Stambolov met an untimely end when political enemies hacked him to death in the streets of Sofia in July of 1895.

As we approached our first road game against Stambolov's school, I knew that Bulgarians never forget their history, and I was hoping that these modern Stambolovs weren't thinking too much about the anger they most certainly held for his brutal murder.

But as we entered the school—my first glimpse at a Bulgarian public school—I realized that my most immediate concerns were going to have nothing to do with Bulgarian basketball. The school was huge, and could be compared in size to an urban American public high school. But that's where the comparisons to America ended. There was graffiti scrawled in Bulgarian all over the outside walls of the school, and where there wasn't graffiti, there were metal cages erected to cover up the classrooms' glass windows. My team thought nothing of this, but I was slightly terrified.

"Coach, are you okay?" Pesho good-naturedly sensed my hesitation. "This is life in Bulgaria. Don't be afraid; we are used to this."

With no other choice than to follow my grinning 6'4" center through the front door of the school, I considered this my most official welcome to a Bulgarian public school. We made our ways through the halls, and my players let me know that they knew where the gym was, on the third floor. This struck me as odd, but I tried to stop myself from pointing out all the things I was finding odd about this school.

As we made our way up the flights of stairs toward the gym, I could hear the bouncing of basketballs, and this was a comforting feeling. Still, as we approached the door to the gym, it appeared to be no bigger than a door to a classroom. I started to wonder what was inside. Menkov had already warned me at practice earlier in the week, but I hadn't given his words much thought.

My first look through the cramped doorway, though, gave me all the information I needed to know—and all the reason in the world to make sure I listened to Menkov in the future.

The "gym" I was looking at was about the size of two classrooms, and it would be generous to say that the court was half the size of a regulation court. The first game of the tournament was in the third quarter. There was no scoreboard, but my players had found out this information, and my initial thought was to have my team go into the gym and watch this game to scout a potential future opponent. But there was no way we were going to be able to enter this gym. There was no space inside for spectators.

That was mostly because there were no out-of-bounds lines in this gym, just four walls. If the ball—or a player—hit the wall, that counted as out of bounds. The floor was wooden, but cracks were seen easily even from a distance. A few of the floorboards were wobbly, and I could see the nails that were hammered home to precariously hold the floor in place. No two dribbles appeared alike, as the ball bounced differently on each replaced floorboard. With each new thunderous step during the current game, I half-expected one of the floorboards to spring up, slapstick-style and whack an unsuspecting player in the nose.

As I looked up to the hoops, their status was as tenuous as the floorboards. Each time the ball hit either rim, it jostled and assumed a new crooked shape. Upon further inspection, I noticed that the free throw lines were at least 12 feet from the hoop, making a free throw flung toward these rusty cylinders probably the least "free" thing I could imagine. Of course—and I'd become accustomed this—there were no nets dangling from the hoops. It was difficult to tell the difference between a made shot and an airball; both plummeted downward and ricocheted off the concrete wall directly behind the hoop.

Unfortunately, as I continued to take in my new—and very Bulgarian surroundings—things weren't getting any better. The ceiling was low and it seemed to threaten any shot that had excess arc on it, but this was no concern at all compared to the far wall. Serving as the out-of-bounds "line," the wall was lined with windows that had steel cages protruded inward onto the court. Any player daring enough to make a beeline down that sideline stood a good chance of getting clipped or clocked by the steel reinforcements that extended onto the court. And even worse than that—I was having trouble believing there could be something else worse—was the rusty and jagged metal pipe that jutted out at least a foot from the wall in the far corner. Well within the realm of the basketball court, this jagged pipe appeared ready to impale any player brave enough to drive the right baseline.

Not willing or wanting to see any more, I turned back to my team members who were stretching in the hallway, seemingly unaffected by all of this. Menkov, though, remembered what he'd told me earlier in practice, and he was glued to my face.

"Coach, you okay?" he asked with concern. "It looks like you're sweating a little bit."

With this, I reached my hand to my forehead and realized he was right.

"Yeah, yeah, I'm okay," I said, pretty sure I was lying.

"You think we can run your motion offense in this gym?" he responded with more than a hint of sarcasm.

Several players laughed, as if they'd known all along what we'd be facing. This gym wouldn't allow for much motion. If my players circled the floor with the reckless abandon I'd criticized them for in practice, criticism wouldn't be their penalty. They'd either run into the wall, a steel cage or a jagged metal pipe. Taking one look back at the gym, it seemed more fitting for a prison dodge ball game than a high school varsity basketball tournament.

"Guys," I alerted them as I could sense my own anxiousness rising, "I've gotta take a pee. Do you know where the bathroom is here? I didn't see one as we walked in."

Pesho, who had already proven eager to be my Bulgarian public school tour guide, was the first to offer his help.

"Of course. We passed the bathroom on the way in, Coach. Didn't you see it?"

Again, this was met with laughter from my team that, while good-natured, didn't make me feel very comfortable.

Pesho started leading me down the hallway and stopped not far from where the rest of the team was stretching in preparation for the game. I knew I'd asked him to show me the bathroom, and I also knew he spoke good enough English and had no trouble understanding what I'd asked him. But that's what made me the most confused. Pesho had stopped in front of an unmarked wooden door that appeared to be a janitor's closet.

"This is it, Coach. This is the bathroom."

I couldn't help but notice that Pesho was smiling. He was enjoying the various looks of astonishment on my face with each new part of this public school "tour."

"Good luck, Coach!" Pesho hollered, turning to head down the hallway and back to the rest of the team.

Looking at the door, I could see the faint outline of a men's bathroom symbol that was also probably etched into the door in 1962. Seeing this, I opened the door and discovered that my initial thought about this being a janitor's closet wasn't far off. The bathroom was tiny, just a dingy little boxed room, and the toilet was nothing more than a hole in the middle of the floor. And it wasn't a port-a-potty type hole either; it was a drain hole, like you'd have in your bathtub.

Despite my own selfish concerns, I started to think about the bigger issues. This was a large Bulgarian public school and this was the bathroom that loads of students used each day. Still standing on the brink of the bathroom with the door open, it didn't take long for me to realize that with everyone peeing on this floor, it wasn't exactly a floor I wanted to step on to take care of my own business. But what choice did I have? What choice did the thousands of students at this school have?

Walking on the same floor that you urinate on seemed incredibly savage and uncivilized, but I couldn't see any other options. Pesho's earlier comment, *This is life in Bulgaria. Don't be afraid; we are used to this*, started to ring far too loudly in my head. I could either go with Pesho's philosophy and suck it up, or there was only one other Bulgarian choice regarding urinating before the game: *ne modje*. Faced with what I thought was the simple task of urinating, I thought I was getting far too much of an education about the Bulgarian condition.

The entire experience had unnerved me to the point of having to urinate even more, so I took two precarious steps into the closet and peed. Exiting with sticky shoes, I sheepishly made my way back to my team trying to focus on basketball, the whole reason for what I already felt was a misadventure.

With the previous game finally ending, we were granted permission to enter the gym. So many things that we'd worked on, and that I'd harped on during practices should've been at the front of my mind, but I was having trouble focusing on the task at hand–something I expected to chide my players for, not myself. As we entered the gym and found our wooden team bench–of course, it was part of the court since there were no out-of-bounds lines–I started to give a quick pep talk to lead us into our team warm-up. But I could tell my players were concerned about something else.

"Coach," Menkov interrupted, "before we start, can you do one thing for us?"

I couldn't claim to know what was coming next.

"Here are all of our cell phones and wallets," he said as he handed me a bag. "We need you to watch these during the game and keep them safe. Bad things can happen here; can you please watch our stuff?"

"Menkov, I don't know how I can watch your stuff," I reacted immediately, "because I'm going to be coaching the game. There's gotta be somewhere here where you can put your stuff where it's going to be safe. Do you really think something's going to happen to your wallets and cell phones here?"

With that, we both looked around the gym–crooked rims, cages on the walls, pipe protruding from the wall—and neither one of us could claim we saw comfort or security anywhere. Standing under the far basket were the two Bulgarian referees for our game. One was talking on his cell phone and the other was smoking a cigarette.

Exasperated, I took Menkov's bag of valuables and set it down on the bench next to my clipboard. My team started their warm-up, and I continued to shake my head in amazement at all that had led up to this game. And no, I wasn't shaking my head to acknowledge Bulgarian agreement.

As we huddled as a team to start the game, I wanted to give a speech about overcoming adversity, standing up and being strong when things weren't going well, and not making excuses for things that were out of your control. But as all these thoughts ran through my head, I realized that this wasn't a speech I needed to give to my players. They weren't fazed by the decrepit and dangerous state of the court, the drain hole for a urinal, or the cigarette smoke from the referee at the other end of the floor. I was the one who was having problems with this; I was the one who needed to hear the speech.

Thankfully, I was the one who was the most affected by the conditions we were faced with, and this was evident from tip-off. Even though there was very little room to move on this court, our practice in a motion offense at least encouraged movement and sharing of the ball. The other team looked mostly uninterested and out of shape. Using the speed and fitness they'd both gained from pre-season running, Menkov and Stefan were both zooming by their defenders and wreaking havoc in the passing lanes on defense. We employed a full-court press because there was no reason not to; the court was only the size of a half court gym anyways. Stefan Stambolov's players quickly became rattled as they threw the ball all over the gym. With each pass that would rattle off the cage wall, my players gained more confidence. And with both teams leery of going anywhere near the wall, the protruding cage or pipe, our press was even more successful. The game was played in an even smaller space where it was easy for us to trap them.

The first time Stefan Stambolov called a timeout, we had a 12-point lead. Or at least I thought we had a 12-point lead. There was no scoreboard, and the time and score were being kept by a kid sitting at the scorer's table. He appeared bored with the game, and perhaps in life itself, but when he told me in Bulgarian we were winning by 12, I figured I could live with that. Looking to the other bench, I was starting to get a better and better grasp on Bulgarian swear words as they shouted their way toward their team huddle. As we broke our huddle determined to keep up the pressure, I could see two opposing players barking at each other, clearly upset about a previous play, and clearly not focused on moving on. It was no surprise at all then that they turned the ball over once again on their next possession. The yelling between teammates continued, while the cheering got louder from our bench.

So many of the things I'd become accustomed to in our practices were coming to fruition in this game. Thankfully, though, it was the other team who put this on display. They were fighting amongst themselves, they were angry, and they were defeated–only one quarter into the game. Thinking back to my experiences as an American basketball coach, I told my players that we had to keep playing hard because our opponent–that didn't lack talent–was certain to make a run and mount a comeback. But just as Pesho had smiled when he gave me a tour of the school and its sanitary facilities, he was smiling now, too. Even with his post moves in a stage of infancy, he was dominating down low, and he knew exactly what was going on in this game. This Bulgarian team had already folded up into itself. I wasn't sure how to feel about the fact that I knew my players knew exactly what was happening with Stefan Stambolov: one quarter into the game, they had already given up.

And Stefan Stambolov never did make a run to get back into the game. They were content to launch long-range jump shots at rims that were anything but forgiving. During each timeout, I continued to harp on getting the ball inside.

"Look at those rims," I told my players repeatedly. "What chances do you think you have making a jump shot on that crooked rim? We need nothing but layups today."

It didn't occur to me until after the game that while I was giving my players sound strategy and logic for this basketball game, each time I pointed to rims, I was indirectly criticizing their country. But on this Saturday, most of the criticizing came from the other team. In the second half, the coach got into a profanity-laced Bulgarian shouting match with his point guard, and it looked heated enough for the two of them to come to blows. As my jaw dropped at what I was watching in front of me, I once again noticed that this didn't affect my players at all. This wasn't unusual, embarrassing or out of character; it was normal. Perhaps the most unusual thing was that I didn't yell at them this way.

With Menkov smashing into the metal cage once, Stefan running into the cement wall behind the basket, and Ivan tripping over the protruding metal pipe, the game ended with only minor scrapes and bruises which is probably the best outcome we could've had. The outcome of the game itself was never in doubt; we won by 30 points to advance to the next round of the Third of March tournament.

My players once again were very jubilant, though it was hard for me to join them in their celebration. While better than the first disastrous team we'd played, our competition once again was not very strong. And while there was talent on the other team, there was a sense of fracture and frustration that permeated their every move. The minute they'd fallen behind in the game, there was no coming back.

It startled me that our opponent had given up so soon, and this dominated my thoughts as I hopped back on the 76 bus and headed home for the afternoon. Every time I told my players to expect our opponent to come back, to fight, to have pride and play harder, it never happened. Their play represented no qualities befitting their school's namesake, a modern Bulgarian hero. And while my team humored me by listening to my speeches and continuing to play hard themselves, they must've all been thinking that I had no idea what I was talking about. Early on in the game, they knew the other team had already quit. *This is life in Bulgaria. Don't be afraid; we are used to this.* Pesho probably had no idea how prophetic his words were. He was talking about Bulgarian public schools, but he might as well have been talking about the life under the Turkish yoke, the loss of Macedonia or 50 years of Soviet domination.

A rain-snow slushy mix was falling as I sat near the window on the 76 on my way home. The bus windows started to fog up, and I attempted to clear up my view with my winter gloves. But as I wiped away the gray, disillusioning mist from the window, my view didn't change all that much; the outside row house world looked gray and disillusioned, too.

I got off the bus early, several blocks from home because I needed to stop at the cell phone store. Earlier in the week, my cell phone stopped making or receiving phone calls. In Bulgaria, to pay your cell phone bill, it was necessary to report to the cell phone provider, and I'd done this only a week before. It made no sense to me why the phone was no longer working. I tried my best to explain this to the woman behind the counter at the cell phone store.

Half-understanding my Bulgarian and somewhat understanding the charades I used in place of some Bulgarian words, she told me in Bulgarian that she would have to find someone else to help me with this problem. When I was ushered to the next customer service woman, I was given the opportunity to butcher the language once again trying to explain the problem. I had the same result: she told me to go talk to someone else.

On my third try, I was both gaining confidence in my Bulgarian and brimming with frustration over their lack of willingness to help me. But luckily, the third time was a charm. This woman was willing to look up my account on her computer.

"Ahhhh," she emoted.

"What is it?" I responded in Bulgarian.

"The problem is simple," she told me in simple Bulgarian language that I could understand. "Your phone was turned off because you are from America. You are from America, and we are concerned."

I was dumbfounded.

"But now that you are here, I can turn your phone back on. You have come here, and we are no longer concerned."

I walked out of the cell phone store relieved that my phone was once again functional, and also relieved that Bulgaria was no longer concerned about me. But that didn't mean I didn't have some concerns about Bulgaria.

Chapter VIII
Commie Central

Living in Bulgaria is certainly the best way to get clued in about the country. But you can still learn a lot simply by reading the in-flight magazine. On my first Bulgaria Air flight, I was pleased to see the in-flight magazine included a tips section on how to handle life in a country, the magazine claimed, where "the East meets the West." To help curious newcomers navigate this new Wild East, the magazine ran them through the basics–how to say *good morning, good afternoon,* and *good evening.* Those first three helpful phrases seemed right in line with the kinds of things you'd want to learn when arriving in any country. But it was the fourth phrase that jumped out to me: *Please write me a ticket. I will not give you any cash.*

I laughed when I read this because I naively assumed that something like *please, thank you,* or *I'd like a beer* was coming next. But no, in Bulgaria it's most important to know how to avoid the rampant corruption that plagues the country. According to the Center for Democratic Studies, Bulgarian traffic police receive more than 100,000 bribes every year. So when a cop makes any kind of traffic stop, odds are generally considered good that a bribe could end up being part of the deal. And while in-flight magazines are generally known to present rosy pictures of wherever your travel destination may be, this Bulgarian in-flight magazine got right to the heart of corruption. It was hard to believe this was much of an advertisement for the country.

But during the entire Cold War, there was no such thing as advertising in Bulgaria, and it's clear that the art was still being formed. Usually advertisers seek ways to play loosely with the truth, but in Bulgaria, there was no masking the truth: the country was riddled with corruption.

Following the model that had been so successful for the EU up to this point, it was widely assumed throughout Europe that Bulgaria's corruption problem would be solved by its ascension into this new governing body. So many countries previously admitted into the EU had swiftly cleaned up their acts following admission in order to impress the group they had now joined. But in 2008, one year after being accepted to the EU, the Transparency International Corruption Perceptions Index lowered Bulgaria's world ranking, which was already the lowest in the EU. After EU admittance, Bulgaria's rating worsened, and this was the first time in 10 years this had happened. This prompted an official for the Index to remark, "Apparently Bulgaria's EU membership did not automatically lead to a decrease in corruption practices."

On the contrary, it seemed that to some in Bulgaria, entrance into the EU just allowed for more opportunity to money grab. The model previously followed by other entrants to the EU had represented how much countries were eager to prove they belonged. Bulgaria, on the other hand, seemed eager for its slice of the pie. Once the EU started doling out money for projects that were dedicated to serving some of the country's desperate infrastructural needs, the money started disappearing. Or it started going to family members of government ministers. In the summer of 2008, the EU announced that 670 million dollars of funding scheduled to go to Bulgaria would be frozen because, after only a year and a half as an EU member, the country could not be trusted to ethically handle the money. Great portions of the money already doled out to Bulgaria to improve infrastructure and education had simply disappeared—or so said the Bulgarian government. Most likely, and this was understood by anyone who had any understanding of the way Bulgarian politics operated, the money had been parceled out to various members of the mafia in the form of bribes and payoffs. When the Bulgarian government reported to the EU with answers of "I have no idea what happened to the money," this did not sit well with Europe's governing body.

The first serious sanctions that were levied upon Bulgaria should've served as a warning sign to a country that had so recently joined the EU. But Bulgaria's response to the EU was not one of contrition, but a response that tried to shift the blame: *What about Romania?* Bulgarian officials complained to the EU, indicating that their neighbor to the north who had been admitted to the EU at the same time was having similar problems with corruption.

This response—akin to an 8-year-old trying to get his parents to focus on his 6-year-old brother's behavior, not his own—did not sit well with the EU. A British diplomat overseeing Bulgaria and Romania's case responded to Bulgaria's defense in a manner that left no doubt about his frustration: "In Romania, the structural problems in government are much worse, but the behavior of the Bulgarian politicians in the EU was exceptionally presumptuous and disrespectful. They believe themselves untouchable and that nothing can happen to them regardless of what they do, which is why Bulgaria will suffer the consequences."

That harsh language like this directed at Bulgaria became commonplace so soon after EU admittance should have been appalling to Bulgarian politicians trying to govern the country. But when not immaturely pointing the finger at Romania, those Bulgarian politicians who weren't "presumptuous and disrespectful" generally weren't able to offer much more than their standard response of, *It's not my fault. I can't stop the corruption.* And in many ways, the honest members of the government had a very good point. That's because the government wasn't particularly in charge of Bulgaria: the mafia was.

This was another point of contention—and certainly an alarming one—with the EU and the rest of the Western world. The mafia seemed to have an influence on Bulgarian governing far more than most countries this side of Russia. Many of the Bulgarian wrestlers who had enjoyed steroid-induced fame and eventual infamy in the 1980s during communism saw their opportunity once capitalism slowly came to Bulgaria. Capitalism and democracy just meant more freedom for them to use tough-guy tactics to run roughshod over any sense of laws that may have existed. And now, without the Big Brother-esque watch of communism and the secret police hovering over them, Bulgarian tough guys—wrestlers and bodyguards—started experiencing a renaissance, a mafia renaissance.

A former member of Bulgarian parliament and former counterintelligence chief in Bulgaria, Atanas Atanasov, described the mafia influence in Bulgaria both succinctly and correctly: "Other countries have the mafia," he said, when interviewed by the *New York*

Times. "In Bulgaria, the mafia has the country."

As a teenager growing up, Kapka Kassabova noticed who the "real men" were in her world, and who was truly running things in Bulgaria. Her description of the mafia renaissance is as follows: "Real men, collectively known as *mutri* (gangsters) or 'ugly mugs,' put together racketeering businesses, bought up government factories for small change and turned them into private businesses, trafficked drugs, weapons and women, laundered money, and felt like the winners they really were—until a rival racketeer shot them in the face."

So it should be no surprise then, that in a 10-year period starting in 1999, there were 150 mob-style murders in Bulgaria, and not a single one of these cases was solved. It seemed that getting shot in the face was not only a likely end to a *mutri* life, but a "crime" that wasn't even really a crime. In this 10-year period, not a single person was convicted for any of these murders.

To me, as a foreigner, statistics like this were staggering, though I was reassured by Bulgarian colleagues on several occasions in a similar manner: "Don't worry, Andy. The mafia has no interest in shooting foreigners. They only shoot other mafia members."

How about that for comforting.

Out of curiosity, I'd tried to get to know as many of my players and their families as possible. And I found right away that most of my players were eager to open up about their families and tell me about their lives away from school. But Kosio Dimitrov was one player who didn't display this trait. After Menkov had told me all about his father's concern about his employer's fate now that Western cigarettes had moved into Eastern Europe, I turned to Kosio and asked him what his father did for a living.

"Business," the normally smooth-talking forward said bluntly.

"Okay," I said patiently, "what kind of business?"

"He's a businessman," Kosio retorted defiantly, "and that means he does business."

I looked at Kosio, not sure where the hostility was coming from, and also not sure if it was acceptable to continue with what I thought was a harmless line of questioning. Perhaps he could sense the internal debate swirling inside my head, and he took the initiative.

"I don't have to tell you what kind of business he's in."

With that, Kosio walked away. I was left feeling as if I'd violated some kind of unwritten law regarding the occupations of my players' fathers. But I'd asked the question at one point or another to nearly every player on the team, and none of them had responded with the dismissive tone I just heard from Kosio. But that's because there seemed to be no doubt about the legitimacy of the occupations of the rest of the players' fathers. Kosio, though, was different from many of my other players because it was clear he had money. He had new basketball shoes and basketball shorts, things many of my players didn't have. But it was also becoming clear to me that those nice basketball shoes and shorts were being provided by his father's "business" interests, which I was left to wonder about how ethical his business might be.

In April of 2008, this issue made international headlines when two men were shot in broad daylight 50 minutes apart sitting in two different cafes in downtown Sofia. Both victims had recently spoken out against the mafia control of Bulgaria, and conveniently, there were absolutely zero witnesses to either of these murders. I was appalled by the obvious lack of ethics and justice that this crime, and so many others, represented, and used this as a discussion topic in my English classes. I soon discovered, though, that while my students might have at one point felt this same sense of outrage, they'd learned to accept these mafia killings as a part of life in Bulgaria.

"I just don't understand why they have to shoot people downtown," one of my 11th grade students commented in class. "Why can't they shoot them somewhere else? The murders downtown just make traffic absolutely terrible."

Functionally speaking, my student was correct. I was learning that the only thing the authorities could be counted on for was stopping traffic to clean up the mess from the killings, not daring to deal with the much larger judicial mess at hand.

Whether I was reading the newspaper about Bulgaria's corruption, or seeing it first hand, it was difficult for me to fathom how a country could function like this. It was clear that so many of my students and players had grown to accept this as life in Bulgaria, but I wondered, *Was life always like this in Bulgaria?*

I posed this question to my Bulgarian language teacher, a 40-something woman who had lived as a teenager during the Cold War, and then become an adult as Bulgaria once again became a free country. What was her life like during communism? Was it this rife with corruption?

"No way, no way," she responded immediately with a trademark finger wag of disapproval. "We had rules during communism. It's not like life now. We had lots of rules during communism."

"Then what happened?" I asked. "How did everything change so much?"

She gave me a sad smile before answering.

"*Democratsia.*"

Democracy, according to my Bulgarian language teacher and many others, was the cause of all of Bulgaria's problems. While the majority of Eastern Europe reveled as the chains of communism were broken, this wasn't necessarily the case in Bulgaria as the Berlin Wall fell. And it still wasn't the case in Bulgaria when I arrived in the fall of 2007. A good portion of the population—many people told me the number was around 50 percent—preferred life under communist rule to the free and "democratic" Bulgaria. While democracy had ushered in a brand new era of freedom, this freedom seemed to most directly allow for the freedom to cheat. Without the iron fist of communism pounding down on the people, democracy unfortunately allowed for all sorts of illegal behavior to flourish. The Bulgarian brawn, the wrestlers and bodyguards who held high positions in communist Bulgaria, quickly saw opportunity to make money through extortion, graft and violence in their new democratic country. As a result of this, Bulgaria became one of the few countries in the world to have a decrease in population from year to year, a statistic that still holds true today. Many who didn't feel like they could deal with the new *democratsia* in Bulgaria just decided to leave, a wish that nearly everyone on my basketball team shared.

Those who stayed, it appeared, had mixed emotions about democracy in Bulgaria. Consequently, there were images of communism all over Bulgaria. In other countries like Hungary, all communist statues had been dramatically torn down and kept in one place as a memoriam to a dark part of history. In many places, the statues were torn down and destroyed, never to be seen again. But in Bulgaria, the communist statues remained. At *Orlov Most*, the Eagles' Bridge that represents the entrance to Sofia's downtown, a majestic Russian soldier holding a rifle looks toward the sky with proletariats huddled behind him, and hovers some 50 feet above the pedestrian and car traffic below. This staggering entrance to downtown caught my attention right away, but even as a young child, author Kapka Kassabova reflected the most typical Bulgarian attitude regarding the statues: "You didn't really notice these statues: they were everywhere, they were identical, and somehow you sensed they were fake."

But to a foreigner experiencing the Eastern bloc for the first time, even though I knew they were fake, there was no mistaking the oppressive power of communism looming over you all the time. While a similar hovering image of Stalin was finally taken down after the Cold War, Sofia's largest and most populated park, *Borisova Gardina* (Boris' Garden), is littered with Soviet communist shapes and images, and highlighted by another 50-foot monument to communism that looks like a miniature version of the Washington monument, commie-style.

When one of these monuments was desecrated—at least that was the official term—it provided a humorous look at Sofia's attachment to its communist statues. At the base of one of the Soviet monuments was a sculpture showing numerous people surging forward behind a flag in defense of the Motherland. In the middle of the night, an artist—though the official term was "vandal"—decided to have a little fun with the sculpture. He came armed with plenty of colorful paint. The presence of color itself represented a distinctly un-communist approach to statue making. All of the communist statues in Sofia were different versions of stone and iron, gray and black in color. But it wasn't just the color of the paint itself that garnered so much attention. This artist/vandal painted each one of the members of the proletariat in the sculpture as a different Western superhero.

What was a monument to the power of the common man bonding together for a greater idealistic force had been turned into a celebration of some of the West's most well-recognized superheroes. Captain America, Batman's Robin, the Joker and even Ronald McDonald now stood as the driving force behind support for the Motherland; they were now unified behind the American flag. Even Santa Claus joined in for part of the fun. The artist included an inscription along with the colorful new superheroes that read, "Rolling with Time." Sofia officials, though, were not ones to roll with time in any way, shape or form. They were not amused, even though the new artwork became a hotspot for foreigners who wanted to take pictures. Socialists in government demanded that the "vandalized" monument quickly be washed. There would be no rolling with time in Bulgaria.

During one of my early Bulgarian language lessons, when grammar gave way to discussions about communism, my teacher told me a story she remembered from her adolescence. She recalled attending a rally in the center of Sofia after the Berlin Wall had fallen. People in the crowd were eager to see the demolition of a giant statue of Lenin. The event was to take place at noon on a Friday afternoon, and many workers were given the afternoon off so they could celebrate the demolition of the statue, and metaphorically enjoy the shackles being lifted from Bulgaria. But as the clock struck noon and the explosives were set to go off, nothing happened. The explosives didn't properly detonate, and the crowd was left to mingle, wondering if anything was actually going to happen. In the end, nothing did. The huge crowd had showed up to revel in the splendor of Soviet communism's defeat, but the explosives couldn't bring down Lenin. This seemed to foreshadow the way communism would still linger in Sofia by the time I arrived in 2007. Even with the strongest explosives, Mother Russia just wasn't going to go away.

When monuments in Sofia weren't dedicated to Soviet communism—or Western superheroes—even Bulgarians themselves seemed to have an odd way of celebrating their nation. In another key part of downtown, the monument to the founding of the Bulgarian state stood out for all to see. The problem was, though, that most people decided this wasn't something that celebrated anything, and therefore did not want to see it. The English language guide to Sofia, *In Your Pocket*, accurately described the monument in the following text: "Sofia is probably unique in Europe in being the only capital which can boast a decaying pile of junk as one of its major downtown focal points. Unveiled in 1981 to mark the 1300th anniversary of the founding of the Bulgarian state, this unimaginably shoddy memorial is an eloquent metaphor for much that has happened in Bulgaria in the intervening 25 years…. An angular piece of modern sculpture with statues emerging absurdly from its summit, the monument has long been the object of popular scorn—'the seven-angled thing with five pricks' being the most enduring of its many nicknames."

The absurdity, though, was not simply limited to Sofia. Any trip through the country would inevitably lead to discovering another key to Bulgaria's communist past. In particular, the Soviets relished placing their most demonstrative monuments as high as possible, as symbols of majesty and power. Early on in my Bulgarian tenure, I went on a hike with the school's hiking club, and we reached a picturesque peak that looked down on the wintery village of Lakatnik. Stopping to admire the view and take pictures, I was distracted by a student who was in turn distracted by a large brick structure with a giant red star adorning the highest point of this beautiful peak.

"That's great," he spit out in Bulgarian, "just more stupid communist crap."

I found this comment to be a sign of things changing for the youth in Bulgaria, but without a doubt, this was a rare comment. To many Bulgarians, especially the older generation, communism represented a safety and security that had been much more difficult to find during nearly two decades of capitalism and democracy. Maybe this was because of the extensive propaganda ingrained in the minds of Bulgarians who grew up before the wall fell. Drilled and schooled in the evils of capitalism, Bulgarians during the '60s, '70s and '80s weren't sure what to believe. Or, even worse from my Western point of view, maybe they knew exactly what to believe. As a child growing up in the '80s, Kassabova remembers the Berlin Wall in a far more amicable way than most would imagine: "It was a collective state of mind, and there is something cozy, reassuring in all things collective. Even a prison."

I guess even if Bulgaria was a prison, it was a Cold War prison that many of its citizens felt comfortable with. And maybe so many people still revered communism for its sense of fairness—a prison-like fairness—because the modern-day version of *democratsia* in Bulgaria was riddled with corruption and cheating.

That's why I was overwhelmed during my first months at the American College of Sofia by the numerous staff meetings that were held solely to focus on prevention of student cheating. The College, seen as the most dignified educational institutional in the country, was determined to keep its standing. But that was no easy task, as the American College was one of the few schools in Bulgaria not tainted with a reputation of dishonesty and cheating. And maybe, as I'm sure my Bulgarian teacher would argue, that's because of the strong links to communism the American College had all throughout the Cold War.

The American College of Sofia is one of the oldest American schools (outside of America) you'll find anywhere in the world. In 1860, the college was founded by American missionaries in a small town south of Sofia. By 1926, the school had expanded and moved to Sofia where it began to develop a strong reputation as an excellent educational institution. The school was valued by Bulgarians and the few Americans who had invested in it, namely the president Dr. Floyd Black. Black increased the school's prominence and even oversaw the construction of the best English language library in the Balkans at that time. With life at the American College moving swimmingly, there didn't seem to be too much that could derail an institution that was so widely respected.

Well, that is, not until Bulgaria declared war on the United States.

Hoping to appease their new allies, Nazi Germany, at the beginning of World War II, Bulgaria declared war on the United States. It's a move that most people at the time saw as foolish, and most historians today still agree. There was no need for Bulgaria to publicly declare the United States as its enemy, especially since the U.S. and Bulgaria had a friendly relationship. R.J. Crampton echoed this sentiment with his commentary: "In December 1941, Bulgaria bowed to German pressure and declared war on Britain and the United States. The war, insisted the Bulgarian government, was merely 'symbolic', but the declaration of war had a deep psychological impact. Bulgaria, it was widely and correctly assumed, had succumbed to German will; and few could understand why Bulgaria should pit itself against the USA with which it had remained at peace during the first world war."

In a sign that this war declaration was purely symbolic, Bulgarian authorities encouraged Americans, their declared enemy, to stay in the country, and allowed the American College to remain open. But as a sign of their capitulation to Nazi Germany, the Nazi Commander of Sofia ordered all Americans out of Sofia in 1942. Given 48 hours to pack up and leave, the ACS faculty had no choice but to hop on the next train to Istanbul. As the train left Sofia, Bulgarian alumni of the school paid a touching tribute to their American teachers by "waiting on the platform and singing, in English, the College song and other American songs which they had learned." This would be the last time an American would set foot on the campus of the American College of Sofia for 50 years.

That's because the American College of Sofia was turned into the training facility for the Bulgarian Secret Police, which was more or less an extension of the KGB. Most books and classroom supplies were destroyed. The faculty houses, though, remained intact and were even used for official state visits by Russian leaders. It's safe to say that living on the ACS campus offered me what will most likely be a once-in-a-lifetime opportunity to spend a significant amount of time in a house that Khruschev slept in whenever he came to visit Bulgaria (which I still imagine was not all that often).

With the Bulgarian Secret Police in charge, the vestiges of an educational institution were quickly forgotten. And it wasn't until the Berlin Wall fell that there were even discussions about re-opening the campus as a school. In 1992, however, an American board of trustees who still hung onto their ties with ACS from 50 years previous sent an American administrator, Dr. Roger Whitaker, to Sofia to attempt to re-open the school. With no books, no buildings, no classroom supplies and no students, Whitaker entered the country with one suitcase full of clothes and one suitcase full of a 1991 PSAT exam that he'd had translated into Bulgarian to use as the school's entrance exam. Per strict—and very communist-seeming—Bulgarian rules, the only way the school's entrance exam would be deemed as valid by the Bulgarian Education Ministry is if the seals of the test hadn't been broken and the test hadn't been looked at by anyone before the test date. Whitaker brought 500 copies of the entrance exam on the plane with him as his carry-on and prayed that Bulgarian customs agents wouldn't inspect his bag and break the tests' seals. Luckily, they didn't, but I'm sure it was clear to Whitaker that while the previous American educators were sent off 50 years ago with songs of tribute, his welcome to the country wasn't going to be as warm. Suspicions of American capitalist attitudes still ran high in Bulgaria, and it'd been 50 years since the two countries had had any form of significant contact.

But that didn't dampen enthusiasm from Bulgarians who wanted to attend the school. As Whitaker declared that the top 50 boys and top 50 girls would be admitted to the school starting in the fall of 1992, three thousand 7th grade students from all over the country registered for the test. Following this unprecedented registration, the Bulgarian Education Ministry responded by saying that the school would not be allowed to open. They did not offer any specific reason, other than the assumed, "We're not interested in letting American capitalists have a school here," rationale. This left Whitaker in quite a bind, and one of his issues was money. The only way to pay for the entrance exam— and raise much-needed funds for a school that, again, had no classroom supplies whatsoever—was in cash. Bulgaria, which was far from a credit card society when I arrived in 2007, barely even knew what a credit card was in 1992. Whitaker, with anti-American sentiment running high from all corners of the education ministry, couldn't trust the money in any Bulgarian bank. So, in perhaps an ode to the mafia that would soon be flexing its muscle in Bulgaria, he put the piles of Bulgarian *leva* in the only place he could think was safe: his freezer.

On the eve of the entrance exam, the education ministry once again told Whitaker that he wouldn't be allowed to administer the entrance exam, this time using communist bureaucracy to claim he hadn't appropriately acquired all the necessary licenses. He was told that if he administered the exam, he'd be arrested. Apparently a man either naïve to or undeterred by stories of Eastern European gulags,

Whitaker decided to call their bluff. When masses of students–along with the media–showed up in the morning for the test, he was going to dare the Bulgarian police to arrest him.

He gambled right. Press coverage glowed with stories of the school as a beacon of light, a symbol of the new, free Bulgaria. The police didn't arrest him. In fact, they issued all the appropriate licenses the next day.

This rocky, but successful, beginning was emblematic of the relationship Bulgaria would have with the American college throughout the 1990s and 2000s. While the education ministry had virtually no reason to take issue with the school–the best in Bulgaria—they always seemed to find some issue with the school. And perhaps that happened just because the school was the best in Bulgaria, and it was run by Americans.

For Whitaker, even after the entrance exam was issued, he still had many cross-cultural battles to fight. This was the American school, but the Berlin Wall had only fallen three years ago, and communist paranoia still ran high. That's why when Whitaker ordered the giant bust of Vladimir Lenin that was displayed outside the school's auditorium to be taken down, none of the Bulgarian maintenance men were willing to do it. "If I do this," one Bulgarian worker told him, "then I don't know what will happen to me. I cannot take this risk."

At first Whitaker had to think they were joking, but no matter what reasoning he tried, no maintenance worker would go near the sacred Lenin statue, an iconoclastic symbol in Bulgaria for 50 years running. So he had no choice but to take a very American approach to fixing this communist problem: he got a sledgehammer and knocked down the bust of Lenin himself.

This was one relic of the communist past that was gone by the time I got to ACS, but there was still plenty left to remind me of the fact that this school didn't have what anyone would call a normal history. The first time I entered the English department office, I had an odd feeling, almost like my voice was trapped in a vacuum. Then I looked back at the padded door. This English office was a soundproof room. It had been used by the Bulgarian Secret Police to interrogate suspects. At that point of realization, I tried not to think why it would be necessary to have interrogation rooms be soundproof. Maybe, though, it was just so Lenin, perched not too far away, wouldn't be bothered by the all the noise.

When the school was able to regain its rights to the campus, the

Bulgarian government still made life as difficult as possible for the American intruders. They granted half of the land back to the school, but insisted upon keeping the remaining half to use as police training grounds. This was the best compromise the school was able to broker, and as a result, every time I entered the American College's gates, I was met by an armed Bulgarian guard, inevitably smoking a cigarette and looking disenchanted, as I showed my government-issued ID to enter the school's grounds.

When the police weren't smoking cigarettes and giving Americans dirty looks, they were embarking on all sorts of training routines–preparing for the next invasion of Macedonia, I assumed. As a teacher in the States, I'd become inured to noise in the hallway or noise out the window causing distractions for my students, but the Bulgarian police took "noise" to a whole new level. Their regular war games frequently occurred in the forested area outside my classroom window. As I attempted to get Bulgarian 11th graders to focus on *Macbeth* on a rainy autumn day, it was hard for me to focus as we all gazed out the window to the war game that was occurring right below us. As the witches creaked, "Double, double, toil and trouble," gunfire erupted as soldiers could be seen hurling their bodies behind trees and into bushes for cover. It's safe to say that Shakespeare lost out on the battle to capture their attention.

But at least in this situation, the shooting occurred in a field while we were safely in our classroom. One of the first times I heard gunfire during class and brought it up to my students, they were very excited to tell me what had happened last year during P.E. class.

"Mr. Jones, did you hear what happened to Kliment last year? It was incredible! We were playing football on the pitch over by the broken-down building they use for urban warfare training…"

At this point, I was keenly aware that this was the first time any student of mine had seriously and correctly used *urban warfare training* in a sentence.

"… and he got shot! They shot Kliment right in the ear! I mean, it was just a rubber bullet, but it still almost took off his ear."

I looked over to Kliment, who solemnly nodded in agreement with the re-telling of the story.

"Seriously, Kliment?" I had to ask. "You got shot in the ear by the police during gym class?"

"Yeah, that's right, Mr. Jones."

I was dumbfounded.

"Actually," and here came the beauty of the male teenage mind, "it was pretty cool. How many people get to skip the rest of classes for the day because they got shot by the police while playing soccer?"

When I probed deeper to find out about the repercussions of this debacle, I found out that when the school contacted the police about the incident, they were told that students needed to be more careful during P.E.—and not play soccer, I guess. When the school pressed the police for an apology and assurances that live rounds wouldn't be fired onto the soccer pitch again, the police refused. This was reflective of the co-existence on the same campus: both sides accepted that the other was there, but neither was happy about it. It wasn't until the U.S. Embassy intervened that the guilty soldier trudged over to the school and offered up an apology for shooting a high school student when he was supposed to be aiming at fellow cadets.

It seemed to me like every day in Bulgaria, I was introduced to a new way that "East meets West." Whether it was East and West butting heads over a school, literally taking down the head of Lenin, or bullets aimed at the heads of my students, my impression was that in Bulgaria there was no shortage of conflict. And we'd only played two basketball games; I hadn't even truly discovered how much conflict could exist in basketball.

Chapter IX
Cheater Cheater

"We want to know," the coach said in defiant Bulgarian, "how you can assure us there won't be cheating."

"Yes," came the immediate and similarly defiant continuation from another coach, "how will we know you have not paid the referees?"

More questions followed:

"How can we be sure all players are legal members of opposing teams?"

"Will someone be checking school IDs of players to ensure they aren't fake?"

"How do we prevent coaches from using players who have already graduated or don't attend the school?"

I wasn't sure what was more alarming for me: the rapid-fire, quick-speaking, harsh Bulgarian that was flying out of these coaches' mouths as I desperately tried to translate in my head, or what they were actually saying. Were all of these coaches really that concerned about cheating in a high school boys' basketball tournament?

This was the coaches' meeting for the American College of Sofia Open—ACS Open—which was held every year at our school. We were sitting in a second floor classroom listening to Nikolai lead a meeting regarding tournament rules. I had assumed this meeting would mostly focus on the random drawing for the two different groups the teams would compete in for opening rounds. Nikolai started the meeting focused on this random draw—but almost immediately the other local Sofia coaches started launching into diatribes about cheating and injustice.

Nikolai, displaying attributes that I would define as un-Bulgarian, calmly addressed the group of coaches, saying that this tournament had been held at ACS for many years, and there had never been problems with cheating before. The school prioritized the integrity of the tournament and would take all appropriate measures to ensure that rules were followed and fair play observed.

After living in Bulgaria for three months, my Bulgarian language comprehension wasn't great, but I was determined to learn more than just *ne modje*, something I was still hearing all too frequently from my basketball team and my students. I understood the gist of what Nikolai was patiently saying to the other coaches.

But what Nikolai had to say didn't seem to matter much to them.

"Of course you say this tournament will be fair. That's probably because you'll be the one doing the cheating; it'll be fair to you when you win!"

Nikolai sighed audibly, but I was the only one who noticed this. The other coaches now collaborated in a series of salvos about the last comment accusing our school of cheating. I found this comment particularly ridiculous especially relating to my team. This wasn't because I expected the other coaches to see me as honest and full of integrity, but the real truth was I had no idea how I would cheat in the first place.

Pay the referees?

How would I even begin to know how to do this, and when would I do it? Before the game, when they smoked cigarettes and talked on their cell phones?

Use illegal players who didn't go to our school?

I knew so few people in Bulgaria that I was hard-pressed to think of *anyone* I knew who wasn't associated with the school.

Once again, Nikolai tried to calm the crowd of coaches by assuring them that ACS was committed to running a fair tournament. This, I was learning quickly, was no easy feat. The coaches in the classroom continued to object. And as much as I was trying to translate their Bulgarian angst into my English head, I got lost in the various intricacies of how they were positive everyone else in the room was a cheater. At this point, I started to take a look around the room at the different coaches who were representing their teams.

Nikolai was standing up in front of the room, trying to assuage the barrage of insults being hurled around the room. He was wearing warm-up pants and an ACS girls' basketball polo shirt. He very much looked the part of a basketball coach, and his patience during the meeting was truly astounding to me.

I had no idea what this meeting would be like so I just wore the same shirt and tie I'd been wearing all day. But as the meeting dragged on, I also wore a look of disbelief on my face. My head already started to hurt from concentrating so hard to try to translate what was going on, but what little translation I could manage was making my jaw drop.

Clearly, the angriest of the opposing coaches was a short and fiery woman who had strutted into the meeting wearing a shirt that couldn't accurately be described as tight—suffocating was more fitting. Her bright purple skirt barely started at her thighs and then led up to an even tighter black top that engulfed her torso and chest. I was floored by her outfit which would most likely have been deemed inappropriate for a bar, let alone a school. Her outfit could have been sultry in a classless way, but this woman was in her forties—and she was missing several teeth. The teeth she had remaining had eroded into a faded yellow, evidence of a life spent smoking, I assumed, since I'd had to ask her not to smoke in the school when the meeting began. The mere suggestion that she could not smoke in the school might have been the trigger she was looking for to get her ire elevated in order to rage on against cheating.

Next to her was the second most active participant in what I could inaccurately call a "conversation" about cheating. He was wearing jeans and a sport coat and at least dressed the part of a coach. Sweat, though, was pouring off his bald head as he emphatically slammed his fist—with a pencil in it—down each time he became more suspicious of the other coaches sitting around the table. He had a huge gap between his front teeth, and spittle flew out from the empty space with each new outrageous remark. I imagined he'd studied Khrushchev's shoe-slamming moment religiously and now sought to make it part of his daily repertoire.

The coach next to me was wearing a Megadeth t-shirt. His hair matched the depiction you get from the t-shirt. With each new conspiracy theory he laid out, his hair flew in all directions like he was banging away on the drums on stage.

The coach at the end of table had the same Charlotte Hornets

Starter jacket from 1993 that so many of my players loved. He had been an ardent participant in the rage spewing from all angles of the table, but soon lost interest. As I looked over at him, I wasn't sure if he was even awake anymore.

And the final two coaches weren't even coaches at all. They were players. Two Sofia schools hadn't bothered to send their coaches, but simply asked representatives from their teams to go to the pre-tournament meeting. In both cases, I would watch their eyes dart from one coach to another as the debate escalated. And with each new comment by a coach determined that other coaches would be cheating, their countenances reflected the same emotion: terror.

In general, when Bulgarians speak to each other about any matter of importance, they don't speak; they yell. That's exactly what these coaches were doing right now—vigorously yelling at one another, accusing their opponents of paying referees and playing with illegal players. The two student representatives were dismayed, intimidated and silent.

And I felt a very strong bond with them.

"She used a 23-year-old player in her last tournament!" Megadeth howled, split ends shooting out left and right.

"He takes the referees out for drinks after every game!" Yellow Teeth hissed.

"None of his players even have school IDs!" Khrushchev slammed away at Starter Jacket who by now was definitely asleep. The pencil breaking woke him up, though, and alerted him to rejoin the carnage.

"How can we trust him?" he wailed away at Nikolai. "He's hosting the tournament. There's no way he won't cheat!"

With this latest salvo fired at Nikolai, who I knew to be incredibly honest and fair, I'd had enough. I couldn't take the headache from the loud Bulgarian angst any more. And I could no longer endure the nature of the conversation.

"Is it possible," I started, in meek Bulgarian, which surprised everyone at the table. They'd forgotten I was even there, and certainly never considered I could understand or speak Bulgarian.

"Is it possible," I repeated, trying to remember all the words in Bulgarian for what I was going to say, "that all of us in this room could just agree not to cheat? We are all adults and can agree to do what's right."

With this, I thought a breakthrough might be achieved. After I finished the boldest statement I'd ever made in my life in Bulgarian, there was a pause for silence–easily the first time this had happened at the meeting–from everyone around the table. What I was proposing seemed so simple that it had to be understood. We were coaches in charge of the education of our student athletes. It was our job to teach them much more than just how to play basketball, but how to live life the right way. While in the States, it was understood that cheating was wrong, Bulgaria's attitude toward this seemed to be much different. But maybe, just maybe, my comment had made sense to this irate round table of coaches. Maybe that's why they were all silent for a few moments–moments that allowed them to ponder the wisdom of what I'd just proposed.

Or maybe they were silent because it took them a few moments to make sense of my butchered Bulgarian.

"There's no way I'd ever come to an agreement with him!" Yellow Teeth attacked Khrushchev. "He's a cheater!"

"Agreement?" Khrushchev's eyebrows raised. *"Ne modje, ne modje, ne modje!"* With the last *ne modje* he broke his second pencil of the night.

The yelling continued from one coach to the next, and the furious pace of speech didn't provide me a chance to make out too many specific details. I should've realized that I never had a chance to begin with. In a country where hope constantly ran low, I learned all too quickly the danger of having those hopes to begin with. Having them crushed should always be half expected.

As the bickering continued, I glanced up at Nikolai who had been determined and strong throughout the meeting. But now his shoulders sagged and he moved forward to drop his arms down on top of a desk. I saw his entire posture slump, and he made eye contact with me as if to say, "I'm sorry."

But he didn't need to apologize to me. This was all new to me and I was just learning. Nikolai had spent his entire life with this, and he wasn't learning anything new. This was normal for him.

As he rose up and tried to summon energy to regain any semblance of propriety to the meeting, he was once again rebuffed. He looked over at me and, in what seemed like slow motion, shrugged his shoulders painfully.

In her memoir about life in Bulgaria, Kapka Kassabova had written about this shrug. Now, looking at Nikolai, I recognized the accuracy of her description immediately as his burdened shoulders moved in this distinct and "deeply Bulgarian way: resigned, fatalistic, almost mystical."

As the cheating cacophony reached its crescendo, I felt I'd taken another step in my Bulgarian education. Concerning this meeting, I was resigned, I was fatalistic, and I had no choice but to tune out and enter a mystical world that was far, far away from this one.

Mercifully, the meeting ended, though I don't know that there were any resolutions to the cheating issue. But this didn't seem to matter much to Yellow Teeth, Khrushchev, Megadeth or Starter Jacket. All of them gave me warm handshakes on their way out of the meeting, and they even seemed to leave together as friends–friends who had just spent the last hour accusing one another of cheating. The rude comments, harsh tones and yelling all seemed to be a part of the experience, and though my temples were pounding with frustration, the other coaches seemed completely content with how the meeting had transpired. I was baffled, but happy enough since at least the meeting was over.

This caused me to reflect on the verbal discord I'd just witnessed for the better part of the last hour, and wonder how anyone could leave this meeting with a smile on his or her face. But Robert Kaplan, the author of *Balkan Ghosts*, had a similar experience upon first arriving in Bulgaria and making contact with a Bulgarian journalist who would provide him with a good deal of the Bulgarian information for his book. His experience seemed akin to the shouting match I'd just witnessed, and he remarked that, "the fact that I would shout and argue and drink with him [his Bulgarian journalist contact], I think this was the moment when our long and ongoing friendship began, and when I really began to understand about Bulgaria."

I, too, tried to look at this coaches' meeting as an opportunity to understand Bulgaria, but I didn't feel as if I'd become friends with Khrushchev, Megadeth, Yellow Teeth or Starter Jacket. I was just happy they'd all walked out of the room without any blood being shed.

Like the other coaches, Nikolai was also smiling, but his smile spoke of much more relief than actual happiness. He had survived the meeting, and it was over. There didn't seem to be more to say. I think he could tell that I had many questions about the raucous nature of the meeting, and he summed it all up before I could even ask.

"Andy, I think you can see," he said, measuring his words, "that we Bulgarians operate a little differently than you."

It wasn't an explanation that offered any details, but it was an explanation I certainly couldn't disagree with. So I nodded my head in agreement, and then realized that he might've thought that my nodding actually meant I didn't understand. It was probably good that we moved on to the next topic.

"Andy, this will be an interesting tournament," he once again seemed to be measuring his words.

"Interesting how?" I responded. "Interesting because of all the potential cheating controversies?"

"Oh no, not interesting because of that. The cheating controversies will happen no matter what. This is just what we do. Many of those coaches just want somewhere else to place blame if they lose the game. This is normal for Bulgarians—not even interesting, just normal."

"Yeah, I noticed."

"But what will be interesting is how your team does. The other two teams in your pool, 35th School and Spanish School, they are the two best teams in Sofia."

"The two best teams in Sofia?"

This sparked my interest.

"Yes, it is one of these two teams that usually wins the ACS Open every year, and 35th won all of the major city tournaments last year. You will have two very difficult games. And to advance to the elimination round, you will need to win one of those two games."

This was the news I took with me to practice, and my players saw exactly what Nikolai saw.

"Whoa!" Stefan reacted immediately. "We play Spanish and then we play 35th? That's not going to be easy."

"Coach, Coach," Pesho yapped at me like an over-sized dog, "do you realize how good Spanish and 35th are?"

"Those guys are good," Dimov piped in. "They killed us last year."

"Well then," I tried to stem the tide, "I guess that means we need to have some really good practices to prepare for next week."

I hoped this would resonate with the team, but I was also realistic. At this point, I still didn't have a team that particularly enjoyed practice. But Menkov was starting to buck this trend.

"Come on guys, they're good. But we can be good, too. We've just gotta work hard. We can beat those guys."

A few of his teammates smiled, clearly in approval of his enthusiasm. Several of his teammates' expressions didn't change, though. They probably wanted to be optimistic, but as Bulgarians, they'd been trained dealing with the concept of hope: it wasn't worth it to get your hopes up because they might come crashing down quickly.

But the practice was spirited nonetheless. I didn't feel like I was watching good basketball, but I was witnessing examples of good effort. And something else started happening as we finished up the week: players whose attendance was irregular at best were now coming every day. Players who didn't deem it necessary to run hard–Kosio–now saw the urgency. As a whole, the players knew the ACS Open was coming up and they wanted to play. This added more life to practice, but I wondered if these players knew I wasn't planning to play them in the games just because they came to practices a few days before the games. I harkened back to the first days of tryouts when one hopeful team member told me he "wanted me to see how committed he was." As the season had started, I got a great glimpse at what commitment meant for many of my Bulgarian players. It generally meant they were committed when they wanted to be and/or they were committed when they knew there was a big game coming up.

We normally practiced three times a week–one more time than in past years–and the third practice was on Friday mornings. Practices on Friday mornings started at 6 a.m., and the first week, only four players showed up. When I asked those four where the rest of the team was, Menkov responded with honesty that scared me.

"Coach, I don't think the rest of the guys thought you were serious. No one ever has 6 a.m. practice in this country. I think they thought it was a joke."

This wasn't a joke to me at all, so that first Friday morning I ran those four players through as many shooting and ball-handling drills as I could think of. The next Friday, six players showed up at 6 a.m. practice– an improvement, but not much of one. In the following weeks, eight to nine guys would show up for these morning practices, with half of them complaining about the inhumanity of practicing while it was still dark and cold outside.

Stefan, though, didn't complain about practice, but told me all he had to go through just to get to practice in the first place.

"Coach, my parents are really unhappy about this," he explained. "They don't want me getting up this early to go to school. They say it's unhealthy for me, and my mom's scared I'm going to be attacked by stray dogs on the way to the bus stop. I get up at 4:30 so I can catch the 4:55 bus from the station near my house. Then I take that bus for about a half an hour so I can get to the next stop where I get the 76 bus to come to school. There's no heat on the buses so when I get here I'm pretty cold. But at least that means when I get here I'm ready to run. I'm too cold not to."

As Stefan told me this, guilt seeped through my entire body. Six a.m. practice in the States just meant that Mom or Dad had to get up a little early and drive their son seven minutes to school in a heated and comfortable car. Six a.m. practice in Bulgaria meant fighting off stray dogs and freezing temperatures for an hour in the dark just to get to practice. This was what Stefan was willing to do every Friday morning, but he was the exception not the rule. Several team members flat out told me *ne modje* regarding Friday morning practices. When I pressed them for reasons, sometimes they didn't even give me an answer; they just responded with that same fatalistic shrug I'd seen from Nikolai. Six a.m. practice wasn't even an option for at least five or six of my players.

What that left me with was a smaller roster of players who showed up on a regular basis. Regardless of the talent of some of the irregular attendees, I already knew I would have a team focused on the likes of Menkov, Dimov, Stefan, Ivan, Vassy, Kosio, Sasho, Pesho and Pavel. I didn't have much interest in the others who rarely came to practice, and even though I explained this to them, it hadn't set in yet. It became clear to me that in the past it wasn't necessary to come to practices – the practices at 6 a.m. or the ones after school. In the past, if you were good enough, you played in games. It didn't matter if you came to practice or not. They fully expected to play in the ACS Open.

And I fully expected not to play them. They didn't deserve it like the others did.

Regardless of being told that we would be up against a superior opponent, my players exhibited excitement all day long during school on the Wednesday the tournament started. Pesho came whizzing by my room and hurriedly came through the door—almost like Kramer in *Seinfeld*—to show me how jazzed he was for the game.

"Look, Coach! Look, Coach! New haircut, I gotta new haircut!" he said as he smoothed his hand over his new buzz cut, the most popular Bulgarian male haircut. "This will be perfect for tonight. You want to give me a slap? Come on, give me a slap. You're a Bulgarian today!"

With that, I grinned as I reached up and slapped 6′4″ Pesho's near-bald head.

Dimov was the next to stroll by and express his confidence.

"Coach, we can take these guys. I've been working on my behind-the-back dribbling. They won't know what's coming."

"That sounds good, Dimov," I smiled in response, "but I'll be happy if you keep the dribbling simple."

Stefan came in not too long after this to let me know what he was thinking.

"Coach, I never got to play in any important games before. This is really, really exciting. You said the guys who come to practice and work hard are going to play, and I'm really excited about playing tonight."

Stefan couldn't have been more right. He was a Bulgarian rarity; he never missed a practice, and no one deserved to play more than him. I just wondered if he had the talent to compete with one of the best teams in the city.

And this was exactly what I was thinking as I was watching warm-ups before the game. Our warm-up, which we'd spent too much time on just trying to remember the order of drills, still looked discombobulated. Even though we were now getting the hang of the drills, none of them looked particularly fluid as passes were chucked at teammates' ankles and layups caromed too hard off the backboard. Dribbling was arduous since my players' eyes were glued to the ball completely obscuring any notion of floor vision.

The perfect contrast to this was occurring on the other side of the floor. The 35th School looked poised and confident, like they'd gone through this warm-up 100 times together. In fact, their warm-up wasn't even scripted like ours. It was a random assortment of different guys stretching, dribbling and softly banking layups. Their coach, Khrushchev, calmly strolled the sidelines; he hadn't deemed it necessary to have a set warm-up, and his players seemed to mingle on their end of the floor without a care in the world. I wondered if all the fire he'd showed in the meeting had just been bravado. He didn't seem remotely concerned about cheating now. Maybe, I thought, that's because he was the one who'd brought some 23-year-olds to play. Several of his players looked bigger, older, more mature and—most importantly—far more talented than our team. From my vantage point, I gazed out at a monstrous group of Eastern European players, none of whom smiled, and all of whom looked angry. In an ode to communist times past, most Bulgarian public schools were simply named by numbers, and 35th looked like they had plenty of pent-up communist rage to take out on us.

I watched as a 6'6" forward smoothly took two dribbles and soared toward the backboard to dunk the ball, a rim-rattling dunk that awed the crowd—and also one that would be a technical foul in the States where you can't dunk during warm-ups. I had now been in Bulgaria long enough, though, to not mention this fact. Dunking during warm-ups certainly wasn't a technical foul here in Bulgaria, and to add to it, another dunk was slammed home a mere five seconds later. My players heard the clamor and looked over at the 35th players who were laughing and enjoying themselves. I told them to focus on their layup lines, not the other team. Then Pesho went up and tried to dunk, but was rejected by the rim. He fell backwards awkwardly, and the clamor of his fall led to laughter from the fans and the other team.

As a coach, I try never to judge too much from warm-ups, certainly not the warm-ups of the other team. But as my stomach started to turn, I couldn't help but make judgments. From all angles, it appeared we were in big trouble.

Everything about our team seemed to connect to one common descriptor: awkwardness.

Looking at 35th, the exact opposite could be said: they were fluid and confident. In fact, they didn't even seem remotely concerned about the game we were about to play.

Since we were playing in our bubble gym, this meant there actually was a crowd in attendance, unlike the third floor cage we'd played in the previous Saturday. The crowd mostly spent its time "oohing" and "aahing" as the 35th players continued to dunk during warm-ups. The reason dunking in warm-ups is prohibited in the United States is because it's seen as a lack of sportsmanship. Players shouldn't be showing off or trying to intimidate their opponents before the game. "It's a matter of class," I'm sure is the reason you'd get from anyone in the States explaining the genesis of the rule. I'd learned in Bulgaria, though, that class was always an option. For each of our first two games, I'd insisted that our players line up to shake hands with the other team after the game. In both cases, my players quizzically looked at me and said, "Why would we do that?" In both cases, I made them do it which resulted in an awkward chasing down of the opposing players so we could shake hands. They had no intention of shaking hands after the game and were completely befuddled as to why we were approaching them trying to do it.

But as this first game of the tournament was about to start, class was one of the last things on my mind. I had watched numerous 35th players dribble confidently with both their right and left hands—something that only Menkov and Dimov on my team could do—and those who weren't dunking in the layup lines were smoothly taking off on the correct foot and making left-handed layups. Honestly, there wasn't a single person on my team who could do this two times in a row. Kosio made one left-handed layup and almost made his second one. With this, I almost considered starting him, but thought better of it because he still hadn't shown he'd consistently work hard in practice.

As we huddled up to start the game, though, I didn't let my concerns show. I had our starting lineup written down on a basketball whiteboard and went over our keys for the game. With the listing of five players who were regular attendees of practice, but not necessarily the five best players, I noticed several sets of eyes roll. Players with more talent would be sitting on the bench at the start of the game, and they didn't like it. I could already sense that I was going to have a battle over this within the larger battle of trying to win the game.

I was careful not to talk too much about winning in my opening huddle, too. In the back of my mind, I might've already thought this was unrealistic. So I focused on playing hard and playing together. Menkov, I could tell, was fired up. He started patting guys on the back and encouraging them in Bulgarian, telling them that we could do this.

But as the game started, we really couldn't do it.

Thirty-fifth won the jump ball and immediately fed the ball into the post where their 6'6" dunker made a drop-step move on Pesho for an easy lay-in. Pesho immediately looked to the bench as if to say, "How did he do that?" I wanted to pull him to my side and respond, "That's the move I've been trying to teach you for a month now," but we were headed back down to the other end of the floor.

Actually, we didn't get very far, though. Thirty-fifth was employing a full-court press and trapped Menkov in the corner. He launched an ill-advised pass to no one in particular, and this resulted in a steal that led to the second layup of the game. I could see the frustration on the faces of our players less than 25 seconds into the game. Players on the bench were already yelling out to the floor in Bulgarian, "Come on! Don't be so stupid!"

On our second possession we were able to break the press, but the minute the press was broken and I called for motion offense, the only motion Pavel seem to understand was his barreling motion of wildly dribbling to the basket. Unable to cross over to dribble with his left hand, he had the ball stolen at the three-point line. And then we were headed the other way for a left-handed reverse layup from 35th. Less than a minute into the game, we hadn't taken a shot yet and were down 6-0. I felt like I had no choice but to call a timeout.

I noticed the toothless grin on Khrushchev's face as his players confidently sauntered over to his bench. Unfortunately, my players were sauntering, too, but not due to confidence; they were already frustrated. In fact, they already started to look like the two previous teams we'd beaten—defeated in a hurry.

The first point I made in the huddle was about not running to the bench for a timeout. My second was about competing, and how we were going to have to work together on both ends of the floor. My third was a form of foreshadowing: no matter what the score is, we have to play our hardest and fight for everything out on the floor. I told them it was still early, and we had plenty of time to come back.

And a ray of hope appeared on our next possession. Menkov was able to break the press, we passed the ball three times before getting it into Pesho in the post. From this point, Pesho took one dribble and launched a ridiculous fade away 10-footer that clanked off the back of the rim. But at least we'd gotten a shot up; that was the ray of hope.

On the other end, 35th wasn't having problems getting shots up. And when the shots didn't fall, they also weren't having problems getting rebounds. It was clear that most of the guys on my team hadn't ever had to box out a bigger player before, so most of them just forgot about boxing out altogether. 35th scored to make it 8-0, then stole our inbounds pass to make it 10-0. Vassy committed a foul on the shot so the 35th player went to the line to try to complete a three-point play. As I was desperately racking my brain trying to figure out what to do—who to instruct, who to encourage, who to yell at—I noticed 35th's two starting guards had taken a seat at half court. As their teammate was about to shoot his free throw to try to extend the lead to 11, they'd decided to take a break and enjoy the moment. I furiously shouted instructions while they sat with their legs splayed across half court, looking like they didn't have a care in the world. As my shouting of instructions to my team got louder and louder, I realized that I really wanted to yell about the lack of class I was witnessing sitting down at half court.

With the free throw missed, Menkov took it upon himself to shoulder the burden and dribbled the length of the floor to hit a six-foot floater. We were on the scoreboard and the bench jumped up for joy. But this was short-lived as 35th came down, missed two shots, but got the rebound both times and scored to push the score to 12-2. With this latest score, Pesho frantically waved his arms in the air, looked at me and said, "Coach, it's impossible!"

And with that, I started substituting. Pavel picked up a charge on the next possession by rumbling right into two 35th players. It actually should've been called traveling, too, but the referee decided Pavel had earned the charge–and he had. I took him and Pesho out of the game to try to calm them down.

"You can't get frustrated and get out of this game," I told them hurriedly. "If you're angry and frustrated, that's fine, but you need to use that energy to make something good happen."

Right as I said this, Dimov tried his behind-the-back dribble but spun the ball too far and had it stolen. Down at the other end, it was now 16-2. Dimov watched the rest of the play from half court, not too interested in running back on defense. It was now time for him to come out of the game, too.

Five minutes into the game, I'd subbed all five starters out of the game and we were down 24-4. Thirty-fifth had hit two consecutive threes to end the quarter, shots that I told my players we should never take because we had no one on the team who could make a shot from beyond 15 feet. Thirty-fifth played zone, a defense set up to make us shoot jump shots from the outside. With each new player that joined the bench came a new comment of frustration, a new expression of *ne modje*.

"Coach, there's no way, Coach. There's no way," Pesho kept repeating. "He's so much bigger than me."

"These refs have been paid, Coach! Every time I get the ball, they blow the whistle–every time! They've been paid!" Pavel was howling out.

"Why aren't we playing zone defense?" Dimov howled. "This man-to-man does not work in Bulgaria!"

"Coach, we're losing by too many! This sucks!" Kosio groaned. "You have to let me shoot threes!"

There was plenty more frustration all down the line, but Menkov was the one who worried me the most. His head was down and he wasn't saying anything.

"Hey, Menkov," I went over to him. "This is just the first quarter, and we're going to come back. You're our leader. You're our positive energy. I need you to lead us and show that we can come back."

He just looked at me. He didn't say anything.

The second unit wasn't faring much better as I looked out at the floor. Stefan had managed to steal the ball from the 35th point guard, but then clanked his layup off the backboard–the easiest shot we'd had in the game so far. Ivan was actually battling under the boards and was more than holding his own, but he was missing every follow-up shot.

106

When he finally got the benefit of a foul call, he went to the line and immediately hoisted up an airball. Vassy was far too undersized to be able to guard the twin towers down low for 35th, but he was playing with a determined passion. He'd already taken an elbow to his cheekbone, though, and from my perch on the sideline, I could see he was going to have a black eye.

Mercifully, the first quarter came to a close with us trailing 31-8. While I'd thought my job as Bulgarian basketball coach was difficult up to this point, now I sensed it was going to get even tougher. I spoke in positive tones during our huddle about playing with pride and winning this quarter so we could get back in the game. But as I looked at the eyes around me, I could already sense the skepticism. The minute our huddle broke, I could hear more than just skepticism. Dimov was yelling at Ivan about missing shots. Pavel was chastising Dimov for not passing the ball. Stefan was yelling at both of them for yelling at each other. This disintegration of teamwork was exactly what I'd seen as we started the season, and exactly what I'd seen from our first two opponents when they were losing. At that point, I'd been grateful that my team seemed far more together than our opponents, but now I was seeing the truth: we were only together when we were winning.

As the second quarter started, there were more pressing issues, though. I was starting to get very skeptical about Khrushchev's coaching strategy. With a 23-point lead against a clearly inferior team, he was still employing the full-court press. The lead ballooned to 27 in 40 seconds. I looked over at him and yelled in Bulgarian, "Are you having fun with the press?" Apparently, he was, as he laughed and showed off his missing teeth. The press continued.

But thankfully, our effort improved—perhaps because we had nothing to lose. Menkov and Stefan led the way by diving all over the floor, and I tried to point this out to the bench.

"This is how we'll become good, and this is the only way we'll become good," I told them. "Only with effort like this can we succeed. This is the kind of effort we need."

Some of the players on the bench shook/nodded in understanding. Others, who hadn't been coming to practice, had a look on their faces as if to say, "He can't be serious."

Menkov went on a mini-6-0 run and Pesho was able to score twice underneath before halftime. Ivan continued to grab rebounds—and also continued to miss shots. We finished the half, though, at least competing with 35th. The score at halftime was 41-22.

For the rest of the game, I hounded each one of our players to continue working hard–to take pride in putting forth their best effort. I warned them that if they failed to run back on defense, yelled at a teammate, or waved their arms in frustration, they'd be on the bench immediately. I already sensed that giving up at this point was innate, and that drove me crazy.

Dimov tried a behind-the-back pass and then fulfilled all of these requirements. He sat.

Stefan and Menkov continued to play hard and battle with 35th guards. They did a better job handling the press–which continued for the whole game. Pavel ran over two more 35th players while he had the ball, and each time looked over to me and said, "I don't understand, Coach. Why can't I do that?"

Eventually I had to take Vassy out of the game because I was worried he'd end up with two black eyes. I let Kosio take his place and saw a great deal of his smoothness at work–on defense. He smoothly managed to get out of the way anytime a 35th player got near him, terrified they might make contact with him. When he hit consecutive three-pointers at the other end of the floor, he wanted to celebrate and didn't understand when I took him out of the game.

"Kosio, you hit two shots which gave us six points, but you gave up at least eight points by not playing any defense on the other end," I told him calmly. "If you're not going to work hard and play tough defense, then you're not going to play. I don't care if you hit three-pointers or not."

He looked completely befuddled by my logic.

I let Ivan continue battling, but also had to take him out because his confidence for making a shot–any kind of shot–was completely gone. He finished the game with 14 rebounds and 2 points. He shot 0-9 from the floor and was 2-10 from the free-throw line.

I'd given Sasho numerous chances, but he was so slow that the ball was routinely stripped from him as he tried to make moves. Each time I took him out of the game, he came to the bench with his uncharacteristically Bulgarian grin. "Coach, this is very difficult–very, very difficult."

The remaining quarters were all better than the first quarter, but the game was never close. We lost 71-52.

As I instructed my team to shake hands with each of the 35th players–something they protested–we had to wait as the entire 35th team gathered in a circle at half court and all fell backwards in unison to celebrate their 19-point victory. They bounced back up and began hugging each other, and I forced my way into their celebration to try to shake Khrushchev's hand. When I finally found him and said "good game," in Bulgarian, he just laughed and continued to take part in the celebration at half court.

After the game when I talked to my team, I tried to stress the positives, but I was addressing a glum, fatalistic bunch. As bad as the score had been, we'd played 35th even for three of the four quarters. The first quarter, though, had been brutal. No matter what I tried to say about moral victories and what we could build on from here, though, it didn't seem to matter. One thing, and one thing only, was very clear to my players: we had lost. And if we needed a reminder about the fact that we had lost, at half court off in the distance, the 35th players continued to dance.

The good thing about a tournament is that you have the chance to bounce back quickly in the next game. This was what I was hoping for as we squared off against the Spanish school the following night in our next game. They were dubbed the Spanish school because these students had chosen Spanish as their primary foreign language. But the Spanish school consisted of all Bulgarian student athletes.

As I had time to reflect on our deflating loss against 35th, I looked back on the game and realized that while 35th was far more talented than my team, they weren't exactly world-beaters. They weren't disciplined, didn't play hard consistently, and mostly took winning for granted. They had many flaws that we were able to expose as the game wore on. And for the bulk of the game, we'd played with three sophomores and two juniors out on the floor. Our team had little experience and got better as the game progressed. But I didn't know if I was able to find comfort in the fact that a team that had beaten us by 19 points wasn't actually that impressive. And I knew for certain my team wouldn't take solace in this fact.

So maybe it was good that we were back on the court so soon against the Spanish school. As down as most of the players had been following the 35th loss, they seemed to understand that we'd have another chance against the Spanish school, our last chance to advance to the elimination round of the tournament.

"What happened against 35th," Nikolai told me, "happens to our teams a lot when we play them. We are intimidated at the beginning, and then lack the confidence to beat them. This year, though, your players thought it would be different."

"Why did they think it would be different this year, Nikolai?" I responded.

"Because this year, they have you as a coach, and you make them feel like they should be confident."

I realized this was a compliment, but Nikolai kept going.

"This is great; to have confidence, it is great. But with our kids in this country, now that they have this hope you have given them, those hopes fall hard. You have to be ready for this."

I certainly wasn't ready for this. As I walked to the gym in the soggy, icy December air and tried to think about the game, I had trouble coming up with just about any aspect of Bulgarian coaching that I considered myself ready for.

Menkov was the first person I had to talk to before we tipped off against the Spanish school.

"Are you okay?" I asked him.

"Yeah, Coach, I'm fine," he responded right away. "We're going to win tonight."

"I hope so, Menkov, but I also want you to understand it's most important for us to come out and play hard from the beginning. We need your leadership to get us off to a good start."

"I know, Coach. I know what you mean. We're going to win tonight."

With this, he flashed me a smile and jogged over to his teammates. I was reassured by his confidence, but concerned by the fact that he repeated "we're going to win tonight" twice. As much as I hoped this would be true, we were going to have to pull off an upset against a superior team to win. I wasn't sure if "winning" represented a realistic option. I was thinking about small steps and just getting better. But as Nikolai had alerted me, small steps weren't a part of the process for my team. They had hope and therefore they wanted to win. They had hope, and they expected results.

On this night, we got off to a better start and by the end of the first quarter, I could at least tell the boys in the huddle that we had a chance. I wasn't talking about moral victories and winning a quarter, but talking the specifics of strategy. The Spanish school was good, but not as good 35th. I'd even seen Starter Jacket get upset on the sidelines with his players' lackluster effort going after rebounds. Our team still couldn't shoot straight, but Pesho had scored on three offensive rebounds and

Vassy on two. At the end of the first quarter, we trailed 16-11.

I was excited, as was the team. But once again, we were outmatched. They had guards who dribbled with their heads up to see the floor, and big men who were able to catch the ball in the post and make strong moves to score. But they also didn't work very hard. They were lazy getting back on defense. I continued to stress out-hustling them—perhaps our only chance, but still a chance nonetheless.

As the second quarter started, though, an alarming trend reared its ugly head once again. Menkov turned the ball over at half court, giving the other team a layup at the other end. As he brought the ball up the floor once again, he was met by Dimov's mouth, scolding him for turning it over. In a show of frustration, Menkov flipped the ball to Dimov who immediately took the ball to the basket and rocketed a wild shot toward the basket. As it careened back toward the foul line, Dimov, under the basket, let loose a rage of curse words as he watched the Spanish team run the other way.

I grabbed Stefan from the bench and sent him in the game for Dimov.

"Do you see what happens when you don't run back on defense?" I said to the remaining players on the bench. "Does it do us any good to spend energy yelling at each other and yelling in general? Does that help us get back and play defense?"

The players on the bench understood me, but also seemed to empathize with Dimov. Many of them, it seemed, would've done the exact same thing if they were in his shoes.

When Dimov trudged over to the bench, I repeated the same things to him.

"But Coach, that's how I play. That's my game. Nobody else seems to have a problem with it—just you."

"That's fine, Dimov, because I'm the coach. And if I have a problem with your attitude on the floor, then that means it's a big problem. It means you're going to sit."

Fuming, I couldn't believe how difficult it was for me to explain my logic to him. And now I had an even bigger dilemma: we really needed him in the game, but I didn't think I could stomach putting him back in the game.

Trying to focus on the game in front of me and not my own burgeoning sense of anger, I watched Kosio give us a boost by doing something extremely rare for our team: he hit a jump shot. With this, he raised his arms in the air and pointed to the sparse crowd that was cheering us on. In the process of celebrating his shot, he completely lost his man who scored on an easy layup while Kosio's mind was still in the stands. I took him out of the game as well.

So the second quarter sloshed along. Stefan played with heart and hustle, but had two shots blocked because he released them too slowly and nervously. Pesho picked up his third foul reaching in because he didn't want to move his feet.

"Butt down! Butt down! Don't you remember the drills?" I pleaded with him.

"Yeah, Coach, I remember," he sheepishly replied, "but it's really hard. It's easier to just try to steal the ball."

Vassy was undersized once again, but battling down low. His now black eye might've given him respect from the other team, I surmised. And Pavel was ineffective in the traditional offensive manner, but scaring the daylights out of the man guarding him because he continued to approach his offensive game as if he were a battering ram.

The horn went off for halftime and we were down 31-21.

It was difficult to find too many positives in terms of the beauty or style of play, but we were playing harder than the Spanish school. We were fighting for loose balls, getting rebounds and playing with the heart I'd hoped we'd have. They were playing zone defense, and while we couldn't hit a shot from outside, we were being a little more patient to get the ball inside.

"We can win this game!" Menkov shouted to his teammates at halftime. "They're not playing as hard as we are! We can win this game! *Haide! Haide! Haide, momchetas!*"

Right along with *ne modje*, I'd learned the defintion of *haide* early on in my Bulgarian tenure, and I heard it with great frequency on the basketball floor. *Haide* roughly translates to "Let's go!" or "Come on!" and could be used to express either happiness or frustration. I just got used to hearing *Haide!* no matter what was going on out on the floor. A bad defensive play? *Haide!* A made shot? *Haide!* A missed layup? *Haide!* Drawing a tough foul? *Haide!* In this case, I was happy that Menkov was using it as a motivational tool. And it seemed to have some success.

Menkov was exhibiting the exact leadership I'd hoped for, and we started the second half on an 8-0 run. Starter Jacket slammed down his clipboard and called a timeout. My team came rushing to the bench slapping high fives all around. In the corner of my eye, I noticed three players who didn't bother getting up from the bench to join the huddle. They hadn't come to practices and still expected to play, and sat dejectedly on the end of the bench while the rest of the team was full of exuberance.

As we broke the huddle, Sasho, in all his awkwardness, came up to me with a big smile. "Coach, this is fun. This is really fun. We're going to win this game."

I smiled back at Sasho, and noticed the contrast between him and the three players on the end of the bench. Sasho had only played about two minutes in the game, yet he was having fun.

But soon, Sasho would have to play much more than two minutes. Pesho picked up his fourth foul, reaching in once again, and I had to put Sasho in to guard their best post player.

"I know, I know, Coach," Pesho said as he came to the sideline. "Butt down, butt down, don't reach in. It's just hard; no one's ever told me I needed to do that before."

This was the first time one of the players had directly told me that, but I sensed they'd all said it to each other. I was preaching hard work, intelligence, togetherness, resilience and teamwork—things I thought were cornerstones of a good team. These were also things I'd gotten used to taking for granted with my teams in the States. For Pesho and the rest of his teammates, the things I was saying certainly represented a foreign language, and not just because I was speaking English.

With only a two-point lead, the Spanish school now realized they were in for a game. As a result, they started doing what they should've been doing the entire game–playing hard. Pavel had the ball stolen from him as he tried to cross over to dribble with his left hand, something I'd been begging him to do. As he headed back on defense he looked at me as if to say, "See Coach, I told you I can't dribble with my left hand. Why would you ever encourage such a thing?"

Baskets were traded back and forth, though with Pesho on the bench we were struggling. I'd put Dimov back in the game, and he'd managed to keep his mouth shut and his dribbling in front of him for a stretch of several straight minutes. Along with this, he'd made two nice passes–one to Menkov and one Kosio, who both finished with floaters in the lane. Determined to do exactly what I'd told Pesho I wanted him to do, Sasho was sliding his size-14 feet clumsily in the lane trying to stay in front of the Spanish big men. Watching his effort and seeing how receptive he was to coaching was heartwarming, but that feeling slowly dissipated as Spanish's much quicker and more experienced post players slid by him time after time to score. While Sasho was trying his hardest on defense, Kosio continued to only show interest in playing offense. After a Spanish possession where he stuck his leg out to trip one of their guards instead of moving his feet, I took him out of the game, deciding that I'd seen enough.

As we entered the fourth quarter, Spanish led by six points. In our team huddle, I decided to gamble and implement our own full-court press.

"Whenever we score, whenever they have the ball out of bounds, we're going to run our press," I explained while drawing everyone's position on my clipboard. "It's absolutely essential that each of you know where you're supposed to be. This is a zone trap; we've worked on it in practice. Make sure you're in the right spot. We're in better shape than they are; we're going to work harder than they will. We can win this game."

With that, a spirited group jumped back onto the floor for the fourth quarter. I could sense the excitement in the gym, the chance that we could advance in the tournament, and a belief that maybe this would cause the team to believe, bond and buy in to what we were doing.

"Coach, Coach, please," Pesho pleaded from the bench, "I promise I won't foul. I promise I'll play nice. I can move my feet. I will move my feet. Just put me back in the game."

Even in the heat of an intense game, there was something comical about a 6'4" buzz-cut Bulgarian pleading with me to be put back in the game. His innocent and youthful tone made him sound like Borat as a teenager. And it made it hard for me to say no.

With no scoring for the first two minutes of the fourth quarter, I put Pesho back in the game. He flew to the scorer's table and loped into the game with an urgency I'd never seen from him during any of our box-out drills. Sasho returned to the bench with the same goofy smile he always wore on his face.

"Did I do good, Coach? Did I do good, Coach?" he asked. "I moved my feet just like you wanted me to. I moved my feet every time on defense. Did you see?"

"Yeah, Sasho," I couldn't help but smile back at him. "You did great."

And Pesho was great upon re-entering the game. He stole a post-entry feed then sprinted down the floor creating his own one-man fast break. Amidst my shouts of, "Hold up! Get the ball to a guard!" Pesho was a runaway freight train with no eyes or ears for anything else. He contorted his body awkwardly as he soared through the air to heave in an ugly-looking scoop shot. He pumped his fist in the air and sprinted back on defense.

The only problem was that he was supposed to be front man on the press. The other four players were pressing; Pesho was not. This immediately led to yelling from his teammates. The press, as I had forewarned, would not work with only four guys. The Spanish school easily broke the dysfunctional press and headed down the court for a 2-on-1 fast break. Pesho was the one man left. And using the same awkward energy that allowed him to miraculously score on the other end, he went up to block the layup attempt.

The ball went in the hoop. The whistle was blown. Pesho had fouled out.

With that, frustration returned. Pesho waved his arms in the air, hoping he could find someone else to blame other than himself. Dimov, who had been remarkably and effectively silent in the second half, looked at me and said, "See Coach, I told you we never should've pressed."

Pesho trotted to the bench. I grabbed Stefan to go get Dimov. He trotted to the bench soon after.

"At some point, Dimov," I sternly warned him, "you're going to have to understand that your mouth only gets you in trouble."

Menkov tried to lead us out of frustration, but tried to do too much. He dribbled the ball off his foot driving the baseline. Spanish came right back down and scored another three-point play. This time Pavel mauled his man going up for a short jump shot.

"But Coach," he pleaded, "I barely even touched him. If that's a foul, he must get tougher."

This comment made Pavel sound like one of Borat's bodyguards.

Spanish had extended the lead to 10 and I called a timeout. But even with around five minutes left in the game, I could sense 10 points was going to be too much for our offensively-challenged team to recover from. Plus, two of our best players were now permanently planted on the bench, one due to fouls and the other due to attitude.

Menkov and Stefan played their hearts out, usually running a two-man press when the rest of the team forgot where they were supposed to be. Vassy battled under the boards, but was limited offensively because the Spanish team was starting to realize that he could only go left—he was our one left-handed player—and only finish on the left side. Pavel got frustrated when his attempts to steal the ball were deemed as muggings—which they were—and told me he was certain "the refs were out to get him." In order to spare him the agony of things getting worse and me the agony of watching it, I took him out of the game as well.

Menkov hit a three—a rare feat for our team—to cut the lead to five points with a minute to play. I called a timeout to try to diagram strategy for the last minute. While the players on the floor had the right intentions and played hard for the last minute, not a single one of my strategic commands was followed. We failed to score for the remainder of the game and lost by nine.

When the horn blew, our deflated team slowly made their way back to the bench as the Spanish showed their level of sportsmanship by celebrating loudly. Their starting point guard turned in the direction of the crowd and pounded on his chest. Shaking hands, once again, was an arduous undertaking. The Spanish players were perplexed as we approached them with our hands extended. They looked as if they thought we wanted to fight them, not congratulate them.

Starter Jacket told me in broken English as I shook his hand, "You play well. You play much more good than I think you will."

This comment actually sunk in, and he was right. We'd played much better than the previous game. Any observer could easily comment on how much we'd improved from the last game. Even though we weren't advancing in the tournament, we were making strides toward getting better. I planned to say all of these things to my team in my post-game comments.

But as I turned to find my team to prepare for our post-game talk, I wasn't sure if I'd be able to make any comments. Several of them had already headed for the revolving door bubble exit. And since we didn't have a locker room, we did all of our talking in the gym. Several of the players were just taking off. I saw Menkov trailing them, about to head out the door, and called to him.

"Menkov! Where are you going? We're not done yet."

He glumly turned and walked back to me.

"Of course we're done, Coach. We lost. We're done. I thought we were going to win, and we lost."

"Menkov," I tried to console him, "I know we lost, but you played a great game. You were a leader out on the floor. You played your hardest the entire game. And we played a much better game. It was close the whole way."

"That doesn't matter, Coach," he snapped back, and I noticed his entire tone and demeanor as an enthusiastic leader had changed. "We lost. That's what matters. Some of the guys want to quit. We thought things could be different this year."

Want to quit? Already?

"Things are different this year, Menkov. We're playing hard, we're playing together, we're getting better—but it might take some time for us to start winning. It's all part of the process."

"Coach, I thought we were going to win. And we didn't. Our tournament is over. I just don't know if I see the point. I thought this year would be different."

"This year will be different, Menkov. You'll see. We're going to keep getting better, and you're going to be our leader."

"Coach, I don't see the point. There's no point in being the leader of a losing team."

I felt like I was talking to a petulant five-year-old kid who wanted to eat dessert without eating his vegetables. I'd run through several motivational and consolation speeches with my most important player, but now I was reaching the point of exasperation. If I lost the leader of the team, the student council president, and perhaps the only player who had a positive attitude that the other players would follow, then what did I have left? And if I couldn't convince them that winning wasn't everything, what could I do?

I was fairly certain we were going to lose games. We weren't a very good basketball team. But I was hoping they'd see the value of playing hard together even if we did lose. This had always been my experience with teams in the States. But this team—this Bulgarian team—was unlike any team I'd ever had in the States.

"Menkov, I want to talk to the team. You guys can't leave before we've had a chance to talk. We're going to win together, and we're going to lose together."

"Some of the guys have already left, Coach. And I don't think they're coming back," he offered begrudgingly, but then he conceded. "But I'll get the guys who are still here."

With this, he took his deflated body over to the other players and told them we were meeting for a post-game talk. From the body language of the players he talked to, I could see they felt the same way he did. The game was over. We had lost. Nothing else mattered.

Pesho was immersed in his cell phone, not even looking at Menkov when he was talking. Vassy's black eye drooped as Menkov told him I wanted to talk to them. Ivan dragged his bag along the floor, ensuring it would make noise as he shuffled over to the bench. And for the first time today, Sasho didn't have a goofy smile on his face.

In that moment, it was hard for me not to panic. The fact that we'd lost was not good, but not surprising, and also not that bad—at least from my vantage point. From the moment I'd looked at our team, I knew we were going to lose games. But I didn't think that losing games necessarily meant we were going to have a bad season. To these players, though, all my rhetoric about working hard and playing together would only be tolerated on one account: if we were winning games. Hard work and teamwork didn't matter if we were losing. I watched them collectively trudge over to the bench and I wondered what in the world I was going to say. I'd already had several players walk out of the gym, frustrated either at losing or not playing enough. Those who stayed didn't particularly look any better.

So as I assembled them for the last time that night, I told them how much we'd improved, how proud I was of their effort, and how we needed to continue to improve. I told them that we'd played better than the game against 35th; this game was close the entire night. I said that I was proud of their effort; they'd played hard and never gave up. I told them that if we kept working hard, we would beat teams like this in the future. That needed to be our goal—to work hard and beat teams like this in the future.

During my speech, I scanned the group of boys to look for any acknowledgment of what I was saying, any belief in what I was saying. But no eyes met mine. No heads were raised proudly. At some point, I realized that all my words, though I meant them sincerely, were hollow to my players.

As I brought the team together and each put their arms in for our team break, they collectively uttered a defeated "TEAM!" and headed for the exit. I stood and watched as they wandered dejectedly toward the revolving door.

Four players had left without even staying for the post-game talk. They were upset I hadn't played them in the game even though they hadn't come to practice. Two of them I'd never see again at practice. Those who did stick around seemed to have given up all hope a mere four games into the season. These were two losses—two losses against superior teams at the beginning of the season. But they certainly didn't see it that way. All the lessons I was trying to teach were falling on deaf ears. I wondered how many of them were even going to show up at practice on Monday.

Bulgaria was a country that was used to losing. They'd lost their culture to the Ottoman oppression, lost land to all their neighbors, lost their gold medals to positive drug tests, and had currently lost their government to the mafia. They were tired of losing. And on this night, no amount of American optimism after a loss was going to matter.

Watching them walk out, I dropped my head. I felt like a failure. Nothing I had done, nothing I had said had made a difference. In the end, we had lost and I felt like I'd lost the most.

Pavel was the last to leave the gym, and he came up to me–the only player who came up to me after the game.

"I'm really upset we lost, Coach," he said, and looked visibly shaken, "but I promise you I'm going to work my hardest for the team. I promise."

I flashed back to the first day I'd met Pavel when he'd told me the same thing.

"Thanks, Pavel. I promise I'm going to work my hardest for this team, too."

As he walked away, I seriously began to question whether Pavel's hardest or my hardest would be even close to enough. I felt like I was up against cultural forces I couldn't even begin to comprehend. The tournament experience had started with rabid and illogical arguments about cheating, something that seemed like ancient history to me. All I could think about now was how my players were so deflated and perhaps ready to quit because we'd been beaten by two teams far superior to us.

As I walked slowly out of the gym in the shadow of the giant dilapidated row house, I found Khrushchev outside smoking a cigarette and bellowing loudly; his team's game was about to start in a few minutes, but he hadn't finished his cigarette yet. The only other sound I could hear was the distant rattling sound of police gunfire.

Chapter X
A Corrupt Christmas

"So, how much do you think this is gonna cost me?" I asked as we walked out to the car.

There was no audible response from Igor, the school's driver, just a subtle finger-wag—which was the Bulgarian charade form of *ne modje, it's not gonna happen.* It was clear to me that I wasn't supposed to ask that question, no matter how innocuous I thought the question was.

I'd figured that Christmas was a joyous time, and since Igor was driving me to go pick up the Christmas package that my mother had so generously sent all the way from the capitalist West, I figured that Igor and I could have an enjoyable trip to go pick up the presents. But his finger-wag, accompanied with a Bulgarian scowl, told me that I should be quiet—we weren't going to have any more discussion. So, I obeyed, put my head down, and got into the car.

Igor lit a cigarette before he turned the key in the ignition. With it dangling precariously from his lips, he had a tough-guy Humphrey Bogart look to him. And as the stray dogs started yelping and growling as the wheels of the car started moving, he didn't seem affected at all. I noticed this mostly because I still jumped as the dogs chased the front wheel, teeth snarling, even though I was well protected inside the car. The car had rumbled its way out of the college and over numerous potholes when Igor finally decided to open up the dialogue.

"We do not talk about this outside—only in car," he said to me carefully in English with smoke blustering my way.

This gave me the impression that we weren't embarking on a normal pick-up of Christmas presents. We were about to undertake a mission far more serious.

And this was exactly what I was hoping to avoid. When the school's secretary told me that a Christmas package for me was being held at customs, I was initially excited because it meant I had a Christmas package coming. Even though it still remained difficult for my mother—or anyone for that matter—to understand why I'd left the comforts of home for the Eastern bloc, she still had enough goodness in her heart to ship me a Christmas package, across some 5000 miles. And in between losses on the basketball floor, slips on the Bulgarian ice and my continued fear of feral dogs, I was elated for a touch of comfort from the States. But when the secretary said the package was being held by customs, she didn't smile. Nor was she smiling when she said with a Dracula-like drawl, "You *vill* have to go *vith* Igor."

It appeared to me that my Christmas presents weren't simply being held by customs; they were being held *hostage* by customs. Even though I'd chosen to go into this experience with a positive attitude, Igor was doing nothing to assuage my concerns.

"If you want your package," Igor started and looked for me to assent that yes, I did want the package, "you have two options. One option is just to pay customer tax." (It took me a little while to realize that "customer" meant "customs.") "I think this customer tax will be ... um ... probably 150 *leva*."

"Whoa," my reaction was immediate. One hundred fifty *leva* was somewhere in the neighborhood of 110 U.S. dollars.

"Or," Igor could sense my displeasure, "you try option two."

The way he said "option two" made me wonder if he was going to put me in a room with four rabid dogs and let the five of us fight for the package.

"Which is?" I gulped.

Taking the cigarette out of his mouth, he smiled slyly.

"Well, we pay them."

"I don't understand. Isn't that just like option one?"

"No, no," Igor gave me my second finger-wag. "How you say in English ... we don't pay them, but we *pay* them.

I thought I might be catching on, but my understanding of Igor's ambiguity didn't calm my nerves.

"You mean we bribe the customs' officer?"

This time Igor smiled at me, the first smile I'd seen from him this afternoon.

"Yes, that is the word, but I don't like that word so much. But that is what we can do—if you want. We will not do this if you do not like."

Yet again in Bulgaria, I was entering completely uncharted life experience territory.

"Well, I don't know," I stumbled a bit, searching for guidance in how to deal with this situation. "I'd like to spend as little money as possible, but I don't want to get in trouble."

With this, Igor laughed heartily, the cigarette bouncing up and down as his head bobbed.

"Get in trouble? Andy, you know better than this, do you not? This is Bulgaria. There is no—how you say?—*trouble* here."

Even though I had no idea how I should handle this situation—much like so many I'd faced on the basketball floor—I still admonished myself for not being able to understand quickly and decide what to do.

"Igor, I'd like to spend as little money as possible. These are my Christmas presents. What would you do if these were your Christmas presents?"

"Oh," he raised up proudly, "I would not pay customer tax. I would talk to them first, and then *pay* them—no doubt. This is how we do things here."

This is how we do things here was most directly a reference to my Christmas presents, but I knew it meant so much more than this. *Things* seemed to range from paying referees to mob hits in broad daylight at crowded cafes with no witnesses to playing 23-year-olds in a high school basketball tournament. And *here* didn't refer specifically to the customs' office; *here* meant Bulgaria.

I found it curious that as our conversation continued and I agreed to bribe the customs' officers, bribe was a word that Igor knew and understood, but refused to ever say. He continued to refer to *paying them* like it was a normal occurrence—and I was pretty sure it was—but never used the word bribe. It seemed to me that he held the logic that as long as he didn't use the actual word bribe, then he wouldn't have to actually admit that a bribe was occurring. I was certain he'd learned this version of plausible deniability at a young Bulgarian age, and it was working well with an American who wanted his Christmas presents. On the grander Bulgarian scale, though, this same attitude was not ingratiating Bulgaria to the ministers of the EU.

Earlier in the fall, the EU's anti-fraud official—clearly curious about where so much of the EU's money had disappeared to—had arrived in Sofia to discuss corruption in Bulgaria. When he landed at the Sofia airport, he hailed a cab to take him to the center of town. When reading about this episode in the *Sofia Echo,* the local English language newspaper, I was surprised by the fact that an anti-fraud expert representing the entire European Union would not be picked up at the airport by some member of the Bulgarian government. Seeing that Bulgaria was already on EU thin ice, why would they not attempt to roll out a red, or even faded pink, carpet for an EU official who was taking the time to come visit the country? This slight, though, was not what put the official's visit in the news.

He took a Sofia taxi from the airport to the parliament in the center of the city where his meetings would be. Normally, this cab ride costs 10 *leva*—about 7 U.S. dollars. And the EU anti-fraud official— who was from Spain—felt comfortable in his taxi because it had a meter, a sign of regulation he was familiar with from his country and other European countries. But when he got out at parliament in the center of town, the cab driver pointed to the meter which showed a fare of 102 *leva*—a whopping 10 times what the ride should've cost (and a sum in the neighborhood of 70 U.S. dollars for a 12-15 minute ride in the poorest country in the European Union). The official sensed something was wrong, and did the best he could to argue the fare, but the cab driver continually pointed at his posted rates on the side of the cab, which represented the extremely high cost of a ride in his cab. In the end, the exasperated minister gave in and paid the cab driver the exorbitant sum of 102 *leva*, about as much as a legitimate cab driver might make in one full day of driving.

What happened to the Spanish official is something that could happen to anyone not inured with the way that corruption and cheating rules Bulgaria. When the cab driver pointed at his posted rates, he was correct in saying that his rates were reflected on the window. But to a foreigner from another country used to taxi regulations, it would be very difficult to discern what the small print on the window of the cab actually meant.

Legitimate taxis in Sofia—most were run by the OK Taxi company— would charge 0.68 per kilometer. This meant 68 *stotinki*, or about 45 U.S. cents. If you approached the taxi and saw 0.68 on the window, you were in good shape. But not all taxis were legitimately run by the OK Taxi company. And the ones that weren't flocked to places like the airport or train station, eager to pick up foreigners. In fact, one of the best pieces of advice I ever received in Bulgaria was to never take a taxi from the train station. All the taxis at the train station were illegitimate, and if I wanted a taxi home, I should walk to the bus station across the street. Getting out at the train station, though, it would be very difficult to see the ruse right away.

Illegitimate taxis in Bulgaria looked very similar to legitimate taxis. Most were run by the CK Taxi Company, and their version of "C" was shaky at best. To the naked eye, their logo looked exactly like the OK Taxi logo, except their first letter became a "C" by leaving a sliver of space disconnected on the right side of the oval. Looking very closely, you could see that this letter was not a complete "O" because the oval wasn't attached on the right side. There is, however, a miniscule likelihood that someone like the transportation official—or any foreigner for that matter—would have ever noticed the difference. And if he happened to look at the rates posted on the window, he would've seen the same sets of numbers that were on all the legitimate taxis: 068. But in this case, the decimal point was moved slightly; his rates were listed as 06.80 *leva* per kilometer, a price 10 times as much as a legitimate taxi.

Though there were most likely many taxis at the airport, and many taxi drivers who could've alerted this well-dressed foreigner he was making a big mistake, no one spoke up. And since Bulgarian politicians refused to regulate taxi rates, this situation occurred over and over again. This was the Bulgarian form of capitalism: since it was every Bulgarian's right to make money, many dropped ethical concerns and looked for the best way for this to happen. In many cases, this meant swindling those who were unsuspecting—swindling those who came from countries where taxis meters were regulated (most countries in Europe).

The Spanish EU anti-fraud official entered his first meeting with Bulgarian politicians feeling befuddled and betrayed. How could at 15-minute ride from the airport cost him 50 Euros? That was an obscene amount of money in a country with such a low cost of living.

He brought this question to the attention of the Bulgarian minister of transportation, who sheepishly had to admit to the EU anti-fraud official that he'd been swindled by an illegitimate taxi. These taxis were not registered taxis and took advantage of people who didn't realize what the rates actually should be.

The Spanish official was appalled. He questioned his Bulgarian peer about this practice, and couldn't help but ask him how this problem could still exist so commonly, especially if the Bulgarian minister seemed so aware of the situation.

The Bulgarian minister could see that life in Spain and the rest of Western Europe was very different than life in Bulgaria. He must've told him that Bulgarian lawmakers were well aware of the prevalence of illegitimate taxis ripping people off in Sofia and the rest of the country. Alas, though, this is just part of life in Bulgaria.

The Spanish official still had to have trouble understanding. There had to be something that could be done to change this. People were entering the country–perhaps for the first time like this official–and immediately being ripped off.

I'm sorry, the Bulgarian minister told him in response. We know this is a problem in Bulgaria, but nothing can be done.

Ne modje, he was telling the Spanish official.

The truth was, things could be done to rectify this grievous wrong, but nothing was going to be done.

At the end of his cab ride, the Spanish official was left feeling baffled and angry, and the official response from his Bulgarian counterpart in charge of these matters was a shrug of the shoulders– sorry, but there's nothing I can do. Also at the end of the cab ride, that cab driver drove away knowing that he'd charged a fare so ridiculous that he'd made enough money to keep him solvent for quite a while. But because he'd charged the far, however illegitimate it was, that was posted on his window, he could drive away with a clear conscience as he was about to pick up his next unsuspecting customer. He could plausibly deny that he'd done anything wrong. This was capitalism at its finest in Bulgaria.

As Igor motored along through the slushy streets of Sofia toward the customs' office, I was starting to realize that I was now going to partake in Bulgarian capitalism very soon. I was going to make some lucky customs' officer solvent for the week by bribing him to receive my Christmas package that was being held hostage. I was faced with paying an absurd customs' tax of over 100 U.S. dollars, a tax that was possibly set so high to encourage the unlucky recipient to find some other reasonable way to receive a package. That reasonable way, of course, would be completely to the benefit of the lowly paid customs' officer.

We pulled into the customs' office parking lot, a swampy mixture of snow, ice and water, and I stepped out of the car into four inches of a freezing cold puddle. My attire for the day—teaching clothes of slacks, a shirt and a tie—now seemed ill-fitting for this experience. The customs' building in front of me looked far more like an old barn than an official government building. My professional dress—with one pant leg now soaking—was not going to make a difference here.

When we entered the building, I could see my breath and noticed that it seemed colder inside than it was outside. Parts of the building were open-air—clearly not the most effective design for mid-December Sofia. Several people inside—workers included—were wearing stocking caps to stave off the cold.

And inside, there was lots of Bulgarian haggling going on. I tried to translate, but the pace of speaking was an impediment, and I was also putting quite a bit of energy trying not to completely stand out as the foreigner inside the customs' office. I probably had little chance of this, but in the moment, I was telling myself otherwise.

Igor led the way to the first window where we were sent to another window. After waiting in line for about five minutes at this window, we were then sent to another window. I wanted to ask Igor how things were going, but I didn't want to tempt fate. His expression, solemn and Bulgarian, hadn't changed since we entered the customs' barn, and I remembered his earlier warning about when it was okay to discuss this: *only in car*. I also didn't want to speak English in this place, so I stood silently next to him as we waited in our third line.

When Igor made it to the window, there was more haggling between him and the woman behind the counter. When she spoke, I deciphered "*Chaka, chaka tuka*," which meant "wait, wait here." Igor looked at me and raised his eyebrows. This could have meant that things were going swimmingly, or that things weren't going well at all. Bulgarians, I'd learned quickly, were not easy to read from their various solemn facial expressions. Georgi Markov, the Bulgarian dissident writer, had astutely pointed out that due to their long history and mutual understandings, Bulgarians "can converse for hours without speaking a word." Unfortunately I didn't share this common Bulgarian trait with Igor and started to wonder if we were going to be in this customs barn for hours.

The woman returned to the window with another man, and more discussion ensued. The wooden floors creaked as people scrambled through the five-foot wide hallway. Some had packages and appeared to be hurrying out as if there was a chance that someone, anyone, could rip them from their grasp if they didn't exit quickly. I could see my breath as I stood waiting next to Igor. He continued the back-and-forth with the customs' officers, and they reached a level of conversation that I was having a lot of trouble translating. So I looked around for comforting images—perhaps even a Christmas image—anything to help make me think that this would all work out. But all I could come up with was a life-size poster behind the desk of a bikini-clad girl holding a giant chainsaw. At that point, I decided that "comforting" was going to have to be a relative term.

The conversation at the window continued and Igor turned and directed me. *"Tam,"* he said, meaning "there," as he pointed straight-faced to a new window.

We then went to our fourth window. Nothing was said. A piece of paper was pushed in my direction with a signature line. I signed it. There were no smiles.

Igor headed through a door to a back room after telling me in Bulgarian, "Just wait here. Don't say anything."

Seeing that waiting and not saying anything constituted everything I'd been doing since we entered the barn, these weren't difficult instructions for me to follow. I watched as a bird flew in through the open-air section of the barn. He perched himself on a wooden support beam for a few seconds, looked around, and then decided to fly back out of the barn. I couldn't blame him.

A minute passed.

Another minute passed.

Then Igor re-appeared, stone-faced as before, but this time he was holding a package in his arms. He didn't smile; he didn't speak; he just pointed toward to exit door. I followed.

My heart was racing, wondering what had happened behind those closed doors. He had a package in his hands, and I assumed it was mine, but his expression hadn't changed—and he hadn't given me the package either. Trying desperately to remain faithful to the *only-in-car* rule, I continued my silence. Once we got in the car and the doors were closed, I finally felt free to speak.

"So what happened in there?" I asked him in English.

He slowly slid a cigarette out of its pack, and I could see his lips turn upward as he looked over to me. This was the first inkling of a smile, or any emotion for that matter, that I'd seen since we'd entered the customs' office. His response was only one word:

"Talking."

He laughed deliberately and heartily.

"Yes, yes, we talked. Then we came to a—how you say?—an agreement."

He looked straight ahead to the road, and he looked happy. His mission had been successful, and even though it wasn't Igor's package, I sensed that he felt a sense of accomplishment from this entire enterprise.

"So how much do I owe you, Igor?"

With this, he smiled again.

"Forty *leva*."

"Forty *leva*?"

"Yes, I paid them 40 *leva*. This is not bad, no?"

"Not bad at all, Igor," I replied as took out my wallet to pay him.

He had saved me 110 *leva* with his bribe—though I didn't use the word bribe with him either—and even though it was hard to fathom that it was necessary for me to pay money to receive this package in the first place, I couldn't have been happier in that moment. I suppose the same could be said for whoever received my 40 *leva* under the table. Bulgarian capitalism had worked for all parties involved—just in time for Christmas.

After our ACS Open two-game debacle, I'd hoped that possibly Christmas could infuse a more enthusiastic spirit into my basketball team. Though I wasn't disappointed by losing the two games, it was near impossible for me not to be disappointed by the response from my players following the games. I'd grown used to Bulgarian men and boys not expressing happiness through their countenance, but Menkov saying there was no point to playing if we weren't going to win, and the team not even willing to make eye contact with me after the game seemed extreme.

Thankfully, Menkov showed up in my classroom the next day apologetic; he'd had a change of heart.

"I'm sorry, Coach. I was just really frustrated," he told me. "I don't want to quit. I think we can get better, and I know it's a long season."

"I'm glad to hear that, Menkov," I told him.

"But I can't guarantee all the other guys feel the same way."

"What does that mean?"

"Well, I think some of them aren't going to play any more. They were upset they didn't play much in the tournament, and thought it was embarrassing to sit on the bench."

"Are these players who didn't come to practice regularly?" I responded.

"Yeah, it's all guys who haven't been coming to practice, but they still thought they'd play."

"And you understand, Menkov," I was deeply hoping he'd understand, "that it's not going to work that way this year. The guys who work hard and come to practice will be the ones who play."

"Yeah, Coach, I get it. And I think you're right. But this isn't easy for most of us to learn. No one's ever had rules like these before."

He wore a sympathetic look on his face, and I knew he was serious.

"Well, Menkov, I understand what you're saying, and all I can tell you is that the rules won't change. They'll always be the same."

"I know, Coach. It's probably just going to take a while for us to get used to them."

Our next game, the second round of the Third of March tournament—a name that still made no sense to me as it was now December 18th—made me worried that my team was getting used to one thing in particular: losing. We'd regained enthusiasm in practice, but this might've been because we lost some players who didn't want to put up with sitting on the bench. Menkov, Stefan and Pavel led the way with positive energy, and we went eagerly into our second round game.

But positive thoughts and energy didn't seem to make a difference once the game started. In the first quarter, our defense watched two dunks get slammed home behind them. This team was huge, and I tried not to think about the fact that the 6'8" center might be 23 years old. We were down 10 at the end of the first quarter and had more turnovers than shots attempted. The second quarter didn't make it any better. Menkov, clearly playing proudly like he didn't want to get blown out of this game, made two consecutive shots, and then followed that up with two consecutive turnovers. Stefan stole the ball at the other end of the floor, then went up for a layup at the other end and was clobbered by a player twice his size. No foul was called.

"How is that not a foul?" I tried to yell to the referee in Bulgarian, but then switched to English as my ire elevated. "He got mugged! He's on the ground! That's an obvious foul!"

The referee, ignoring the fact that Stefan was still on the ground, jogged by me, waving his finger in my face. Whether it meant simply stop talking, he didn't understand me, or *ne modje*, this did nothing to satisfy me. Stefan limped to the bench on the next whistle, and Pavel headed into the game telling me, "They'll pay for that, Coach. I can play like that, too."

I tried to tell him that we weren't going to play like that, but it was too late. Fifteen seconds into the game, Pavel gave a shoulder shiver to an opponent sending him flying out of bounds. The whistle blew this time, and the foul was called. I pulled Pavel out of the game, and tried to explain to him why I didn't want him to play like that.

"Coach, you don't understand," he said, "these refs, they hate us. They hate us. We're the American College and they hate us because we're the *American* College. They hate America. It doesn't matter what we do; they won't let us win this game."

At this point, I wanted to launch into a speech about sportsmanship and taking responsibility for our own play—and not blaming the referees. But as I was about to say this to him, Vassy went up for a left-handed hook shot and was whacked in the head from behind. His shot sailed wide of the rim as a result. No foul was called, and our opponent headed to the other end—and dunked again. I didn't say anything to Pavel. I was seriously concerned he might've been right.

This wasn't the first time I'd heard that Bulgarians weren't fans of the American College of Sofia—and mostly because of the *American* part. It made little sense to me that people would harbor negative feelings against the best school in the country that happened to be run by American money, but this was Bulgaria. As much as things had changed since the Berlin Wall fell, I was living in a country that was still Russia's closest ally.

At a banquet I'd attended with an American friend and softball player celebrating the end of the Bulgarian softball season, the speaker, the head of the Bulgarian Softball Federation intended to celebrate softball's arrival in Bulgaria, but couldn't resist starting his speech like this:

"Twenty-one years ago, when we first thought of softball, we thought of America. And that meant evil."

As Ivan had the ball stolen from him by an opponent who slapped both of his hands, he looked at me and said, "Coach, what am I supposed to do? Why won't they call a foul?"

This seemed to be a question that I would have no ability to answer. In the meantime, the lead ballooned to 24.

The rest of the game continued in a similar fashion. Our motion offense had improved, and some possessions involved good passes and cuts. But the majority of our possessions consisted of rushed shots, errant passes, and fouls that probably should've been called. Pesho once again struggled against players bigger and more experienced than him. Sasho continued to smile, but moved far too deliberately to have a chance to score down low. Kosio hit a few jump shots, but shied away from contact, giving up several offensive rebounds. Stefan's defense was effective and he caused several turnovers, but he still couldn't make a jump shot. Menkov was a bright spot, but he was a bright spot in an overall dark and ugly game for us.

No matter what the referees had in store for us, it wouldn't have mattered. We were crushed by 27 points, with the opposing coach leaving his starters in until the final whistle so they could try to get one last dunk against players from the end of our bench.

At the end of this game, our players didn't seem nearly as disheartened, possibly because losing had become more expected at this point. Plus, this tournament game had started at 8 a.m. on Saturday morning, a ridiculous time for a game, in my opinion. It's possible that some of them weren't even awake. Or, maybe even worse, as Dimov was able to point out.

"I'm sorry about the game, Coach," he offered. "I had way too much to drink last night. We were out at the club and I really should've come home earlier than three. It was really hard to play this morning so hungover."

I just stood in front of him with my jaw dropped. *Should have come home earlier than three? Really hard to play so hungover?* It was one thing when the team had invited me out to have celebratory drinks after a game; I found that rather bold. But now, I had one of my starting guards admit that he was hungover for the entire game. And this didn't seem odd to him at all; it was just part of life in Bulgaria.

Since it was our last game and last time together as a team before Christmas, I decided not to focus on us getting blown out, the referees who might've hated America, or my hungover starting point guard. I focused more on the importance of Christmas and hoped they all would appreciate the time they'd have with their families. As I spoke about how important it was to be with ones you loved and appreciate the time you had together, I realized how much I really meant what I said. For the first time in my life, I wasn't going to be spending Christmas with my family. Instead, I was spending Christmas in Bulgaria.

When I arrived in Bulgaria, I was told that in all the countries in the world, Bulgaria was the third least religious. I wasn't sure what a statistic like this could even be derived from, but numerous people told me this was not a religious country. Maybe it was because during communism religion wasn't allowed, or maybe it was because this was a country that didn't seem to have a lot of faith or hope. No matter the reason, I didn't really start to notice the lack of religion until Christmas rolled around.

And while my American version of Christmas certainly doesn't always link to religion, I started to notice in December how few Christmas decorations were up in Sofia. Even downtown, which I anticipated might have a Christmas market, offered very little in the way of Christmas decorations other than a series of giant lighted blue balls that hung from one of downtown's busiest streets. These didn't seem to celebrate Christmas nearly as much as they pointed out that it was cold outside. I knew that the Soviets had banned Christmas during the Cold War, but I'd expected more of a Christmas spirit rebound in the time after the Berlin Wall fell.

As I rode home from our 27-point drubbing, a loss that knocked us out of another tournament, I looked around at shops and houses for Christmas decorations, but didn't see many. Once we exited downtown and were only offered a view of row houses, any evidence of Christmas seemed to disappear altogether. But looking at the row houses—drab and dreary—I wondered if I would put up any Christmas decorations if I lived there. No matter how many decorations you could put up, it wouldn't make the row house buildings any more attractive.

Soon my view was completely blocked by more people getting on the Bulgarian *mashrutka*, a glorified minivan used as public transportation. Pavel and Pesho were taking the *mashrutka* with me because they both lived close to school, where I was headed. Even though we were speaking English together and getting stares from close range from several other people on the minivan, this didn't seem to bother Pavel or Pesho.

"Coach, you will spend Christmas here in Bulgaria, no?" Pesho asked.

"Yep, I'll be here, Pesho."

"Oh, this is nice. This will be very nice," and again, I couldn't help but notice that he sounded like Borat.

"Coach, Coach, we have to get you a present. Yes, we have to get you a present," Pesho was gaining momentum for his thoughts as he continued.

"It's okay, Pesho," I told him. "I appreciate the thought, but you certainly don't have to get me a present."

"No, no, Coach, I don't think you understand what kind of present I am talking about."

He grinned at Pavel who seemed to understand. I definitely didn't understand.

"A nice girl, Coach, a *very nice* girl, just for you, Coach," he schemed.

Now I understood.

And now I definitely didn't want a present.

"It's okay, Pesho, I don't need a present."

"No, Coach, I have connections, and I can find you a girl for the right price. She will keep you warm. You know it is very cold here in Bulgaria right now. You will need a girl to keep you warm."

There were many things I wanted to say to Pesho in response, but I didn't even know where to begin. I was huddled in a minivan that now contained 18 people—at least 10 more than it should—and my starting center was towering and grinning over me as he planned to hire me a prostitute for Christmas. There were so many things wrong with this entire situation that I was left speechless. At least, and I took solace in this, there was little chance anyone else on the *mashrutka* understood English and could grasp what our conversation was about.

"Coach, Coach, I'm not talking about one of the girls who stands outside with the tires on fire," Pesho continued. "I'll find you a really nice girl. Then you'll really see how nice Bulgaria is."

Apparently Pesho, a 16-year-old, already knew how *nice* his country was, and at least he wasn't afraid to show his pride. But in the moment, I did all I could to deflect his urgings and change the subject. The fact that he wouldn't get me "one of the girls who stands outside with the tires on fire," was at least comforting in knowing that Pesho would look out for my best interests. These girls he referred to would stand on the corners of streets in the winter waiting for a man to drive by and pick them up. With no easy way to stay warm, the girls would light car tires on fire and stand close to them to stay warm while they weren't working. The smell of burning tires would permeate street corners, and served as a signal that there were working girls in the area. Anytime I'd pass one of these corners I couldn't help but have my heart drop down in my stomach based on the sadness of this situation. But Bulgarians didn't bat an eyelash; like the commonality of paying bribes, this was just a part of society.

To get off the *mashrutka*, I had to push my way through several people who couldn't even move to clear space for me; there was no extra space. I had to jump out of the minivan which caused me to slide on the ice. I barely gained my balance without falling as the *mashrutka* sped away to take Pavel and Pesho home.

I started walking toward the armed guard at the gate as I headed to my home for Christmas break. As I approached the guard, I said *Vesela Koleda* to him, wishing him Merry Christmas. He acknowledged that I'd spoken to him by looking at me, but he said nothing in response. His expression didn't change. He just looked at me.

For me, the realization set in that I was going to have a hard time making this seem like Christmas as I knew it. While I'd been constantly awed by how different life was in Bulgaria, and sometimes frustrated by the differences, I hadn't experienced homesickness before that moment. I tried to walk carefully so as not to fall on the ice as the stray dogs started to mount their approach. In my head, I started to reassure myself that everything would be okay; I still had a Christmas package waiting for me in my house.

Chapter XI
Tom Robinson
Visits Bulgaria

As I settled into life in Bulgaria, there was one unsettling aspect of everyday life that I realized I would have no choice but to get used to: getting stared at in public. On the bus, in the supermarket or walking the streets downtown, it was commonplace for me to feel the eyes of a stranger on me. And when I'd turn to meet these eyes–Bulgarian eyes–they didn't typically look away, worried they'd been caught staring. They just kept on staring right at me.

These stares definitely stemmed from curiosity, but still fell short of a curiosity that made me feel comfortable. As time went on in Bulgaria, I just realized that I'd have little choice in the matter. Bulgarians were going to stare at me because I looked different than them.

With blondish-reddish hair, a beard to match, and fair white skin, there was no way I'd ever be confused for a Bulgarian. To make matters worse, I smiled a lot, something Bulgarian males seemed to have been trained not to do. Basically I didn't have a chance at fitting in, and I relented to the expectation that when I left the American-friendly world of the college, I would be stared at.

Being stared at creates a sensation of unease no matter when it happens, but this wasn't the intention of Bulgarians who stared at me. They were staring at me because throughout the country, even in its capital city of some two million people, it was truly out of the ordinary to see someone so different-looking. It was almost unheard of to see someone from another country. And that was primarily because Bulgarians felt that after having been wronged by so many other neighboring countries, it was best to go it alone. They had little interest in diversifying the population. I found this extremely ironic considering the linguistic origins of the name Bulgaria. The word *"bulgar"* is derived from a Turkic verb meaning "to mix." But in my Bulgarian experience of being stared at because I was so different looking, I didn't see a whole lot of mixing going on. Bulgaria was a country mainly for Bulgarians; and as a result, there were few people in the country who didn't look and act like Bulgarians.

Author Robert Kaplan appropriately described the entire Balkans as a "region of narrow visions," then went even further to describe the genesis of Bulgaria's homogenous population. Writing about Bulgaria's history, he described the country at the beginning of the 20th century as "a bitter and irrational nation," due to betrayals from other Eastern European nations. He went further to say that at this point in history, "Bulgarians hated everybody: Serbs, Romanians, Turks."

Nowhere in this description did it say anything about Americans, but the more and more I got stared at by suspicious eyes in public places, it gave me pause to wonder. No historical description of Bulgaria I could find said it was a place that opened its arms up in a welcoming fashion to foreigners. But I could take solace in the fact that most Bulgarians didn't consider Americans as the foreigners they most had to worry about; they spent far more time concerned about the Turks.

Preying on centuries of pent-up anger toward the Ottoman Empire centered in Turkey, Bulgaria's communist dictator Todor Zhivkov enacted a desperate plan to regain support for his party in the 1980s when it seemed communism was falling apart. In his eyes, though, the Bulgarian communist state was falling apart because of one specific reason: the Turks in Bulgaria. Much like what happens in any time of financial crisis, Zhivkov sought to assuage the concerns of the masses by picking on a minority.

Birth rates for Bulgarians of Turkish ethnicity were much higher than birth rates of other Bulgarians, and this greatly worried Bulgarian communist officials. There were food shortages in the country already, and this Turkish trend seemed to be even more of a threat. And to top it off, Zhivkov believed that the modern-day Turkish people had "an invoice to pay for killing Levski," the Bulgarian freedom fighter hanged in Sofia more than a century ago.

So he launched an assault on the Turkish population in 1984 that was labeled as an attempt to "regenerate Bulgarian consciousness." What really was happening, though, was an attempt to wipe out the Turkish culture within the population. Zhivkov had a strong desire to "erase all traces of Bulgaria's Muslim past, present and future." His first decrees banned several things that were common for Turks living in Bulgaria: speaking Turkish in public was outlawed, Turkish newspapers were shut down, and any television or radio broadcasts in Turkish were no longer allowed. Finally, the most severe law in the eyes of most Turkish Bulgarians mandated that all Turks acquire a Slavic name. As a result, more than 900,000 people—about 10 percent of the population—were forced to change their names. Mehmet became Mikhail, Ercan became Ivan and so on. Zhivkov threatened that in relation to these laws, especially the name change law which was highly controversial, "anyone who resists will be killed like a dog." In some cases, this is exactly what happened. In others, when Turks refused to legally change their names, wives and daughters were raped by Bulgarian police and soldiers. Thousands were imprisoned, and many were killed, though the exact death tolls are still a subject of great debate. Mosques were destroyed, and it seemed there was no place safe in Bulgaria for Turks.

This cultural regeneration lasted about five years before Zhivkov declared in 1989 that all Turks were free to leave the country. At this point, many had already left due to the oppression they'd experienced or witnessed. But one Bulgarian Turk reported the problem with leaving Bulgaria to return to Turkey: "In Bulgaria we are Turks, and in Turkey we are Bulgarians." Deciding the former was worse than the latter, some 370,000 Turks left Bulgaria in mass exodus in 1989. This figure only represents how many left in 1989; many had left before for fear they would lose their identity or be killed. Zhivkov's invitation for Turks to freely leave the country sounded like the act of a benevolent leader. But Kapka Kassabova, living in Bulgaria at the time, points out the hypocrisy that existed: "The citizens had departed voluntarily, just as they had changed their names and religion voluntarily."

Before the cultural regeneration and expulsion of the majority of the Turkish population, Bulgaria was a relatively closed society. The exodus just made things even more closed off, and Kassabova goes on to describe her sentiments about diversity while growing up in Sofia: "Diversity didn't exist in the glossary of our lives."

She was referring to life in Bulgaria in the 1980s. But I found it hard to believe much had changed as I sat on the 76 bus being stared at by an elderly woman across the aisle from me and a middle-aged man two rows ahead who'd taken the opportunity to turn himself completely around in his seat to gaze at my out-of-place red beard.

Like most cultural observations I was able to make about Bulgaria, there was usually a difference between generations—those who had lived under communism, and my students who were all born after the fall of communism. But as far as the diversity and Turkish issue, there still wasn't a big difference. In the run-up to Christmas, I'd told my students that I'd planned to spend three days before Christmas in Istanbul. I said this excitedly, eager to tour Hagia Sophia and stumble my way through the Grand Bazaar. My students, though, did not see why I was enthusiastic about going to Turkey.

"Why would you go to Turkey, Mr. Jones?" one student blurted out in front of the whole class. "They are our enemy. They are terrible people. Why would you go there?"

I was taken aback, but thought I'd respond with the truth.

"Well, I'm curious, and I've heard Istanbul is beautiful."

"No, it's not," snapped the response.

"Well, have you been there?" I had to ask.

"No, I haven't. And don't worry, I don't ever plan on going there either. I hate those people."

This made me want to delve into a teachable moment about judging without actually knowing, and discussing the nature of prejudice, and how it usually stems from ignorance. But as I looked around the class at my 11th graders, there didn't seem to be anyone who found this student's comments inappropriate or wrong. No one was raising his/her hand to defend Turkey or wish me a good trip, so I decided to bite my tongue. There were clearly generations and generations of hatred that I was not going to be able to unwrap in the beginning of just one class period.

So I didn't mention my trip to Istanbul again, but the same topic reared its ugly head after the Christmas holiday when I returned. In the middle of a lesson about Matthew Arnold's poetry, I was interrupted by a different student.

"Mr. Jones, is that a Turkish water bottle?"

This seemed like an odd question, but I looked down at the plastic water bottle that I was using in class that day. I hadn't put much thought into my water bottle, but yes, I noticed it was Turkish. I had bought the water in Turkey and saved the plastic bottle to keep refilling. I hadn't thought twice about it, but clearly I should have.

"I can't believe you brought a Turkish water bottle into our country, our classroom. That's disgusting. Their water must be disgusting."

The only thing I found disgusting was the continued blind hate for anything and everything Turkish, but once again, I didn't know how I could fix this in the middle of a poetry discussion. I went home dejected that afternoon and tossed the water bottle in the garbage. As much as I was being stared at on the bus, at least I just looked weird to Bulgarians, not Turkish. This would've made things even worse.

Unfortunately, the Bulgarians' fiercest wrath was not saved for the Turks. Throughout Zhivkov's process of regeneration so many had left the country that there wasn't much of a Turkish presence left. And the majority of that presence was in the far east near the Turkish border. Sofia, where I lived, was in the far west, an oddly-placed capital considering Bulgaria's contemporary geography. Actually, Sofia used to be in the center of the country—back when Bulgaria possessed what was now Macedonia. Being situated so far west of Turkey, there wasn't a great Turkish presence in Sofia.

The only presence in Sofia truly deemed as an outsider presence—it can be safe to say that the Bulgarians didn't even classify the smattering of Americans in the city, probably less than 150 in total—was the Roma population, referred to as Gypsies by Bulgarians. And without the Turks to worry about, the Bulgarians directed most of their hatred toward this extremely impoverished and uneducated portion of the population. Like many countries in Eastern Europe, Bulgaria had few plans to increase the standard of living for the Roma population which would decrease their involvement in crime; they just wanted the Roma gone.

In the 20th and 21st centuries, Bulgaria never experienced a period of great prosperity, and as a result, there have always been populist campaigns to rid the country of those who don't belong, those who are different and therefore must be the problem with the country. In recent years, the focus had not been on the Turkish, but on the Roma population, most of whom live in shanty-like houses that don't have heat or electricity.

The attack on the Roma population has not been as efficient as the attack on the Turks, but it still had political backing without a whole lot of opposition from the Bulgarian people. Ataka is a political party headed up by Volen Siderov based on the ultra-right platform of ridding the country of all minorities, most specifically the Roma population. Siderov's two main slogans are "Give Bulgaria back to the Bulgarians," and "Stop the Gypsy terror." His terror-inciting voice has gained more and more attention and notoriety in Bulgaria, but Kassabova indicated how his really is a voice that had been heard many times in the past: "They are the same voice, the same continuous screech of fear and hate, and today's paranoid Siderovs are the malformed offspring of yesterday's paranoid Zhivkov's."

The "paranoid" Siderov's "screech of fear and hate," though, garnered him 25 percent of the vote in the 2006 presidential election. And his party, Ataka, which would hold neo-Nazi-type rallies in the center of Sofia, held 15 percent of the seats in parliament in 2008. Siderov doesn't only have hatred for the Roma population; he holds similar feelings for his enemies. His party came under fire in 2006 when one of his subordinates openly instructed political enemies—both inside and outside of Bulgaria—to "buy a Gypsy girl, around 12-13 years old, to be your loving wife."

Siderov did not back down from the crude statement made from his party member, and in some circles it even gained the party even more popularity. It shocked me to have someone like Siderov rising in popularity at the same time Barack Obama was closing in on his historic bid to become the first African-American president of the United States. Reading *To Kill a Mockingbird* with my 9th grade students in Bulgaria, we discussed all things Tom Robinson, Barack Obama and Volen Siderov. In the process, I tried to bridge the gap between racism in the U.S. in the 1930s to the treatment of Roma in Bulgaria in modern times. The universal connection I was trying to make, though, didn't go over too well.

"Mr. Jones, I don't understand what you're trying to say. I don't see a connection at all. African-Americans in the United States; the way they were treated was terrible. But the Gypsies here in our country; they don't deserve to be treated like human beings."

I could feel my blood begin to boil.

"What do you think people said about African-Americans in the United States? They said the same thing you just said—'they don't deserve to be treated like human beings'—and you just told me that was ignorant and hurtful. How can it be any different with the Roma here in your country?"

"Because they aren't human beings," came another voice from the class. "They live in filth, they act like animals. They aren't human beings."

Unlike I had done during the Turkish conversations I'd had previously, I wasn't willing to bite my tongue on the Roma issue. I prodded with different questions and fought with different arguments, but by the end of the discussion, I don't know that I accomplished anything. According to my students–the brightest students in Bulgaria who were desperate to leave the country and open their minds to the rest of the world–there was no connection between Harper Lee's book and their lives in Bulgaria. African-Americans were human beings worthy of fair treatment; Roma were not. I ended class that afternoon feeling more defeated and deflated than I had after any basketball game.

A few months after arriving in Bulgaria, I attended a Euro Cup qualifying soccer match between Bulgaria and Romania. And though, as I mentioned earlier, it was not well attended, that didn't mean that the fans in attendance weren't vociferous. As the Romanian national anthem was being played before the game, the Bulgarian crowd rose as one and chanted, "*TSIGANI! TSIGANI! TSIGANI!*" *Tsigani* is the derogative Bulgarian term for "gypsy," and it rained down on the Romanian fans during their entire national anthem. And once the national anthem stopped, the Bulgarian fans took a break–and then continued the *TSIGANI* chant once again three minutes into the game.

I turned to a Bulgarian friend who was immersed in the chanting and had a question for him.

"You're calling them gypsies, and they're chanting right back at you. If you call them gypsies, what do they call you in return?"

He pondered the question for a moment, and then seemed to figure it out.

"They're saying the same thing. They're calling us gypsies, too–just in another language."

I suppose that meant I was supposed to be comforted by the fact that the ignorance and hatred wasn't solely confined to Bulgaria.

As we were about to start our first game of 2008, I found myself far less concerned about basketball, and far more concerned about Bulgarian diversity and attitude toward the Roma population. That's because we were squared off in the first game of a tournament against a Roma team. This in itself was shocking to most of my players; a similar refrain was heard up and down the bench as they laced up their shoes.

"I didn't even know they had schools. I didn't think any of them went to school," Pavel wondered aloud.

"Do you think it's safe to leave our cell phones on the bench?" Kosio wondered, genuinely nervous.

Their eyes were being opened up to a new reality, so I didn't jump into the conversation. The message about judging all Roma as dirty, uneducated thieves–or wives ready to be bought at the age of 12–was being sent by what my players could see in front of them, a team that was working together to warm up for the game.

Our warm-up began, and I had to admit I was a little curious, too. When Nikolai had told me who we were playing, the name of the school meant nothing to me. That's because Bulgarian public schools are communistically named by number–and other than hearing that the 35th school was the best in Sofia–none of the other numbers meant anything to me. But now watching this team of Roma warming up, I realized that it wasn't just me who was entering a new Bulgarian world; the same could be said for my team as well. Several of them pointed out to me that they'd never actually spoken to a Roma person before. It was clear they were nervous, and their nerves had nothing to do with basketball.

And watching their warm-ups, I could see that we had nothing to worry about in terms of basketball. While my team still bickered over the exact order of our warm-up activities–I couldn't understand why it was so difficult to remember–and had trouble with left-handed layups, the Roma team was having trouble dribbling. There wasn't a single player on their team who could confidently dribble the ball from half court to the basket. Based on their living conditions I'd seen on the outskirts of town, I was shocked to discover there even was a Roma basketball team. Most Roma housing developments that I'd seen were entrenched in mud, not an ideal surface to learn how to dribble a basketball.

Their ragged yellow jerseys had numbers taped onto the backs; their tallest player was just below six feet. Their shortest player looked like he could've been in the fourth grade. And all of them looked like they were much better suited for the soccer field than the basketball court.

In terms of appearance, their skin was noticeably darker than my Bulgarian students, and many had longer hair that was begging for a cut. Each of the Roma players presented his own version of disheveled– from a jersey that was too big to shorts that were too small. Watching them warm up, it was clear that whatever disadvantages I might've thought my players had, this was nothing in comparison to the Roma team. Everything about them reeked of poverty. And to make matters worse, they reeked, too. The scent of their body odor was starting to waft over to our bench, and it was clear that many of these boys hadn't had a shower in quite some time. This could be used as criticism against them—and was on a regular basis by many Bulgarians—but I doubted whether any of them actually had showers in their homes.

As my team came over to our huddle before the game, my pre-game talk had little to do with the game. I was nervous about what was going to happen, and my nerves had everything to do with intolerance, not with basketball.

"You have to respect your opponent today, and I want you to realize that you have opportunities that others don't have. But this opponent is an opponent like any other we've played. You know what it's like to feel good when you're winning, and you also know what it's like to lose badly. No matter what happens today, I want you to keep that in mind. At no point will it be acceptable for you to show up your opponent. And at no point will it be acceptable for you to make derogatory comments about your opponent. They are people just like you and me, and I want you to treat them that way."

Several players in the huddle looked at me befuddled. They'd just finally gotten used to the fact that I expected them to pay attention to our strategy during each huddle, and now I wasn't talking about strategy at all. Menkov and Stefan, though, completely understood what I was saying and Menkov was the first to speak up.

"We got it, Coach. There won't be any problems with these guys today."

With that, my team headed to half court to start the game. Once again, in an opposing gym, half court was a relative term because it would've been the three-point line in most gyms. This was another bandbox gym with cages on the windows, walls as out-of-bounds lines and no scoreboard other than a Bulgarian sitting at a table with a pencil and paper.

Before the game started, my players were caught off-guard as each one of the Roma players shook hands with our players on the floor, wishing them good luck. Pesho looked over at me confused and then jogged over to me.

"This," he stammered, "this is not normal, Coach. I have never had anyone shake my hand before the game like this."

"That's okay, Pesho," I laughed. "There's nothing wrong with it, is there? They're just being friendly."

With my last comment, I felt like I had the task of explaining some kind of alien race to my team. And that's basically what I was doing. Though there was a significant Roma population in Sofia, no one on my team had ever spoken to a Roma before. They'd just relied on stories from so-and-so who had this-and-such happen to him/her because of those filthy, uneducated, savage Roma. And now these same Roma were showing the best sportsmanship I'd seen from any Bulgarian team we'd played.

It would make for a great story to have the Roma team find success against a much bigger, stronger and more talented opponent. But that wasn't the case. As I'd seen in warm-ups—and I'd learned to rely on my warm-up impressions in Bulgaria—the Roma team had a lot of trouble with the fundamentals of basketball. Many looked as if they might've just started playing a few weeks ago. Several still seemed confused on the rules. But, in typical fashion, it wasn't as if the referees were paying much attention to the rules anyway.

That didn't mean crazy things weren't happening out on the floor, though. Menkov blew by his defender at the top of the key and finished a nice scoop shot in the lane. There was an audible response from several of the Roma players. They weren't upset they'd been beaten for a basket, or upset at each other for not guarding Menkov well; they were impressed by the quality of his shot. As he turned to go back down the floor on defense, one of the Roma players held up his hand to give him a high-five. He wanted to celebrate the nice shot Menkov had just made.

A few minutes later, as we'd built a 12-point lead, I took Menkov out of the game.

"Did you see that, Coach?" Menkov was still stunned. "I scored, and that guy gave me a high-five. He told me it was a great shot. Can you believe that?"

Once again, I didn't have to say anything in response for the message to be learned.

"They did the same thing with me," Ivan chipped in. "After I scored, my defender said I was awesome and he hoped he could play like me one day."

Looking back out to the floor, the Roma team scored the first basket which led to jubilation from the five players on the floor and their five remaining players on the bench. Even though the score was now 15-2, they were elated that they'd scored. As I looked down at my bench, I noticed that Sasho and Vassy were clapping, too.

"What, Coach?" Vassy defended himself. "It's cool; look how happy they are."

That's how the game continued—in a manner unlike any basketball game I'd ever experienced before. Both teams played hard, scrapped, clawed and fought for loose balls and baskets. And every time someone scored—which still wasn't very often; our shooting hadn't improved—both teams cheered. There were high-fives exchanged amongst teammates and between the two different teams. Several times, the Roma team kicked the ball somewhat intentionally and the whistle was blown for a violation. There appeared to be mass confusion within the Roma team about the nature of the kicking rule. Stefan stepped in at one point to explain to the Roma players that kicking was illegal in basketball. They seemed truly enlightened, as soccer was the only other sport they'd ever played.

When the final horn sounded to end the game, I didn't bother asking the scorekeeper the final score, and neither did any of my players. We'd played our own version of ugly basketball, but still won very easily. For the first time in my Bulgarian coaching career, I didn't have to instruct my players to go shake hands with their opponents; it happened naturally. The Roma players spoke quietly—probably a result of their status as second-class citizens—but I could hear some of the things they were saying in Bulgarian to my team.

"Thanks. That was a great game."

"Thanks. We had a lot of fun."

"Thanks. I learned a lot from playing against you today."

"Thanks. I hope we can play against you again."

We walked out of the gym together as a team that had advanced to the second round of a new Bulgarian tournament, but that didn't seem to be what was on the minds of my players.

"Coach," Menkov still seemed amazed, "I can't believe those guys. They were so *nice*. That was so much fun to play against them."

"Why is it so unbelievable, Menkov?" I asked.

"Well," he paused, a bit embarrassed, "I guess it shouldn't be unbelievable. I'd never met a Roma person before."

Pavel was the next to speak.

"Yeah, I feel a little bad right now."

"Why?" I probed.

"Well, it's just that—it's just that...."

Pavel's voice trailed off as he had trouble coming to grips with his own thoughts. Stefan picked up the slack.

"It's just that none of us really know any Roma people. All we know is what everyone else says–and that's only the bad stuff. And today," Stefan was also coming to grips with his thoughts, "today was pretty cool. They were pretty cool guys."

I thought that this would probably be a great moment for me to finish the lectures I'd started in class talking about Turkish people or *To Kill a Mockingbird*. But I also thought that maybe the problem with tolerance and diversity was never going to be solved with lectures. Little had I known, though, that a big step to solving the problem began with basketball.

Chapter XII
Thank God You're Not Bulgarian

One of the reasons I fell in love with basketball both as a player and a coach in the United States was Friday and Saturday nights. There was nothing that compared to the electricity and excitement inside a packed high school gym on a cold, wintery night. With winds blustering outside and no one wanting to move an inch outdoors, inside gyms on Friday night, there was liveliness and everyone wanted to jump and yell. It would become so hot that everyone took off winter coats, hats and gloves. Friday and Saturday nights during basketball season would break everyone out of the doldrums of winter. Students, parents and community members would shovel their cars out of the snow, scrape the ice off the windshield, and head for the only game in town–and they'd cheer raucously for their team, heating up an entire gym.

Bulgaria, however, didn't view winter Friday and Saturday nights the same way. For whatever reason–and I was never given a reason other than the communistically traditional, "That's just the way it's always been"–Bulgarian high school basketball tournament games were almost always played on Saturday mornings. This meant waking up early, stumbling out of bed, bundling up, and then sliding on the ice on my way to the bus. By the time players and coaches arrived at the gym—almost all rode the freezing public buses–they were all equally chilled to the bone. And at 9 a.m. on a January Saturday in Bulgaria, no one would come to watch the tournament games. Of course 9 a.m. probably had a lot to do with this, but most of the gyms we were playing in didn't have any room for spectators anyway. Our team benches typically were part of the playing floor. The only thoughts I'd have regarding electricity had nothing to do with the environment created by the gym and the fans inside; I just hoped the gyms had electricity and heat.

Aside from the early start times for our weekend games, I also had trouble adjusting to the fact that we were always playing in tournaments. Of course I was used to basketball tournaments being a part of the season, but in Bulgaria basketball tournaments were the season. There were no conference or league games because conferences didn't exist, even though they could have. There were plenty of teams in Sofia, and plenty of teams close enough to our school that could constitute a conference. I'd slowly prodded Nikolai about this, asking him if it was possible to create a league for us to play regular games against.

"Andy, I went to America once," he told me, acknowledging that I had made a valid point, "and it was incredible to me. It was incredible to see an entire basketball schedule set at the beginning of the season. This must be so nice for coaches and players, so nice."

He paused at this, and I just waited for him to continue since this was the exact point I was trying to make.

"But here in Bulgaria, I just don't think we're capable of something like this."

He said this sadly, and I sympathized with him, but still didn't completely understand why.

"Andy, these athletic conferences, these schedules you have in America–they require planning ahead of time. They require cooperation. I would love to do this here, too. But here in Bulgaria, I just don't see how it is possible. You have met some of these coaches already. Do you think they will want to plan ahead of time? Do you think they will want to cooperate? Do you think they will want to change the way things have always been done?"

I thought of Khrushchev breaking two pencils at our last meeting, Starter Jacket falling asleep and the two schools that didn't even bother to send actual coaches. I didn't need to respond to Nikolai's question. I just remembered the defeated shrug he emoted at that last meeting; it would probably be too deflating for him to even try to institute changes—changes he was already a believer in.

And changes, though they seemed highly unlikely, would have greatly helped my team. Without a set schedule, I never knew when we were playing our next game. I just had to find Nikolai on a daily basis and ask if he'd heard anything about an upcoming tournament. And when he didn't have any news about a tournament, attendance at practice decreased. Players had no idea when we were going to play next, and some saw no need to come to practice as a result.

What made matters worse for my struggling team was that most of the tournaments we played in were single elimination. A tournament that would start in November and end in March could be over awfully quickly for a team that lost in the early rounds. And I started to discover that tournaments started four months before they finished not because these were long tournaments with lots of games; it was just easier to do it this way because coaches never felt pressured to organize anything. Even if there wasn't a game played for an entire month because no one scheduled it, this wasn't a problem. Coaches gave themselves leeway to not schedule games for long periods of time by making tournaments last this long.

Since my team had yet to advance past the second round of any tournament, we hadn't played nearly as many games as I would've liked, and not nearly as many games as were needed for us to improve. Following our easy victory over the Roma team, as much as it was never easy to get fired up for Saturday morning 9 a.m. games in the freezing cold, I was eager for our next game, hoping we could advance in this tournament past the second round for the first time.

But once again, warm-ups seemed to provide a cautionary tale of hope for me. As I watched our team sleepwalk its way through the warm-up, the other team was dunking. They didn't have any semblance of a set warm-up, but more of "Let's see who can dunk the best" competition going on at the other end of the floor. Their coach was wearing an Allen Iverson 76ers jersey far too small for his corpulent figure. His gut protruded out and he looked more like an Iron Curtain John Belushi than Allen Iverson. When I shook his hand to greet him as we walked onto the floor, he stunk of booze—either from the night before, or perhaps the night before hadn't ended for him yet. With each new dunk, he emitted boozy cheers and loud laughter. There seemed to be quite a bit of camaraderie on the other end of the floor; I wondered if maybe they'd all gone out drinking together the night before. Once again, looking at this other team, I wouldn't have been surprised if I was told that half of them were 23 years old. When they weren't dunking, their faces were long and sullen, and each player looked as if he could tell you a grisly story about what the Cold War really was all about.

I couldn't focus too much on the other team, though, because there seemed to be enough problems with my team. With 10 minutes to go before tip-off, Dimov still hadn't shown up yet. I asked Menkov about this and he looked like he didn't want to respond, but finally acquiesced.

"I think, I think ... he had a long night, Coach. I don't know if you should expect him to show up. And if he does, he might not be in great shape."

Kosio had shown up at the game with a knee brace, saying that his knee hurt too much for him to play. This was new, as he usually only tried to sit out practices but was miraculously healthy for the games. To top it all off, Sasho was sitting on the bench with a cast on his hand, a hand he'd broken in P.E. class two days earlier.

With three of my top eight players out of commission for one reason or another, I started to wonder why I'd been so excited about the game when I woke up in frosty Bulgaria early that Saturday morning. What made the sour feeling in the pit of my stomach a little worse was the notion that I didn't think I was the only one who was low on confidence this morning. I could sense that the core of the team, while they were showing up for practice and working hard, didn't have much confidence. As the season—and the blustery winter—wore on, they were becoming more and more aware that we hadn't beaten a single good team all season long. We'd had victories over teams who appeared to have never played basketball before, but every time we matched up with a talented or experienced team, we were losing by 15-20 points—or even more.

As a coach in the States, I'd always valued senior leadership because it meant that the team had experience and basketball savvy, an understanding of the game and a confidence, a "we've been here before," that helped win games. But in Bulgaria, senior leadership meant something much different – and something much more significant. It meant that players had played that much more basketball.

On my Bulgarian team, leadership wasn't so much the issue. And we weren't being beaten due to basketball intelligence or basketball savvy—we had none of this, and neither did our opponents. We were being beaten because our players hadn't played very much basketball in their lives. The sport was still new to them.

I wrote down my starting lineup on a whiteboard and considered each one of my starters' history as basketball players:

Point Guard: Menkov, junior. He had played a little in previous years, at least enough to have confidence in himself and say he was a basketball player.

Shooting Guard: Stefan, sophomore. He had barely played at all in the past, and had always been told he was too small, not quick enough, and couldn't dribble well enough, all criticisms that were likely true.

Small Forward: Pavel, sophomore. Watching Pavel play basketball nearly convinced me that he'd spent an inordinate amount of time playing fullback for an American football team.

Power Forward: Vassy, junior. He had never played organized basketball before this year, just thought it would be fun to come out and play against opponents at least a head taller than him.

Center: Pesho, sophomore. He had experience playing with a club team, but I'd learned quickly that this experience taught him how to try to steal the ball instead of move his feet, and just try to jump over everyone instead of actually boxing out.

Those were the five I was starting with plus Kosio and Sasho sitting on the bench looking glum. If it was hard to get up early on a Saturday morning to come play a game, I couldn't imagine what it was like getting up early on a Bulgarian Saturday morning just to sit on the bench. Dimov came running into the gym two minutes before tip-off and hurriedly started putting on his basketball shoes. As I walked up to him, he greeted me happily.

"Coach, Coach, what's up?" his speech was a little slurred, but his smile was big. "Sorry I'm late, Coach. But I promise I'm going to make it up to you when I get out on the floor. I'm ready to play."

I paused, understanding that he was serious. He really thought he was going to play. When I told him that he was late, most likely hungover, and not fit in any way to play basketball, he seemed astounded. I was hoping that some of his teammates would reinforce my decision to keep him on the bench, but they seemed confused, too. Why should it matter if you were late for the game and hungover? That shouldn't be a problem, should it?

Despite our rather obvious shortcomings, we started off the game well. Stefan led a fast break off a defensive rebound and finished at the rim with his right hand. Following the next missed shot from our opponent, Pesho saw it as his turn to go coast-to-coast, pummeling the ball into the floor with each new dribble, head down as he chugged toward the basket. He elevated and also finished at the rim, getting fouled in the process. He made the free throw and it was 5-0. Obviously excited, Menkov came running over to me at the bench.

"This is a great start, Coach! Great start! I think they're tired, or hungover–or something."

And he was exactly right in his assessment of the other team. They'd spent their entire warm-up session trying to dunk, and now they seemed either uninterested in anything other than dunking, or as Menkov had pointed out, maybe they were hungover. As I looked over to tubby Allen Iverson with froth now flying from his lips, I could tell that he didn't care they were hungover. He was solely unhappy that the score was 5-0, and in a loud, violent and Bulgarian manner, he was screaming across the floor at his team.

The screaming served the purpose of waking his team up, as they made their way back down the floor and fed the ball into the post where their power forward, four inches taller than Vassy, scored on a smooth-looking baby hook shot. Menkov drove the ball back the other way to find Pesho in the post who performed a move that should've been similar to the one he'd just witnessed on the defensive end, but his version of a baby hook shot turned into a whirling-Dervish 12-foot fadeaway that clanked off the backboard. Our opponents took the long rebound and headed the other way. Pesho looked like he was limping coming back down the floor, and his man beat him down the floor for a layup to make it 5-4.

"Are you okay, Pesho?" I hollered out to the floor, and he gave me a thumbs-up to show that he was. "Well then start running!"

The game see-sawed back and forth with Pavel plowing his way to the basket, bricking a layup, getting his own rebound, bricking another layup, getting another rebound, and then finally coaxing the ball through the net. But once again, Pesho was slow getting back on defense and gave up an easy basket in transition. I was infuriated; we'd gotten off to a good offensive start against a superior team, and now we were giving up baskets because Pesho couldn't make it up and down the floor. I had no choice but to take him out.

"Pesho, what the hell is going on? Are you hurt?"

He shook his head, which didn't help matters.

"What does that mean? Are you shaking your head 'yes' or shaking your head 'no'?"

"No, Coach, I am not hurt," he said meekly.

"Then why aren't you running?"

"Coach, you see—I have this problem, you see," he replied.

"What problem, Pesho? If you're not hurt, then why can't you run back on defense?"

"Coach," now his voice lowered as if he were going to tell me a secret, "it's the beast."

"The beast?" I was not particularly in the mood for some kind of joke.

"It's the beast," he said again, pointing to his stomach. "I need to let the beast out into the wild."

With this, he held his stomach and doubled over. I thought only native-speaking high school boys had idiomatic English expressions for bowel movements, but clearly Pesho was teaching me otherwise.

"You need to go to the bathroom, Pesho? Is that what you're saying? You need to go number two?"

Again, he shook his head, but this time I sensed that his head shake meant yes.

"Then just go, Pesho! What are you waiting for? We're in the middle of the game? Just go!"

"But Coach, have you seen the bathroom here? I need to let the beast out into the wild, but I cannot do it here. There is no bathroom; it's just a hole in the floor. There's no paper, no paper!"

I knew exactly the kind of bathroom he was describing because he'd introduced me to this kind of bathroom during our first road game. But I couldn't believe that I was spending my time during a competitive first quarter discussing "letting the beast out into the wild" with my starting center—a starting center I needed out on the floor.

"Pesho, I don't care what you do, but I'm not putting you back out onto the floor until you're able to run full speed."

"But Coach," he pleaded, "I can't run full speed with the beast inside of me."

"Then you're either going to sit on the bench, or you're going to go get rid of—get rid of the beast."

I couldn't believe that I was now speaking his language.

With my latest response, Pesho looked more in pain than ever, and it wasn't from the "beast" inside him, but the notion that he might have to get rid of the beast in a disgusting Bulgarian closet bathroom. Dimov, who was slowly realizing he really wasn't going to play, at least came to my aid.

"*Haide*, Pesho! Just go to the bathroom. We need you on the floor!"

With this, Pesho looked questioningly at me, then skeptically at Dimov. He started trotting toward the hallway, headed to the bathroom. As he reached the doorway, he looked back at the bench as if to say, "You know, I might not make it out alive."

Thankfully, even with Pesho and his "beast," we made it out of the first quarter alive. We were only trailing 13-12, and there was an enthusiasm in the huddle, a feeling that we could play with these guys, especially since they still weren't taking us very seriously. Every time they'd run a play to get the ball inside and get a good shot, they'd get good results. But they didn't do this very often. Like their coach who was still spitting boozy venom on their bench, they were impatient and not willing to share the ball. Many times down the floor, they took the first shot that became available.

"Guys, we've got to keep boxing out, and when we get the rebound, we've got to run. They don't want to run back on defense, so we've got to push the ball. They don't want to work as hard as you."

I could see the nodding and shaking of heads in my huddle and understood that all of these gestures served as an assent of what I was saying. And it was true. We were once again playing against a team that had more talent and experience, a team with players who might or might not have been 23, and a team with players who probably didn't study at night like some of my players did. They had talent, but they wanted to solely rely on that talent. I didn't sense there was any urgency for them to work hard.

And my rough translation of Iverson's rants didn't indicate he wanted them to play any harder. He was yelling at them for missing shots and not grabbing rebounds, but he wasn't saying a word about the obvious; this was a close game because his team wasn't playing hard.

That's what continued throughout the second quarter. They'd take a bad shot and Menkov and Stefan would race the other way to get us a good shot. Then they'd figure out—for a possession—that they should be patient and get a good shot, feed the ball into the post, and then Ivan, Vassy and Pesho— now without the beast—didn't stand much of a chance.

But overall, we still stood a great chance because of our hustle and effort. Watching from the sidelines, I was thrilled as Stefan continued to shoot into the passing lanes and Pavel plowed through anyone in his path for a loose ball, or fumble, as he still looked like he was playing football. At halftime, the score was tied at 27, and our team was as energized as I'd seen them in a long time. I didn't have too much to say at halftime other than to keep playing hard; we were going to have to out-hustle them to beat them.

As the second half started, that's what we continued to do. We headed back out to the floor to face a team who hadn't even had a halftime meeting; several players just sat down on their end of the floor, and several others continued practicing dunking. They weren't concerned that the score was tied, and as a result, I wanted to beat them more than ever.

"They don't respect you," I told my players as the huddle was about to break for the second half. "They're not taking you seriously, and they don't want to win as badly as you do. They didn't practice hard this week like you did. This is your game. Go out and take it."

We couldn't have started the second half with a better attitude or with more passion. As the ball was entered down low, Pesho anticipated the same move he'd been beaten on several times, timed his jump perfectly and swatted their taller player's shot back to the foul line. Stefan was waiting there to snatch it and led a 2-on-1 break with Menkov. Their speed was too much for our dragging opponents, and Stefan fed Menkov with a perfect bounce pass for a layup—just like we'd worked on in practice so many times.

Menkov missed the layup.

With this, he let out a Bulgarian howl, something uncommon for him. I knew he sensed we had the momentum and we could beat this team, but we had to make shots, especially layups. At the other end, our opponents knocked in an 18-foot contested jump shot, portraying the perfect contrast of the two teams: we were doing everything right and getting open layups, and they were doing everything wrong and getting guarded jump shots. But we were missing our layups, and they were making their jump shots.

This sequence provided a microcosm of the entire second half. Vassy would make a strong move to the basket, get fouled—and then miss both free throws. We would force them into a difficult jump shot, and they'd rattle it home. Pavel would take a charge when they drove, but then drive out of control on the other end and lose the ball out of bounds.

At the end of the third quarter, it was still a close game, as we trailed by only four points. Despite the fact that it was a freezing Saturday morning at 9 a.m., despite the fact that we were short three key players, and despite the fact that we were short on talent and experience, our effort was incredible. We just needed a few shots to fall in the fourth quarter and we would win this game.

But the shots didn't fall.

Sticking to our game plan of running on the fast break and only taking shots in the paint, we continued to get one good shot after another. And they continued to clank, roll and drop off the rim. The spring was back in Pesho's legs, but this just led him to spring the ball off the backboard, too hard every time. Menkov's floaters and scoop shots were always the right plays, and almost every time, they rimmed out.

By the time the game had ended, I didn't even want to know what our shooting percentage was. We'd out-worked, out-hustled and out-played our opponent—a supremely-talented opponent that just didn't care that much—and we'd lost by seven points because we couldn't make a shot.

Nearly everything we'd done out on the floor represented huge leaps forward in terms of how we played as a team. But in the end the result was the same: we'd lost in the second round of a Sofia city tournament—again.

In my postgame speech, I focused on nothing but positives because I knew the effort was there; they clearly weren't missing shots because they weren't trying. But I also was getting to know my team pretty well; positive speeches after losses didn't have much of an impact on them. In the end, they still lost. Menkov came up to me after the game, and I could already sense my nerves were on high alert, wondering what his reaction was going to be.

"Coach, we played so much better today. This is probably the best we've played as a team."

"I know, I'm really proud of the way we played today," I said honestly, thrilled that he saw the improvement, too.

"But it's really tough. Whenever we play a good team, we just keep losing. And when we go home, and go back to school on Monday, all everyone asks is if we won or lost. All we have to say is that we lost."

"But Menkov," I didn't want to feel desperate, but I was a little bit, "you know it's about more than winning and losing. You know we're getting better. And you know we're going to win these games in the future."

He looked up at me as I said this, and I could see uncertainty in his eyes–probably the same uncertainty he'd tell me his father had about the future of the only company he'd ever worked for, Bulgarian National Tobacco.

"I know you're right, Coach. I think we're going to win these games in the future," he said, half-believing what he was saying. "But right now, it's hard to feel like anything other than a loser."

Svetla Mironova was anything but a loser. In fact, if she'd heard what Menkov had said, she probably would've scolded him–*Haide*! Not only was she one of the top students in my class and the entire 11th grade, she had an indefatigable positive attitude and outlook for the future. She was determined to succeed in my class and certain that her academic success would lead her to a bright future–somewhere outside of Bulgaria. Svetla was the kind of optimistic student I tried to focus on when other Bulgarians I knew–my players, my students, Nikolai–seemed to be at a loss for hope. Skinny and wiry with black hair and glasses, she would consistently flash a smile full of braces that stood out amongst what many times was a canvass of blank Bulgarian gazes. These blank gazes were the same I faced after our latest loss, and I would've given anything to have one of my players react like Svetla–see the positives and smile knowing she'd do better next time. As I left the gym that day, I thought about Svetla because she'd told me confidently that she wasn't bothered by the lack of opportunity in her country; she wasn't worried by her classmates who had negative attitudes or pessimism about the future. She knew she was going to succeed. She just knew it.

"Mr. Jones, I can't wait to have a chance to go to university. This is such an amazing and incredible opportunity for me, and I just know it's going to happen."

When Svetla said "university," she didn't mean Bulgarian university; she meant a university in Britain or the States. Her optimism and enthusiasm were contagious, but even I had to wonder a little bit if her excitement was tinged with naiveté.

"Svetla, I know how excited you are for university in a foreign country, but have you ever been to a foreign country?"

"No, Mr. Jones," and with this she paused, "I've never been outside of Bulgaria. In fact, I've never even been on an airplane before. But I hope I'll like all of it–airplanes, airports and new countries."

Even in admitting something that was hard for me to fathom–never even having been on a plane–she still said it encouragingly. She didn't see any of this as anything more than a positive challenge, not a hurdle over which she would stumble.

That's why I was surprised when her mother showed up to parent-teacher conferences and requested the first meeting of the night with me during the first semester. I couldn't fathom why she'd need to meet with me. Svetla had the highest grade in the class, and there shouldn't have been any reason for concern. My only concern was that Svetla had told me her mother wanted to speak with me, and her mother didn't speak any English. I was going to have to do the conference in Bulgarian.

"*Gospodin* (Mr.) Jones," she told me in very polite and slow Bulgarian so I could understand, "I am a fifth-grade teacher at school 12 here in Sofia."

This introduction told me why Svetla had never been on an airplane before. Public school teachers in Bulgaria made somewhere in the neighborhood of 350 dollars a month.

"I would like for my students to have the chance to meet with an American teacher, and I am wondering if you would be willing to visit our class. They would be very excited to meet their first American."

With this, I now understood the reason for the parent-teacher conference, and as the bus home from the game chugged along at a communist slow pace, I thought back on my trip to school 12 earlier in the week.

For the first time since I'd known her, Svetla seemed nervous and a bit uncomfortable as we hopped off the 76 bus and walked toward her mother's school.

"I just want you to understand, Mr. Jones," she cautioned me, "that this school is not like ACS. Bulgarian public schools are different, and I just don't want you to be afraid."

I appreciated her concern, but let her know that I'd visited many Bulgarian public schools for basketball games; I wasn't going to be too surprised by her mother's school. But, as we approached the school, I quickly stopped trying to reassure her.

On the giant brick wall leading up to the stairs to the school was a massive mural. It contained all sorts of images of war—from tanks to guns to planes to soldiers—and then it was highlighted by a large and striking portrait of Osama bin Laden.

"Wait a minute, Svetla," I hesitated, "is that—is that who I think it—"

"Yes, Mr. Jones," Svetla sighed, "it's Osama bin Laden."

"And why does your mother's elementary school have a giant portrait of Osama bin Laden on its outside wall?"

"Uhh ... this is kind of what I was trying to tell you about Bulgarian public schools being different. I think the bin Laden portrait is supposed to be part of an anti-war message, but I think they kind of screwed up. That portrait with all the tanks and guns around it makes it look like a tribute to bin Laden."

"That's exactly what I was thinking," I said, trying not to sound too worried.

"Yeah, Mr. Jones, I think they just screwed up. It's not really the best way to welcome someone into the school."

With this, I stood mesmerized by bin Laden, unable to move.

"So why don't we go inside? Let's not focus on bin Laden for too long."

But really it was hard not to. The mural was gigantic and bin Laden's head dwarfed the other images on the mural. Once again, I found myself pausing trying to figure out where I was. I knew there was anti-American sentiment in Bulgaria due to Bulgaria's close ties to Russia for so many years, but anti-American sentiment and pro-bin Laden sentiment seemed to reside in entirely different neighborhoods. Many people take issue with the States for various reasons, and living abroad, I'd grown accustomed to this. Despite this fact, I'd still been a little alarmed by the news I'd read in the *Sofia Echo* of a Bulgarian cabinet member who publicly referred to the U.S. ambassador to Bulgaria as "scum," and then went further—if that's possible—to slander him as a "liar and a drug addict." This was all because the ambassador had denied this particular cabinet member a U.S. visa because he was currently on trial for committing a crime in Bulgaria. The ambassador's decision seemed rather run-of-the-mill, but the cabinet member's reaction was anything but.

Even with outlandish statements like this, and even if the cabinet member harbored bitter rage toward America, I still seriously doubted that he was a fan of Osama bin Laden. That would be taking things to a whole new level.

And that was a level that I could sense Svetla was a little nervous about. She was proud of her mother, and proud of her country unlike any other Bulgarian I knew. She wanted me to like and be impressed by her mother's class. As I walked into the school with her, I realized that this wasn't just a big moment for the fifth-grade students who were meeting their first ever American, it was a big deal for Svetla, too. She didn't want to talk about bin Laden any more. And honestly, neither did I.

Luckily, when I entered the fifth grade classroom, I quickly entered a whole new world. Students hushed themselves quiet and all stared up at me as if I were some kind of movie star. As I had just previously been mesmerized by bin Laden on the wall, they were now entranced by the sight of their first-ever American. I greeted them in Bulgarian first, and this just seemed to throw them off even more. Not only was I an American, but I was speaking Bulgarian. To them, this was too much to handle.

But I noticed that it wasn't the students who were having the most trouble as I walked into the room; it was Svetla who was upset with her mother. I could hear her trying to speak quietly, but clearly not speaking quietly enough as she approached her mother.

"Mom, how could you put that up on the board? Is that really the best representation of our country? Seriously, Mom, how could you put that up on the board?"

Understanding the gist of Svetla's rushed Bulgarian, I looked up to the chalkboard where a giant sign read "WELCOME, MR. JONES." It wasn't the message that was bothering Svetla; it was the two images below the greeting.

Under the heading of "UNITED STATES" was a large printed image of the Statue of Liberty.

Under the heading of "BULGARIA" was a large printed image of a donkey cart.

This was a meeting of two different worlds, an introduction of the United States to Bulgaria and vice versa. The United States was represented by an enduring symbol of hope and freedom, a statue that makes people believe anything can happen, that dreams can come true in America. Bulgaria was represented by an out-of-date form of transportation, a symbol that the country hadn't advanced into the 21st century. It was stuck in the past. There wasn't a whole lot of hope inside that donkey cart.

And Svetla was not happy about it at all. She continued to scold her mother, asking her how she could view the comparison between the two countries this way. The students in the class—who could definitely understand Svetla's Bulgarian better than I could—seemed just as confused by this conversation as they were by having an American walk into their classroom and greet them in Bulgarian. To them, the comparison—Statue of Liberty to donkey cart—seemed completely accurate. Svetla was the only one in the room who saw a problem with it. Well, Svetla and me, too.

My celebrity visit as the first-ever American these fifth graders had met was filled with wonderfully innocent questions from students admirably doing their best to speak English. They covered a broad range of topics from, "What's your favorite color?" to "Where is your favorite place to visit in Bulgaria?" to "How much money would it cost for me to go to America?" to "Is life in Bulgaria different than life in America?"

With this last question, I couldn't help but laugh, but didn't want to seem rude by indicating just how different life in America truly was. When answering the question, I referred to differences like the language and the food, the countryside and the traffic, American football versus European football—all tangible things that I knew the kids would understand. But this wasn't what I was thinking about as I answered the question. I was thinking about Menkov telling me he felt like a loser, knowing I now had an image of a donkey cart looming behind me.

As we walked out of school that day—and I walked out with arms full of Bulgarian gifts the students had saved money all month to buy me—both Svetla and I were in good spirits. The warmth and innocence of the fifth graders had caused me to forget all about Osama bin Laden and Svetla to at least push the donkey cart to the back of her mind. But still, I had to ask her about it.

"I noticed in there," I pried, "that you were a little upset with your mom about the two images on the board."

"I know, Mr. Jones, and I'm sorry about that," she was frustrated, but very sincere.

"You don't need to apologize, Svetla," I told her.

"It's just that when you look at things that way—one country has so much hope, and the other has a donkey cart—it's hard to believe that things are really going to change that much in my country."

I wanted to empathize, but found it difficult to know what to say. After all, I was represented as the Statue of Liberty, not the donkey cart.

"I'm not really upset at my mom," Svetla continued. "She's lived in this country her whole life; she knows how things are, and she's been through a lot. But I just wouldn't want her students to think it always has to be this way. I wouldn't want them to think that the symbol of Bulgaria, the best of Bulgaria, is a donkey cart. If they really believe that, then how are they supposed to have hope for the future? I don't want hope to exist only on the day an American comes to visit their class."

Once again, there wasn't much I could say to Svetla. We walked back to the bus together in silence—not an awkward silence, but a pensive silence. She had hopes and dreams to go to school and create a new life somewhere like the United States, and she believed that everyone else in her country should have these same hopes and dreams, too. But clearly, she was the exception more than the rule.

I thought about my basketball players and wondered if they would have been upset by the donkey cart on the board representing Bulgaria. I wondered if they would've reacted like Svetla did, or would they have just shrugged like Pesho and said, *This is life in Bulgaria; we are used to this.* And even worse, I wondered if they would've looked up at the Statue of Liberty-donkey cart comparison and felt like losers.

Following our latest loss, I had plenty of time to ponder all of these things. As a basketball coach, I typically used the time after the game to start going through different plays, different sequences in the game and figure out where things went right or wrong. But on this Saturday, I wasn't thinking too specifically about the game itself. We'd lost pretty much for one reason: we couldn't make shots. And after the game, I was left with a team that had done nearly everything I'd asked and completely outplayed its opponent—but still lost. They were deflated, and I was trying my best not to be deflated, too, but their attitude had become contagious.

I wasn't lying to them when I told them we were improving. I wasn't lying to them when I said that I was proud of their effort. And I wasn't lying to them when I said I thought we'd win games like this in the future.

But I wondered how many of them really felt proud about their improvement, felt proud to be working hard, and looked to the future optimistically thinking that we'd start winning. If the leader and most positive person on the team, Menkov, felt like a loser because we couldn't beat good teams, how did the rest of them feel? If I couldn't teach them to find pride regardless of winning, where was the sense of pride and self-worth going to come from? If it was so easy to see themselves as losers or drivers of donkey carts as the world excelled around them, how difficult was it going to be to change that mindset?

In the first decade of the 21st century, at a time where the world population was booming and overpopulation was a concern, Bulgaria would experience a population decrease of 582,000. In fact, in Eurostat's study of the entire European continent, they predicted that Bulgaria would lose 27 percent of its population by the year 2060, the equivalent of the "disappearance of 28 medium-sized Bulgarian towns."

While many Western European countries' populations were booming with predictions of drastic increases–both from native populations and an influx of immigrants–Bulgaria stood out as an exception to this. Some of those predicted to leave Bulgaria would be the country's best and brightest like Svetla. Based on the statistics, it was clear that regardless of Bulgarians' feelings about their home country–regardless of their level of pride–many were eager to take the risk to find a better life elsewhere.

I struggled with all of these thoughts as I was enjoying my time living in Bulgaria. But I was enjoying my time as an outsider, someone who had been raised in a different country and was now living and observing the country and its people as someone who sometimes understood what was going on, and sometimes didn't. That Saturday following the game, I thought I might get more of an understanding about Bulgaria by visiting its medieval capital, the historical capital of the Second Bulgarian Empire, Veliko Turnovo.

Most of my research regarding Bulgaria had led me to understand its oppression by outside forces, but this Saturday trip was taking me to a place that was a capital of the Second Bulgarian Empire. Veliko Turnovo was a source of pride for Bulgarians, an epic city on three hills referred to as the "City of the Tsars." During the 14th century, Veliko Turnovo was even dubbed a "Third Rome" based on its cultural pre-eminence in the Balkan world. Of course, with the invasion of the Ottoman Empire, Veliko receded into a stature of much less renown, similar to what happened to the rest of Bulgaria. But in contemporary times, Veliko was highlighted in *Lonely Planet* guidebooks as the best tourist destination in Bulgaria with the potential to become the next Prague.

Needless to say, I was excited to get a glimpse of this old city about three hours northeast of Sofia. The bus glided smoothly–with the aid of new roads constructed with EU funds–through the Stara Planina Mountains providing snapshots of rolling hills in the forefront and snow-capped icy ledges in the background. As a tourist seeing this for the first time, I was soaking it all in and appreciating the beauty of Bulgaria. I looked around the rest of the bus to see if anyone else had his/her nose pressed to the window like me to see outside, but didn't find any kindred spirits. The woman sitting next to me was bundled in various cloths and scarves, and had fallen asleep about four minutes after the bus started moving. The two men in front of me were sharing a bottle of Bulgarian *rakia*–liquor native to Bulgaria with a potent taste that would make most people think of rocket fuel–and I sensed that they were either going to be boisterously ready to invade Macedonia by the time they finished the bottle, or fall asleep like the woman next to me.

I was in my own world, though, enjoying the beauty of a country that had so much history, and I felt like I was traveling to the center of it. Unfortunately, though, the outskirts of Veliko Turnovo didn't look much different from the outskirts of Sofia; they're filled with drab, gray row house buildings. Since I was headed to what many viewed as the cultural capital of Bulgaria, I suppose it was fitting that all elements of culture be on display. The first element in nearly every Bulgarian city seemed to be Soviet communist architecture.

But gradually the road gave way to the hills that the guidebooks had promised me in Veliko Turnovo, and soon after getting off the bus, I was perched high on a cobblestone road overlooking the snakelike, winding Yantra River. It became clear to me early on that Veliko was the kind of city that felt like a town, a place where even though it was large, you could wander around its cobblestone downtown streets and feel like everyone there had known each other–perhaps since the Second Bulgarian Empire. The shops downtown were traditionally Bulgarian, and while they became tourist stops for me, I got the impression that I was buying things–pottery and jewelry–that the locals would buy, too.

There was a pleasantness to Veliko that took my mind away from the earlier basketball game, and calmed things down from the traffic-weary streets of Sofia. I found a restaurant overlooking the river and ordered a *shopska* salad–the traditional and delicious Bulgarian salad containing tomatoes, cucumbers, green peppers and *cyrene* cheese–a cheese similar to feta–and *mousaka*, a Greek/Bulgarian eggplant dish that had also become a wonderful staple of my Bulgarian diet. As the sun started to fade in front of me, I glanced down the hill at Bulgarian orthodox churches and Bulgarian national revival architecture–an entire scene that seemed to be a poetic ode to the 19th century.

Wandering back to my guesthouse, I perched myself on the balcony to gaze out at Veliko Turnovo's most famous landmark, Tsarevets Castle. The castle was built in 1185 and served as the empire's fortress for more than 200 years. It wasn't difficult to see why Bulgarians chose this location perched high upon a hill overlooking the river and the city. It offered vantage points that spanned for miles, and while I was focusing on the majesty of medieval castle in front of me, I could also easily see its strategic value as a stronghold. The castle's walls seemed to cover the entirety of the circular hill, and from a distance, I could see several old stone buildings and towers as part of the castle grounds, as well as a cathedral perched at the peak of the castle. This castle was built to exhibit the glory of the Bulgarian Empire, and from where I was sitting, it had certainly stood the test of time.

I was hoping to see the light show, a laser-light extravaganza I'd read about that lit up the castle with various vibrant colors for a span of 15 minutes. I was told that the laser light show occurred on weekend nights when someone was willing to pay for it. When I'd asked my waiter at dinner how much it cost to make the light show happen, he just laughed at me and walked away. I later learned that this show usually went on when someone with big bucks–a mafia-type–was hoping to impress a date, and was willing to fork over several hundred Bulgarian *leva* to make the evening special. I held to my hopes, as I sat on my balcony, that the laser light show would light up the night, but it never happened. Apparently, there would be no overt displays of romance on this night, but I went to bed far away from basketball in Sofia. I went to bed in the cultural capital of Bulgaria feeling happy about life.

I got up early the next morning hoping to spend my morning touring the castle. I'd just viewed it from afar, but I wanted to have the chance to experience the castle up close. I wandered through town on a sleepy Sunday morning, and even though I could see my breath and slipped on the cracked icy sidewalks, this didn't deter my optimism for the conquest of this castle. I found the entrance and it appeared to be the same entrance the Bulgarian kings had marched through nearly 1000 years before me. The cobblestones were sprinkled with ice and snow and led the way to a giant stone drawbridge that marked the beginning of the castle. As I looked around me, I didn't see another soul, and I swore I couldn't hear another soul either. When I walked up to the gate, I expected to pay a fee to enter the castle, but couldn't find a ticket booth, and couldn't find anything that even indicated this was a tourist attraction, though it most definitely was. So I just walked into the castle and started hiking up the hill.

I walked by the remains of old stone houses, small churches and plenty of craftsmen's workshops. When I wove my way around to the other side of the castle, I found myself on Execution Rock, a stone plateau where unlucky traitors would be pushed from, crashing down on rocks and eventually tumbling to their death either on these rocks, or a little farther off into the Yantra River. From Execution Rock, I glanced back at the panorama of the river, the churches, the national revival houses, the cafes and guesthouses that now made up modern-day Veliko Turnovo. I still didn't see another soul up on the castle grounds, and I started to swell up with a pride, a sort of tourist discovery pride that I had this ancient castle on this brisk Sunday morning all to myself.

I kept thinking that this castle, this town, should be flooded with tourists, but I didn't see any. I didn't even see evidence that any kind of tourist operation was being undertaken on the castle. As I bumbled my way along the castle's numerous paths, all I could hear was the slow rustling of the winter wind. All I could see were rocks upon rocks used to fortify the castle grounds that hung over the river gorge. This Sunday morning in the 21st century might as well have been Sunday afternoon in the 12th century.

That is, until I spotted something on the ground ahead of me. It was black, plastic and rectangular, and stuck out because everything else on the castle grounds was brown and made of stone. I approached this object, and my first thoughts were confirmed. It was the most anachronistic object I could possibly spot in this setting as I reveled in Tsarevets' antiquity: it was a snazzy new Motorola flip-phone. And it was lying right off to the side of the castle's stone path.

I picked up the phone wondering if it was broken and this was just someone's frustrated manner of ditching it. I hoped this wasn't the case because the castle should be the last place for littering. When I opened up the phone, though, I realized this wasn't the case. The phone worked, and Cyrillic letters flashed at me in a hurry to confirm this.

I looked around the castle once more. There was no one. That was the incredible thing I'd been taking note of for the entire hour I'd been touring the grounds of the castle. I hadn't seen a single soul. So where did this phone come from? And what was I supposed to do with it?

I felt fairly certain the castle didn't have a lost-and-found department, and though there might have been one somewhere in the town of Veliko Turnovo, did I want to take this expensive phone to the police station and try to explain in Bulgarian that I'd just found it? Even if I managed to find the police station, how did I know the Bulgarian police wouldn't accuse me of stealing the phone? Or knowing how things worked in Bulgaria, what were the chances the police would just keep the phone for themselves? There seemed to be too many cross-cultural dangers associated with carrying the phone with me.

So I did what I thought was the most sensible thing: I took the phone with me toward the entrance to the castle and placed it on top of a four-foot tall rock. The rock was highly visible from many locations within the castle, and I figured the phone would now be visible as well. Of course, it was now visible to anyone who wanted to steal it, but I was hoping whoever had lost the phone in the castle would come back to find it. And if he or she came back to find it, the odds of it being found where I spotted it–around the back side of the castle path–were much smaller than the odds of it being found closer to the entrance. I tried to convince myself that this plan was going to work, but in the back of my mind kept thinking, *If you found someone's phone in the States, is this the way you'd try to handle the situation–by placing it on top of a giant rock?*

Thankfully, it didn't take long for me to find out what was going to happen with the phone. As I headed down the path and exited out the drawbridge entrance, a family of four came rushing back up the path headed my direction. As they approached, the daughter who appeared to be in her early 20s immediately started speaking Bulgarian–fast and rushed Bulgarian–to me.

I couldn't understand every word she spoke, but I understood the last one: *telefona.*

This was the owner of the phone, and she'd come back to look for it.

"*Da,*" I responded eloquently. "The telephone is there," I told her in simple Bulgarian. "Come with me."

While the family seemed frantic with excitement and nervousness, I calmly walked them back toward the big rock where I'd put the phone. They were speaking quickly and asking all sorts of questions–it was clear they were very concerned–and I had trouble understanding them. I mostly just kept pointing and saying, "Your phone is up here." Once the rock came into view, I pointed to it, and they could see the phone resting on top in plain view. They smiled and rejoiced, and this was accompanied by more rapid-paced Bulgarian that I couldn't understand. As they hurried along the path in the direction of the phone, I started heading back down the other way, happy and a bit incredulous that my "put the phone on the rock" plan had actually worked.

It was about 45 seconds later–I had already exited the castle once again–that I heard someone yelling in English.

"Wait, wait! Wait a minute! Please, wait a minute!"

I turned slowly to see the mother of the family clutching the cell phone and rushing toward me. I wasn't sure what to make of this, but I also couldn't pretend like I didn't understand her. She'd been speaking Bulgarian before, but now she was speaking English.

She came hurtling down the path, and as she got closer to me, her arms spread out. I was hit head-on with a tackle form of a hug, complete with gracious and effusive cries.

"Oh, thank you, thank you! You saved me! You saved me!"

I thought this was a bit much—it was just a cell phone—but I wasn't going to ruin the moment. She started kissing my cheeks, my neck, anywhere she could find to express her appreciation. And to say she was appreciative would be a massive understatement.

"Thank you, thank you! You are wonderful!"

Much like listening to Svetla reflect on the hope for her country, there wasn't much I could say to this woman. I found myself nervously laughing and smiling as a 40-something Bulgarian woman was hugging and kissing me, madly telling me that I'd saved her. Finally, when I was able to disengage from this onslaught of thanks, I told her in English that it was not a problem, that I was happy to help.

The mother looked like she was going to cry. Thankfully the rest of the family had now caught up with us, and we discussed in English how she'd lost the phone yesterday afternoon and this was the last place they'd come to look to see if they could find it. I told them where I'd found it, and how I'd come up with the potentially dim plan to put the phone on top of the rock.

It took a moment for the matriarch to compose herself, but then she rejoined the conversation.

"Oh, you aren't Bulgarian," she emoted.

I figured that was rather obvious for many, many reasons, but also felt compelled to reply.

"No, I'm not Bulgarian."

"If you were Bulgarian," she continued in English, "there's no way we would've gotten our phone back. You'd still have that phone right now, and we'd never see it again."

I had to laugh at this as well because I wasn't sure how else I was supposed to respond. Unfortunately, though, I knew exactly what she meant. I was getting used to how Bulgarians viewed themselves. Whether Nikolai had no faith in other coaches' ability to cooperate, Khrushchev was accusing everyone of cheating, my basketball players felt like losers, or Svetla's mother represented her country with a donkey cart, I worried that Bulgarians didn't view themselves with a lot of pride.

"Well, I think you can tell by my English that I'm definitely not Bulgarian," was the best response I could come up with.

"Thank God!" she exclaimed. "Thank God you're not Bulgarian!"

And then she hugged me one more time.

I walked back down the castle path with this friendly Bulgarian family that spoke surprisingly good English. They insisted I come to lunch with them, but I politely declined.

As left them, I gazed back up at the castle one last time and saw a majestic structure that represented the true pride of Bulgaria. Looking up at Tsarevets, I felt thrilled to be in this unique and interesting country, and proud I'd made the decision to come experience Bulgaria. But I was still stumped as to how to infuse this sense of pride into Bulgarians, and most specifically my basketball team.

Chapter XIII
The Jewish Question

Bulgarian 20th century history is unfortunately littered with many instances of what went wrong, and this includes being on the losing side of both World Wars. But Bulgaria's actions during World War II actually make it stand out in a positive way when compared to other Eastern European nations. That's because during World War II, Bulgaria was the only country in all of Eastern Europe to save its entire Jewish population. The Jews in Bulgaria experienced discrimination–they were prohibited from voting, holding political office, marrying ethnic Bulgarians or owning rural land–but the Jewish population of 48,000 remained intact throughout World War II. In fact, Bulgaria was the only country in Europe to have a larger Jewish population after World War II than before it started. Ed Gaffney, a professor of law at Valparaiso University who has studied the Jews in Bulgaria, has described Bulgaria's actions with their Jewish population during World War II as "extraordinary, stunning and staggeringly wonderful."

One of the main reasons that Bulgaria was motivated to save its Jews was because Jews were far more integrated into the regular culture of Bulgaria than they were in the other Eastern European countries. Gaffney points out that in Bulgaria, unlike so many other countries in Europe at the time, "Jews were common labourers and artisans." Jews in Bulgaria weren't necessarily seen as the "other"—and they certainly weren't viewed as the part of the population that ran the country's finances, a claim that Hitler would exploit all too well in the majority of Europe. Bulgarian Jews were forced to wear the Star of David, but it was a smaller version of the Star that Hitler placed on Jews in Germany. I don't know that this reduced the stigma of being Jewish, but Bulgarian Jews still were viewed as more acceptable in society than they were anywhere else in Eastern Europe. As a result of this, they weren't subjected to living in ghettos to further stigmatize them. They were allowed to remain as part of the population, and this allowed them to survive at a time when six million Jews were being murdered in Europe—an average of roughly 2,000 a day.

I first learned about the history of Bulgaria's Jews from my students, who displayed pride that their country had been the one country in Eastern Europe to save its Jews during the war. I was thrilled to see them displaying this rare form of Bulgarian pride. Hearing stories about Bulgaria saving all its Jews piqued my interest and made me want to learn more. With more research, though, I learned that Bulgaria saving its Jews during World War II wasn't exactly the entire story.

"All by itself, it's a beautiful story," Ed Gaffney writes. "What's wrong with it from our point of view as journalists, is that it's not a complete story."

The feel-good part of the Bulgarian Jews story is that Bulgaria saved all 48,000 of their Jews during World War II. The "complete story," though, illustrates what happened to Jews in Bulgarian-occupied territories. The reason Bulgaria joined the war on the side of Germany was due to Germany's promise to restore Macedonia to Bulgaria. And since Germany had easily conquered Macedonia and parts of Greece already, Hitler saw Bulgaria as a convenient ally, a country that could take care of the day-to-day operations in Macedonia and Greece. So during World War II, Bulgaria was officially in charge of both Macedonia and Greece.

These were two countries that had significant Jewish populations, and even though Bulgaria had gone to great lengths to save their Jews—and somehow Hitler had allowed this—they did not expend any effort to save Greek or Macedonian Jews. All told, Bulgaria handed over between 11,000-14,000 Greek and Macedonian Jews to the Nazis who were sent to Treblinka for extermination. Bulgarian officials justified this decision by saying that these Jews weren't Bulgarian nationals, and therefore they had no duty to save them. Considering that even in the present day

Bulgarians consider Macedonia to be part of their homeland, this claim that Macedonian Jews were not Bulgarian nationals can be considered tragically ironic.

In his study of the Bulgarian Jews, Professor Gaffney goes on to point out the truth about human nature when considering the two sides to this story: "One of the extraordinary things about the Bulgarian story is that we expect our rescuers to be 100 percent saints and never get anything wrong. The very improbability of the Bulgarian story makes it a compellingly human one because most of us are like that; we're not saints and we get it wrong as often as we get it right."

As a result of the very human questions this study provides, I thought I'd bring up the issue of the Bulgarian Jews with my students in class in connection with reading Elie Wiesel's Holocaust novel, *Night*. Most were aware of the first part—the happy part—of the Bulgarian Jew story, but not as many were aware of what happened to Jews in Bulgarian-occupied territories. I encouraged them to debate Bulgaria's actions dealing with the Jews in World War II, and the discussion that followed was fantastic.

There were those who said Bulgaria could not be held responsible for what happened in Greece and Macedonia. There were those who said Bulgaria was completely responsible for what happened in Greece and Macedonia. And there were those who tried to understand the time period—the virulent anti-Semitism—and grasp why Bulgaria had saved some, but not others. By the end of the class period, there were no concrete conclusions, and I didn't think there should be. The Bulgarian Jew story presented some murky ethical questions, as did nearly every story related to the Holocaust.

That day, a Bulgarian history teacher had been observing my class. She had asked me if she could come and I invited her since we were reading *Night* and spending part of the day on an historical debate regarding Bulgaria. I thought it would be relevant to a history teacher, and I was interested to hear her perspective on the debate. It turned out, though, the discussion left a far greater impression on her than I had ever intended.

"Andy," she told me, "I know you probably don't know this, but this kind of discussion you just had—it is not allowed here in Bulgaria. It is very dangerous to do this; you must be careful."

Because we had a friendly and usually humor-filled relationship, I wasn't sure if she was serious or joking. I couldn't fathom what was wrong with the discussion, especially since my students all had an opinion and wanted to share it and had been thoroughly engaged in the debate during the entire class period. But her countenance didn't change, and I realized she actually was serious.

"What kind of discussion? A discussion about history?" I asked.

"No, no. This was not history. You were also talking about politics," she quickly reprimanded me.

"Well, I guess so, but history and politics are always wrapped together. I'm sure that's the way it is in your class, too."

"No, this is not the way in my class," she said as she gave me a Bulgarian finger-wag. "You just brought politics into the classroom, and there is a Bulgarian law against this. No politics in the classroom."

"You can't be serious," I replied incredulously, "there's an actual law that says you can't discuss politics in the classroom?"

"No, no, it is too dangerous," she responded gravely, her head bowing lower and her voice dropping to a hushed tone. This gave me the impression she thought it was dangerous we were even having this discussion between the two of us. With a glance sideways, and then a firm stare back into my eyes, she declared, "We shall speak no more of these things."

"That's ridiculous," I exclaimed. "Even if there is a law like that, you can't actually agree with the law. Teaching history as just facts with no discussion doesn't allow kids to think. How can you teach history and politics without having discussions? That's complete suppression of freedom of speech, freedom of thought."

"Andy," her tone now was scolding, "I said we shall speak no more of these things."

With that, she gave me her final finger-wag and marched out of my classroom.

I watched her walk away and was stunned. She was one of the Bulgarian teachers I'd gotten to know the best and admire the most, but now she was telling me that a discussion where students had different opinions based on a political matter from the past was illegal based on Bulgarian law. And I couldn't blame her for the law, but I found it even more astounding that she actually followed the law—and encouraged me to do so as well. The Bulgarian Jew question, like so many questions and issues in Bulgarian history and politics, was a multi-faceted story that could be looked at in many different ways. But according to Bulgarian law and my colleague, discussions like the one I just had were actually illegal, and I needed to be careful.

I was learning that Bulgaria was a place that had rules that baffled me, and a lack of rules that also baffled me. Taking my colleague's advice that I needed to be careful made sense to a foreigner in a very foreign land. But in many circumstances, I had no idea how I should even be careful. I didn't think I'd need to be careful during a coaches' meeting before the ACS Open tournament, and that meeting turned into an all-out war. On the other hand, in my previous life I couldn't even imagine getting myself into a situation where I'd need to bribe a customs' officer, and it turned out that was just business as usual in Bulgaria.

Thankfully, our next basketball tournament wasn't business as usual, and this meant that the games weren't being played on Saturday mornings. I was thrilled when Nikolai told me that I could sleep in on Saturday and not worry about my players showing up hungover. But then he told me when the tournament would actually be, and I found myself possibly even more confused; this next tournament would be held on Thursday morning.

"The school hosting the tournament wanted to reward basketball players and give them the day off school, so they've organized the tournament for Thursday morning. This is the Mladost Tournament, so this will be a big deal to your players." (Mladost is the Sofia neighborhood where the college is located.)

I also assumed that missing school would be a big deal for my players, as apparently this was their "reward" for playing basketball. At least, in the case of this tournament, though, we didn't need to take a long public bus ride to the game. School 144, the host of the tournament, was only about ten blocks away.

February had brought warmer temperatures to Bulgaria, so for the first time in as long as I could remember, the walk out of the college wasn't an icy one. The ice had melted to slush, which then blended to mud, but we all saw this as a step in the right direction. It's easier to slip and fall on Bulgarian ice than it is to slip and fall on Bulgarian mud. Even the stray dogs seemed to appreciate this change. They demonstrated much surer footing in the mud than they had on the ice, although they still barked and snarled at all of us as we marched out of the college together .

This February Thursday was also a special day because it was Valentine's Day—or at least that's what was marked on my American calendar. The Soviets, though, had outlawed Valentine's Day, which seemed to me a bit of an overkill. But considering they had also banned

Christmas, I suppose I shouldn't have been too surprised they banned a holiday most strongly supported by a capitalist American greeting card company. February 14th was, however, a Bulgarian holiday for Trifon Zarezan, the Bulgarian patron saint of wine. In Bulgaria, there seemed to be no traditions associated with this holiday other than drinking a lot of wine. Most of my players seemed to think was a far better tradition than having to worry about buying chocolates and flowers for your girlfriend. As much as I didn't want to encourage them to drink wine, I had to admit they made a great point.

"You see, Coach," Pesho was telling me as we walked to the tournament, "tonight you Americans are stressed about Valentine's gifts. In the meantime, us Bulgarians—you see, we will be drunk on wine."

"I suppose that'd be okay," I told my players, and my consent was instantly popular with all of them, "but I'd like to be drinking wine celebrating the three victories we're going to get today in this tournament."

While School 144 reminded me of so many other Bulgarian public school gyms, our first game was not reminiscent of our past failures. In this instance, the team we were playing was not supremely talented, although they still had more talent than our team. But what they had in talent, they were completely lacking in composure.

Dimov, who was sober and playing point guard confidently, was finding openings in a porous defense that enabled him to pass to Menkov who could cut to the basket for some easy scores. Pesho's post moves were far from what any basketball aficionado would call post moves, but his incessant motor was helping him jump like a pogo stick for rebounds and put-backs. At the end of the first quarter, we had an eight-point lead and our team huddle was energized.

The second quarter was more of the same, and I started to think that maybe there was something special about Trifon Zarezan. Pavel had taken my advice and was at least trying to dribble with his head up. On one particular drive as he burrowed down the lane, he spotted Ivan underneath the basket and recorded—unofficially, of course—his first assist of the season. Kosio's knee seemed to be magically healed and he made two jump shots and a scoop shot in the second quarter. I could also tell that he was benefiting from the extremely small court we were playing on; it didn't require him to run back that far on defense.

In the second quarter with our lead pushed out to 15 points, I was able to put a different Sasho in the game to serve as a replacement for the smiling version of Sasho who was currently sitting on the bench with a cast on his hand. There were actually a lot of similarities between the two of them, and most of these dealt with their awkwardness on the basketball floor. The healthy Sasho I'd just placed in the game was tall, about 6'3", and considered basketball a game that should only be played with elbows. This meant that whenever he got the ball on offense, he would swing both his elbows in the general direction of anyone crazy enough to get near him. On defense, while guarding people, he always made sure to have at least one elbow in his opponent's ribs or back. Sasho played the last two-and-a- half minutes of the second quarter. He picked up four fouls. And as he headed back to the bench for halftime, he was certain that he'd been wronged on each one of the foul calls.

"Coach, it *eessn't* fair! It *eessn't* fair!" he howled.

"I don't know, Sasho," I wanted to agree with him, but just couldn't do it. "You're swinging your elbows an awful lot. They're going to call fouls on you when you do that."

"Yes, this is true," he responded, seeming to have a moment of clarity. "But those ... those .... *sons-of-beeetches*, did you hear what they say to me?"

Some of his teammates started laughing because Sasho was one of the few players who seemed to enjoy swearing in English–though it never remotely sounded threatening, just comical.

"Who said what to you, Sasho?" I asked.

"Those guys, those ... those ... stinking referees!"

"The referees?" I looked over to the opposite corner of the floor where the refs were currently smoking.

"Yes, those ... those ... *sons-of-beetches*, they said bad things about my mother!"

"The refs said bad things about your mother?" I was finding this hard to believe.

"Yes," Sasho was still fuming, "they said things ... things ... oh, I cannot repeat these things!"

I wanted to laugh out loud at Sasho and his flying elbows and foul mouth, but then Pavel interrupted.

"He's telling the truth, Coach. I don't know who these refs are, but they said things to me about my mother, too–things I'm not going to repeat."

Wonderful, I thought, as I once again looked over to the corner where the refs were now on cigarette number two. *The referees–*

supposedly the voice of maturity, fairness and reason—are insulting my players' mothers. What's going to happen next?

Well, as the second half started, I made a point of paying attention to the referees, who were clearly spending far too much time talking to my players. Early in the second half, I saw Menkov intervene between a referee and Pesho, as apparently the referee had commentary to share on Pesho's mother as well. This baffled me and I felt completely helpless. I had spent so much time preaching to my players about playing the right way and not talking trash, and now the referees were instigating verbal confrontations with my players.

I turned to Nikolai, who had also made the trip to School 144 because his girls' team was playing in a tournament as well. Before I could even say anything to him, he started shaking his head, which this time I knew was not the Bulgarian version of "yes."

"Andy, I do not know what to say," he mused sympathetically. "This is wrong. These referees continue to say things to our players, and I do not know why. But I also don't know what you can do. These are the referees. They are supposed to be in charge. It is impossible."

With Nikolai's official *ne modje* response, I decided there wasn't much I could do other than ensure that my players continued to play the right way. As this thought was firmly implanted in my mind, Dimov stole the ball at half court and cruised to the other end for a layup. At this point, our lead was more than 20 points. As the whistle was blown due to the ball being deflected off the cage wall, the coach of the other team subbed out the point guard who had just had the ball stolen and not bothered to run back on defense. He made his way to the sideline, ignored what his coach said to him and then went after the bench. With his right leg, he wound up and soccer-kicked his team's empty wooden bench. This created a loud crash and the bench started to slide. One kick, though, was not enough, and he followed this up with two more swift right foot punts that flipped the bench and sent it hurtling onto the playing floor.

My jaw dropped. I had never seen anything like this before. The offender just looked at his team's bench—now in the middle of the floor—and then walked out of the gym. I had no idea what to expect next, but it was clear this incident was a bigger deal to me than it was to anyone on the other team. The opposing players still seated on the other remaining bench feigned indifference at the violent outburst they'd just witnessed. I mistakenly assumed several of them would run out and drag the bench back to its expected location to end this embarrassing debacle, but they did nothing.

Stefan and Menkov, eager to continue playing, trotted across half court and replaced the other team's bench. All the while the other team's coach and players continued looking on as if nothing had happened. And maybe in this world I was living in, nothing had happened. No technical fouls were assessed, and when the point guard came back into the gym a few minutes later, the coach re-inserted him into the game without as much as a word about the bench-kicking tirade. I thought at least once the point guard re-entered the game, the referees might want to say something to him about his mother, but they seemed to save these comments for my players.

To their credit, my players kept their cool, which was really all they needed to do to win this game. With things spiraling downward, our opponents resorted to yelling at each other following missed shots or bad passes, and most offensive possessions consisted of us playing 5-on-4 or 5-on-3 because some of their players didn't bother coming back on defense. This led to an easy victory, and it even gave me a chance to put Elbows Sasho back into the game to pick up three more fouls. Apparently, they weren't keeping a close count at the scorer's table because he finished the game with seven fouls, two more than the limit. My starters enjoyed the scene from our bench—a bench that had thankfully remained in place for the duration of the game.

As we'd done in the past, we'd defeated a team we should've defeated in the first round of a Bulgarian tournament. Spirits were high—possibly because we now had a chance to advance the farthest we had ever gone in a tournament—but more likely because this meant we would have a second Thursday game and not have to return to school.

I was happy with our team's performance and proud that they hadn't succumbed to verbally sparring with the referees or throwing temper tantrums like our opponents. These thoughts were at the forefront of my mind even though we had won the game. There seemed to be so many obstacles that had nothing to do with the actual playing of basketball—gyms that were too small and too dangerous, referees verbally insulting my players, and opposing teams with no idea what class even meant—that it seemed impossible to me that anything I was trying to teach was going to resonate with my players.

"Andy, I am sorry about this," Nikolai apologized to me after the first game. "What I am watching—this is not right. This is not the way the game is supposed to be played."

"Thanks, Nikolai," I responded, knowing full well that it wasn't his fault, and feeling badly that he felt responsible. "I feel like I'm not even focusing on basketball here. I'm spending all my time trying to keep everything else under control. I hope the second game will be better."

When I said I hoped the second game would be better, I told myself that I didn't think things could get too much worse. The referees would be different for the next game, which should mean fewer cigarettes and fewer motherly insults. And the team would be different, so I hoped that meant the coach would not tolerate a player kicking the bench onto the playing floor. In truth, neither of these things appeared to be an issue as we warmed up an hour later for the second game. I'd told myself that the only thing I could control was my own team, and tried not to pay attention to what was going on at the other end of the floor.

This worked well—for about three minutes.

Stepping out of our layup lines during warm-ups, Stefan came trotting over to me, his eyes big and terrified.

"Uhh, Coach, uhh … Coach," Stefan stammered, clearly having lost all of the confidence I generally knew him to have. "Coach … do you see what I see? That's … uh … that's…."

As he struggled to finish his thought, I looked at the other end of the floor where the other team was warming up. Once again, it looked like we were going to be facing a bunch of bad-ass Eastern European dudes—some of whom might be 23 years old. But this was nothing new to Stefan; half of our games had been against teams like this. What Stefan was looking at, though, wasn't the team in general; it was one player.

He was looking at the back of one player who stood about 6'3", and was warming up with his shirt off.

"That's ridiculous," I said. "I can't believe he's allowed to warm up without a shirt."

"No, Coach," Stefan replied as the player now faced us. "Look at him. Look at his chest."

Now I saw clearly why Stefan was so shaken. As this player faced our end of the floor, I could see his shaved head, his rigid jawbone and the entirety of the sculpted pectoral muscles. But none of this made an impression; it was what was *on* one of his sculpted pectoral muscles that both Stefan and I were staring at.

On his right pec was a jet-black tattoo of a swastika.

"Oh my God," I uttered out loud, completely forgetting that I was supposed to be the voice to comfort Stefan, my scrawny sophomore guard, who was currently mortified.

Since the rest of the other team were all wearing uniforms–matching uniforms for a change–it was clear that this player's shirt was off for a reason, and that had little to do with his muscles. He wanted everyone to see the swastika.

Without even thinking, I marched over to one of the referees and demanded in pidgin Bulgarian that the player be forced to put his uniform on for warm-ups. The referee pretended not to understand my Bulgarian, but most likely just didn't want to deal with the situation. Our conversation ended with him wagging his finger in my face; he wasn't going to do anything about this. I hollered over to the other coach, telling him to have his player put a shirt on, but he just smiled back at me. This was all fun and games to him.

When I went to Nikolai, he had his head in his hands. I thought of asking him for help, but I knew this wouldn't make a difference either. He was appalled, and even more appalled because he knew that nothing would be done to change this. Bulgaria might've saved its Jews during World War II, but nothing was going to be done to save a sense of integrity and dignity for this tournament.

Our warm-up continued, but word about the swastika tattoo had spread throughout our team. Each of them was taking furtive glances to the other end of the floor to see if it was really true. When the swastika owner took the ball and hammered home a dunk, he let out a primal howl and turned to face our end of the floor. The pure blackness and evil of the tattoo seemed to leap out from his chest and attack our end of the court. My players cowered as if a Nazi invasion was imminent.

And maybe it was.

In the huddle before the game, I was fuming with anger. How could something like this be allowed? How could the other coach smile about his tattooed anti-Semite and the referees pretend it wasn't a problem? Regardless of how much my players were thinking about the larger implications of the tattoo–and I was guessing most of them were–his pre-game antics served the purpose of intimidating my entire team. I wasn't sure if I was more intimidated or angered, but either way, I tried to shift the focus of our pre-game talk to actually playing basketball.

"You need to go out and play hard, and you can't play scared. Play our game, stay together and play the right way. You dictate how this game is going to be played, and we can beat these guys."

I could sense that my players didn't completely believe what I was saying, but they headed out onto the floor with spirit anyway. Stefan remained on the bench looking shell-shocked. It was his dream, he'd told me many times, to explore the world and meet new people. He'd never left Bulgaria, and believed the outside world was a wonderful place with good people. His eyes, though, now just stared straight ahead; he was in a trance, and I could sense that he was starting to question his view of the world being full of good people.

From our vantage point, the other team appeared to be full of large, ripped, hateful people. Our only saving grace was that Swastika Tattoo, now that the game was about to start, had finally put on a jersey. With a shaved head that seemed be more than just a fashion statement, Swastika Tattoo was one of three starters for our opponent who was 6′3″ or taller—and all of them had shaved heads. I'd been able to use our game against the Roma team the month before as a lesson on diversity and tolerance. Now it appeared that we were facing the opposite situation—a team of neo-Nazis.

From the opening tip, it was clear this was going to be a physical game. Swastika Tattoo got the ball in the post, threw an elbow into Kosio and went up for a short jumper. Kosio went flying and immediately starting yelling at the referees, who shrugged in the same manner when I had pleaded with them about the shirtless warm-up. Thankfully, though, Swastika Tattoo did not appear to be able to shoot very fluidly, and he bricked the jumper. Pesho grabbed the rebound out of the air and passed the ball to Menkov who took it up the right side of the floor. Before he got to half court, though, he was body-checked into the side wall. This was an obvious foul, and perhaps even a flagrant foul.

The ref's whistle blew. Out of bounds, he called. No foul. The ball went over to the other team.

I was outraged, first yelling in Bulgarian, and when this seemed to attract no attention, I started yelling in English. Nikolai seemed to be the only person who understood and acknowledged both my Bulgarian and English, but he just looked at me helplessly. His head sunk further into his hands.

Their second possession was similar to the first, though this time when Swastika Tattoo lowered his shoulder into Kosio, Kosio just got out of the way. Part of me was frustrated by his lack of toughness, but the other part of me understood. The refs weren't going to call a foul, so was he supposed to stand in there and take a beating? I had no choice, though, but to put Vassy in the game. While offensively he was far inferior to Kosio, who had played great in the first game, I knew he wouldn't back down. And this was clearly going to be a test for our team—to see how much we could take without backing down.

The first quarter resembled a rugby game far more than a basketball game. These referees were not smoking cigarettes or insulting our players' mothers, but they seemed to be enjoying watching the physical pummeling that was occurring on the floor. Our team was significantly smaller, and as long as Swastika Tattoo and his teammates were allowed to push, shove, elbow and shoulder their way up and down the floor without fouls being called, the result was our players flying all over the court.

Pesho continued to jump down low, though, and was able to score on a couple of rebounds. Dimov quickly realized that dribbling behind his back or through his legs made no difference; every time he made a move right or left, he was pushed by his defender—and no foul was called. Menkov, our best chance at scoring, had driven the lane twice, been hacked twice with no call being made, and now looked like he wanted no part of driving to the basket.

Miraculously, when the first quarter ended, we were only trailing 8-6. For all of the neo-Nazis' thuggery, we'd been saved by the fact that they couldn't shoot. But it was difficult for me to even get a word in during our team huddle at the end of the quarter. Voices were ringing out from all angles.

"I get fouled every time I touch the ball!"

"That guy is completely dirty; he just wants to hurt people!"

"This is impossible; the refs think it's funny. They won't call anything."

I gave them my best, "Don't worry about the refs, don't worry about the other team, just play your game speech," a speech I'd given several times before in the States. But in the States when I'd given this speech, the other team did not have swastika tattoos and shaved heads—and the referees did not find this amusing.

In the second quarter, the neo-Nazis seemed emboldened by their ability to wreak physical havoc all over the floor. After checking Dimov into the wall—and this time, finally a foul was called—Dimov responded by getting in the face of a player much bigger than him. This resulted in two more skinheads surrounding him, and Dimov trying to get out of the situation. I looked down the bench to Stefan, who had found a steely determination. He looked me in the eye and said, "Coach, I won't play scared. I'm ready."

With that, I subbed Stefan in for Dimov, both to talk to Dimov about playing the right way, and to save him from further physical damage.

"I know, I know, Coach," Dimov blurted out before I could even talk to him. "But look at these guys. Look what they're doing to us out on the floor. How am I supposed to not react?"

He had a valid point, but I was determined that we weren't going to play like them.

"I know, Dimov, but we're not going to stoop to their level. That's not how we're going to play. You have to keep your mouth shut and just play ball."

"I know, Coach, I know," Dimov responded sincerely. "It's just really hard with these guys."

He was exactly right, and I was finding it difficult to keep my composure on the bench. Menkov was getting abused every time he touched the ball, and since Vassy, as I had predicted, refused to back down against bigger players, he was getting beaten up even more. Pesho continued to try to jump over and around them, but wanted nothing to do with actual contact. Pavel, who I could usually count on to play like an American football player, appeared to be shrinking before my very eyes.

We were hanging in the game, but having great difficulties scoring due to being physically and psychologically intimidated. With two minutes left to go in the half, Swastika Tattoo found himself alone on a fast break–after not running back on defense–and slammed the ball home with authority. Upon landing on the ground, he pounded his chest and flexed his right bicep. I noticed every player on the bench slump further in his seat.

At halftime, we still only trailed 20-13, which meant we were still in it, but it seemed like very few people–myself included–could even focus on the actual game of basketball. Too many things were running through my players' minds, and I only got 30 seconds into my halftime speech when Menkov pointed behind me and said, "Look, there he goes again."

Swastika Tattoo had taken off his jersey once again, and was proudly marching around his half of the court. With this, my ire rose and I lost focus on my halftime speech. But it didn't matter. All eyes from the huddle seemed entranced by the black Hitler ink. I wanted to turn to some kind of authority–or even express my own authority–and demand that he put his jersey back on, but I realized this wouldn't make a difference. I was helpless. Nikolai looked even more helpless, and I knew that he felt even worse because he'd always hoped to show me the positive attributes of his country. On the other sideline, it was business as usual; the shirtless warm-up was a part of their normal routine.

In the second half, my team continued to fight—literally—to stay in the game. Vassy managed to make a left-handed hook shot while getting knocked to the floor. The same thing happened to Pesho, but his didn't go in. He started barking at the referees and didn't run back on defense. When I took him out of the game as a result, his reaction was similar to Dimov's.

"I know, I know, Coach," he said, waving off my comments before I could even start.

"Pesho, you can't focus on the referees. You have to keep playing hard no matter what. Focus on yourself and our team."

"But, Coach," Pesho was pleading with me now, "look at what's going on out there."

Swastika Tattoo took the ball from the top of the key, took two dribbles and chucked Vassy out of the way with his left arm. Vassy went careening into the cement wall while Swastika Tattoo finished with a layup. I was trying to maintain my sense of dignity—exactly what I was asking of my players—but finding it very difficult.

"That's a foul!" I yelled in Bulgarian, and then continued in English, my blood pressure rising. "There's no way you can't see that. He's going to hurt people!"

The referee jogged by me and wagged his index finger in my general direction.

The deficit ballooned to 12 points and I had to make some substitutions. Some players out on the floor didn't seem in danger of getting in altercations with our opponents, but just seemed demoralized by the physical beating they were taking.

"Coach, this is just impossible," Pavel told me as he took a seat.

Menkov regained courage to drive the lane and beat his man with a crossover dribble. As he went up for a floater, he was pushed from behind, causing him to lose balance and miss long. No foul was called. Vassy boxed out and overcame his size disadvantage to get the rebound. As he soared toward the rim to follow up Menkov's shot, Swastika Tattoo's right arm came crashing across the bridge of his nose. The ball went flying errantly and Vassy's head went whiplashing backwards. No foul was called.

Once again, I started yelling at the referees, and this time I gave up on even bothering with translating to Bulgarian. I knew they weren't going to listen to me no matter what language I was yelling in; I just wanted them to hear my yelling and understand how upset I was in any language.

His head still raised, unable to accept defeat, Vassy jogged over to the sideline to meet me face to face. Blood was streaming out of his nose and I could already see the black circle starting to form under his right eye.

"You need to come out of the game, Vassy," I told him. "You're hurt."

"No, Coach, I'm fine," he said defiantly. "It's not broken; it's just bleeding."

He was right, and I was so exasperated that I didn't know what to do or say.

"But what do you want me to do?"

"What do you mean, Vassy?"

"I mean, Coach, you keep telling me to play the right way. I know I'm not supposed to retaliate, but what choice do I have? They won't call a foul and he just keeps on hitting me. Can I hit him back?"

I was lost in too many things, and swimming in too much anger. I couldn't even respond to a question that I should never have had trouble responding to.

"Coach, Coach," Vassy continued. "What do you want me to do? Can I hit him back?"

"I understand," I told him, "that you have to stand up for yourself."

I turned back to the bench, immediately ashamed that I hadn't unequivocally told him no. Vassy was one of the most intelligent players on the team, and I knew he could read between the lines of my tepid non-response. I was shocked by my own lack of ethics, shocked that I now felt I was stooping to the level I'd implored my players not to. But I didn't know what else to say, didn't know if I had the strength to tell him to keep doing things the right way. It didn't seem to matter in this game; doing things the right way wasn't getting us anywhere other than being pounded by a bunch of a neo-Nazis. Just as so much of Eastern Europe didn't know how to respond to the Holocaust—many didn't approve, but also didn't stop it—I had no idea how to respond to this situation of bullying.

On defense, Menkov slid his feet to stay in front of their point guard, but was then picked off by a forward with both elbows raised. He went down the floor as the pass made its way inside to Swastika Tattoo. As he went up for the shot, Vassy leveled a blow to his chest, a blow he'd felt at least six or seven times at the other end of a floor. He'd intended for this to send a message, but Swastika Tattoo just laughed at him. Their size difference was so significant that even if Vassy tried to rough him up, odds were it wasn't going to work.

Blood was now dripping from his nose and I felt embarrassed I'd left him in the game and embarrassed for my role in allowing him to play like that. I took him out of the game, and tried to reconcile with my own conscience.

"I'm sorry, Coach," Vassy said as he sat down on the bench. "I just— I just don't know what else to do."

I grabbed a towel and handed it to him so he could stop the blood coming from his nose.

"I don't either, Vassy."

I spent the majority of the fourth quarter alternately pleading with my team not to retaliate, to continue to play the right way even if it didn't seem fair, and then yelling at the referees, louder and louder in English. At one point, Nikolai came up behind me, put his hand on my shoulder and said, "You know, Andy, it's not going to make a difference no matter how much you yell."

"I know, Nikolai," I acquiesced, and the truth was that I'd known that for quite some time. But I felt I couldn't just stand on the sidelines and watch what was happening without doing something. I didn't know any other recourse aside from yelling, even if it was an ineffective method.

The score hovered between a 12-14 point deficit, and I had to sub with great frequency to keep my players' heads cool. They either came out of the game because they'd been brutalized out on the floor, or because I was afraid they'd retaliate and make things worse.

I put Elbows Sasho in the game, thinking that his inadvertent elbows might make a difference. But before he even had a chance to get the ball, he was shoved and flung out of the way by his defender. He wouldn't connect with any inadvertent elbows in this game because he was discarded by his opponent before this even became an option.

In the fourth quarter, Stefan continued to prove he wouldn't be afraid, standing in to take a charge that wasn't called, and diving on the floor for a loose ball that sent him sliding into the caged wall. Once the bleeding stopped, Vassy went back in and absorbed more blows, still standing tall and not playing dirty in response. Menkov was like a pinball bouncing all over the court, but continued to drive into the lane, as I'd told him to. And Pesho seemed to find his fight at the end of the game, finally not shying away from contact, as it was coming directly at him with every possession.

When the whistle blew to end the game, we'd lost by 13 points. Throughout the second half, I knew the deficit was too large to overcome—mostly because we could never score enough points because we were being fouled so hard and so often. Vassy came back to the bench first, his nose bleeding once again, and his eye becoming blacker by the moment.

"I'm sorry, Coach. I tried the best I could. I wish I would've done better."

Already, I could feel the tears welling up in my eyes. I told Vassy he had nothing to be sorry for, though one after another, players were coming up to me and apologizing because we'd lost yet another second round tournament game. At half court, Swastika Tattoo had once again taken off his shirt, and had extended his arms skyward in a move that accentuated the black hatred on his right pec even more.

I was half crying and completely disgusted.

"Coach," Menkov said to me, "should we line up and go shake hands with these guys?"

I was impressed by his maturity. This was the rare game I could remember where I didn't have to instruct my players to go shake hands with their opponents. But on this day, at this moment, I couldn't fathom shaking hands with the neo-Nazis.

"No, Menkov," I told him, "we're not shaking hands. We're not shaking hands with these guys. Let's just get our stuff and get out of here."

We exited the gym quietly, and some of my players felt the sting of losing. Others felt the bruising and blood they'd received in body blows from the neo-Nazis. And I felt the sadness of being in a place where I'd felt so much wrong had occurred—not just considering basketball, but considering human decency—and it seemed there was nothing I could do about it.

As my players filed out, Nikolai could see that my eyes continued to be welled up with tears and put his arm around me.

"Andy, I can see what you are doing with the boys, and you're doing the right things."

I looked Nikolai in the eye as he said this.

"Thank you, Nikolai, but none of this feels right. I don't even know if it matters. Doing the right thing shouldn't be this hard."

"No, it shouldn't," was the best support he could offer. But I wasn't expecting much else.

"I don't think we will play in this tournament next year," he said.

As we walked back to school as a team, I felt I'd reached a new level of inconsolable after a loss—and losing the game had very little to do with it. I told my team that I was proud of their effort, and even prouder of the fact that they played the entire game the right way. They should be proud of the class they displayed, and they would grow up to be stronger and better people as a result of their actions today. I didn't mention the swastika because I didn't even know where to begin or how to handle just how wrong it was. In Bulgaria's past, they had tolerated the presence of Jews in their country and been lauded for it. But in Bulgaria's present, the neo-Nazis' behavior was now also being tolerated. I'd been so alarmed at the laws that were thwarting the ability of teachers to have free discussions in class, yet on the basketball floor, it seemed lawlessness reigned.

I wondered what my players were thinking. I wondered if this was just a loss—another loss—or if they sensed there was more to it. Looking at their faces, I could see disappointment in their eyes, but the disappointment didn't seem to simply stem from the missed shots or blown defensive assignments from the last game. I wasn't choked up talking to them because we'd lost the game, and they knew it. I was choked up because on this day—either Valentine's or Trifon Zarezan Day—we'd been up against an enemy of hatred and bullying in an environment where this was deemed by nearly everyone else to be acceptable. I was choked up because it was hard for me to tell them that doing things the right way would always win out in the end.

Stefan approached after I was done speaking and said, "Coach, it's okay. We understand, and we're not going to be like those guys."

Menkov was next.

"Coach, you don't let us get too down after games, and you shouldn't be either. We know how you want us to play, and we know why."

I started my walk home not wanting other players to come up to me for fear that the saline misting my eyes would turn into full-fledged tears. Bulgaria was not a place where males showed their emotions, but I was having an awfully difficult time holding back. I might've been in the middle of a breakthrough with my team, but all I could feel was helplessness.

Thankfully, Pesho garrulously broke the tension.

"Coach, don't worry, Coach. Tonight is Trifon Zarezan. You'll have a bottle of wine and everything will be much better."

"I hope so, Pesho," I laughed as he smiled. "I really hope so."

By the time I got home that afternoon, I was starting to contemplate quitting coaching basketball. While I'd just learned about Bulgaria heroically saving its 48,000 Jews during World War II, that day made me realize that, as Professor Gafney had said, the story wasn't complete. There were always two sides to the story. For the wonderful deed of saving the Jews in their own country, there were thousands of Jews sent to the gas chambers by Bulgarians in other countries. And now for all my talk about playing the right way and having it pay off in the end, I hardly felt that way right now.

I had always believed that taking the hard line about doing things the right way would lead to good results. In my past as an American basketball coach, I felt I could pretty clearly see the positive results of this. But now I wondered how naïve I was to truly believe that in all cases, good really would triumph over evil. We'd left the gym quickly and quietly after trying to do things the right way and getting beaten up in the process. In the meantime, a team full of neo-Nazis was celebrating at center court, and the centerpiece of the celebration was a shirtless player proudly inked to display his hatred.

I failed to see how much of an impact I was making based on what I'd witnessed earlier in the day. I'd even wavered in my principles and tacitly approved of Vassy fighting back, something I'd never previously thought would happen. Later that night, though, I thought about the looks on my players' faces after the game—looks that weren't just depressed by what had just happened, but looks that also contained expressions of anger. There was understanding in their eyes, frustration at what had just happened, and determination to want to change it.

So when I opened up a much-needed bottle of Bulgarian *Mavrud* red wine that night, I thought of Pesho and laughed. And I thought of the rest of my team and how often I'd preached that they couldn't give up. I was in a new place and it wasn't necessarily getting easier on a daily basis, but I didn't come to Bulgaria to give up—no matter how many swastika tattoos I was faced with. I'd started the new year worried that my team didn't have enough pride to fight through tough times, and now I realized that maybe it wasn't just my team I was worried about; I was worried about my own resilience. But there was no way I could ever expect them to be strong and proud if I didn't display those same attributes.

A few weeks after this game, billboards sprung up in several locations in Sofia—most notably one block from the Israeli Embassy—featuring Hitler's face with a caption written in Bulgarian saying, "They Talk, You Listen." No one claimed responsibility for the billboards, and no one was exactly sure what the caption meant. If "they" was people like Hitler, then the billboard seemed to be implying that "you" should listen when dictators—and genocidal maniacs—speak. But this was just one interpretation of the message. Regardless of how you interpreted the billboard, Hitler's face glowering down on the Israeli Embassy was not appreciated by many.

Thankfully, the billboards were only up for a few days before Bulgarian officials stepped in and ordered them to be taken down. I thought of the argument I had with the Bulgarian history teacher where I had insisted on freedom of speech, and then wondered what my definition of "freedom" really was. I didn't have a clear answer to this question, though. For the moment, I took solace in the fact that Hitler's face was no longer hovering over Sofia's streets. I wasn't convinced, however, that his spirit of evil was gone.

Chapter XIV
Things Fall Apart

In many ways, Sofia was a beautiful city during the winter. With the snow-capped Mt. Vitosha looming just beyond the city, its snowy whiteness provided a nice contrast to the gray of so many of the row house apartment buildings. And the snow that would cover the lawns and parking lots of these row houses added a sense of brightness to what could otherwise be described as dreary neighborhoods. Perhaps more important than anything, the snow worked wonders to cover the city's growing garbage problem.

On the one hand, Sofia residents would point to the excess garbage on the city's streets and in its parks and point the blame to the mayor, tough-guy Boyko Borisov, who had had many disputes with the city's garbage workers. This definitely was part of the problem, as the garbage workers would threaten to strike, only pick up some of the garbage, and then go on strike completely. When this occurred, dumpsters would overfill, stray dogs would rejoice and residential areas would start to take on an unpleasant odor, not to mention an unsightly appearance. As I walked to the grocery store—about 10 minutes from my house—I would routinely encounter dumpsters that were overflowing, broken glass on the sidewalks, newspapers that had become playthings for the wind, and various fast-food wrappers swooshing from one side of the street to the other. When snow covered Sofia, most of this was hidden. But as spring rolled around, the garbage problem in Sofia was now blooming, and it seemed everyone had a different theory as to why it was so difficult to put trash in its proper place.

Usually the best and most entertaining theories came from my basketball players, Pesho in particular. We were hosted for our next tournament by the only other American school in Sofia—a much smaller and decidedly more international school—and the break in between games was complete with a pizza lunch. Since I was becoming inured to playing in third-floor gyms with caged walls and peeing in closet drains, playing in a tournament in an American school that had nice facilities and offered a pizza lunch—a pizza lunch!—could only be described as an immense breath of fresh air. My players, too, couldn't believe that an opposing school actually had a locker room for us to change in, and then offered us free food in between our games.

The challenge that resulted from this, though, was getting my players to handle these great strokes of fortune with class. One after another, as players finished gorging themselves on pizza, they got up to leave the lunch tables without taking their trash with them to the garbage cans. When I admonished several players for getting up to leave without throwing their trash away, Pesho was the first to respond.

"Come on, Coach," he needled, though I sensed he was serious, "you don't really expect us to throw our trash away, do you?"

"Yes, I do," I curtly replied. "That's what civilized people do; they throw away their garbage."

"But, Coach," Pesho answered right away, "this is Bulgaria. We aren't civilized. We don't do these kind of things."

As much as it was popular to blame the garbage problems in Sofia on the mayor and the disgruntled garbage workers, it seemed to me they were just convenient scapegoats. Nearly everything Pesho said came with a smile, and a hint that he might be kidding. But in this case, he really wasn't kidding. He was surprised that I actually expected him to throw away his garbage.

In other instances, the throwing didn't represent the actual problem; the issue was where the garbage was actually being thrown. As the school's driver, Igor, had so eloquently told me on my arrival to the ACS campus, this was the nicest campus in all of Bulgaria, and I'd grown to see that he was right. While it could be unkempt when the grass wasn't cut and the stray dogs still ran wild, the campus was set amongst beautiful oak trees with a perfect view of Mt. Vitosha in the distance. Nearly all of my students would list the campus as one of things they loved most about going to school at ACS. And since I'd had the chance to compare it with the other public school choices, and see first-hand that most of the other buildings looked like prisons, I could certainly see their point. That said, though, the one thing that disturbed the beauty of the ACS campus the most was students littering their trash all over it. Though students were quick to acknowledge how fortunate they were to spend their days on a beautiful campus, they were also quick to use the lawn as their personal garbage cans. One Bulgarian tradition my students would inform me about that I was never able to embrace was the celebratory napkin toss. As a means of celebration and expression of joy, Bulgarians would take a large pile of napkins and throw them in the air, watching the paper napkins shower down like confetti. I was told this was a tradition in discotheques, but I'd also seen it happen in school. Of course, once the napkins were strewn all over the floor, it seemed blasphemous when I suggested the napkin-thrower pick them up. The whole fun of the celebration, this student told me, was that you didn't have to pick up the napkins; someone else would do it later.

The juvenile nature of the napkin-throwing bothered me, and it fit in with the general concerns I had about littering in general. The issue came to a head one afternoon in my second-floor classroom while my 11th grade class was studying poetry. In the middle of a partner project, one of my female students stood up from her seat and launched a candy bar wrapper out the window into the courtyard below. This was one of the most absurd things I'd seen. The girl was actually sitting only about four feet from the classroom's garbage can. But instead of throwing her garbage into the can, she turned toward the open window—at least twice as far away—and watched the candy bar wrapper flutter down to the grass below.

I was flabbergasted.

"What in the heck are you doing?"

"I ... uh ... what? It's not like it's a big deal," she shrugged.

"Not a big deal? Why in the world wouldn't you just throw that into the garbage can?"

"What?" she continued, feigning indifference. "It's not like it really matters. There's trash all over the place."

"If there's trash all over the place," I retorted, "then don't you think the country is dirty enough without you adding to the problem?"

The rapid-fire nature of our conversation—coupled with my continued frustration over the garbage issue—led me to cross a cultural line and immediately regret what I'd just said. Foreigners making generalizations about the entire country, even though this one might have been well-founded, typically didn't sit well with Bulgarians, or any people for that matter. And I usually put quite a bit of effort into not sounding exactly like how I'd just sounded.

"*Gaaawwwwwddd*," she groaned in response. "Why does everyone always tell us how dirty our country is? I'm tired of it. You're right, I shouldn't have thrown my garbage out the window, but everybody else throws their garbage wherever they want. I still don't see why it matters."

"Just because everyone else is doing it doesn't make it right," I told her, thinking of all the times I was annoyed as a child when my mother asked me if I'd jump off a bridge just because everyone else was doing it. "Come on, you're way smarter than that."

"But, Mr. Jones," came a voice from the other side of the room. Fittingly it was the biggest fan of napkin-showering. "I don't like what you said about Bulgaria being so dirty. I suppose you're going to tell us that America is really clean and there's no garbage on the ground?"

My regret over generalizing the entire country as dirty continued to grow with this comment, but I thought about what he said and had to respond.

"Well, America is pretty clean. I can tell you with a strong amount of certainty that while there are some dirty places, Americans generally throw their garbage in trash cans. They make an effort to keep things clean and looking nice."

"Hah," came a quick response from a student near the back of the classroom, his finger violently wagging from side to side, "I don't believe this. There's no way this is true."

With that, I decided that my point—whether it had been made or not—was best left to die, perhaps like the death the candy bar wrapper experienced floating out the window down to the ground. I chided myself for making vocal judgments about the entire country to an audience, but still couldn't believe that I was faced with such opposition from a class full of the smartest students in the country. There wasn't much I could say to convince them to respect their school and their country. To them, everyone else was littering, so why shouldn't they?

The one noticeable exception to this attitude was Svetla, sitting near the front of this class. As her classmates spoke of littering not being a big deal, she looked angered and started shaking her head—and this wasn't a Bulgarian head-shake, but a head-shake of frustration. I knew the prideful Svetla wasn't shaking her head because she agreed with her classmates.

Like many things in life, I realized that no matter what country you live in, people act based on their reliance on habits and traditions. In the case of Bulgaria, littering or just leaving trash wherever you chose was so widely accepted that it became habitual for Bulgarians, even my students and basketball players, who so many times represented the exception to Bulgarian rules. Similarly, while we'd made strides as a basketball team, we had also fallen into a comfortable habit: losing. I'd noticed that the level of disappointment over losses—which had been alarming at the beginning of the season—had dropped. This worried me because I didn't see it as a sign of maturity, but as a sign of the acceptance of losing, the last thing I wanted.

So it was good that we were invited to play in the tournament hosted by the Anglo-American School, the newer international school in Sofia. It wasn't just because of the good facilities and free pizza, but mostly because since the Anglo-American School was new, their oldest students were 10th graders. To enter into their basketball tournament, teams had to agree to bring no players older than 10th grade. In the case of most Sofia schools, this meant they would be bringing players who rarely played, and because they rarely played, they most likely rarely attended practice either. But in the case of my young team, I was bringing four of my regular players (Stefan, Pavel, Ivan and Pesho) to play in this tournament.

As a result, we dominated our Friday afternoon game, and I quickly learned that our deficiencies in other tournaments might have been glaring, but might also have a great deal to do with age. Tenth graders from these other schools were significantly smaller than our players, and also far less experienced since there weren't normal 10th grade or JV games. After Friday's victory, I pleaded with my players to have a responsible Friday night. This was something I realized that in the States would be a demand and expectation, not a desperate plea. When I encouraged this group of 15 and 16-year-olds to think about the three games we would be playing the next day and not drink tonight, I was immediately met with a series of protests:

"But, Coach—but, Coach—but, Coach…."

Happily, though, Ivan reported to me his plans for the evening:

"Coach, Coach, all my friends want me to go to a party, but I will not. I am going home. Isn't that good news?"

Without a doubt, I was learning to celebrate the little things in Bulgaria. And Pesho wasn't much different in this regard. When he showed up five minutes late on Saturday morning, he still managed to have a smile on his face.

"Coach, I know you say I must be on time, but this time I have a good excuse."

I stared blankly at him, pretty sure he would not have a good excuse.

"Coach, I was in the bathroom. I had to–you know, release the pressure. The beast, he is gone and now I am ready to play."

I trusted that Pesho actually was ready to play. We dominated both of our Saturday morning games, experiencing fun and enjoyment on the basketball floor that was completely foreign to the experience I'd had coaching in Bulgaria up to this point. After the second game–a game in which Pavel terrified smaller opponents by barreling directly at them, only to have them conveniently get out of his way every time–Pavel came up to me with his assessment on how we were doing:

"Coach, this feeling of winning," he said while pointing to his heart, "is ... *very nice.*"

Still stuck on the same *nice* adjective, I couldn't help but agree with Pavel. For all our hard work in practice and all of the effort we'd put forth against bigger and better teams, it was *very nice* to have some of this turn into wins. The 9th and 10th graders playing in this tournament were having a blast as we were winning by an average of 18 points. My biggest regret was that the 11th graders on the team couldn't have this experience. Menkov was still wondering if his belief in our team, his belief in my coaching, would ever be rewarded. Vassy's eye was purple and his confidence shaken. Kosio could make jump shots but was still afraid of contact. And while Dimov continued to run his mouth and display self-confidence, I knew that he, too, was depressed by the fact that we kept losing.

But for these 10th graders playing in a tournament against kids their own age, their concerns were of a different variety. After the pizza lunch–and after I'd made each of them properly throw away their garbage–Pavel was focused on the upcoming championship game. But his concerns were in a language that made no sense to me.

"Coach, I am worried, really worried. Do you think I should park the tiger on the rock before the game?"

"What? *Park the tiger on the rock?*"

This seemed to catch the attention of the entire team, who clearly understood the reference.

"Really, Coach?" Pavel was astounded. "You don't know what it means to *park the tiger on the rock*? Everyone knows that."

I wanted to point out that *everyone* should know to throw his garbage away, too.

"No, guys," I replied. "I have no idea what *parking the tiger on the rock* means. Please enlighten me."

"It means to throw up," Pesho jumped in quickly.

"Oh," I said, as I started to contemplate the tiger, the rock and how this related to vomiting. "Yeah, that makes no sense to me whatsoever."

"No, no, Coach," Pavel objected. "It makes a lot of sense if you think about it. You see, you have tiger … and you have rock … and you park it. Can't you see it, Coach?"

I definitely couldn't see it, and felt this was a cultural understanding that wasn't even worth gaining a higher appreciation for. I was more interested as to why he was thinking about throwing up in the first place.

"Pavel, do you feel sick?" I asked.

"No, Coach, but I'm worried about all the pizza in my stomach," he replied with consternation.

"The pizza won't hurt you," I reassured him. "You need something in your stomach; you'll be fine."

The look on his face showed that he wasn't convinced. He was still concerned about the lingering grease and carbonation from lunch.

"Look, Pavel," I continued to try, "throwing up—or parking the tiger—is not fun and I don't think it will make you play better. If you're not sick now, you're going to be fine during the game."

"Okay, Coach," he finally acquiesced, "but I try this for just first half. If I play bad first half, though, I am going to park the tiger at halftime."

Thankfully, for Pavel's stomach, esophagus and many other reasons, he played a great first half. So did the rest of the team. We won the game easily, just as we had won our previous games against 10th graders in this tournament, and had a trophy to take home as a result. It resembled a chalice and, of course, since it was Saturday night, my players wanted to take it home to drink from. Since there was no game for us the next day, it was more difficult for me to lecture them about appropriate behavior at night, but there was no way I was letting them take the trophy for their version of a celebration.

As we returned to practice on Monday after a weekend of celebration, I hoped this momentum would carry over to the rest of the team. The younger players were clearly excited by their tournament victory, and I planned to use their enthusiasm to push us forward as we reached the end of our season. Unfortunately, though, too many of my 11th graders were realists and shared their commentary about the weekend right away.

"Big deal," Dimov spouted. "So you beat a bunch of 10th graders. It doesn't mean anything until we start winning some *real* games."

I looked at Vassy, his eye still blackened, and his body language showed he agreed with Dimov. His eye wasn't going to start looking and feeling better because we won a 10th grade tournament. We needed to win a varsity tournament.

Soon enough we'd get our chance. My players would once again rejoice with the return of the weekday tournament; this time it was on a Tuesday morning. Our first game was scheduled for 8 a.m., a time that was usually seen as unrealistic for teaching the poetry of John Keats, and certainly not appropriate for an entire basketball tournament. This time the tournament was being hosted by a school in the center of Sofia, and since the game was scheduled so early, we planned to all meet at the gym at 7:30. Nikolai gave me directions to the gym, and I asked my students if they wanted the directions as well. They all told me this wasn't necessary; they'd been to the school before, and knew where it was.

So on this Tuesday, I braved early morning rush hour on the 76 bus to get to our game. Early morning rush hour in Sofia means there's a chance the bus won't move for periods of six to eight minutes at a time. As a precaution, I left home at 6:30 to head to a destination that was only three or four miles away.

But all criticisms of anything Bulgarian immediately dissipated when I walked into our latest playing venue. While I was expecting something along the lines of an oversized prison cell, what was laid out in front of me was incredible. There was a regulation-size court–probably twice the size we were used to playing on–a wooden floor that had just been swept, no floorboards or nails sticking out, and glass backboards–the first I'd ever seen in Bulgaria. The hoops even had nets. I stood at the corner of the court in awe; this place was amazing. My excitement levels rose as I thought about my team finally having a chance to play on a real and fair playing surface. I was elated and couldn't wait for this tournament to begin.

I was lost in this euphoric state of Bulgarian basketball heaven when I sensed something was about to ruin the moment. I looked down at my watch. It was now 7:40. Where was my team? They knew how much importance I placed on being on time. Why weren't any of them here?

I felt my phone buzzing in my pocket.

"Coach, where are you?" Menkov asked.

"I'm in the gym. Where are you?"

"We're all in the gym, too. But we don't see you anywhere."

As I looked around at a mostly empty gym, I now realized we had big problems. My elation over the playing conditions quickly evaporated. I would soon learn that while the tournament was being hosted by a Sofia school, the tournament was being played at a special gym, the unbelievably nice gym I was admiring. While I was at the gym, the site of the tournament, my team was at the school, the place they'd assumed the tournament was being played since this school was the host. After all the obstacles we'd faced this year, I felt like I was comfortable with always expecting the unexpected. Regardless, I now felt lost. I'd showed up for a game while my entire team was missing.

This left me to plead with the tournament organizers, who were currently getting things set up in the gym, to please delay the start of the game because the American coach unknowingly allowed his players to go to the wrong gym. At that moment, my team was hopping in taxis so they could rush across town and get to the correct gym. I tried to sound as helpless as possible in Bulgarian, and eventually gave way to English when I found someone who could understand me.

"I think it is okay," I was finally told by one of the tournament organizers. "We have no referees, we have no doctor, and they," he pointed to the other team that was beginning a loosely structured warm-up, "have no coach. I think it is okay you have no team."

For once, it seemed Bulgaria's lack of punctuality and efficiency was going to work out in my favor. My eyes were glued to the doors of the gym, anxiously awaiting my team to burst through them. The first of the missing persons to enter the gym, though, was the aforementioned doctor. She didn't give me much comfort. Her middle finger was wrapped in a massive splint and she had a blackened and swollen left eye. I quickly made a note to myself that if my team ever did show up, and if one of them got hurt during the game, I did not want to send them to this doctor.

I continued to wait for my team, and when they finally showed up, the game started soon after. Once the game started, unfortunately, I still waited for my team to show up. Seven minutes into the game, it was 17-0. I'd already called two timeouts to try to stem the tide, but neither had any effect to actually wake up my players. Whether their nerves were rattled by showing up late for the game, or the fact that we were playing in such a nice gym—I would later learn that this was the nicest gym in all of Sofia; Sofia's Bulgarian league basketball team played here—none of this mattered. We were getting annihilated out on the floor, once again by a more experienced and talented team. By the time halftime rolled around, we'd finally managed to score, but the deficit had increased: we were down by 21 points.

All the good vibes from the 10th grade tournament didn't seem to mean much on this morning, although I tried to use memories of that previous success to boost confidence for the second half. While Menkov (11th grade) had handled the ball well and Kosio (11th grade) had made several jump shots, Pesho (10th grade) reverted back to launching fadeaway jumpers that should've been power moves. Stefan (10th grade) was routinely having the ball stolen, and Pavel's (10th grade) power moves were going nowhere against players who weren't opting to get out of his way. The one thing I felt I could count on was the fact that our opponent most definitely wasn't taking us seriously any more. With a 21-point lead at halftime, there was little doubt about what our opponent expected from us in the second half: we were going to give up and fall apart.

I told this to my team at halftime, and told them we had a chance. The last thing they'd expect was for us to continue to play hard and come back. But that's exactly what we did.

Upon my instructions, Pesho started using his jumping ability to jump toward the rim, not away from it. He scored twice in a row down low. Menkov, knowing that our opponent no longer wanted to run back on defense, started pushing the ball every time he got it, sprinting down the court to earn easy baskets. Dimov and Stefan provided pressure in the backcourt and created deflections that turned into steals. The team on the floor was alive with excitement; the players on the bench couldn't believe we were coming back. With less than six minutes to go in the game, we'd cut the 21-point lead down to seven points.

Surprised and frantic, the opposing coach called a timeout. He could sense the game was slipping away from his superiorly talented team. They didn't seem to know how to flip the switch back on to play hard again, since they'd already assumed at halftime that they had this rag-tag team beaten. I continued to harp on playing hard and out-hustling them as my fired-up team huddled around me. But then I noticed that the scoreboard clock–this was only the second time all year we'd played using a scoreboard–was still running. Their coach had called a timeout, but seconds were still ticking away from the clock. He'd called a timeout with 5:50 remaining, and now the clock showed 5:12.

I rushed over to the referees and explained this very basically in Bulgarian. One referee immediately responded with *"Ne modje,"* while throwing his hands in the air, and then another confirmed that the clock would continue running. This was a timeout, and by definition–at least my American definition–timeout means the clock stops. But now the clock was ticking down under five minutes to play. I ordered my team back to the floor as quickly as possible and told them to be ready to go.

Our opponents meandered their way back onto the floor, and I looked over to their coach. He flashed me a cocky smile that seemed to say, "I know exactly what I'm doing." And I found out that this was exactly the case. His team failed to score, and we headed back down the floor against a team that had already run out of gas. Menkov drove to the right and found Vassy underneath for a layup. The lead was cut to five. Immediately, their coach called another timeout.

The clock now showed 4:24, but it kept on running. I didn't allow my players to come to the bench; I told them to stay on the floor because we were ready to play. I continued to plead with the referees to stop the clock. While many bizarre things had happened on the basketball floor during my tenure in Bulgaria, this had never happened, and this wasn't part of the rules. I said this over and over again getting response of *ne modje* and finally finger-wags telling me to shut up. All the while the opposing coach just kept smiling.

The game re-started a minute later and our opponents managed to score to push the lead back to seven points. Dimov hustled the ball down the floor, found Kosio in the corner 15-feet away, and he buried a jump shot. I knew what would happen next.

The opposing coach called a timeout.

Now it wasn't just me yelling at the referees. My players refused to head to the bench and continued to protest what was happening. I'd previously always had a rule that I would not allow my players to argue with referees, but in this case, I'd run out of Bulgarian exclamations and figured maybe something they'd say would make a difference.

It didn't.

All told, the opposing coach called four timeouts in the fourth quarter, essentially erasing four minutes–half the quarter–from the game. With precious time lost and our momentum crushed, the clock ran out on us; we lost by nine points. The opposing coach's broad grin widened as the horn sounded to end the game.

"Coach, I am frustrated, very frustrated," Menkov said to me as we sat in the bleachers waiting for our next game.

"I know, me too," I replied.

"I don't even want to think about what happened during that game."

"Me neither."

"Do you have something I can read?"

"Something you can read?" I said, surprised.

"Yeah, you're an English teacher. I figure you have to have a book in your bag, don't you? I just can't think about us losing games anymore."

Many of the experiences I was having in Bulgaria left me scratching my head, saying, "Wow, that's never happened before," and this fit right in with that general theme. But as I reached into my backpack and gave Menkov a book, I had no choice but to beam about this new experience. The best player on my team–a kid who loved basketball more than anything–wanted to read a good book in between games in a tournament. That was pretty cool.

I didn't think much about the book I gave him, other than the fact that it was good book that I thought he would enjoy. And I only had two books in my backpack, the two that I was currently teaching. But when I saw him start reading right away, I realized that the symbolism behind the title of the book I'd just given him was all too fitting: he was now reading Chinua Achebe's *Things Fall Apart*.

To have a chance to advance in the tournament, we'd have to win our second game, and thankfully we were more ready to begin the second game than the first. While I always worried we were on the verge of a meltdown reminiscent of Okonkwo's downfall in *Things Fall Apart*, in this game, we faced the French school—Bulgarian students who wanted to study French as their main foreign language—and the game started off competitively. In fact, at the end of the first quarter, we were down by two points. At halftime, we were down by two points. We were playing this game the same way we'd played the second half of the last game—with passion and hustle, like we had nothing to lose.

I'd talked about ensuring that the referees didn't have the power to affect this game; we needed to take it into our own hands. This was exactly what was happening. Menkov and Stefan were running and running—and running a clinic on the fast break, where most of our points were coming from. Our half-court offense still far too much resembled a kamikaze attack with players darting this way and that, so I continued to encourage my team to run. That was our best chance to score.

Kosio clearly preferred a half-court game. He had found convenient injuries to hold him out of running in practice all too often. But for Stefan and Menkov—two regulars at pre-season runs, and two I was convinced would be cross-country running stars if the sport existed in Bulgaria—were flourishing with the chance to push the ball. The same held true for Pesho who continued to be resistant to learning post moves, but loved to run and jump on the fast break.

We entered the fourth quarter with the game tied at 46. In all the games we'd played this year, we'd never entered the fourth quarter in a close game like this. We'd either be up by plenty, or much more frequently, down by plenty.

"This is our chance," I told the team in the huddle. "This is our chance to show that we're in great shape. We're physically fit and willing to work harder than they are in the fourth quarter. This is our chance to beat a good team in a big game. You want it more than they do, and now is our time."

I believed all the things I was saying, and honestly felt like we were going to win the fourth quarter. As the huddle broke with a loud, "TEAM!" I saw Menkov and Stefan start to hurriedly strategize on what to do to win this game. I felt confident. The players on the floor looked confident. Even the players on the bench, who too often looked unaffected, were loud and into the game.

And then things fell apart.

On our first possession, Stefan threw a pass to—well, no one in particular. This led to an easy layup on the other end. Menkov brought the ball back down the floor and put up a wild shot that wasn't even close. Pesho committed a foul on the rebound, his fourth. He had to come out of the game. At the other end, the French team quickly scored again. I thought about calling a timeout, but just told my team to calm down, we'd be fine.

But we weren't fine. Dimov turned the ball over on our next possession. Then Vassy sent an errant pass across the court that led to another fast break. Before I knew it, we'd given the ball away and given the French team a 10-point lead. That's the way the game would end. After a hard-fought close game for three quarters, we completely collapsed in the fourth and lost–again.

As we walked out of the gym, Menkov gave me back the book I'd lent him. I told him he was free to keep it if he wanted to.

"Coach, now I'm so frustrated I don't even want to read."

I accepted the book from him and put it in my bag. In the corner of my eye, I spotted Pesho tossing an empty water bottle on the sidewalk. I turned around and told him to pick it up and throw it in the garbage. Begrudgingly, he complied, and we all trudged to the bus stop together.

Chapter XV
Success—That is All

One of the staples of a season as an American basketball coach was dealing with the inevitable opinions parents have based on how the season was going. And especially if you were enduring a losing season– we certainly were in Bulgaria–American parents certainly had opinions on how things should be fixed. It would be these post-game greetings from parents–when I knew the greeting was just the beginning that I dreaded. After the perfunctory, "Tough loss tonight, Coach," this would undoubtedly be followed by, "You know, Johnny probably should've played more. That might've made a difference."

For all the trials and tribulations of coaching basketball in a completely foreign environment, this was one aspect of the Bulgarian experience that I had yet to experience. As our season was about to end –some would say mercifully–I'd only met one of my players' parents. Pavel's father was the only parent I'd met, as he was the only parent who had ever come to one of our games. I was thrilled he was there to support his son, but also aware that he was running a fledgling athletic apparel business. We still didn't have matching uniforms for all of our players, and he was hoping to sell us uniforms for next year. So I didn't pretend like his attendance at one of our games was completely altruistic and solely just to support his son. I asked my players why their parents never came to games–this seemed to be an incredible oddity to me—and got a whole host of responses.

Stefan told me his parents were doctors who worked long hours and couldn't make it to any school events. Menkov said his parents wanted him to focus on school, not basketball. Pesho's parents were getting divorced, and any time his parents were mentioned, he'd lose his normal cocksure attitude. I decided not to bring it up. Dimov's dad would drop him off in his black Mercedes but never stuck around for the games. Vassy had just moved out of his parents' house—at 16—so he could learn what it was like to live on his own. And Kosio's dad? Well, based on his status as a "businessman," I thought it better not to ask.

The grand sum of all these reasons and excuses just made some of our losses more difficult. When we walked out of gyms together, we walked out alone. There were no parents there to provide support—or even criticize the coach—and I wondered how aware these parents were of their sons' involvement in basketball. In some cases, I'm sure basketball was a focus of dinnertime discussion, but in others, I wondered if it even came up. I wondered how much more difficult it was for my players to stomach losing when we were basically playing an entire season without any fans. What we were doing—and in some respects, doing badly—only existed for us and no one else.

It wasn't until our last tournament of the year that parent involvement even became an issue. This was because we were headed to play our last tournament of the year in Thessaloniki, Greece, and in order for our student athletes to be able to leave the country, there was a laundry list of bureaucratic details that needed to be taken care of. For one weekend trip out of a country that I generally deemed to not have or follow rules, I was astounded by everything my players and their parents had to provide to make the trip happen:

- Two different permission slips authorizing their departure from the country
- Bulgarian ID
- Passport
- Two different medical checks (one by the school doctor who apparently couldn't be trusted because a different doctor's clearance was needed, too)
- A notarized declaration from a lawyer authorizing the crossing of the border
- A written promise to name their first-born child after the mayor of Sofia (Boyko)

And it was also my duty to make sure all these Bulgarian documents were in order so that we wouldn't face any difficulties crossing the Bulgaria-Greece border via bus. In the run-up to the tournament, a few of my players indicated they might have difficulty acquiring all of these necessary documents because their parents weren't really aware of their involvement in basketball. This further led me to understand how easy it was for my team to lose their sense of pride: there wasn't anyone at home who was backing them up, encouraging them.

With each new document that accumulated on my desk, I was getting more lost in Cyrillic Bulgarian legalese. Of course, as teenage boys are wont to, my team was full of suggestions for ways that we could skirt some of the regulations. They didn't actually need the notarized declaration, they'd tell me, or their ID card was enough–the passport wasn't necessary. With all of these theories swirling around my brain, I had no choice but to consult the Bulgarian athletic director about the nature of these regulations. A former water skiing champion in Bulgarian university, the athletic director Kaloyan was extremely friendly, but had clearly spent a lot more time on water skis in university than in English class. I had a lot of questions for Kaloyan regarding the upcoming tournament, but unfortunately, his responses were as unaccommodating as they were consistent.

"Kaloyan, can you tell me what time the bus is leaving on Thursday?"

"Andy," he looked at me seriously before responding completely, "we need *success*."

"Okay, Kaloyan," I answered, seeing if a different line of questioning would work. "Is there a schedule of games for the weekend?"

"Andy, we need *success*."

I thought I'd started out with some easy questions before I got to my real concerns, but this still wasn't helping matters.

"Kaloyan, can my players just bring their Bulgarian ID cards to their border, or will they need to show their passports as well?"

"*Success*, Andy, *success*–that is all," Kaloyan replied, gaining more confidence in his catch-all phrase.

At this point, it appeared that language barriers between Kaloyan and me were going to inhibit any form of successful conversation. I told my players they had better have everything possible ready for our border crossing.

And as we reached the border crossing, it was apparent that numerous athletes didn't have all their paperwork in order. You see, this wasn't just a basketball trip to Thessaloniki, but a trip that involved eight different teams from several different boys' and girls' sports. As several Bulgarian coaches assembled the paperwork for somewhere in the neighborhood of 75 kids as we rumbled toward the Greek border, it was clear that we had most of what we needed, but not everything. The Bulgarian coaches huddled and discussed how we should deal with our border crossing shortcomings, and I left them to have this discussion. If the school's driver Igor was with us, I figured he'd know how to fix this, and that they were probably having a conversation about whether we should pay them—or *pay* them. They seemed to come to some conclusions quickly, and as we reached the border I took out my passport to get ready for the border inspection by the Greek customs officers. But as I extracted my blue U.S. passport from my backpack, the girls' volleyball and tennis coaches (both Bulgarians) quickly reproached me.

"No, no, Andy," the tennis coach warned me, "This—this not good. You do not have passport. You must pretend to be Bulgarian."

Pretend to be Bulgarian?

"Yes, yes," the volleyball coach added, "you are Bulgarian; you must remember. You are Bulgarian—just act Bulgarian."

Just act Bulgarian?

All sorts of confusing and culturally insensitive thoughts ran through my head, but I also realized that I had to act quickly. The Greek customs' official had just entered our bus, and it was clear that these Bulgarian coaches were not joking. Apparently it was going to be easier for us to cross the border if I just showed my Bulgarian ID card, and therefore we were all the same nationality. But still, as I'd noticed nearly every day in my Bulgarian life, there was nothing about me that looked or acted Bulgarian. The Bulgarian boys' soccer coach then turned around to face me and tried his best to help.

"Don't worry," he said, "you almost look Russian. You could definitely be Russian."

So in my best attempt to look and act Bulgarian—or at least Russian—I just sat in my seat dumbfounded, not too eager to once again break a customs' law, this time with Greek customs. But as Kaloyan looked at me and gave me a smiling thumbs-up, I could tell that the *success* of our mission depended on me at this point. I handed the border guard my Bulgarian ID and didn't flinch. I didn't smile and showed no expression on my face; just stared straight ahead.

He handed my ID card back to me without incident, and after a meeting between a few coaches and border guards to explain why some of the paperwork was missing–"explain" is the official term I'll use, though I didn't ask what actually happened–we were through the border and into Greece. There was jubilation from all parts of the bus as we starting rolling smoothly on Greek highways, heading south to Thessaloniki.

The jubilation actually was warranted, not just because I doubted whether or not we'd be cleared to cross the border, but because many of the student athletes on the bus had never been to another country in their entire lives. This was astounding to me, if only because the Greek border we'd just crossed was a mere two hours south of Sofia.

Stefan fit into the group of those who had never left the country, and he was wide-eyed and incredulous as we entered Greece. The scenery didn't look any different, but the road signs used a new alphabet, and the smoothly paved road itself represented an entrance into a whole new world.

"I can't believe it, Coach," he was rapt with awe to everything going on around him. "Look at the roads. They're so nice–no potholes, no garbage. Wow, Greece is amazing."

I had to laugh at his pure and innocent enjoyment of things so simple, but I also had no choice but to agree with him. The minute we passed into Greece, there was no more garbage on the side of road, and the ride became very comfortable; there were no more bumps on the highway that bounced and jostled us around.

There were, however, plenty of bumps in the metaphorical road waiting for us once we arrived at the tournament. Though our school had brought eight teams to compete in the multi-sport tournament, we soon discovered that there wasn't actually a tournament for three of the teams that had come along for the trip. There was no girls' soccer, boys' tennis or boys' table tennis tournament being held this weekend. As the Greek athletic director communicated this in English to Kaloyan, I could see they were having the same language barrier issue that I'd been experiencing all throughout the process of preparing for the tournament.

"I just don't understand how this happened," the Greek athletic director said as he turned to me, realizing that I would understand his English without a problem. "We never advertised that we were having a tournament for these three sports. There is no reason that these teams ever should have come."

I looked at Kaloyan to see if he had heard what the athletic director had said. Clearly, he had, but I doubted that he understood it. I decided to focus on my team, which thankfully was participating in an existing basketball tournament, and let Kaloyan figure out what to do with the 30-odd kids who'd come on the trip to find out there wasn't actually a tournament for them to play in. I was reminded of my earlier conversation with Nikolai about having leagues in Bulgaria instead of always having tournaments. He said that Bulgarian coaches would never cooperate and organize these leagues. The Greek athletic director continued to look at me astounded by what had happened, and I wished Nikolai had been there to step in and explain things to him.

We began warm-ups for our first game, and even though there was a boys basketball tournament occurring, I started to wonder what kind of tournament this was going to be. It was common for me to look down at the other end of the floor and wonder if a Khrushchev-esque Bulgarian coach had brought 23-year-olds to play in a high school game. But in this instance, I had trouble believing that any of the opposing Greek players were in high school. They were huge and looked like a college team. With this thought in mind, I had no choice but to ask Kaloyan what was going on.

"Andy," he told me with a sigh, "I think we make small mistake. This tournament is college tournament. In Bulgaria, college is young students. Here, college is different."

What Kaloyan was saying—and I was able to figure it out relatively quickly—was that this was a university tournament. For our final tournament of the year, a tournament we'd been practicing for the last two weeks for, I had brought my struggling high school team to play a tournament against 20 and 21-year-olds, some of whom were on scholarship to play basketball at this college. While my school was the American College of Sofia, we were a high school. Our host school, the American College of Thessaloniki was an actual college. And that meant we were in big trouble.

We had showed up late for the first game because our bus driver got lost, but our Greek hosts were generous enough to give us time to warm up anyway. My players were dwarfed by these much larger university athletes, and I sensed they felt sympathy for us. I also sensed they were wondering, "What the hell are these high school kids doing here?" This was something that was most certainly running through my head as well. This was our last tournament of the year and our season would end in Greece. I'd been hoping to find some positives to finish with and maybe build momentum into next year. I knew we'd be playing in a nice non-caged gym–which we were–and thought that maybe we'd benefit from good gym conditions. But looking at a polished university team at the other end of the floor, I was already struggling to figure out how I was going to spin this positively.

To make matters worse, two days before the trip Menkov had gone up for a layup in practice and landed on a teammate's foot, spraining his ankle. He had to sit out the rest of practice. I had hoped that with ice and rest, his ankle would be okay for the weekend. But it wasn't; it was purple and swollen. I tried to assess the desperate situation laid out in front of me, but it seemed even more desperate with Menkov sitting on the bench in an air cast with his ankle elevated.

"Coach," he said to me glumly, "this is going to be a really tough game for us."

"Yeah," I told him honestly, "that might be an understatement."

"I'm really sorry I can't be out there."

"I know, but we're going to need all the help we can get in this game. Talk to guys on the bench and help them during the game."

Before we could get to the game, though, there was a pre-game ceremony where each of the Greek players came over to our players and gave them a gift–a souvenir from the school. This, I'd later learn, was the tradition for international tournaments, and my players were thrilled to get a pennant and a lapel pin from players on the other team. I was presented with a banner flag with the name of the Greek school. As the last of the gifts were handed out, my team all looked at me as if to say, "What do we do now?"

I had no answers for them. I knew nothing about this international tradition.

We had nothing to give them.

There was a pause during the pre-game ceremony as the Greeks waited for us to have a chance to give them gifts, but I signaled to their coach that we didn't have anything. It was an embarrassing way to start a game that I thought might be an embarrassment anyway.

At halftime, the score was 46-4.

As we rode home from the school to our hotel, I thought back to the game, reflecting, in amazement, that we'd been able to score 20 points in the second half. That had brought our total to a still-not-respectable

24 points for the game. Throughout it all, our team played hard and competed as best they could. But it was obvious there was no reason a game like this should have even be played. I tried to consider myself lucky that at least we had traveled six hours to Greece to an actual tournament, unlike the three other teams who didn't even get a chance to play. But for us, playing a tournament against university teams wasn't going to do much for our wavering confidence—or even my wavering confidence. Not much that had happened during this basketball season gave me cause to believe that things were looking up.

One thing I figured I could do to improve our participation in the next day's game was to follow the international tradition of giving gifts to the opposing team. I asked Kaloyan if he had anything we could give to our opponents to erase some of the embarrassment we had experienced earlier that day. He seemed to understand me for a change, thought about this for a moment, and then produced a bag from under his bus seat.

"Andy, Andy, we have gifts. We have gifts," he said enthusiastically. My spirits rose.

"Here," he said as he handed me the bag, "other teams love these."

I looked inside the bag and saw a bunch of No. 2 pencils with the American College of Sofia logo on them. At the bottom of the pile was a pamphlet and I took it out to examine it. It was a prospective student pamphlet given to the families of 7th graders in Sofia who might want to enroll their son or daughter in the school.

"This," Kaloyan pointed to the pamphlet, "you give to coach."

Looking at our potential gifts, I tried to smile and thank Kaloyan. I now had pencils to give to the opposing players and a prospective student pamphlet to give to the opposing coach.

In my reading about Bulgaria, I'd earlier come across a quote from Winston Churchill as World War II was getting underway. As Churchill had always been one of my favorite sources for inspirational quotes, I wondered what he had to say about Bulgaria. What I found, though, while it may have been insightful, certainly wasn't inspirational. Churchill "described the Bulgarians as a 'peccant people' and told Stalin [his ally at the time] that 'he could not give a damn about Bulgaria'." Maybe, I thought, that's because Churchill believed Bulgaria had little less to offer than some No. 2 pencils and a prospective student pamphlet.

Regardless, I thought it should be up to my team to vote on

whether or not we would hand out the gifts before our game the next day. The vote was quick and decisive: 10-0 in favor of not giving out pencils and pamphlets. They thought it would be too embarrassing to receive a pin and a flag and give a pencil in return.

So we geared up for day two of the tournament without gifts, but at least with an attitude that it couldn't get worse than yesterday. While the team was deflated from losing badly, they also realized that we weren't going to beat university teams. This softened the blow some, and then there were players like Stefan who had never left Bulgaria before this trip. Just being in Greece, regardless of the outcome of the basketball games, was worth it. I tried to look at it this way, too, and to my surprise, the entire team was dressed and ready in the hotel lobby at 7 a.m., ready to leave for the gym the next day. They had always had trouble with punctuality and I was impressed with their enthusiasm so early in the morning—and the fact that everyone was ready to go.

But there was one problem: it didn't seem we had a bus ready to take us anywhere.

As we headed outside to prepare to get on the bus, we couldn't find the bus.

We couldn't find the bus driver either.

I sent Menkov and Kosio back into the hotel to see if they could find the bus driver. They reported back to us that they'd found him—in his room asleep. Twenty minutes later—and overall, we were now 35 minutes behind schedule—the bus driver finally showed up with the bus. As he got out of the bus, I could tell from the stubble on his face, his yellowed teeth, and his mussed up hair that he hadn't had an early night. The bus stopped so all of us could get on. But before that could happen, the bus driver grumpily stumbled out of the bus onto the sidewalk. Without acknowledging anyone—or the fact that he was 35 minutes late—he lit up a cigarette and started puffing away.

I wanted to light into him about being so late and potentially causing us to miss the game, but as I approached him and his cigarette, all I could smell was alcohol emanating from his pores. As repulsed as I was by his behavior, I found myself even more repulsed by getting close to him. He smelled like he'd taken a bath in Greek ouzo. As I stood on the corner, my mouth agape, stunned by his lack of decorum, my players filed on the bus without incident, and seemingly without noticing any of it. I didn't need for Pesho to slap me on the shoulder and tell me, *This is Bulgaria, Coach. We are used to this.* Although we were in Greece for an international experience, I could see that Greece wasn't necessarily having a transformative effect on our bus driver.

The bus finally started chugging along and I looked at my watch realizing the hopelessness of our situation. The game was supposed to start in 20 minutes. The ride to the school was half an hour. None of our Bulgarian cell phones worked in Greece; there was no way we could contact the school to let them know we'd be late—and of course we'd been late the day before as well. None of this seemed to bother the bus driver who figured he was getting paid no matter what happened.

I, however, sitting at the front of the bus, was a nervous wreck. There was no way we were going to make it to the school on time, and this would be the second day in a row that had happened. Even worse, in my eyes, was the fact that my players had shown great respect for punctuality on both days—and on both days they were let down by our bus driver who was far more concerned with booze and cigarettes than anything else. This proved to be even truer when, 25 minutes into our ride, he turned to the Bulgarian girls' tennis coach who was on the bus with us and raised his hands in the air. Even though we'd driven from our hotel to the school yesterday, he couldn't remember the route. He was lost.

"*Ne modje, ne modje!*" he was hollering, indicating that it was impossible to find the school.

I was now fuming, in disbelief that our bus driver was late because he was hungover, and now couldn't even do his one and only job—drive us to the school. His repeated *ne modjes* didn't seem to stem so much from frustration as perhaps his desire for us to say it was okay to go back to the hotel and just forget about the tournament all together. That way he could get some sleep—or some more booze.

My frustration got the best of me and I started telling him in Bulgarian that we needed to go to the school now; he needed to do his job. I was cut off, though, by the Bulgarian girls' tennis coach, who was eager to assuage my concerns and calm my burgeoning rage.

"Andy, Andy," she stopped me, speaking English, "don't worry about being late for the game. Everything will be fine."

I appreciated her attempt to calm me down, but didn't see how it was logical.

"I don't see how everything will be fine. We're almost a half an hour late, and we're lost. In the States, if you're late like this, you have to forfeit the game. You don't even get a chance to play."

"Yes, Andy," she replied with a smile, "but everything is different here. There are no forfeits; this does not happen here. Everything will be fine."

I liked her optimism, but I still wasn't sold.

"I understand the way things work in Bulgaria," I told her, "but this isn't Bulgaria. This is Greece."

"Trust me," she continued, "everything will be fine. They will wait for us."

When the bus driver was finally was able to find his way to the school, we were an hour late for the game. The Greek athletic director met us at the doors of the gym, and told us that because we were so late, the tournament had already moved on. We'd forfeited the game.

Not surprised, but certainly angry, I turned in the direction of our bus and saw the bus driver idly leaning on the bus, smoking another cigarette. The girls' tennis coach started to protest our forfeit; she was clearly dismayed that we'd have to forfeit a game that we showed up an hour late for. While she spoke to the athletic director, she looked to me to continue to protest, but then realized I wasn't going to say anything. What could be said? I thought. We were an hour late, and everywhere other than Bulgaria, the result of being that late would be a forfeit.

My dejected team sauntered over to a couple park benches outside the gymnasium. I started getting a new education in Bulgarian swear words as they directed them at our bus driver. I tried to think of how this could possibly become some kind of teachable moment. But unfortunately, this was just the same as so many other moments I'd had with my team during this year. They had done nothing wrong. They'd done exactly what I'd asked them to do, and in this case, they'd been ready at 7 a.m., eager to go play a game against a university team that was probably going to run them over. But once again, they'd been thwarted by forces—Bulgarian forces—far outside of their control. As a result, we all sat on the benches together, muttering under our breaths.

A few minutes passed and the Greek athletic director reappeared. He was the last person I wanted to talk to. I already sensed how he viewed our team and our whole school. To make matters even worse, he then started telling us how he viewed our team and our whole school.

"You know, we have a saying in Greece," he said, pausing for effect. "When you are wrong once, you are wrong; this happens. But when you are wrong twice," he continued, clearly alluding to us being late the previous day and bringing several teams that weren't even scheduled to participate, "this makes you stupid. You have been wrong, wrong, wrong—many times. In Greece, we would say this makes you very, very stupid."

I just looked up at him as he finished his commentary, but didn't have anything to say. While having salt rubbed into the wounds was never fun, it wasn't like I could disagree with him. I thought of a line from Kapka Kassabova's memoir where she considered how other countries looked at Bulgaria. She felt that "the rest of Europe looks to the Bulgarian 'kingdom' with either indifference or condescension." The athletic director's biting words didn't represent indifference, but I felt plenty of condescension raining down on us.

The athletic director walked away, but his words didn't sit well with Pesho.

"Coach, Coach," he said urgently, "I will not accept this. He cannot say things like this. You want me to go kick his ass?"

Before I could correct Pesho, Pavel piled on as well.

"He can't say things like that to you, Coach. We will take care of this. Let's go kick his ass."

If there was one positive I could take from this, it was that Pesho and Pavel understood the nature of team: we stood up for one another. Vassy and Dimov seemed ready to join them, too. But in this case, the last thing in the world we needed was for them to start a physical altercation with the Greek athletic director. I'd certainly never had any of my players threaten to beat up an adult, so I mentally composed my thoughts on how to best explain why this wasn't appropriate. But Stefan came to my rescue before I could even say anything.

"Guys, why would we go beat him up?" he questioned. "Everything he said was true."

With this, Pesho and Pavel looked Stefan and slowly realized that he was right. I nodded my head, wishing that both the athletic director and Stefan weren't correct, but knowing full well that they were.

Pesho and Pavel eased up from their ready-to-strike poses and slumped back onto the bench. I once again looked back to the bus and this time the driver was no longer smoking cigarettes. He was in the driver's seat, his head down on the steering wheel, asleep.

"I really don't like this feeling," Pavel said. "I don't like what happened today. I just feel–I just feel … very helpless."

With this, we all slouched a little farther down on the benches.

My first season as a Bulgarian basketball coach ended with a forfeited game in Greece. The last game we played was 5-on-5 on a blacktop outdoor court we found on the campus of the school. Our bus wasn't scheduled to return to the hotel until the afternoon, so I figured we should at least find some kind of game to play. Thankfully—and this is one of the best things about 16-year-old boys from any country—once we started playing on the blacktop courts, they got immersed in this game and seemed to forget about the fact that we'd been forced to forfeit the real game we came here to play.

Pesho was jumping all over the place, still refusing to make the power post moves I'd tried to teach him all year. But when he finally hit a 14-foot fadeaway jumper, he let out a scream of celebration, then turned to me.

"See, Coach, see Coach," he grinned. "I told you I can make that shot."

Stefan, playing as if this game mattered more than any other, was blowing by his defenders and finishing at the rim. Ivan didn't have to worry about making free throws, and he seemed much less nervous. Kosio was free to shoot threes without my watchful eye telling him to play strong and go to the basket. Dimov's mouth was running as he whipped the ball behind his back, between his legs and every which way—all things I would've told him not to do. Vassy was still grinding—undersized on any team against any defender, but still not aware of it. Even Menkov, hobbling on one good ankle and joining in during breaks in the game, was laughing as he tossed prayers toward the hoop from 20 feet away. None of them were going in.

I sat in the grass on a hill just behind the court watching it all. With each new basket, each new missed layup, and each new terrible basketball decision, there were roars from my team, some of celebration, some of derision. But in each separate case, the roars were followed by broad smiles from all of my players. They were laughing; they were having fun.

From where I was watching, I could see a whole lot of bad basketball in front of me. It didn't appear to look that different from the day I sat on the sideline and watched my first open gym. But it definitely sounded different. The loud Bulgarian yelling and cajoling didn't express frustration or anger; the cheers and jibes represented friendship and happiness. The teasing and celebrating was immature and befitting of teenage boys, but it showed me that maybe we had accomplished one thing this season: we had a team. We had a team that liked playing together and liked each other.

By all normal standards, my first season in Bulgaria would be judged as a miserable failure. We lost a lot of games, and perhaps lost a lot of hope along the way. We still didn't play anything that a basketball coach would describe as good, fundamental basketball. We'd been beaten down by neo-Nazis and dunked on by university teams. I'd grown frustrated with far too many things I'd learn would become part of the mosaic that was Bulgaria. But it was all part of the experience—all part of the experience that led me to sit on the grass and watch my team enjoy playing basketball together.

I laughed as Pesho tried to call a foul on his latest ridiculous fadeaway attempt and was rebuffed by nearly everyone out on the court. He looked to me to see if I would help him out, but I just shook my head—and made sure he knew I was shaking my head to say no. Menkov limped over to my spot on the grass, finally realizing that his ankle just wasn't fit for any version of basketball.

"It's a lot fun out there, Coach," he said. "It's too bad we couldn't play in the real game, but this game is a lot of fun, too."

For all the times I wondered if we were playing "real" games in Bulgaria, his comment couldn't have been more fitting. As my first season of Bulgarian basketball came to a close, I sat in the grass with Menkov and watched Pavel barrel to the basket and chuck a shot up off the backboard that ricocheted back to the three-point line.

Menkov and I looked at each other and laughed.

SEASON TWO

Chapter XVI
A New Start

"Wow, this really doesn't look like basketball," he said in stunned fashion.

I just laughed.

"Seriously, that kid is wearing ripped jean shorts. The one with the Megadeth t-shirt–his hair is covering his face; he can't even see where he's going. And that kid, he's playing basketball in loafers. This is truly ridiculous."

Sensing he was finished for that particular moment, I decided to weigh in.

"I tried to prepare you for this," I said sheepishly.

"I know," he replied. "But this is pretty incredible. Look at all these Eastern European bad-asses; half of them look completely pissed off. Or at least they're pretending to be pissed off." With this he paused. "But maybe there's plenty to be pissed off about. The basketball being played out there on the floor is terrible."

Again, I laughed.

"I know, I know, but relax. It will get better. This is only open gym."

Michael Branch had emailed me toward the end of my first basketball season indicating he was interested in helping out with the basketball program. Like me a year earlier, he'd been hired by the American

College of Sofia to teach English, and he'd heard there was a basketball team—one that he hoped to be a part of. Branch was from Northern California and had emailed me to say he loved coaching and was interested in infusing his belief in teamwork and hustle into Bulgarian basketball players. Upon receiving his emails, I was elated at the thought of getting an assistant coach for my second year in Bulgaria. There was no shortage of things I could use help with, and I'd be lying if I didn't say that I thought my Bulgarian basketball sanity stood a better chance of leveling out if I at least had another witness to what I was used to seeing on a regular basis on the basketball floor.

But Branch still wasn't completely sold, and before I'd met him, he emailed me saying, "I want to help coach, but I'm really committed to teaching English, too. I'm wondering how much of a time commitment coaching is? How much does it distract you from teaching?"

It took me a while to compose an adequate response to this because my experience as a Bulgarian basketball coach had been the single greatest distraction from teaching I'd ever had in my life. It wasn't that the time commitment was unmanageable, but more so that every new day of basketball seemed to flip my world upside down. I tried to express this sentiment in my response to Branch, and thankfully he didn't seem scared off. By the time I met him when he arrived in Sofia in late August, he was eager to become part of the basketball program.

I thought a good way to introduce him to Bulgarian basketball in general would be to invite him to the weekly adult game I played in on Wednesday nights. Well, originally it was just a game I played in, but as time wore on, it was a game that I was hosting. We played in the ACS bubble every Wednesday night, and typically I was able to recruit some other American teachers to play as well. As my second year rolled around, though, it was not uncommon for me to be the only American, and the one in charge of the gym, playing with 11 or 12 Bulgarians. I brought Branch with me to help create some kind of cultural balance, and I also thought this might give him some insight into just what kind of "distraction" he was in for by becoming involved in Bulgarian basketball.

"Good evening, Andy," came the slow Dracula drawl English from one of the stocky Bulgarian Wednesday night regulars. "Tonight will be different game. You LA Laker, and me Detroit Piston. I play Detroit ball tonight. Detroit ball—Bad Boys."

He finished his declaration with a smile—a rare Bulgarian smile—but I still wasn't entirely sure he was joking. Maybe he wasn't sure either.

"Tonight, you shoot. Nice shooting is okay. But if you drive," he paused, pressing his right fist into his left palm, "you get hurt. Detroit ball—Bad Boys."

Again, he found this uproariously funny, and I played along. Branch tried to as well, but this clearly was not a friendly, Western way to start a pickup basketball game. Then as the game got underway, Branch got a glimpse at the normal progression of events for Wednesday night basketball. While the game itself might've seemed disorderly and chaotic at times, there was a certain rhythm to things—a pattern that was followed pretty closely based on what happened out on the floor:

When a shot was missed? Several loud swear words in Bulgarian would follow.

When a bad pass was thrown? Hands were raised to the heavens with more shouting.

When the other team scored a basket? Requisite yelling at whomever was deemed to be at fault.

When a foul was called? This is when the real yelling would start, or even better, soccer would come into play. A tried-and-true method of Bulgarian protest was taking the ball and punting it the length of the floor.

I wanted to be surprised, shocked or appalled by any of this behavior, but it was nothing new to me. What I attempted to prevent my players from doing during our practices and games were exactly the same things I witnessed up close and personal every Wednesday night when I played basketball with a group of adults who certainly should've known better. I started to figure out a formula for having success in the Wednesday pickup games: the team that yelled at each other the least usually seemed to have the most success. The teams that chided, hollered and criticized seemed to self-destruct much sooner. Whenever I was in charge of picking teams, I made sure my team was stacked with the quieter, calmer version of Bulgarians—and we usually won.

So Branch had already experienced Bulgarian basketball as a Wednesday night player. But that didn't completely prepare him for his first open gym. Now that I was embarking on the second year of my Bulgarian adventure, I tried to tell myself that I was prepared for just about anything. But after a month-long summer holiday in America, my return to Sofia for the beginning of year number two threw me for a loop.

When I arrived back in Bulgaria in August, it was a warm and humid and my house had no running water. I'd contacted everyone I could think of from the school—they owned the house—to try to find a solution. Not having drinking or showering water was not exactly the welcome home present I'd been hoping for. And it was especially hard to take after having spent four weeks in the functional United States.

After the second day without water, I talked to the school's Bulgarian director of human resources. She'd been able to contact Sofiiska Voda, our trusty water supplier. She had asked nicely in many different ways if it would be possible for them to turn the water back on in our house. The first answer she received was, "We will not come out to help with the water, but we will send you a letter."

When she relayed this message to me, I asked her if it was possible for her to call back again. The prospect of receiving a letter to explain why we didn't have water might provide a little Bulgarian peace of mind, but it wasn't going to do anything to actually help us get water. So she called back again, and I asked her what happened this time.

"I asked for help," she told me, "and all they did was start yelling. Just yelling, yelling, yelling."

This at least seemed more promising than receiving a letter, I thought.

"Finally, I broke down," she continued, "because I couldn't take the yelling anymore. I just said, 'what can I possibly do to get you to help us?'"

"Okay, so what did they say to that?" I asked anxiously.

"Their answer was one word," she said stoically. "Beg."

Beg?

Sweaty and thirsty as I was, I felt like I was in a begging mood myself, and I had to ask, "Well, did you beg?"

"Yes," she said quietly. "I cannot believe it came to this. But I begged and begged. I hope this will make a difference."

Three days later, the water was turned back on.

It was entirely possible that the begging had worked about as quickly as it could. Bulgaria, as I'd learned, was not a place where things changed or got fixed very quickly. Even when the Soviet version of communism came to an end in the rest of Eastern Europe, Bulgaria democratically re-elected the same communists who had been running the country for the second half of the century. This was one of the reasons why I knew the changes to the basketball season I wanted to propose weren't necessarily going to be met with open arms. When I explained to Branch several of the things I wanted to do for the upcoming season, his response was simple: "Yeah, all that makes a lot of sense."

But Branch was a curly-haired laid-back guy from California. Everyone I would be talking to about making changes would be Bulgarian. I knew this wouldn't be easy. But as I headed into Bulgarian basketball season number two, I'd already formulated a game plan on how to make the season more manageable and productive—both for my players and myself.

My previous American teams had all experienced difficulties playing away games in other gyms. But nothing compared to what it was like going to other Bulgarian gyms, cages or prisons—however they were most accurately described. And it wasn't just the gyms themselves that presented the problems; it was what came with it: no scoreboards, swastika tattoos and referees smoking cigarettes. So I decided that we could make Nikolai's dream of having a schedule set at the beginning of the year a reality: we'd host a different team at our gym every Wednesday to ensure that we played at least one game a week. Perhaps even more importantly, this would give us control over which teams we invited, and also how much the referees were going to be smoking (not at all was my preference).

This idea went over well with Nikolai and my players, but Nikolai had words of caution for me.

"Andy, does this mean you do not want to play in the city tournaments? I understand why you don't want to, but you have to know that this is tradition for our players. They are going to be very upset about this."

He was exactly right. Even though I was providing a schedule with at least one game a week—in contrast to my asking Nikolai three to four times a week when the next Bulgarian city prison tournament was starting—this differed from what my players were used to.

"But Coach," Kosio crowed, "how can we not play in the Mladost tournament?"

"Yes, Coach, I don't understand," Dimov continued. "What about the Third of March tournament? *Everyone* plays in this tournament."

I was tempted to ask who *everyone* was, especially since the gyms for both of those tournaments didn't seem large enough to fit the 10 players from both teams. In the end, I let my players have their say, but told them things were going to change; they were going to have to adapt.

Not taking the Greece trip was a no-brainer, since we didn't belong in a university tournament, so I sought out a different international trip for our second season. And one change I made that was received well by everyone on the team was the timing of our tournament, the ACS Open.

"I don't want our biggest event of the season to be at the beginning of our season," I told the team. "We weren't playing our best basketball last year in December, but we got a lot better by the end of the year. So this year, we're going to schedule the ACS Open as our last tournament in March."

For the first time during the meeting, this idea wasn't met with Bulgarian bickering. Most seemed to be in favor of the idea, and liked finishing with our biggest event of the year. There was, however, an issue that was raised.

"Coach, I like this idea," Menkov said, "but what if the dates of the ACS Open conflict with the dates of other tournaments?"

"Well, Menkov, here are the dates for the ACS Open," I responded as I wrote them on a white board. "We've already told other schools that these are the dates almost five months in advance. Do you think any of the other tournaments already have their dates scheduled?"

With this, several people in the room started laughing.

"Exactly," I grinned. "So hopefully they will schedule around us—whenever they get around to scheduling."

As the after school meeting ended, I said that I expected them all to be at the first pre-season running of the year, the following Monday. Just like my previous comment about the other schools scheduling ahead of time, this was met with some laughter. Pesho had already begun his protest before I'd even finished speaking, and I sensed that Kosio's hamstring was tightening up just at the mention of running.

When the following Monday came, I once again led a small group of dedicated runners as we geared up for the season. Menkov, Ivan and Vassy were some of the first ones to arrive for running, and I didn't know if it was even necessary to ask about Pavel, Pesho, Dimov and Kosio. Sasho's hand was healed now, though, and he kept my mind—or at least my ears—busy by telling me all about the book he was reading in English class. His chattering distracted me from the fact that half of the team's core was missing. Even more important than those who had chosen not to come was the absence of one player who wouldn't be coming at all.

Stefan had won a year-long scholarship for his junior year to a boarding school in the United States, and was fulfilling his dream to explore and see the world while getting an American education. I couldn't have been more excited for him, and couldn't think of any player or student I knew who was better suited to tackle life in the States. But on a selfish level, his absence was already starting to eat away at me. He was the team's best defender and most fearless player. He never missed practice, never missed a pre-season run, never yelled at his teammates, and rarely ever seemed to lose confidence in himself. He already had many of the attributes I was trying to teach to the rest of the team, and as we started our first two-mile run of the year, I was sad he wasn't with us.

At the same time, on the other end of the Atlantic Ocean, Stefan was using all he'd learned from pre-season running and basketball the year before to become a star on his new American high school's cross country team.

Branch's introduction to Bulgaria probably wasn't too different from mine, though instead of always experiencing things on his own for the first time, he had me there to explain—or at least try to explain what was going on. When Kosio showed up for running one day with a brace on a different knee saying he'd "re-injured" it and couldn't run that day, I was able to explain to Branch the trials and tribulations I'd had trying to get him to run at any time. When Sasho delayed his lumbering two-mile run every week by talking incessantly about Atticus Finch from *To Kill a Mockingbird* or George, Lennie and rabbits from *Of Mice and Men*, I told Branch that Sasho probably belonged in a small, rural U.S. settings with all the heroes of his favorite novels. And when Menkov took more of a leadership role, encouraging other guys to show up for running, and demanding they run as hard as they could, I pointed out to him that our fate as a team this year would probably have a lot to do with Menkov's ability to lead.

But as Branch moved into his new Bulgarian apartment about a mile from the school and told me of his first encounter with one of his Bulgarian neighbors, I wasn't able to offer much of an explanation. This was Bulgaria, after all.

During the move-in process, Branch and his wife had placed some of their things in a basement storage unit until they figured out exactly where they would fit in their apartment. They'd locked the storage unit and assumed all would be well until they returned to the basement with a plan for all of their excess stuff. But when they returned, they quickly discovered this was not the case. The lock they'd used to secure their belongings was no longer there. In its place was a note written in Bulgarian. Attached to the note was a skull-and-crossbones sticker.

After much deliberation and many attempts to translate the note, they discovered that it directed them to an upstairs apartment in their building. Branch and his wife obsequiously followed the note's instructions and marched up to the top floor. After knocking on the door, they were greeted by a large Bulgarian man with giant gold chains around his neck. He sneered when he saw who was at his door, and encouraged them to come inside. Unsure whether he was sealing his Bulgarian death sentence or not, Branch entered the apartment and immediately saw all the boxes that were missing from their storage unit.

Although very little intelligible conversation occurred among the three of them, Branch and his wife started grabbing their boxes. They had no idea why this man had emptied their storage unit to begin with, and nothing about him seemed like this was done due to some misguided sense of good Samaritanism. As Branch carried the last box out, the gold-chained Bulgarian continued to bellow with laughter. Branch and his wife were slightly terrified, though relieved they'd been able to retrieve their belongings from their intimidating Bulgarian neighbor.

As they were about to leave from what would end up being their one and only visit to this neighbor's apartment, the gold-chained man found some basic English to conclude this episode.

"*Americanski, Americanski,*" he jeered at Branch and his wife in his version of English. "You stupid *Americanskis*. I want to teach you lesson. I teach you lesson."

With this, the bellowing continued and Branch and his wife hurried downstairs with their boxes. Even though the storage locker was listed on their lease as part of their apartment, they never used it again. There seemed to be no reason for what had happened, other than their neighbor wanting to intimidate them. While I wasn't with Branch when it happened, he was able to tell me the story, shrugging it off and laughing—a Northern California character trait highly necessary for living a happy life in Bulgaria.

"I don't know, man," he told me afterwards. "This guy was huge— and he looked half-pissed and half-psychotic. I have no idea why that happened, but he certainly thought it was funny to try to scare the Americans."

"Well," I responded, "I'm sorry this happened, but it probably won't be the only time here that you end up in a scary situation."

"Yeah, you're probably right," he said, still going over the whole situation in his mind. "Something tells me that living here is going to be pretty crazy."

With this last comment, I felt like there were about 25 other stories I needed to tell him just to make sure he was fully prepared for life in Bulgaria.

Chapter XVII
A Bunch of Strays

One lived on my front porch and three lived on the back porch. Mama Dog, as she was called, had grayish-black fur and gold eyes that always shone in the dark. She had been living on campus for somewhere in the neighborhood of the last 10 years. The three strays on the back porch, though, were new. They had scraggly gray fur and seemed to be getting bigger by the day. They'd only been born last year–by the police checkpoint front gate–and they made their way to my back porch one day because they could smell food cooking in the kitchen. Seeing three hungry dogs patiently watching me, hoping for something to eat, I couldn't resist and tossed some of my dinner out into the grass. This convinced them that they'd found a place to stay, and it seemed that territories had now been marked. Mama Dog owned the front porch, and the three strays controlled the back porch. Whenever I came back to the school at night, Mama's keen sense of smell led her to know I was coming from a mile away. She'd routinely come sprinting across campus and make her way to the gate to find me. On the one hand, this would provide further proof for why dogs were a man's best friend. And it was nice to see Mama galloping to the gate, ready to walk me home for the night. But the trouble came when Mama attracted more attention than I hoped for.

Mama on my front porch and three strays on the back represented only a small part of the population of stray dogs on the American College of Sofia's campus. And these were the only four stray dogs that I *wasn't* afraid of. Normally at night, if I was walking from one house on campus to another, I'd take a tennis racket with me to ward off any dogs that might start snarling and charging. (I would never hit a dog, but just wave the tennis racket in their general direction.) Other American teachers made a habit of not going anywhere on campus or in Sofia without having some stones and rocks in their hand, ready to fling at the dogs if necessary. All told, there were close to 15,000 stray dogs in Sofia—and most of them were hungry. There seemed to be nowhere you could go without seeing stray dogs, and there were few places you'd go without growing worried they might charge you.

If I was coming home at night from dinner or drinks, I wouldn't have my tennis racket with me. And most times, I hadn't stooped down to pick up a handful of stones either. By the time Mama Dog would reach me, she'd be panting and waiting to be petted, then eager to head back home together. But that usually meant that behind Mama Dog there was a cacophonous pack of strays, teeth flaring, eager to join the action. On most nights, I'd walk home with Mama and just listen to the sound of their barking, howling, yelping and gnashing. But other nights, I'd see their white teeth flare in anger, unsure about whether they wanted to attack Mama Dog or me. At no point during any of these walks did I feel safe; I just felt a great sense of relief once I'd walked across campus and into my front door unharmed.

One day, a mere 10 minutes after school had let out, the stray dog issue came to a head when two entire packs of dogs got into a vicious fight on campus. What I watched was akin to a seven-on-seven rugby match where biting was encouraged. Several dogs left the brawl bloodied and limping. Many students were terrified by the all-out dog war they'd witnessed just outside their chemistry classroom. A few weeks later, several stray dogs ganged up on an American teacher's pet cat. The guards who patrolled campus attempted to ward off the strays, but their attempts were too little, too late. The cat had been killed.

This prompted the president of ACS to instruct Americans living on campus not to feed stray dogs. By giving them food, we were only encouraging them to stay, he said. His logic was definitely right, but the truth of the matter was that the Americans on campus were only feeding about 10 percent of the dogs who frequented the campus. There were so many strays around that there was no way we could even feed half of them. The president's next move was an attempt to deal with the problem much more directly: he gave the Bulgarian guards shotguns to shoot any dogs that posed a violent threat to people on campus.

Having guards on campus walking around with shotguns enhanced my notion that I was living in *1984*. But I did hope the guards with guns would at least create a sensation of security—a "you don't have to worry anymore," kind of feeling. These middle-aged men, though, didn't inspire a lot of confidence in me. They usually had about half of their teeth remaining. While on duty they were frequently asleep, sometimes drinking Bulgarian *rakia*, and other times trying to peep in female teachers' windows. I quickly realized that armed with shotguns, these guards made me even more worried than I had been about the stray dogs. I felt more confident that a bullet would hit me before one ever hit a dog. As a result, when I came home at night, I muttered a quick, "*Dober vecher*" (Good evening) to whichever guard was on duty, put my head down and hurried along my way.

There were many theories as to why there were so many stray dogs in Sofia. I'd heard people tell me that once again, *democratsia* was to blame. People were no longer afraid of communist authorities, and rules didn't apply to them. If they wanted to get rid of their dogs, they just stopped feeding them until the dogs eventually went away. Sometimes when food was scarce in the house, feeding a dog fell pretty low on the scale of priorities. To add to the problem, there was no central agency that took care of animals in the city. There was no dog pound, mostly because Sofia city officials didn't want to spend money on animals when so many people were in need. The result of both politicians' and individual citizens' lack of care for these animals was a chaotic city where stray dogs roamed all day and night. The dogs could be seen simply as a fear-causing nuisance that would perhaps raise your blood pressure a little. But the overall level of fear was raised significantly after a woman took her dog out for a walk one afternoon.

Ann Gordon, a 56-year-old British woman, had moved to Bulgaria to retire with her husband two years earlier. She and her husband had been attracted by the cheap real estate prices, and liked Bulgarian culture. She developed a daily routine, walking her dog Alsatian in a park near her house. But this part of her daily routine hadn't come without danger. Three times she'd been bitten by stray dogs as they lunged at her and her dog. Each time she'd complained to neighbors and tried to register complaints with local officials, but each time she'd been ignored. Her last run-in with stray dogs, though, would not be ignored. It was impossible to do so.

A neighbor and witness to the attack described what she saw from a distance as "the most terrible thing I have ever seen." As Gordon was walking with Alsatian, they were met by a pack of eight dogs, "big, slavering dogs with jaws flashing rows of teeth." It didn't take long for the feral dogs to overcome Gordon, who was on the ground quickly. As described by the neighbor, "the first cut sent them into a frenzy as they tasted and smelled blood." The neighbor rushed over to try to intervene, but could not move very quickly since she needed a walker to help support her failing knees. By the time she reached Gordon, the stray dogs had started to run off, blood smeared all over their mouths. Ann Gordon had been mauled. "The poor, poor woman was like a bloodied rag doll, totally unrecognizable," her neighbor commented.

Her husband, alerted by some children in the neighborhood, rushed out to his wife. By the time he reached her, though, all he could do was hold her in his arms. She was dead.

Another neighbor and friend pointed out what had been obvious to most people in Sofia for a long time when she said, "These dogs have been a problem for some time but no one ever does anything about it."

This killing of this British woman—a woman who had learned to speak Bulgarian and immersed herself in Bulgarian culture because she enjoyed the country so much—made international headlines. With the international headlines, Bulgarian authorities were forced into action—at least some kind of action. They passed laws that mandated that all stray dogs be off Sofia's streets by 2011. Without offering any ideas or funding for how the dogs should be taken care of, they passed laws that dictated that the official in charge of each borough would be fined 2000 Bulgarian *leva* (about 1300 U.S. dollars) for any stray dog found within the borough's boundaries. For repeat offenders—dogs found more than once—the fine rose to between 3000 and 4000 Bulgarian *leva* (between 2000 and 2750 U.S. dollars). If these laws were actually enforced based on the number of strays in Sofia, the Bulgarian government would end up collecting somewhere in the vicinity of 40 million Bulgarian *leva* (27.5 million U.S. dollars) —every day. This solution was tough-sounding, but no one in Bulgaria seemed to remotely consider that these laws would actually be enforced. As a result, with no tenable plan to deal with the dogs other than unrealistic fines, it was clear that these new policies didn't represent a change for victims like Ann Gordon—or anyone else.

The changes I'd introduced as the basketball season got underway didn't seem to ruffle too many feathers–at least not in a way that caused my players to complain too much to me. Branch said he couldn't understand why there'd be anything to complain about, and I tried my best to indicate that any kind of change in traditional Bulgaria was never easy. In the same regard, I had hope for our second season; other than Stefan leaving for the States, everyone returned from the year before. I was hoping that another year of maturity and hopefully some added commitment to basketball would improve our team. In many ways, I thought there was only one direction for us to go: up.

But much like the chaos that Sofia's stray dogs caused, neither open gyms nor tryouts looked anything other than, well, chaotic. Some of the players were in shape from pre-season running and therefore running circles around those who'd come to tryouts in jean shorts and Metallica shirts. But in several cases when Menkov should've had an easy layup because he was outrunning everyone, there were actually two defenders back at the other end of the floor: they didn't have enough energy to actually run past half court on offense.

On day two of tryouts, I had no choice but to pull Dimov aside and talk to him. With Stefan in the States, Menkov and Dimov were the only true guards I had left on my roster. (Pavel was guard-sized, but was still playing like a fullback, which gave me no choice but to play him at forward.) I'd entered tryouts thinking that we had some decent size and strength down low to contend with other teams, but that Menkov couldn't be the only one I could count on at the guard position. The team needed Dimov to have a big year, to stop running his mouth, stop partying too much and become a senior leader.

But during the second day of tryouts, I couldn't believe what I was seeing. Or maybe I could believe what I was seeing–because my worst fears were coming true before my very eyes.

Whenever something went wrong on the floor–and trust me, this happened quite frequently– Dimov would be the first to comment on it. And by "comment," I mean yell, and yell loudly. Since tryouts attracted a wide range of students, and some were playing in jean shorts, others in loafers, it was easy to see that most drills weren't going to be run fluidly. But Dimov must not have noticed this. When a 9th grader missed a layup, he'd hiss at him, making the kid cower into a shell. When a 10th grader didn't pass him the ball during a scrimmage, he'd howl in rage at this perceived sign of disrespect. And then when Dimov himself missed a shot or turned the ball over, he'd snarl at teammates he perceived to be in his way, or loudly shout that he was fouled, even though he knew no fouls were going to be called in tryout drills anyway.

"Is he always like this?" Branch asked, sounding alarmed. "I mean, it seems like nothing happens out on the floor where he doesn't turn and yell at someone else."

I'd certainly seen this before from Dimov in spurts, but this wasn't just a spurt. It had now been two straight days with nothing but his losing his cool on every other possession.

"Dimov," I asked as I pulled him out of the drill. "Is everything okay?"

"Yeah, Coach," he seemed surprised, "everything's great. Everything's great."

"Well, then why are you yelling at your teammates out on the floor so much?"

"I'm not yelling at my teammates," he responded defiantly.

With this I paused and gave him time to assess what he was saying.

"From where I'm standing, you're yelling at your teammates–and you're doing it a lot. This is tryouts, and this is the time you need to start showing you can be a leader. You're a senior now. I need you to be a positive leader out on the floor and stop yelling at other people. If you don't start doing that, then I don't know that I can put you on this team. We don't have room on the team for someone who yells at his teammates."

Now I'd gotten his attention.

"You wouldn't, Coach. You wouldn't–I love basketball. You wouldn't cut me," he protested, trying to figure out how serious I was.

The truth of the matter was that he was right. I wouldn't cut Dimov, if only because I knew that he was now a senior who should be in the lineup giving us the best chance to win. But watching him holler immaturely at teammates for two days had put all my hopes for the upcoming season in question. The only other option at the guard position–as far as I could see–was an 8th grader who had just entered the College for his first year. The problem with this new player, I learned quickly, wasn't the fact that he was in 8th grade. He was big for his age, and as I watched him handle the ball on the second day of tryouts, it was clear to me that he already had more skill and talent than any guard on our roster. That included two senior guards, Menkov and Dimov, who were a whopping four years older than him. The problem with this 8th grader Georgi was that he hadn't shown up for the first day of tryouts. The other kids on the team had raved about him, said that they were excited to play with him, but before day two started, I still didn't know who he was. Finally he showed up on day two, and greeted me right away.

"Hi Coach, I'm Georgi," he said. "I'm here for tryouts."

He didn't say it with that much enthusiasm, though. It seemed like there was some skepticism and more that he had to say.

"I've heard there are four tryouts this week," he continued.

"Yes, this is true," I responded.

"Yeah, umm," he paused, "well, there's no way I can come to all four tryouts."

I thought this was better left unsaid since he'd already missed the first day.

"But I'll be here today, and then I might be able to come again one more day."

This led me to launch into the same speech I felt like I'd given several times about how playing basketball was a commitment, and I hope he wanted to be committed to playing. Each time I said the word "commitment," though, he cringed as if I'd just said the word "gulag."

Branch had been there for our conversation, and, like me, didn't have a favorable impression of what just happened.

"I'm not sure why he's reacting so strangely, but if he wants to be on the team, I don't think it's too much to ask for him to come to tryouts," he mused.

"Yeah, well, it's funny how things work here. When I say tryouts are optional—which of course they are—lots of kids take the optional part of it very literally. They don't seem to understand that I also have the option of keeping them off the team, or on the bench."

"You're right. I don't even see Svetoslav here today," he responded.

I looked around and confirmed that he was right. Svetoslav was a 6'4" Russian who had also given me hope for the upcoming season. He hadn't played on the team the year before because he wanted to focus on practicing for his "professional" team. My players—Pesho especially—were also enthusiastic about Svetoslav, mostly because, as Pesho would tell me, "Coach, he can dunk. And when he dunks, he doesn't miss. It's not like when I dunk."

Svetoslav had told me that his professional team was eating up too much of his time, and he'd rather play for the school team. This in itself served as a cautionary tale for me since he seemed to think that the school team would take up less of his time. Still, he was 6'4", could handle the ball and even make jump shots—a commodity unknown to the majority of my team. On the first day of tryouts, he'd impressed me enough that it was a no-brainer for me to take him on the team. But at the end of practice, he came up to me with a concern.

"Coach, I liked playing today, and I want to keep playing," he told me, "but I need you to do a favor."

I certainly hadn't ever been asked for a favor before during basketball tryouts.

"You see, my old professional coach, he doesn't have a job right now," Svetoslav said, in accented and slightly broken English, "and he wants to coach basketball. So I thought he could coach with you."

I waited to see if Svetoslav was really serious, but then I looked into his solemn Russian eyes and realized he probably didn't even know how to be sarcastic.

"Svetoslav, I'd like to help, but I'm not sure the school would allow it," I told him, trying to come up with a somewhat-true response other than stating the obvious: this wasn't going to happen.

"But my coach, he is really sad right now without job. Can you give him job?"

I had to give Svetoslav credit for loyalty and devotion, though I also had to let him know it wasn't going to pay off.

"I feel badly for your coach, Svetoslav, but Coach Branch and I are already coaching. And the school likes its coaches to be teachers, too. So I just don't see how we could add another coach right now—especially one who doesn't work for the school."

He seemed crushed, and I was half-surprised and half-saddened. It seemed that he really expected me to hire his Bulgarian coach, sight unseen, to come join the staff.

"Well, Coach," he said dejectedly, "if my coach can't be part on this team, I'm not sure if I can be on this team."

This could've been a threat because it certainly sounded like one, but Svetoslav was truly deflated by my responses. I sensed he was speaking from pure sadness much more than an attempt to force my hand. No matter where his emotions were coming from, it really didn't matter. As much as I wanted to believe that Svetoslav had had a great experience with this coach, I'd also had all sorts of experiences with Bulgarian coaches (Nikolai being the exception) that made me want nothing to do with Bulgarian coaches.

"Wait a minute," Branch was laughing. "Do you think he was serious? He won't play unless you hire his coach? That sounds like some kind of shady Russian mob deal to me."

Without the 'shady Russian mob deal,' Svetoslav never showed up again at tryouts. And while Dimov had certainly toned it down, it looked as if he was fighting every urge in his body not to yell at his teammates. Georgi was able to make it to one more tryout, and this convinced me that it was at least worth a shot to keep him on the team. With all the talent he had at such a young age, it was very difficult for me to say no. The rest of the floor certainly wasn't riddled with talent.

Regardless of what I thought the outcome would most likely be, I decided that we should start out our year setting our goals high. So only a week after the team had been set, I got Nikolai to invite 35th school to our gym to play our first Wednesday game. My players were incredulous.

"Coach, 35th school is coming here?" Pavel said, awestruck. "The first week of the season, they're coming here?"

"Wow, wow, wow," Dimov kept repeating.

"This will be an incredible first game," Pesho said, clearly indicating that "incredible" meant "difficult." I wondered if it registered with him that coming to pre-season running might've helped him be in better shape for this first game.

"*Haide!*" Menkov changed the tone. "We can do this! We can beat these guys."

I didn't see Menkov's comment as realistic, but I liked his positive attitude, and liked what I perceived to be the beginnings of leadership emanating from him. Odds were, we weren't going to be able to beat 35th, the most talented team we'd played in my time in Bulgaria, in our first game of the season. But since I was banking on having another chance to play them in the ACS Open to finish our season, I figured we'd start where we planned to end.

As Khrushchev, the volatile coach of 35th, and his troops marched into the bubble for our first Wednesday game, I had to ask two of them to take the cigarettes out of their ears—clearly one of the classier looks I'd seen in a while. Upon being reproached by an American coach in Bulgarian, both players scoffed at me and looked at Khrushchev, who laughed at the notion of being asked to follow rules. I stood my ground, though, and both players gave me their cigarettes, sneering at me as they deposited them in my hand. I half-expected them to pull two more cigarettes out of their gym bags and replace the ones I'd just taken away. Instead, half of the team started jumping up and rattling the rims, finding this more appropriate behavior than smoking for a basketball setting. As I was about to go take on this latest affront to our school rules, I decided against it and focused on my team instead. This game was much more about us than it was about them anyway.

The opening tip led to a fast-break layup for 35th. With the full-court press I knew was coming, they stole our inbounds pass and scored again to make 4-0 in a matter of 12 seconds.

"Holy shit," Branch exclaimed. "I think we're in big trouble."

I knew we were most likely in big trouble, but also knew how 35th was going to play this game. They would be interested in blowing us out early, and then most likely lose interest once they got a big lead. I knew we weren't going to win, and I wanted to get a lot of different players into the game, so I wasn't that concerned about the score in the early going. Thirty-fifth, though, was pouring it on early, running the score to 11-2 before it appeared my team had woken up.

At this point, a 35th player was shooting free throws while one of his teammates had gone over to the bench to sit down. Two others were sitting at half court, legs extended, reaching out to touch their toes to stretch their hamstrings. It was clear that they didn't even consider the game to have even started at this point. I pointed it out to my players, hoping they'd see the disrespect as a motivating factor. Unfortunately, several players on the bench just let their heads droop lower. This just served as confirmation that we shouldn't be playing the game anyway.

The first quarter mercifully came to an end with us trailing 20-6. There weren't many positives to take away from the first quarter, and I'd noticed that Branch had spent the majority of the quarter bouncing up and down at the other end of the bench. He was at times irate at the officiating, at times flabbergasted by our players' lack of basketball intelligence, and at other times incredulous at the disrespect 35th school continued to show toward our players. I looked at him and could see all of these emotions oozing out of his body and he looked very familiar; he must have looked like me one year before.

As much as I'd tried to prep him for the Bulgarian basketball experience, he looked like a madman at the other end of the bench. I'm sure he was thinking there were so many things we needed to change–our fundamental execution, our basketball IQ, the referees' disdain for a school associated with America, and the lack of class shown by 35th–that he didn't know where to start. I couldn't help but empathize with him, and in a way, he made me feel better. His reaction to basketball in Bulgaria was making me think that all the things I'd felt last year for the entire year didn't make me crazy. Maybe you had to be crazy to think what happened at a Bulgarian basketball game was normal.

The 35th players sauntered over to their bench, and their starters took a seat. They leaned back and looked as if they had no interest whatsoever in this game. I wondered if the cigarettes would re-appear in their ears. Khrushchev appeared to be considering whether or not he needed to say anything during the quarter timeout; perhaps it was okay to just laugh with his players and enjoy the blowout.

But I wasn't certain this was going to be a blowout. We'd only been practicing for a week and had been shell-shocked at the beginning of the game. And none of my players were leaning back on the bench, conceding defeat. They knew we had a long way to go, and they knew that if any of them gave up, they'd end up on the bench.

Sasho had started the game as a product of his attendance at all the pre-season runs and practices, but picked up two early fouls. I put him back in the game to start the second quarter, and paired him with Pesho down low; this was the biggest power forward/center combination we could muster. I was already noticing the huge strides Sasho was making now that his hand was healthy once again, and he'd committed himself to working out with the team every time he could. He'd even grown an inch or two, which put him near 6'5"; he was clearly the biggest player on the team. Unfortunately, though, too many of his teammates didn't see him as the asset he was becoming. They saw him more as a liability, since he still didn't move quickly. Even worse, I'd hear his teammates call him "Fat Sasho," and when I admonished them for this, they told me that had been his nickname since the second grade.

"But look at him now!" I told them. "He's not fat; he's just huge. And he's going to be a force down low. Don't call him that anymore."

"But, Coach," came the unified response, "that's what we've always called him. That's who he is."

Thankfully, Sasho was either oblivious to their teasing or was working on tuning it out. I sensed that he knew he didn't fit in—knew that his teammates weren't goofy like him, didn't talk to their coach about literature like he did—and had come to grips with it. Still, the tradition of picking on the biggest kid on the team—and in turn, the biggest kid in the school—baffled me. I was used to the little guys getting picked on because they served no physical purpose to most teams, not the big guys who could actually make a big difference. Earlier in the year, Sasho got into an altercation with another student at lunch when the other student called him some derivation of "Fat Sasho." Sasho, evidently tired of being picked on, pushed the much smaller kid who continued to deride him with insulting nicknames. Not aware of his own strength, Sasho's light push sent the other student flying off his cafeteria bench. The other student broke his wrist as a result.

In the time I'd known Sasho, I'd quickly learned he didn't have a mean bone in his body. He also didn't appear to be aware of how much bigger and stronger he was than everyone else. I knew he didn't intend to hurt the other student, but had probably had enough of being picked on. When I asked Sasho about this, he told me he'd been frustrated and pushed the kid who he'd been upset with. He offered no excuses, just apologized, saying he was wrong.

"But Sasho, those kids were picking on you, weren't they?" I said to him.

He looked at me stone-faced, unwilling to respond.

"Sasho, what you did was wrong, but there was also a reason why you did what you did, wasn't there? How often do those guys pick on you? How often do they call you Fat Sasho?"

Again, he looked unwilling to respond.

"Sasho, the school administration is talking about expelling you for hurting someone else. You need to explain to them that you get picked on. I know you get picked on, and I know it happens every day."

"Coach," he said carefully, "I understand what you are saying. But I pushed him. He broke his wrist. I do not think I should make an excuse for why I did it."

I was floored by Sasho's maturity—maturity in the face of years and years of bullying. And I decided on that day in the fall that if he wasn't expelled for this incident, he deserved to start our first game. In the end, he was given a five-day suspension, but not expelled. When he came back, I knew he was going to face the same boorish Fat Sasho taunts, but I sensed he'd moved beyond being affected by them. And when I put him back in the game to begin the second quarter, he wasn't affected by anything.

Pesho missed an unnecessarily difficult running hook shot, but Sasho was there to box out for the rebound, keep the ball high and score. On the next possession, Menkov found him posting up, and he made the move I'd been trying to get Pesho to make for two years. Sasho took one power dribble toward the basket, sealed off his man, and finished off the backboard for a perfect drop-step move. The whistle blew as he shot the ball; he scored and was fouled. The 35th player guarding him looked stunned. Perhaps he had heard this guy was called Fat Sasho, too, and felt no need to take him seriously. As Sasho ambled to the foul line to complete the three-point play, he flashed me a broad grin as his brown hair flopped harmlessly on his brow.

Khrushchev had taken out three of his starters—his two starting guards and starting center—and they still were resting peacefully on the bench. They didn't seem affected by what was going on. But soon they'd start to take notice.

We put on a full-court press of our own, and Menkov stole the ball in the backcourt. Dimov put up what should've been a left-handed layup, but he launched it with his right hand off the top of the backboard. As I howled, "Left hand!" Pesho came crashing in, jumped over two players, grabbed the rebound in mid-air and tipped it back in. Our bench was electric; the score was now 22-15. Maybe, just maybe, Khrushchev and the 35th players were starting to take notice. He called a timeout to re-group.

"They expect you to quit," I told my players emphatically. "They expect you to roll over and die. But you can out-work them, out-hustle them. If you play harder than them, then you'll get back in this game."

That's exactly what happened. Slowly, the 35th starters matriculated back into the game, but they didn't appear ready to play when they got back in the game. They had hoped that the first quarter—a quarter when some of them were stretching at half court—was all they'd really need to take seriously, or at least half-seriously.

Pesho was now crashing the boards, using his springy legs to continually jump over people. He was having trouble finishing, but Sasho was not. Using his superior size and ability to box out, Sasho was grabbing rebounds high and immediately putting them back in the basket. Our press seemed to surprise 35th, and Menkov flicked the ball away from the point guard and headed the other way for a layup. Following another 35th miss, Pesho grabbed the rebound and dribbled like a runaway freight train down the court determined only to stop when he got close to the basket. With me screaming, "Find a guard! Find a guard! Pass the ball!" Pesho jumped into the last remaining 35th defenders, flung a horrible shot up toward the rim—and it went in. Our bench went nuts, and Pesho came back down the floor grinning, yelling to me, "See, Coach! See, Coach! I no need to pass!"

On our next possession, Menkov and Dimov patiently passed the ball on the outside until Sasho flashed open at the elbow. When he caught the ball, he turned deftly and launched a 15-foot jump shot. As he released it, I realized that with all the work he'd put in, all the open gyms he'd come to, and all the times he'd asked me if he could stay after open gym to shoot more, he now had the most pure looking jump shot on the team. Considering how the rest of the team shot, this wasn't saying much, but I watched the rotation of the ball as it fluttered toward the basket, and I was impressed. As it descended down toward the rim, it touched nothing but net.

We were now winning 25-24.

The bench was ecstatic.

"Coach, Coach," Pavel was hollering, "we can beat these guys! We can beat these guys! They don't take us seriously."

Now that they were losing, though, 35th seemed to realize they were going to have to start playing harder. For the rest of the half, the score seesawed back and forth. I could sense we were gaining more confidence with each new basket we scored. Outside of Sasho's jumper, we still couldn't score from the perimeter, but we were more patient working the ball to the inside of the zone. Ivan was also crashing the boards, and that gave us a formidable trio inside to continue pounding away trying to get rebounds. Thirty-fifth seemed to regain their balance and exploit the talent differential as the half wound to a close. As the horn sounded, the scoreboard showed a score of 37-33. We were only down by four points. As my team headed to the bench, there were high-fives all around; they were pumped.

But I was a little worried about what the second half would bring. I'd played my regulars far more than I'd wanted to. This was the first game and I'd wanted to get everyone in. And there were several players who were sitting out the first half because they'd missed practice; I wanted to give them a chance as well.

"Andy," Branch said to me honestly, "I think we can hang with them if you keep this lineup in the game for most of the second half."

"I know, I think we can hang with them, too."

"But do you want to go with these five or six players only for the rest of the second half?"

I thought about what he said and it only further served to reinforce what I'd been thinking about as the first half ended. In my eyes, winning this game didn't matter. I wanted us to compete, and I wanted a lot of people to have a chance to play. But now it looked like we had a legitimate chance to win. We'd outscored 35th 27-17 in the second quarter—an amazing feat for our team.

"I don't know what to do," I told Branch. "I don't think the point of this game is to stick with five or six players. I wanted to play everybody."

"Yeah," he seemed to understand. "But don't you want to beat these jerks?"

I looked over at Khrushchev who was now laughing uproariously about something while the rest of his team mingled about, looking more like they were at a cocktail party than a basketball game. I wanted to beat them more than anything.

So we started the second half with the same group that had played so well to end the first half. Soon, though, I'd be given no choice but to make changes to the lineup. Foul trouble gave me no choice. Sasho picked up his third almost immediately after the half started. Then Pesho was called for a charge– and it was a questionable call–and he responded to this call by spewing venom toward the referee. This earned him a technical foul, and a permanent seat on the bench. I didn't agree with the referee's charge call, but I'd made it very clear that I would not tolerate them getting technical fouls on the floor.

"Coach, Coach," Pesho came running over to the bench. "He hates me. He hates me. *Thees ees* terrible call!"

"Pesho," I said calmly, "I don't care how terrible the call is. You don't argue. Let me argue. You can't get technical fouls; I won't stand for it."

"But Coach," Dimov came to his defense, "this is Bulgaria. Everyone gets technical fouls."

Branch looked at me and raised his eyebrows. I wandered his end of the bench and told him that he should probably get used to be told, "This is Bulgaria," followed by a statement that might shake the foundation of his world.

As the carnage started to pile up for our team, I morphed back to my original plan to give more players a chance to play. With Pesho and Sasho leaving the game, we lost our advantage on the boards, and the lead ballooned to 10 in a hurry. Thirty-fifth poured in two consecutive three-pointers–something we could never dream of doing–and their lead was up to 16. I started substituting, eager to make everyone feel like he was part of the team. When I left Menkov out on the floor with four other non-regulars, I could see he was seething from my coaching decision. He played with these four for several minutes and did an admirable job of keeping us in the game. When I took him out of the game, though, I made sure to talk to him right away.

"Menkov, I want you to understand," I told him, "that it's our first game. I want to make sure—"

"You want to make sure that everyone gets a chance to play," he finished my sentence for me. "I know, Coach; I get it. I just really want to beat these guys."

I'd put the 8th grader Georgi in the game to replace Menkov, and figured I'd give him a chance to play point guard to see what he could do. He was about Menkov's size, and already dribbled the ball with his left hand better than anyone on our team. I sent him into the game to run the offense and instructed him about how we wanted to move the ball from side to side to beat the 35th zone.

On his first possession in the game, he dribbled the ball up the floor and immediately launched a three-pointer. It was nowhere near the rim.

"Georgi, Georgi," I called to him, "just calm down. Be patient. Pass the ball."

I figured it could be expected for an 8th grader to be nervous in his first game and make a bad decision. But then he brought the ball up the floor a second time and did the exact same thing.

"Pass the ball!" I shouted with a little more urgency in my tone this time.

His third time up the floor, Georgi again refused to pass the ball and tried to dribble to the basket against the 35th zone. He was double-teamed and had the ball stolen. Thirty-fifth headed the other way for a layup.

I had no choice but to take Georgi out of the game. Our talented prodigy looked anything but talented in his short stint in the game. He'd made three terrible decisions, and the troubling part about this was that I'd sent him in the game to play point guard—a position centered on passing the ball.

When he came out of the game, I drew up our offense on a whiteboard and started explaining to him that he was the point guard, the player who needed to start the offense by passing the ball. I showed him on the whiteboard how offensive opportunities would come to him if he'd trust his teammates and be willing to pass the ball. But in the middle of my explanation, he interrupted me.

"No, Coach, I don't want to run offense like this. Here," he grabbed at my marker, "we do something different."

I'd never had a player do something like this before, but Georgi certainly seemed confident and saw no problem with telling his new coach how he wanted the offense to be run. He wanted me to run plays designed for him so that he could shoot. I quickly rebuffed him and told him that we were running a team-based offense where anyone could shoot. I re-drew what our offense looked like, and asked him if he understood. He looked at me skeptically, but indicated that he understood. I wasn't sure quite how to deal with him, so I asked Branch to go talk to him about the nature of team basketball.

In the meantime, 35th's lead hovered around 15 points. Ivan had made a couple of short jumpers, and Vassy, as always, was willing to battle with players much larger than him to at least make life difficult for them. As a guard, Pavel was a disaster; it appeared like he not only couldn't dribble with his left hand; he couldn't dribble with his right either. But as a forward, he was at least getting opportunities inside the paint by pushing, shoving and bullying his way toward to the hoop. His shots, though, were rarely falling.

Branch approached me and said that he thought Georgi now understood what we were looking for in our offense. He suggested I give him another try and put him back in the game.

When I did, I just saw more of the same. As the point guard bringing the ball up the floor, he only motioned for his teammates to screen for him; he wouldn't pass to them. And screening the ball against this zone wasn't going to work; I'd already talked to him about this. But he still tried it anyway, and this resulted in another long jump shot that clanked off the backboard. At this point, I had no idea what to even say to him to change what was happening. The next possession was more of the same. His teammates on the floor who had heard me preach about team for so long now were baffled by his unwillingness to pass the ball. I pulled him out of the game quickly.

"Georgi, you have to pass the ball! This is a team game; you have to pass the ball," I told him, exasperated.

"Coach, you no run plays for me. I don't like this. Why you no run plays for me?" he quickly responded in English that still needed quite a bit of work.

"Georgi, this isn't about you; this is about the team," I said, speaking slowly to make sure he understood.

"I no like this," he replied. "You no run plays for me."

As he headed toward the end of the bench, I felt lost about what to do. He clearly had the talent to step in and help the team right away, but the word "team" seemed to be an entirely foreign concept to him.

"Coach," Pavel tapped my shoulder, "on these professional teams, they don't talk about team like you do. They just run plays for the individual. That's why he's so confused. He's never heard a coach talk about team before."

I just looked at Pavel while considering his words.

"In fact," he continued, "most of us had never heard of a coach talking about team like you do."

Taken at face value, this was a compliment, but the look on Pavel's face told me more what I needed to know: my consistent talk about teamwork had befuddled all of them at one point or another.

The game ended with us losing by 19 points. Khrushchev led his team in another tasteless half court celebration, complete with dancing. As I assembled the team for our post-game talk, I focused on only one thing: when we'd play them next.

"There were parts of this game where we were playing right with this team. In fact, there were parts of this game where we were beating them. You can't forget that because this is just our first game of the year after only a week of practice. I know you're going to practice harder than they will, and I know you're going to improve so we're ready for the next time we play them."

"When are we going to play them next?" came a voice within the team huddle.

Before I could respond, Menkov knew exactly what I was thinking about.

"The ACS Open," he said resolutely. "They'll be here again for the ACS Open, and we can beat them when it really matters."

With this, several eyes within the huddle made contact with each other, heads shook or nodded according to the Bulgarian or rest-of-the-world custom, and I sensed a determination that I hadn't seen the previous year. Post-game speeches the year before had been beyond arduous. Half the players wanted to leave before I could even speak, and then when I did speak, it seemed no matter what I said, all any of my players could think about was the fact that we'd lost. But this huddle felt different. We were approaching our season with a goal in mind. This was just game one, but we'd be playing every week, and we'd finish our season with the tournament that mattered the most to us. I could talk about goals realistically because I had some idea of what actually lay ahead of us.

The 8th grade point guard Georgi would never come to practice again, and though I knew there were some on the team who wanted him there because of his talent, there were too many who had been on the floor with him when he wouldn't pass the ball. I wondered if I needed to address the fact that we'd had a player quit after one game, but none of the other players seemed surprised that someone would quit. *This is Bulgaria*, they'd most likely tell me, *and this sort of thing happens all the time.*

As Branch and I exited the bubble following our first game of the year, we volleyed different ideas about the game back and forth. We considered different lineups and did the best we could to laugh at Khrushchev's antics and his players' cigarettes. And as we walked down the stairs of the bubble to head home, we couldn't help but notice that there were three new puppies huddled together for warmth. They looked up at us, wondering if these new, larger creatures above them might provide them with food or shelter. I couldn't help but feel badly for these newly-born pups as they were about to be tossed into the chaotic survival-of-the-fittest Bulgarian stray dog world. I wanted to take them home and offer them some kind of hope for the future, some belief that they wouldn't be thrust into the world with so little of a chance.

Branch was talking about hope for our basketball team and I was wondering about the future for these innocent new puppies. But in the end, we kept walking in the shadows of the broken down row houses. There wasn't much I could do for the puppies; my front porch and back porch were already occupied.

.

Chapter XVIII
The Cold War

As we started the new season, I started to warm up to the idea that we could have a competitive season. My players had a year's experience with me as their coach under their belts, and spirits weren't too down after our loss to 35th. There seemed to be an understanding amongst some of the players that this season could be different. It might not be riddled with double-digit losses, swastika-inflicted bruises, and numerous urination experiences in Bulgarian public school closets. Pavel's dad had even come through with a full set of uniforms for the team. Gone was the Mavericks-and-76ers mish-mash of the past; now we actually looked like a cohesive team with the same uniforms. The school would not provide any money for uniforms, so the players had to pay for them themselves. Dimov, unbeknownst to me, had ordered a jersey with the number 69 on the back. It was moments like these where it felt great to have an assistant coach, not only to help develop our players, but more importantly, help me keep my sanity. Branch was even more astounded than I was at Dimov's jersey number choice.

Our second Wednesday game of the year was a game against a faculty team from ACS, and this game gave me an up-close-and-personal look at our team. I had Branch coach our team, and I was playing on the faculty team against the team I'd spent so much time coaching. And to my great delight, every time I drove to the basket, I was met by a wall of defenders. If I went up for a rebound, Ivan and Vassy thrust their bodies into me. If I tried to get in front of Menkov on defense, he was determined to use his fitness to blow by me each time. Even though the faculty team was nothing worth writing home about, it was composed of several Americans. I thought we'd be able handle my team relatively easily, but this wasn't the case at all. During one timeout, one of my colleagues leaned over to me and said, "Coach, your players are certainly physical, and they want to win. I'm glad we aren't playing another one of these games."

I looked at the several bruises I'd acquired during the game and had to smile. My team who had wanted nothing to do with diving on the floor or box-out drills was wreaking havoc on the ACS faculty team.

With three minutes left in a close game, I shot out on a fast break determined to take the ball to the basket to score. The only defender to beat was Kosio, and I knew he generally had no interest in moving his feet to play defense. As I approached him at the three-point line, I crossed over right to left, and saw him awkwardly adjust far too late. But instead of reaching in with his arms to commit a foul, or just letting me go, Kosio stuck out his leg and tripped me. I went flying headfirst into the lane, and got up quickly with anger boiling inside of me. There are many types of acceptable fouls in basketball, but tripping someone intentionally is not one of them. In soccer, it would earn you a yellow or red card. In basketball, it would earn you the wrath of your opponent.

As much as Kosio had talent, he was one player that I worried was never going to get it. It was one thing to get beat on defense—this would happen to him routinely—but it was entirely another thing to play dirty as recourse. Too often, when Kosio would give me excuses for not running, playing defense or avoiding physical contact, I tried to bite my tongue and tell myself, *Remember, this is Bulgaria. Things are different here.* But when he tripped me, there was no biting of my tongue. Thankfully, though, before I could pick myself off the ground, Branch had literally yanked him out of the game and, judging by his body language, he was saying exactly the same things I would have said. As I reflected on this later, the outrageous nature of the trip incensed me more and more. It was one thing to trip an opponent you didn't like— something that would rarely ever be condoned—but entirely another thing to trip your coach, the person who was in charge of your playing time for the rest of the year.

The faculty-student game went into overtime, and that's when the physical nature of the strong high school bodies took their toll on the group of 20 and 30-something teachers. Even though they couldn't shoot straight, with Pesho, Sasho, Vassy and Ivan alternating turns crashing the boards, the game was decided quickly in overtime. Never being one who likes to lose, on a personal level I was frustrated by the outcome of the game: my team, the one I was playing for, had lost. But then I looked over to the other end of the floor and saw high-fives and hugs all around. My real team was elated. This game had mattered to them, and they won.

Before I knew it, and without being told, each player made his way over to the faculty end of the floor and congratulated each of us on a good, hard-fought game. My players were thrilled with their play and their victory, and I was thrilled with their sportsmanship and maturity. My heart started to warm up, thinking that maybe things were starting to change.

The next day, all the warmth was sucked out of Bulgaria.

Actually, "sucked" isn't the most accurate descriptor. Most accurately, the warmth was drained and siphoned. That's because, as January temperatures dipped well below freezing, Russia shut off the natural gas supply to the majority of Eastern Europe.

As the year 2008 came to a close—a year Bulgaria had declared "The Year of Russia"—Russia and Ukraine continued to squabble over whether or not gas pipeline bills had been appropriately paid. This story had grazed the news, but wasn't making too many waves outside of Russia and Ukraine. Usually in smaller print toward the end of articles, it would be noted that the gas dispute had the potential to cause much bigger problems: Russia supplied the majority of Eastern Europe with gas, and the only pipeline out of Russia ran through Ukraine. Throughout the month of December, Russia continued to say it would shut off the gas in January if Ukraine didn't pay its debt—a debt to the tune of $1.67 billion dollars. At the last minute, Ukraine, frustrated by what they believed to be unfair Russian tactics, still anted up and paid the debt. Then to initiate a new contract, Russia raised the prices for the following year. In the cold of winter, this seemed like a Stalingrad stalemate, but all Bulgarian reports on this issue pointed to the fact that the gas dispute shouldn't have an impact on Bulgaria. Prime Minister Sergei Stanishev indicated that aside from the normal supply of gas Bulgaria received from Russia, the country had one month's worth of gas reserves for the entire country.

The first week of January, without a new price for natural gas agreed upon between Russia and Ukraine, Russia turned off their natural gas pipeline. In turn, no Russian gas flowed into Bulgaria. No Russian gas flowed into Poland. No Russian gas flowed into Romania, or Serbia, or Bosnia, or Turkey, or Macedonia. Russia, which supplied 25 percent of the natural gas used for heat to European Union countries, had completely shut off the flow of gas from their pipeline.

Now this story started to garner international attention. No matter whose side you took in the dispute—and both Russia and Ukraine seemed equally stubborn—it was hard for me to side with Russia, the more powerful and wealthy country who seemed to be holding all the cards in this equation. And considering this situation, mighty Russia was not just denying customers access to some kind of insignificant product; they were depriving a frigid Eastern European population of a primary heat source in the throes of a January freeze. Cries rang out throughout Eastern Europe for the problem to be fixed soon; otherwise countries would run out of their remaining gas supplies.

When the story broke, I took notice, but I didn't take close notice until I noticed something far more pressing: there was no more heat coming out of the radiator in my classroom.

This didn't make any sense to me. I'd read the prime minister's comments about the reserve gas supplies that would last Bulgaria a month. As much as I expected Russia and Ukraine to stand firm and not back down, I was certain the gas dispute wouldn't last for a month. I figured we were good until February. But then why was I starting to see my breath while teaching my fifth period class?

I asked my students what their other classrooms had been like. Did they have heat in their other classrooms, too? No, was the resounding answer, they didn't have heat anywhere. *But what about the reserve supply of gas? I thought we were good for a month?*

All these questions might as well have been rhetorical because they were just met with a series of fatalistic shrugs from my students. They were cold, and they were miserable, but they weren't surprised. I suppose I shouldn't have been either.

Soon, the prime minister released a statement regarding the lack of heat in Bulgaria. When he'd spoken before about the month's worth of gas in reserve, he wasn't lying. This was the backup plan the government had had ready. But when government officials went to tap into the reserve supply to provide the country with natural gas heat, they discovered that all of the gas had been stolen. Someone from within the government had gone into the reserve tanks and managed to siphon out the entire reserve supply and sell it to the highest bidders—presumably Bulgarian business types who also dabbled in midday assassinations in crowded cafes.

Hearing this explanation, not to mention that my fingers were turning different shades of blue, I was dumbfounded. The prime minister's story about an entire month's worth of natural gas being stolen from right under his watch sounded similar to a high school student stealing his parents' vodka supply and refilling the bottles with water, hoping they wouldn't notice. But in this case, the thieves stole the supply of heat destined to warm up an entire country in January. The prime minister, while seeming apologetic, didn't appear to feel responsible for what was now a Bulgarian heat crisis. According to him, he shouldn't be held responsible for guarding the country's precious supply of natural gas, and now that it was gone, no investigation would be performed. This was no longer a Bulgarian problem. Stanishev told CNN that now that Bulgaria was in the EU, this was a problem the EU should fix.

The heat ran out in the morning, and I tried to have basketball practice in the afternoon. Several players didn't show up. Pesho later told me, "My mom says that since we don't have heat, we should go on holiday. She wanted to find a country that had heat."

I suspected that other players with far less economic means were not able to flee the country to find heat in other places. Those who did come to practice looked forward to running like never before. It offered their only chance to stay warm. Several players practiced with stocking caps on, and while I'd been critical of the ridiculous outfits players had worn to practice in the past, there was nothing I would say about their stocking caps. I was huddled inside a hooded sweatshirt, joining as many drills as I could to try to stay warm. Sasho asked if he could play with gloves on, but I couldn't justify going this far.

Coming off a victory in the faculty-student game, some good moments against 35th school, and seeing the smiles on my players' faces and the confidence that seemed to be coming with it, I expected to have a spirited practice to recognize the fact that we were getting better. But at this practice, the basketballs clanged heavily off the floor like lead weights, echoing ominously throughout the icy bubble. There was very little talk between teammates; it seemed to be too cold to even communicate.

The frigid nature of, well, everything, brought me back to a quote from the Bulgarian dissident writer Georgi Markov referring to life in Bulgaria: "In this unbelievably tight proximity," he wrote about the borders closing in on Bulgaria, "we feel the warmth of each other's bodies, our slightest shivers, … we can converse for hours without speaking a word."

Markov was writing about a seemingly cold Bulgarian world, but he was long gone by the time Russia shut off the heat. He had no idea how cold it was in Bulgaria now.

And for the most part, the rest of the world didn't either. International news reports started springing up with colorful maps showing the various countries in Eastern Europe that were affected by the gas dispute. The one thing that stood out about Bulgaria was that it was an entirely different color than all the other countries in Eastern Europe; that's because Bulgaria had a color all to itself. Bulgaria was the only country in Eastern Europe that received all of its natural gas supplies from Russia. The result of Bulgaria's complete dependence on Russia was that the country was now plunged into a deep freeze. Other countries relied on Russia for *part* of their natural gas supply, but they also hedged their bets and received gas from other places. Bulgaria, though, was the only country that received all its natural gas from one place, Russia.

Bulgaria's first communist leader in the 1940s, Georgi Dimitrov, had once addressed the Bulgarian people, telling them that "friendship with the Soviet Union is just as necessary for life as the air and sun is for any living creature." Dimitrov didn't mention anything about the necessity of heat in the winter, so perhaps his quote still rang true to cold Bulgarians.

No other country in Eastern Europe was completely dependent on Russia, and no other country in Eastern Europe had had its reserve supply of gas stolen. Regardless, there were problems all throughout Eastern Europe based on the gas dispute between Russia and Ukraine. But in Bulgaria, there was an all-out gas crisis.   And the first places to feel the brunt of the crisis were some of the places that needed heat the most: schools, hospitals, and public transportation.

Schools immediately started closing, deeming it unsafe to house students for entire days without any heat. In most cases, this allowed students to spend their entire days in their row house apartment blocks without any heat. Hospitals had no choice but continue helping people, but babies were born into frigid conditions, and the elderly were being tended to with blanket upon blanket. There appeared to be no other choice.

But that wasn't the entire story. While there wasn't any heat at school, and there was a trickle of heat coming from a generator at my house, there seemed to be plenty of heat other places. The first day the heat was turned off, I called a restaurant to see if they were open for dinner and if they had heat. I was much more interested in heat than dinner, to tell the truth. Of course, was the response, of course we have heat.

What I soon started noticing was that private restaurants and businesses had heat. The general public, and all public services, had no heat, but this wasn't the case with private businesses. All the heat that had disappeared from the government's reserve supply was being put to use in some places by those who were capable of paying mafia prices for the natural gas. As a result, many businesses in Sofia saw no change in their daily operations. At the same time, the general public froze.

We were given a long weekend as school closed and the American president said they'd spend the weekend coming up with solutions to the gas crisis. He was determined to have heat in school by Monday. I liked his resolute tenacity, but had no idea where this gas was going to come from. It seemed that only the highest bidders were getting natural gas, and our school didn't even have enough money for basketball uniforms. Where was the money going to come from for natural gas to heat an entire campus of more than 700 students?

This question remained unanswered as we returned to work on Monday and entered our Siberian classrooms. The school's Bulgarian secretary sent out a school-wide memo in halting English indicating how we should proceed based on outside temperatures that were well below freezing, and inside temperatures that were only a little bit better:

DUE TO THE DIFFICULTY GETTING TEMPERATURES TO NORMAL LEVELS. PLEASE DRESS APPROPRIATELY.

In my earlier years as a teacher in Southern California, I'd been a part of too many staff meetings where we discussed "appropriate dress" for female students, and how exposed midriffs could be detrimental to student learning. In this case–this very Bulgarian case– dressing appropriately meant putting on as many layers as possible. As I started teaching that Monday morning, I was wearing my winter coat, a winter hat and gloves. Looking out at my students, they were all dressed similarly.

I'd already received an email from a colleague explaining her fate in her classroom on this first day back in the cold. It read, "I don't understand how it can be this cold in here. My feet and hands are freezing right now. Before I went outside for lunch duty, I had to change into long underwear, and I was angered by how seriously freezing it is in my room."

I asked my students about their experiences so far without heat, as nearly all of them had already indicated they didn't have any heat in their row house block apartments. One 9th grade girl was quick to offer up the details of her family's fate: "My family bought four space heaters last week," she told me. "Our medicine bills when my little brother and grandma get sick will be much higher than our electric bills for trying to stay warm."

One after another, students told me how they were worried about younger siblings or older grandparents, all of whom lived in the same apartment with them. Perhaps the only ray of hope that could come from this predicament was that so many family members lived in the same apartment that their body heat would have to have some kind of warming effect. But there was only a small amount of solace that could be taken within a much bigger, and colder, problem.

With my next class, I tried to steer the conversation away from solely the misery associated with the lack of heat. I asked for my students' opinions regarding what had happened, and how it had happened. There were several who were quick to point out that the Bulgarian government was doing nothing to help solve the problem. Since Stanishev's CNN interview where he said the EU should be responsible for fixing the problem, he had yet to release any plans for solution—or any indication that he was going to find all the gas reserves that had been stolen. He seemed content to sit back and wait for someone else to swoop in and end the crisis. Bulgarian 19th and 20th century history was littered with instances of the rest of Europe not being interested in helping Bulgaria, and it seemed to me that Stanishev was determined to make a point of having this happen in the 21st century as well. Aside from getting Russia to turn the heat back on, there was very little the EU could do.

With my class, I shared a *NY Times* article about the gas crisis in Bulgaria, and I made special note of the description of Bulgaria's long-standing relationship with Russia. "During the Cold War," the article stated, "Bulgarians were inculcated with the lesson that Russia had twice liberated the country, from the Ottoman Empire in the 19th century and from the Nazis in WWII." The article seemed to point out that Bulgarian sentiment toward Russia could be reaching a crossroads since Russia was now withholding the gas that was making the country freeze. But this crossroads, I soon learned, was not nearly as imminent as the *NY Times* was indicating.

"This is blown way out of proportion and over-dramatic. I'm tired of people saying it's Russia's fault," came the first response from one of my highest-achieving 12th grade students.

"*Ukraina* stole the gas! They're keeping it all for themselves! They stole the gas. This isn't Russia's fault," was soon to follow afterward.

I tried to stem the tide of anti-Ukraine sentiment, but it fit right in with the *Sofia Echo* article I'd read before class that said that pro-Russian Bulgarians planned to stage a protest rally outside the Ukrainian Embassy in Sofia. As I tried to prod my students with questions to see if there were other points of view, there were some in the class who pointed out that Russia had plenty of blame in this mess. But then there was still plenty of pro-Russian sentiment in the classroom, as each new comment came with a visible display of icy breath shooting out from my students' chapped lips.

"Russia is our friend, Mr. Jones," one student pleaded with me. "Russia is so good to us. They have saved us twice; they are our friend."

This impassioned plea made Russia sound like the winner of some kind of international good Samaritan award, and just didn't seem to fit with the fact that we were all bundled up, making sure our fingers and toes could still move because Russia had shut off the gas.

"You have to remember," I pointed out, realizing I was running the risk of offending my pro-Russian audience, "that Russia is the same country that sent its own people to suffer in Siberia for entire winters as punishment."

Before, responses from my students centered on Ukraine's blame in the gas crisis. But now that I'd pushed the envelope, they targeted their angst on the real culprit: the United States.

"This whole crisis was created by the U.S. in their attempt to make the Russians look bad. This is American propaganda just like during the Cold War," was the first response spouted out from a frantically waving hand.

"Are you serious?" I was flabbergasted. "You really think the U.S. is to blame for the Russian-Ukraine gas crisis that's affecting all of Eastern Europe?"

"Yes, I do. Americans are so concerned with their image. They all just want to *appear* to be doing good. Now their main goal is to make

Russia look bad so America looks good. This is *so typical* of America."

With this last statement, the girl speaking let out an audible sneer, saying *so typical* as if she was referring to her mother not letting her go to a party on Friday night. In this case, though, she was already certain she knew what *so typical* American behavior was like. Her teenage disenchantment had passed over the typical culprits—parents and teachers—and moved on to a bigger enemy, the West.

From where I was standing—in hiking boots with two pairs of socks on—there was a dispute between Russia and Ukraine over natural gas that led to Bulgaria receiving no natural gas. There was no heat in my classroom, and most of my students didn't have heat in their homes. I had a little bit of heat in my house, and though it was still chilly inside, I felt very fortunate. The Bulgarian government supposedly had a month's worth of reserve supplies of natural gas, but it mysteriously disappeared, and no investigation would be conducted. Now the only people in Bulgaria who had full use of heat seemed to be affiliated with the mafia. With all of these details, according to some of my students, our anger should be directed at the United States of America.

"What do you guys think of her opinion?" I asked the class, trying to diplomatic, but hoping someone would say this U.S. conspiracy theory was absurd. "Do you agree with placing the blame on the U.S.?"

As looked out at my students, heads started intermittently shaking and bobbing. I wanted to ask what each of these gestures meant, but I stopped myself, worried that all of them actually agreed the U.S. was to blame. With a series of head shakes and bobs, I was once again confused by Bulgarian gestures and the Bulgarian mindset, so I changed the subject to something related to literature.

The gas crisis lasted for more than two weeks. January temperatures didn't get any warmer, and it became common for students to enter my classroom with a thermometer, curious to find out if my classroom was colder than their previous classrooms. They were also working on their own conspiracy theories based on some obscure Bulgarian ministry law that stated that it was illegal to teach classes if temperatures inside were lower than eight degrees Celsius (about 46 degrees Fahrenheit). My classroom, they told me would hover around 10 degrees Celsius, and that wasn't low enough to cancel school. It was low enough, though, to make each new day's cold arduous and piercing.

Basketball practices continued, though attendance was dropping like the temperatures. My promise of games every Wednesday had already fallen flat because we'd had to cancel a couple Wednesday games. No other schools in Sofia were playing basketball without heat. My players would dutifully point this out to me as I shivered while telling them that we had to endure adversity in order to become better. I'd thought we were picking up steam and momentum like never before, but the mention of steam just brought us all to warmer places where we dreamed of not having to sleep every night fully-clothed with three or four blankets.

The international news media continued to pick up the gas crisis story, and I would spend portions of my school day hitting the refresh button on the BBC's homepage, hoping there would be a headline reading, "Russia and Ukraine Broker Deal: Heat to be Turned Back On." Most days, though, the headlines just indicated that talks were occurring to try to resolve the crisis. Nothing had changed.

Bulgaria got more international media coverage, though, than I'd ever noticed at any time during my life. Tuning in to CNN International, I saw a journalist was standing on a bleak Sofia street, taking the brunt force of bitter winter winds in his face and pointing to row house apartment buildings all around him. "These are the people who are the hardest hit by this crisis," he pointed out, showing the world gray dilapidated buildings in various stages of disrepair. The image was a powerful pathos-driven one, and would make any viewer think, *Oh my God, I can't imagine how bad it would be to live there.* The reality of the situation, though, struck me as sadly ironic. The journalist was pointing to crumbling communist architecture and showing how bad things were in Bulgaria, as if this had all been caused by the lack of heat. As a Sofia resident, I knew the truth: those apartment buildings looked gray and desolate whether the natural gas was flowing or not. The reporter could've come to Sofia any time to point that out.

News agencies like BBC showed numerous images of elderly Bulgarians looking miserable riding public transportation, clearly cold and smashed inside buses that looked as unwelcoming as the shabby row house apartment buildings. Again, looking at these images, it would be hard for any rational human being not to think that life in Bulgaria without heat appeared to be raw and grim. But I felt the same way as I did while I was watching the news reports. A BBC photographer could come to Bulgaria any normal day in the winter or summer and take a picture of elderly Bulgarians riding ramshackle buses and see people looking crestfallen. This wasn't life without heat in Bulgaria; *this was life in Bulgaria.*

International newspapers also displayed photographs of Bulgarians chopping wood to use for fires since there was no gas to heat their homes. These images were usually accompanied with captions about the struggles Bulgarians now faced since Russia had turned off the heat. But once again, these images missed the point of real life during Bulgarian winter. The Bulgarians who were out chopping wood in the winter didn't have natural gas heat to begin with. They chop wood every winter, all winter long because that's the only option they have for heating in their homes. They chop wood for survival regardless of what Vladimir Putin and Victor Yushchenko were doing in Moscow and Kiev.

Finally, another CNN International report used its cameras to pan a crumbling Roma neighborhood, showing broken-down homes and hopeless people who looked freezing. As the camera was rolling, a donkey cart wheeled by carrying a flock of children in the back. This image was used to show the hardship Bulgaria was facing during the Russian-Ukraine gas crisis. But again, this wasn't an image that had anything to do with a heat crisis, or lack of natural gas. In fact, it was most likely that the Roma in the shot had no idea there was even a gas crisis to begin with. They didn't have heat or electricity, and the problems the journalist was describing had nothing to do with them. Their life in the winter was always extremely difficult, and international politics rarely had anything to do with it.

As the CNN reporter finished broadcasting from a decaying Bulgarian neighborhood, he remarked that people in Bulgaria were wondering how long it would take before things returned back to normal. He had no idea, though, that he was standing in the midst of what was normal for many Bulgarians, a normal the rest of the world had no idea about.

More than 20 years previous, writer Robert Kaplan had visited Bulgaria during the Cold War, and became educated in what it really meant to be cold. During one winter visit—a visit where heat existed, though it was limited—he discussed the nature of life in Bulgaria in the winter: "I was still cold," he wrote, "and not the pleasant, temporary cold of the West, where you get warm as soon as going indoors; but the grinding, continuous cold of Eastern Europe, where your stomach and ribs ache from clenching your muscles for hours on end, bent over, trying to keep warm."

I'd grown up in several different places in the Midwest and lived my adult life in Chicago. Cold winters were nothing new to me, and in general, I found that I'd always liked the cold better than the warm. But cold weather in Chicago meant that I'd have a brisk walk from my heated car to my heated apartment, or from my heated classroom to my heated car, or from a heated coffee shop across the street to a heated friend's place. In all equations during my Western winters, there was always a warm place to contrast the biting cold outside. It wasn't until this January in Bulgaria that I learned what winter truly meant. It meant being cold all day long without respite. It meant waking up in the morning and realizing that once you got out of bed, you were going to be fighting the elements for the rest of the day. It meant that there was nothing beautiful or majestic about snowy afternoons and flakes falling in the black sky at night; they were just simply cold. Cold War was no longer a term I applied to Russian history; I was living it in Bulgaria.

With protests based on the heat crisis occurring outside the Ukrainian embassy regularly during the days, another group of Bulgarians formed to protest. This might've stemmed from a true desire to cause policy change, or perhaps protesting just sounded like it would be a warmer option than sitting in a refrigerated apartment with chattering teeth. The second group of protesters aimed their frustration at the Bulgarian government, and staged rallies outside of parliament in downtown Sofia. The purpose of their protest, they said, was to rail against, "the Mafia, corruption, lousy politicians, and everything that's not right in the state."

The English teacher in me couldn't help but notice the unintentional Shakespearean connection to snowy Scandinavia in *Hamlet*, when the guard outside the palace famously said, "Something is rotten in the state of Denmark." In terms of the Bulgarian protest with "everything that's not right in the state," I was hoping that the protesters would begin with the fact that we were all living life as icicles. But the more I thought about it, they probably wouldn't make the Shakespearean connection; it wasn't possible for anything to be rotting in Bulgaria in temperatures this cold.

Chapter XIX
The Turkish Toilet
Turning Point

The day Russia and Ukraine brokered an EU-sanctioned agreement to start the gas flowing again, there was much rejoicing in Bulgaria, especially by frozen ex-pats like me. The new agreement in place seemed to put Russia and Ukraine on friendlier terms, or at least terms that would prevent something like this from happening in the future. Many had speculated that the entire crisis had nothing to do with financial terms to begin with. Since its Orange Revolution in 2004, Ukraine had shifted further and further West politically, and further and further away from its longtime ally, Russia. As the Ukrainian president Victor Yushchenko—the same candidate who had been poisoned during his campaign, most likely by a wing of the KGB—moved to take steps to gain Ukraine's entrance into NATO, Russia fumed at this perceived act of disloyalty. Ukraine had been part of the Soviet Union, and for years after the fall of the Berlin Wall, still deemed to be an unofficial part of Russia, even though it had its own sovereignty. The real reasons behind the gas crisis were never spoken about on the record, but when it came time to renew the pipeline contracts, it just so happened that this time around, with Yushchenko making more and more contacts in the West,

Russia wasn't eager to cut a deal with Ukraine. If Ukraine wanted to cozy up to the West, perhaps they'd have to cozy up to a West without any heat, Russia in effect, was saying. Russia had sent a message reminding Ukraine of who was really holding all the power. Even with the signing of a new deal intended to provide uninterrupted natural gas service to Eastern Europe, many European countries started looking for ways to broker new deals with different natural gas suppliers. These countries didn't want to be dependent on the political whims of Russia and be left in the cold again.

But as far as Bulgaria was concerned, Russia's temperament wasn't the problem. Bulgarian politicians started working on plans to create a pipeline that went directly from Russia to Bulgaria without needing to go through Ukraine.

The day the heat came back on was a day of celebration for Bulgaria. But two days before the crisis was resolved, there was a planned celebration for all of Europe in Brussels, as the EU Entropa exhibit was set to be unveiled. The Czech Republic held the rotating presidency of the European Union, and had decided to unleash an art display that celebrated the countries of the European Union. David Cerny, a Czech artist, was commissioned to lead an art project along with 27 artists. They sought to represent the European Union artistically and an eight-ton sculpture was unveiled to a large crowd in Brussels.

But when the sculpture was unveiled in its entirety, many in attendance wondered what they were looking at. This didn't look like a conventional art sculpture, and it also didn't seem to represent a traditional celebration of the European Union. Each country in the European Union was represented within the massive structure, but perhaps not in the way that it had expected.

France was depicted as an entire nation on strike. Holland was displayed under floodwater. Luxembourg was simply represented as a "For Sale" sign. Romania was a Dracula theme park. Italy was a giant soccer pitch. Germany was portrayed as the Autobahn in the shape of a swastika.

Cerny had supplied the names of 27 different artists who were helping him best symbolize each of the countries in the EU, but it turned out it was a hoax. He'd made up the names of the artists and done the entire sculpture himself—with the help of two other artist friends. He intended to represent each country in the European Union however his sense of humor best saw fit. The fact that he was able to pull off such a hoax and have it prominently displayed in Brussels, the capital of the

EU, was astounding. Most countries expressed dismay at how Cerny was able to get away with such an elaborate ruse, and seemed to have no idea how to respond to his art. As much as it was a hoax, though, it was still artwork. And looking at the sculpture and its representations of different countries, it was clearly very funny as well.

Well, it was funny to all countries except one: Bulgaria.

Cerny had chosen to represent countries in different ways. Some were victims of a darker sense of humor (Germany's swastika), and others were certainly given lighter treatment (Denmark was built entirely out of Legos). But no country received a fate quite like Bulgaria's.

Bulgaria was represented as a toilet.

Check that, a whole series of squat toilets.

With each new part of his sculpture, Cerny was quoted as saying he was trying to see if Europe had a sense of humor about itself. There was a resounding answer to this question from Bulgaria: *No.*

Bulgarian politicians were outraged, saying that representing the country as a toilet "offends the national dignity of Bulgaria." They insisted on the sculpture's removal and that they receive apologies in person from EU officials for the abuse they'd received.

In response to Bulgaria's outrage, Cerny was unsurprisingly unmoved by the offense Bulgaria took to its representation in the exhibit. "No other country in Europe has those kind of toilets," he was quoted as saying matter-of-factly in an interview.

Those kind of toilets meant squat toilets where you had to fit both feet into recessed areas on the floor, almost like you were starting the 100-meter dash in the Olympics. The rest of the toilet consisted of a round hole in the ground where you'd deposit whatever you needed to rid yourself of. For a male who needed to urinate, these toilets certainly weren't attractive, but also weren't problematic. But for a male needing to defecate or females needing to go either number one or two, these squat toilets provided quite a challenge. The holes in the floor weren't very large, and that meant any problem with your aim could result in a nasty brown or yellow splashing on your pant legs. Since there was nothing to sit on, balance was also an issue. Using one of the squat toilets was like doing a wall-sit–without the wall. Trying to remain steady without tipping one way or another while aiming for the small hole in the middle of the floor required great acts of strength and balance. If you found toilet paper accompanying a squat toilet, this was a major boon. But if you were looking for soap to wash your hands with after this particularly grimy experience, the odds weren't in your favor. Most squat toilet experiences did not include any nod to cleanliness or sanitation. And unfortunately, these toilets weren't present in a just a few places in Bulgaria; they were everywhere.

Kapka Kassabova explains that when growing up in Bulgaria, you quickly learned to avoid having to go to the bathroom in public at all costs. "Now there is something I must explain about Bulgarian public toilets," she wrote in her memoir. "First, they were generally a hole in the floor. Secondly, and more importantly, they were the ante-chambers of Hell. Wherever you were, however desperate your bladder and bowel situation, you held it in. You didn't eat, you didn't drink, you didn't go, until such time as a home toilet became available. At school, at university, at work, in hospital, and especially at railway stations, toilets were for dire emergency only. And it showed."

I sensed the outrage in Bulgaria coming from all angles, but it was difficult for me to look at Cerny's artwork with anything other than two predominant sentiments: he was right, and it was funny. My experiences in Bulgaria had confirmed Cerny's choice of artwork, and Kassabova's reflections just backed it up. Of course, having your country referred to as a toilet certainly wasn't flattering, but even the metaphor was one that I'd heard before.

Early on in my Bulgarian tenure, one of my students said that as far as the continent was concerned, "Bulgaria is the Mexico of Europe."

Not entirely sure what he meant by the Mexico reference, I asked him to clarify.

"What I mean," he said, "is that we're the toilet of this continent."

I was disheartened by this student's view on his homeland, and the country I was now calling home, but Bulgaria's standard of living was very low, and its politicians were notoriously corrupt. To top it all off, there were disgusting squat toilets everywhere. When Cerny produced his artwork, it seemed to fall right in line with what Bulgarians had already told me. Similar to my student who threw her garbage out the window and said, "I don't see why it's a problem. Everyone else is doing it," most Bulgarians didn't seem hesitant to view their country disparagingly. So I expected the response to the toilet sculpture to be tinged with a mix of acceptance and sadness. But that wasn't what happened. My students were outraged.

"This Czech artist is a bad, bad man," one student told me, "and I hope he pays for this."

"It's just art, though," I responded. "Isn't he allowed the have his opinion?"

"Mr. Jones," another student chimed in, "the problem with the toilet isn't so much that it's a toilet."

With this, several eyebrows were raised. Many people in the class had a problem with the exact fact that Bulgaria was a toilet, and didn't understand what he could be saying.

"This is not just a toilet," he continued. "It's a *Turkish* toilet! That bastard is comparing us to those dirty Turks!"

Now the class was in an uproar, angered even more because their country was not just represented as a toilet, but a Turkish toilet. My student was right, the most common name for these squat toilets was Turkish toilets, and now it appeared we were on the brink of ethnic warfare in my classroom. For those who weren't offended by the toilet itself, they were now given another option for their rage: Bulgaria was being linked with their hated enemy, Turkey.

One issue I'd been dealing with throughout my time in Bulgaria, and especially with my basketball team, was how to build up a sense of pride and self-esteem—whether this was an individual, team or whole-country issue. It seemed that pride was severely lacking in Bulgaria, and too many Bulgarians I knew would be quick to point out the faults of their country, throw their hands up in the air, and say *ne modje*. But I was finding that there was some consistency about when pride would show up: when Bulgarians were offended. Just like when the Greek athletic director called us *stupid, stupid, stupid* and Pavel and Pesho were irrationally ready to take him out mafia-style, now that Bulgaria had been offended on the world stage, many of my students now appeared ready to put up their dukes and beat up the Czech artist. The problem with this equation, as far as I could see, was that the pride only showed up as a response to something bad happening, but wasn't noticeable beforehand.

My parents had come to visit me my first year in Bulgaria, and my father, a journalist for the *Chicago Tribune* at the time, decided to write an article about his experiences in Bulgaria for the Sunday travel section. The piece was run a few months after his visit, and encouraged people to go visit Bulgaria because it "is a dark, fascinating and, unfortunately, forgotten country, an Iowa-sized Balkan beauty with snow-capped mountains and lush green fields." He went on to point out the uniqueness of Bulgaria, encouraging readers with this statement: "Don't come to Bulgaria if you're looking for some glossy European elegance interspersed with Starbucks and all those Western, touristy accoutrements that make travel so comfortable and reassuring. But do come if you're up for something a little wild and pretty rough around the edges. Come if you're interested in watching the noisy, tectonic shifts of a former communist satellite in awkward transition to wherever it's going. Come if you'd like to see the Old World, before it's gone." He finished the article by remarking that Bulgaria "is one of the best and most interesting bargains in Europe." But as he sent me the draft that was about to go to the printers, I asked him to take my name out of the article, worried about how Bulgarians would interpret some of his statements meant to encourage people to travel to the country. I knew they were a sensitive bunch, and while my dad's words were meant to show how different and interesting Bulgaria was, I wasn't sure Bulgarians wanted to be seen that way. Europe was moving forward and modernizing, and the article was pointing out that Bulgaria was unique because its modernization was far from complete. Since the largest Bulgarian population in the United States was in Chicago, there were plenty of Bulgarians who would read the *Tribune* story. And the reader responses my dad received eclipsed the amount of responses he'd ever received for any story he'd written in more than 30 years as a journalist.

"Shame on you, Tim Jones!" was where the Bulgarian responses began.

"In your article, you sound very incompetent and therefore not worthy of any attention," one reader wrote, contradicting himself by giving my dad attention through the very act of writing him a letter. "I am sure you have not experienced the real beauty of your shabby American hometown."

Another reader encouraged my father to respond by threatening him: "If you are man enough, you will respond … if not you will crawl in the smallest hole in the world and be quiet!!!"

As if these responses weren't harsh and inflammatory enough, other Bulgarian readers went even further.

"Sorry that the banks are not only Jewish-owned like your country," was one irrational response that not only sadly displayed anti-Semitism, but had nothing to do with the article itself.

"It's a fact there is a $5000 reward for your head," wrote another Bulgarian, and this is when I asked my dad to stop sending me his fan mail. I was getting the picture very clearly.

My dad's article had intended to advertise for Bulgaria; that's what travel articles do. In fact, Bulgarian tourist agencies even picked up his article and posted it on their websites to encourage people to come visit. But for the Bulgarians who were able to find any slight directed toward their country, they fired back with a vengeance. He'd gone nowhere near comparing Bulgaria to a Turkish squat toilet; in fact, he was attempting to rave about how different and interesting the country is. But Bulgarians' defensive sense of pride kicked in–I'm also guessing some Bulgarian readers had shortcomings in their understanding of English–and they lashed out with venom at his travel article.

Regarding the toilet sculpture, which, unlike my dad's article, was clearly offensive, Bulgarian politicians continued their fervent calls for the artwork to be taken down. This was a clear nod toward censoring something they didn't like. As much as the sculpture could clearly be deemed as offensive to Bulgarians, the same could be said about many other pieces of art regarding many other people. In fact, I felt rather offended that the Bulgarian public school I visited had a bin Laden mural on its outside wall. I definitely thought the mural was in bad taste and it made me worried about the school I was about to enter, but I don't know if taking the mural down crossed my mind.

Slavenka Drakulic, a Croatian author who writes about the Balkans, penned a column for the *Guardian* indicating her views on the Bulgarian protest to the toilet sculpture: "By issuing this official objection 20 years after the fall of communism in Bulgaria, the bureaucrats at the culture ministry ... reveal that they haven't yet heard that art should be an act of freedom, not a propaganda tool, regardless of how tasteless or offensive a particular work might be." It did seem very odd that the new democratic Bulgarian state was objecting to a piece of art because it didn't represent the country in the way the state wanted the country represented. In modern and supposedly free Bulgaria, this seemed like a throwback to the way things used to be during communism. Drakulic continued on to say that while "the political system might change overnight, the old way of thinking is alive and well."

Without a doubt, January was a rough month for Bulgaria. After the country spent the better portion of the month without natural gas from Russian gas pipelines, then it was represented to the entire European Union as a Turkish squat toilet. It had certainly been an arduous month, and it just seemed like the toilet sculpture was doing nothing but pouring salt in the wounds. But I quickly realized that that idiom wasn't going to be useful in Bulgaria; my second winter of sliding on the ice had firmly cemented one thought in my mind: Bulgaria didn't have any salt for its sidewalks.

With the heat back on, we got back to our scheduled Wednesday games. And my rationale for hosting these games was so that we'd have some control over the environment. Our court, while far short of sublime, was close to regulation size and didn't have caged walls or protruding pipes. We could hire referees that Nikolai trusted, and that came with the understanding that they would not be smoking cigarettes or talking on their cell phones during the games. We could ensure that we were inviting teams that would uphold some semblance of non-swastika decency on the floor. And as for Bulgaria's Turkish toilet issue, we could provide real toilets that offered the option of sitting down.

The Bulgarian schools we invited to play were thrilled to play in a real gym. It wasn't difficult to find teams eager to travel to our campus. But I also wondered in late January how prepared other teams were going to be to play against us. When there was no gas flowing through Bulgarian pipelines, many teams had stopped having practice. This wasn't the case with us, though, much to the dismay of my players. We'd kept practicing, and by the time the heat was turned back on, I knew we were ready to play.

Our opponent, one of myriad numbered public schools in Sofia that made it difficult for me to ever tell the difference—35 was the school number that seemed to matter—came into the gym with a swagger. But that swagger was gone soon after tip-off.

Menkov was blowing by their defenders, and our full-court press was making it difficult for them to even cross half court. Halfway through the first quarter, even though we were stealing the ball so often that the game was mostly being played in our offensive end, the other team already looked out of shape, dragging and exhausted. Their coach was wearing a Metallica shirt, and his long hair was rocketing all over the place with each new turnover. At the end of the first quarter, we were up by 14 points.

"This is fun, isn't it guys?" I said to the huddle and could see smiles all around. We'd been in this position before against really bad teams, but our opponents this time were actually halfway decent. They just weren't in shape and hadn't been practicing like we had.

The second quarter—and rest of the game—was more of the same. Menkov would shoot up and down the floor, creating opportunities for himself and others. The combination of Pesho and Sasho down low was killing our opponents on the boards. We'd stopped the full court press because our lead had ballooned, but our half-court defense was still wreaking havoc. It appeared this team had never seen a Bulgarian team play man-to-man defense.

"Coach, Coach," Pavel told me excitedly, "they have no idea what to do on offense. They've never seen a man-to-man defense before. They just stand around and have no idea what to do. They have no idea!"

The truth was, we still lacked any idea of what to do on offense either. But we were creating so many turnovers with our defense, running out on the fast break and crashing the boards, that our lack of offensive fluidity didn't matter too much. Ivan made a couple nice moves inside, Vassy finished on the fast break and Kosio hit a three midway through the third quarter. We were now winning by more than 30 points. Metallica Shirt had given up on being enraged. He was now sitting in his coach's chair, leaning back with his legs crossed. From my vantage point, I couldn't tell if he had his eyes open or not.

We played the rest of the game with substitutes who were eager to be part of the action. I noticed that the regulars sitting on the bench were having fun, enjoying basketball and enjoying each other. I still had to caution them, though.

"Look, you all know what it feels like to be losing by a lot of points. You've been in the other team's shoes, and you know how much it sucks."

For once, there were nods up and down the bench, and I thought this might've meant they'd all converted to nodding to say yes, a victory in itself.

"So you will not taunt the other team, make fun of them or say anything negative as this game finishes. We're going to do this with class—win with class."

My players assented and conducted themselves appropriately as the game finished. On the other sideline, though, as the horn sounded, several members of the opposing team took the water bottles we'd given them at the start of the game and started kicking and throwing them across the floor. Water was shooting across half court, and my players were soccer-trapping the water bottles as they went over to the other team to try to shake hands. At this point, Metallica Shirt looked confused. He didn't know whether he should shake my hand or start throwing water bottles himself. His team had lost by 28 points.

"This is ridiculous," Nikolai told me after the game, as we were mopping up the wet spots on the floor. "We will not invite them to come play here again."

If nothing else, I felt like I was always being provided with examples for my players of what *not* to do and how *not* to act. With each time I'd point out the inappropriate nature of another team's actions, it seemed to me that half the team already understood, and the other half would have an "ah-hah" moment: *Oh yeah, I guess it does look bad when you do something like that.*

As much as Nikolai and I now felt like we had control over which teams to invite, it became difficult to find any Bulgarian team to come play in our gym who would purport themselves in a dignified manner. My concern was centered much more on the play of our team, and the fact that we were playing some of the best basketball since I'd arrived, but this didn't take away from the fact that I was astounded by the conduct of our opponents.

"When you told me we were going to play all of our games at home to avoid the problems you had last year," Branch told me before our next game, "I thought that meant things might be a little bit boring. But this isn't boring at all."

Using our superior fitness and willingness to work as a team, we sped out to another big lead in the first quarter of our next game. Menkov started to understand that the biggest decision we'd face in the first quarter was when we should stop pressing, aware that I didn't want to run up the score on a deflated opponent. At the end of this first quarter, our lead was 12 points. And once again, I remarked to Branch that while our opponent was slowly becoming dejected and clearly on their way to losing, this wasn't an opponent that lacked talent. But the talent this team had—a shooting guard with a smooth three-point shot, and a center who could post up Pesho with relative ease—wasn't interested in playing together as a team. Once the ball was advanced past half court, it seemed that whoever had the ball first was going to shoot it.

This played right into our hands. No matter who was playing the forward positions—Vassy, Ivan or Pesho—they were pulling down rebounds and finding Menkov and Dimov on the fast break. The other team was demoralized by missing shots, and any time we pushed the ball, we usually ended up with a 3-on-2 or 2-on-1 fast break. These shouldn't have been fast breaks, but they were because half of the other team didn't feel like running back on defense. And we'd run enough fast-break drills where I emphasized passing the ball, that even when passes were chucked at players' ankles, we were still converting a high rate.

Sometimes we were even able to start fast breaks off made shots because the opposing players were spending so much time admiring their last basket. The three-point specialist in particular enjoyed interacting with the sparse crowd whenever he scored. His version of a salute to the fans in attendance—an even split between our school and our opponent—was to stop, face the crowd and point at them with one hand. With his other hand, he'd grab his balls. In the meantime, we were headed the other way while he was playing with himself. I pointed out to the players on the bench the stupidity of celebrating while the game was still being played, and also cautioned them not to get fouled by that guy. They were aware of where his hands had been spending a lot of time.

Of course the opposing coach had no problem with his players' celebrations, even though they were trailing the entire game. By no means were we playing a beautiful version of basketball—Pavel still appeared eager to hurt the backboard with his shots and Pesho was fading away trying to sail circus shots into the hoop—but our effort was far superior, and as a result, we were easily winning the game. Once again, the fourth quarter was dominated by subs who got a chance to finish up the game with the outcome already determined. With two minutes to play, a 5'6" opposing guard sneaked in for a rebound, pulled it down and launched an unorthodox hook shot that found the bottom of the net. Upon making the shot, he turned toward our bench, flexed both of his scrawny biceps and growled.

His hook shot had just cut the lead to 23 points.

The bench loved it, and started laughing uproariously with Pesho in the lead. I tried to calm them down, warning them that we knew what it felt like to lose, and we were going to win with class.

"But Coach, Coach," Pesho protested, "when we were losing by 25 points, we never do stupid things like this. *Thees* guy, *thees* guy, he is a real idiot."

I wanted to reiterate my point about winning with class, but Pesho did make me pause for moment.

"Okay, I'll agree with you for a change, Pesho," I told him. "That guy really is an idiot."

With this, the bench roared in approval.

In the waning seconds of the game, one of our subs had to come out of the game because the ball had been deflected into his face, giving him a swollen upper lip. I knew we had a doctor on hand, and had never actually seen him do anything, so I was curiously eager to see how he would handle this puffy lip. Assessing the situation, he dug into his supply kit and produced a bottle of Bulgarian *rakia*. I couldn't believe my eyes. *Rakia* is Bulgaria's national drink, a grape brandy and rocket-fuel mix that seems to be every Bulgarian's favorite version of moonshine. In fact, for the duration of the heat crisis, I knew several Bulgarians who figured they could somehow manage to survive without heat—as long as they had *rakia*. Immediately upon ingestion, *rakia* would scorch your throat and esophagus, making its way down to your stomach, producing a subtle boil in your abdomen. There were innumerous types of *rakia* and each had a different taste. But regardless of the taste, all forms of *rakia* warmed you up in a hurry—and got you drunk just as fast.

That's why I was astounded to witness the school's doctor pull out a bottle of *rakia* from his first-aid kit. Bulgarians had already told me about the mythical healing power of *rakia*: *Got a stomach ache? Have a shot of rakia. Your nose is running? Drink rakia. Your knee just won't stop hurting? Rakia will fix it.* But still, this was a doctor who worked for the school. Was he really going to give one of my players *rakia* to drink? I couldn't believe it.

It turned out, though, that he didn't want my player to drink the *rakia*, but merely place the *rakia* bottle on his swollen lip. In lieu of an ice pack, he was using a frozen *rakia* bottle.

"I save these bottles," the doctor told me in Bulgarian, "just for moments like these."

If you were watching from the stands, you would have seen a bench full of players laughing and enjoying the end of our third victory in a row. Filling out the scene was a backup forward sitting on the end of the bench, sucking on a *rakia* bottle. In a very Bulgarian way, I figured, the entire canvas was just about perfect.

That night, as Branch and I were about to walk out of the bubble together, he pondered how things were going so far this season.

"Andy, you told me all about last year," he said, "and so I tried to prepare myself. And when I watch us play basketball, it certainly isn't pretty. We can look pretty terrible on offense sometimes, and we make some horrible basketball decisions. But," and he paused here, "we've won three in a row, and these kids are playing hard. This is a lot of fun."

I stopped and thought for a second about what he'd said. The heat had been turned off, the country had been disgraced as a toilet, and I'd watched water bottles fly and crotches grabbed, but none of this had affected our basketball team. In the meantime, our basketball team was winning games and having fun.

Menkov and Pavel had hung around, still laughing about the victory, and now came up to the two of us.

"Coaches, this is a lot fun," Pavel said, beaming from ear to ear.

"I can feel it," Menkov said, and clenched his fists as if he really could. "This is our year. This year, we're going to win the ACS Open."

Branch and I both patted them on the back and walked out of the bubble into the slip-and-slide that was Bulgaria's ice. I was thrilled by their optimism, and realized that I was far more prepared to handle things going wrong than to handle winning three games in a row.

Chapter XX
Tough Guys

Bulgaria is a nation full of politicians that the general public loves to hate. Boyko Borisov was the exact opposite of this. Putting the words "popular" and "politician" together seemed like an oxymoron during my time in Bulgaria, but Borisov would provide the exception to the rule. As the mayor of Sofia, Borisov enjoyed high approval ratings and was the overwhelming favorite to become prime minister and unseat Sergei Stanishev, most infamous for having no solutions for how to deal with the heat crisis. Stanishev and Borisov couldn't have been more different either. While Stanishev was educated at the London School of Economics and looked professorial, Borisov was a former bodyguard and black belt karate champion. Stanishev looked like someone who enjoyed discussing policy and economic issues, while Borisov looked like someone who enjoyed beating people up.

That's probably why he was so popular in Bulgaria. Borisov might not have been able to stack his resumé with educational qualifications, but he could promise to act instead of just talk. His political career got its start in an unusual way—at least by Western standards—when he was communist leader Todor Zhivkov's bodyguard in the 1980s. In 2009, polls were showing Borisov would defeat Stanishev in the upcoming election for prime minister—and most of this was based on the people's belief that Borisov, while unconventional and thuggish, would actually get things done.

It's also possible that there were a great deal of Bulgarians who liked the idea of having a prime minister who could kick butt.

While Stanishev was clearly the worldlier of the two candidates—he'd lived in Russia and England, while having family from Ukraine and Macedonia—Borisov seemed to speak to Bulgarians in a way they could understand him. His large frame, no-nonsense demeanor and boisterous attitude made him recognizable to Bulgarians. He was a tough guy who wouldn't give in to outside pressures, and would lead a straight talk express candidacy, a la John McCain in the U.S. in the 2000 presidential primaries. Borisov claimed he would lead to refreshing changes in Bulgaria, and create a transparency and honesty that had been sorely missing as one administration after another seemed to be beholden to mafia interests far more than the interests of the general public.

As Bulgaria came of age after the fall of communism, this didn't lead to an intellectual and cultural revolution like the Czech Republic aimed for with their Prague Spring, a celebration of freedom, artistry and writing. Even Estonia's revolution following the fall of the Berlin Wall had friendly and artistic connotations; the Singing Revolution sought to emphasize the power of Estonian culture through song. In Bulgaria, though, arts and culture didn't seem to be a part of this modern and free country. As a country that was most known on the world sporting stage for its success in weightlifting, brawn still held sway over brains in many circumstances. As Bulgaria was released from the grip of the Soviet Union, Kapka Kassabova remarked on what was most important in the new Bulgarian world.

"One thing was clear: money was king," she wrote in her memoir. "Education, culture, and the life of the mind were for sissies, and sissies sold pantyhose on the street, walked the streets with a lunatic grin, starved to death and were run over by speeding black Mercedes."

She was referring to life in Bulgaria in the 1990s, but I still saw many of these same similarities in the first decade of the 21st century. For Halloween, far and away the most popular costume for male students at our school was a mafia member. Black slacks would be accompanied by a tight black shirt and a gold chain. Some would wear top hats to put the icing on the cake; a few others would walk with canes, and say they needed the cane to help them walk due to an injury suffered during a mafia shootout. Of course this was just Halloween, but it was particularly noticeable that all these males dressing up as mafia members—or *mutri*—were not mocking the mafia. They really idolized these people, the people who many believed were running the country.

While riding in a taxi in Sofia, it would not be uncommon for numerous black Mercedes to whiz by us. More times than not, the taxi driver would turn to me and grumble, "*Mutri, mutri, mutri. Vsyakade.*" He was expressing his frustration that the mafia and their Mercedes seemed to be everywhere. In the poorest country in the EU, it was astounding to see how many Mercedes would be on the road. The socio-economic equation certainly didn't add up—unless, of course, you considered that the middle class in Bulgaria barely seemed to exist anymore. There were just the black Mercedes and then everyone else.

There were two schools of thought regarding Boyko Borisov and how he would deal with the mafia presence in Bulgaria. His supporters would point out that this was a man who didn't back down to anyone—either physically or psychologically. He would stand up to the mafia because he wasn't afraid of them. And his campaign promised to root out corruption and fight drug bosses who currently held great power in Bulgaria. He even threatened to have Stanishev arrested for alleged involvement in corruption. Unlike Stanishev, who had a superior academic background, Borisov was a fighter. He was tough and not afraid to change things.

Borisov's detractors, though, would say that while he represented change from the current prime minister, that was because he was already basically a member of the mob himself. It was easy for him to talk tough because he was so immersed in the corruption that life was good for him. Zhivkov's former bodyguard had learned the ropes from some of the masters, and now he had his fingers in many different pots. Instead of having government officials who had ties to the mob, some believed that Borisov actually was the mob.

These opinions on Borisov were merely opinions, and neither side could definitely prove Borisov's motivations and qualifications either way. But on the whole, he remained a popular figure. My students, who were about to become legal to vote, either liked him because he was a tough guy, or because they were simply exasperated by the status quo.

As the elections started to heat up, Borisov provoked Stanishev over and over again, seemingly unafraid of the incumbent prime minister. In one episode, Borisov both challenged and mocked Stanishev at the same time regarding a televised debate that had gone awry. For whatever reason, Stanishev didn't show up for the debate. It wasn't clear if the debate had actually been agreed to, but in Borisov's mind, it certainly had. And when the TV cameras showed up and there was only one candidate, Borisov certainly had an audience.

"As you can see I am willing to talk to Stanishev," Borisov declared to the cameras. "I was playing football when the invitation came and I had to change quickly."

In a football-crazed country, having to stop a game early to deal with such pithy concerns as how the nation should be governed could be considered an affront to a man's dignity. But clearly in Borisov's case, he was willing to make the sacrifice to stop playing soccer in order to focus on the fate of his nation.

"I am here and waiting and if Stanishev doesn't come than he is a coward," Borisov announced, clearly hitting his stride. "In my neighborhood if someone asks you to fight you either do it or you run away. I used to fight as a child. Stanishev's media advisers are very good and have thought of everything except for the fact that I am fearless."

Stanishev never showed up for the debate. Nor did he respond to such heavy-hitting criticism as being a coward or deal with the fact that Borisov was fearless. The London School of Economics graduate wanted to take the high road. But Borisov's outlandish speech was highly popular. Bulgarians like that he declared himself fearless, and liked his back-alley, neighborhood mentality. When someone challenges you to a fight, you show up and defend your honor; it was as simple as that. That was how honor was defined in Bulgaria. And it was probably how Bulgaria held tight to its own sense of identity even amidst one defeat after another. Even though they'd ended up on the wrong side of two Balkan Wars and two world wars, they'd showed up for the fight. They hadn't backed down. When you don't win, you have to be able to cling to something.

None of what Borisov was saying seemed even remotely worthy of someone who could hold the highest office in the country, but that was just my American perspective. What I saw as Borisov's *schtick*, Bulgarians saw as the strong, karate-chopping mentality of someone who would change the country by kicking some butt.

I discussed the nature of Borisov's caustic tone with my students, and most supported his fiery, and rarely ever policy-driven rhetoric. I had to ask them then if it worried them that Borisov made so many references to fighting, and treated running for political office more like the run-up to a boxing match than anything else. Again, not too many had problems with this. In fact, the same male student who had been angered by the *Turkish* toilets, a student who dressed in mob-like all black every day, wanted to take the time to explain to me the difference between his country and my country.

"In your country," he said calmly, "if you get in a fight with another guy and you beat him up, you will most likely go to jail and then he will probably sue you."

With this, I nodded, agreeing that he was probably right.

"In my country," he continued, and now seemed a little more fired up, "if I beat someone up, I can just keep beating him. I can beat him as much as I was want. So, in my country, I'm able to be a real man, and I like that."

Several female students slumped down in their chairs as he said this, but the majority of the males in the classroom used gestures—head-shakes, head-bobs and fist-pumps—to indicate they were on board with what he was saying. This was further supported by the country's most popular football club, CSKA Sofia. As fans started protesting at games, upset with the managing directors' decisions regarding the club, CSKA's owners had no intention to try to win back the hearts and minds of their fans. To quell the uprising, which was simply being launched by fans sitting in the stands holding up homemade signs that said "PROTEST," the owners hired a group of thugs—60 men who showed up in the stadium in jeeps—to go into the crowd of protesters and start beating them up. This outrageous incident made the news, but it wasn't portrayed as something the owners should be ashamed of, or even something illegal. It was simply the owners' decision on how to deal with the problem. In Bulgaria, it seemed to me that the best solutions were directly linked to the manliest solutions. I was starting to learn that there was great honor placed upon being a "real man" in Bulgaria, whether this meant you were involved in a high school fight, driving a black Mercedes, in charge of a football club, or running for the highest office in the land.

Our next Wednesday game put me face to face with a "real man," the coach of the Italian school, who had been playing in the adult game once a week as well. The adult pickup game, as I've chronicled before, was regularly littered with Bulgarian yelling and angst. The Bulgarian coach of the Italian school was a stocky six feet tall and he liked to use his broad shoulders to barrel into his defender, and then usually call a foul on his defender. The yelling he either instigated or conducted had caused several Bulgarians to come up to me after one of our pickup games and ask me if I could ban him from ever coming back to play. Several of the Bulgarians who were asking me to not allow the Italian school coach were not exactly quiet themselves; they spent the majority of the game yapping and arguing, but it was nothing like this guy. I was put in the completely unenviable position of talking to the Italian school coach in a combination of Bulgarian and English, indicating to him that he'd have to tone it down if he wanted to keep playing with us. He patted me on the shoulders and explained to me that in his country, everyone yells at each other. This is just for fun, and I didn't need to worry. He saw this as an enlightening cultural moment for me, but the reality was he wasn't telling me anything I didn't already know. I was accustomed to Bulgarians yelling at each other in all types of situations.

But as our game against the Italian school tipped off, I don't think my players were used to the volume and pace of the verbal assault that came from the Italian coach. From the very first possession, he was storming up and down the sidelines, spittle propelling from his lips with each new ostentatious display of displeasure. He was howling at his Bulgarian players, screaming at the referees, and most certainly cursing the heavens all at the same time. If I'd have asked him how he was doing, though, I could rest assured that he'd say this was just for fun; I didn't need to worry.

And quite honestly, I wasn't worried. His behavior should have had nothing to do with my team's play. As far as I was concerned, he was irrelevant to our performance on the floor. The only impact he had up to this point was earning a technical foul a mere two minutes into the game. He was shouting so loudly, I actually thought he might get two technical fouls and be thrown out of the game right there. He continued his verbal barrage of the referees as Menkov went to the free throw line and proceeded to miss both free throws. When he looked back at me after missing the second free throw, I couldn't tell if he was apologetic or scared.

At the end of the first quarter of an ugly game, we held a 7-6 lead. Everything about our game seemed off up to this point. There was a carnival side show occurring on the other bench, and as a result, I'd hardly shouted any instructions to my team. There was no way they'd be able to hear me over the clamor of the Italian coach. As my players came into our huddle, though, I looked at their faces and they seemed genuinely afraid.

"Guys, what's going on here?" I questioned them. "There's a lot of yelling going on, but am I the one yelling at you?"

This gave them all a pause, and then Pavel was the first to speak.

"No, Coach, you aren't yelling at us at all."

"Okay then," I smiled at them, "then why are you scared because of all his yelling? He's not yelling at you, is he?"

Again, they paused and a few more started grinning.

"I mean, I'd be scared if he was yelling at me, but he's yelling at his players and the referees. If you want to be scared of someone, be scared of me. But that guy," I said, trying to remain appropriate, "he's a joke. He's ridiculous. He's going to keep yelling, and you can't let that intimidate you. You need to focus on working together, listening to each other, and most importantly, listening to me. To hell with him."

The huddle broke with smiles and laughter. I usually avoided making reference to other coaches during the game, but in this case, it seemed necessary. The Italian coach was so loud and out of control that he'd intimidated my players.

We started the second quarter on an 8-0 run; that was one more point than we'd scored the entire first quarter. With each new basket, the Italian coach got louder. He grabbed one of his players by the jersey and started screaming in his face. To replace him in the game, he yanked another player out of his seat on the bench and hurtled him toward the scorers' table. Now the run had increased to 12-0. His players seemed deflated, and my players had finally started ignoring him.

Unable to stay focused on any one problem for too long a period of time, the Italian coach left his players alone for a little while and went back after the referees. He was a good three feet onto the floor, and his venomous rant was escalating with his wildly gesticulating fingers pointing from one referee to the next. I was able to understand some things in translation, but turned to my bench, curious if they could enlighten me about the finer details of what he was saying.

"Coach, it is very interesting what he is saying," Kosio told me with a smile, "but I don't think I should repeat it."

The bench laughed, and at that moment, the Italian coach was hit with his long-awaited second technical foul. This caused him to wave his arms maniacally and go even more berserk. A second technical foul meant two more free throws–Menkov made them this time–and an automatic ejection from the game. But the Italian coach refused to leave the floor. The referees indicated that, by rule, he had to leave. He'd been ejected. Still, he wouldn't budge, and stood on his sideline arms crossed with his head back, looking like a defiant teenager.

I assumed that sooner or later he would have to give in and leave, but he didn't. And as the referees approached me, I could see from the looks on their faces that they didn't know what to do. They were scared of him—and rightfully so.

"Okay, here's what we can do," said one referee, who surprisingly was speaking English. "He has been ejected but will not leave the gym. We can compromise with him and allow him to stay for the rest of the game. But he must sit down in his seat. He cannot talk to us anymore."

I looked over to Nikolai at the scorers' table, wondering if there was any kind of Bulgarian precedent for this decision. He raised his eyebrows and shrugged his shoulders as if to say, "Do you want to try to get him to leave the gym? I don't."

In the end, I didn't see that I had much choice but to agree, and I also thought it might be just as entertaining to see if the Italian coach could just sit in his seat for the rest of the game and not talk. This might've been more of a punishment than getting ejected from the game.

With one eye on the floor and one eye on the opposing bench, the rest of the game was a breeze. After we conquered our initial intimidation, we had little trouble causing turnovers and running the other way on the fast breaks. This team really only had one talented player, and he started to give up soon after our lead reached double digits. We cruised through the second half, and picked up our fourth win in a row by a wide margin.

The atmosphere after the game was reaching all-time levels of excitement. The previous year, we'd barely won four games, and these had come against teams who didn't appear they'd ever played basketball before. This year, winning was becoming a habit. We still hadn't played a truly strong team like 35th or Spanish, but we'd played teams that had talent. These teams just didn't play as hard or as together as we did.

After the game, though, as some of our team quietly mocked the Italian coach, I wanted to focus on more than just basketball. I could tell that while some of my players found his antics amusing, others saw him as embarrassing. He wasn't just a representative of the Italian school basketball team, he was a Bulgarian—a volatile and irrational Bulgarian similar to people that many of my players knew. The reminder didn't strike them as pleasant.

"You're always going to have a choice," I told them, "based on how you want to act. Whether we had won or lost the game today, we've chosen to do things the right way, to show our character and play with pride. I know the coach from the Italian team, and I know he responds to everything in basketball by yelling, screaming and getting upset. But I hope you see that nothing good comes of that. In the end, it doesn't help anything, and he just ends up looking bad. Keep that in mind—not just for basketball, but for life. Think about how you should act in all situations."

My last piece of advice ended up being far more relevant to our situation as a team than I'd ever hoped it would be. We were riding high, on a four-game winning streak. Practices were energized since we were playing at least one game per week. It was now Monday, and we had two big days of preparation ahead of us. On Wednesday, we had a game scheduled against the Spanish school, one of the two favorites each year to win the ACS Open. Now we would have a chance to actually measure how much we'd improved. We knew this was one of the best teams in Sofia, and I got the sense the team felt we could finally win a game like this. But as practice started on Monday afternoon, something seemed amiss.

"Coach," Branch approached me and said, "weren't Vassy and Dimov in school today?"

I thought about this for a moment.

"Well, I definitely saw Dimov in school...."

"And Vassy was here, too," he added.

"But they're not here now."

Practice had just started, and while there was a possibility that they were late, this seemed unlikely. We had the late time slot for practice, 5 p.m., because the girls had practiced earlier. There were usually no problems with any players arriving late for the 5 p.m. practice since they just hung out on campus after school, did homework, and waited for practice to start. All of the other regulars were on the floor, beginning their warm-up, but Vassy and Dimov were nowhere to be seen.

"Menkov," I briskly jogged over to where he was warming up, "where are Vassy and Dimov?"

"Uhh ... I don't know, Coach," he said hesitantly. "I guess they're not here."

I looked at him an extra second after he responded, feeling certain that he did know something, but just didn't want to tell me. Both of their absences struck me as odd since they'd both been playing so well, and I knew both were excited about the game against the Spanish school on Wednesday. Dimov had learned to stop criticizing his teammates, and while he still wasn't quite a leader, he was our best ball handler. This took some of the burden off Menkov from having to be responsible for having the ball so much. Vassy, while still too small and not exceptionally talented, had been steady throughout his two years on the team. He never complained, never backed down and relished the challenge of banging with players bigger than him.

Practice began without them, and it finished without them, too. I wanted to address the fact that they weren't on the floor with us, and the consequences that would result. Missing a practice two days before a game–especially missing a practice without telling the coaches beforehand–would mean that each of them would sit out for at least the first quarter, maybe even the first half of Wednesday's game. I was frustrated by their absence, and when I'd brought it up a few more times to other players, they gave me quiet mumblings as responses. It seemed something was going on, but I didn't know what.

"I'd just let it go for today," Branch told me as practice was wrapping up for the day. "We've got so much good momentum going; you don't want to focus on this right now. Just focus on who's here practicing and playing hard."

He was right. I knew he was right. But it still irritated me that two seniors, two regular contributors had missed practice and not bothered to talk to me beforehand. We finished practice and talked about strategy for Wednesday's game against the Spanish school. I issued a stern reminder that attending practice on Tuesday would be critical for Wednesday's game.

Vassy came to see me second period on Tuesday, and I was at least glad he realized there was a problem with what had happened yesterday. Early on in my Bulgarian tenure, players seemed shocked when I indicated that I expected them to be at practice every day. Now at least we'd moved into a new realm of accountability. He knew he should've been at practice, and knew he needed to talk to me.

"Coach, I'm really sorry about yesterday. I didn't mean to miss practice. I know these are big practices before Wednesday's game," Vassy said, with a serious look on his face.

I tried to assess the seriousness of what was going on based on his facial expressions. As a result of living on his own without parents, Vassy was one of the most mature guys on the team. But I also knew that living on his own gave him some freedoms that most parents would shudder to give a 17-year-old.

"Thanks for coming to talk to me, Vassy. What happened?" I responded.

"Well, Coach, first of all, it's not a big deal," he said.

That statement, in and of itself, already signaled to me that this was a big deal.

"A couple of us left campus after school to go get something to eat, and then when I was walking out of the restaurant, I got mugged."

"You got mugged?" I was incredulous. "What do you mean?"

"Well, there were two guys, and one of them hit me. The other took my wallet."

"Oh my God, are you okay?"

He looked more embarrassed than hurt, but I couldn't be certain.

"Yeah, yeah, yeah, I'm fine," he quickly tried to reassure me. "It's just that after it happened, I had to go to the police to report what happened. They'd taken my wallet."

"But physically, you're okay?"

"Yeah, yeah, yeah, I'm fine, Coach."

Eager to end the conversation, he started to walk out of my room.

"I'll be at practice today, Coach. Don't worry. I'll be there today."

"Okay, Vassy, because we need you. You can't miss another practice before tomorrow's game."

"I'll be there, Coach."

As he was about to leave my classroom, many different questions were running through my head, but the first one that came out was dealing with Dimov.

"Vassy, wait," I said to him. "Was Dimov with you yesterday?"

Vassy turned and gave me a pained expression, an expression I realized that hadn't left his face since he'd walked into my room.

"Yeah, he was with me. We were both going to come back to practice together."

"Okay," I replied, waiting for more.

"But he, uh, he got the tires on his car slashed."

"What? Are you serious?"

"Yeah, so, uh, he had to go to the police with me to report what happened to his car."

I hesitated, trying to take all of this in, and that gave Vassy the opportunity to leave my classroom. It was clear he didn't want to talk about any of this, and that was odd coming from one of my more self-confident players. He loved to talk, and had come in second in the race for student council president to Menkov the year before. But regarding yesterday afternoon, he wanted to keep it short and simple—and then get the heck out of my room. I was digesting everything he told me when Branch came into my room.

"What'd he have to say?" Branch asked, having just seen Vassy scurry out of my room.

I relayed to him what Vassy had said to me.

"Mugged? Tires slashed? What the hell is going on?" Branch's reaction re-affirmed my earlier confusion. This all sounded bizarre.

As chaotic as life in Bulgaria could be, muggings and tire-slashings were not common. Sure, there was mafia violence, but what I'd been told numerous times before had held true: mob violence only affected the mob. In general, I never felt unsafe walking around on Sofia's streets, even at night. The only thing most people worried about in terms of safety was stray dogs. They represented an omnipresent threat that was far more unpredictable than any thief or mugger. But in general, I rarely ever heard or read about things like muggings or tires getting slashed. Aside from the fact that I'd never want my players to be in danger, I was also alarmed by the fact that all of this seemed so odd.

"Wait a minute," Branch mused. "He said they went to the police to report what happened?"

"Yeah, that's what he just told me," I responded, not sure what Branch was getting at.

"Does that make any sense to you? If something like this happened, would they really go to the police?"

Now I understood what he was getting at. The police—similar to most aspects of the Bulgarian justice system—were notoriously corrupt. People rarely relied on them to solve any crimes, and high school students especially didn't have any desire to be involved with the police.

"No, I guess it doesn't. But that's why he said they missed practice. They had to report what happened to the police."

"Were these guys that attacked them people they knew?"

I hadn't asked this question, but now was thinking that I should've. Vassy had made it sound as if they were attacked by random hooligans or muggers, but now I was starting to wonder if this was the case. Mugging might be done randomly, but slashing someone's tires? That wasn't usually a random act. That was an intentional act of revenge. And as far as I knew, Dimov was one of only two players on the team who had a car (Kosio was the other one). His car, which I assumed was a gift from his Mercedes-driving father, was a luxury car.

"Well, what do we do?" I asked Branch.

"I don't know what we can do," he seemed as lost as I was. "Vassy said he'd come to practice today, so if we want to deal with it then, we can. But what about Dimov?"

"I have no idea. I haven't seen him."

At this point, I felt myself falling into the, "If I was in the States and this happened," trap, and I could sense that Branch was right there with me. But we clearly knew we weren't in the States. There weren't mechanisms in place to help us in this situation. It was clear that two of our players were involved in some kind of bizarre altercation outside of school, and from Vassy's demeanor, I didn't get the impression I was being told the entire truth. But even if I knew the entire truth, I still had no idea what to do about it. Neither did Branch. We decided there wasn't much we could do but see what happened at practice.

Tuesday's practice was at 3:30, and Vassy was one of the first ones there. I inquired right away if he was okay, and he brushed any concerns aside, saying he was fine and eager to start practice. Knowing I probably wasn't going to get any more information from any of the members of my now tight-lipped team, I still tried anyway, asking Menkov if everything was okay with Vassy.

"Sure, Coach, sure," he said.

With that, he put his head down and dribbled to the other end of the floor. I wasn't convinced.

"No sign of Dimov yet," Branch said, as practice began. "And I saw him walking the halls this afternoon. He was in school today, but he's not here now."

I wasn't sure how I should feel. Part of me was pissed off that he was on the brink of missing two consecutive practices before an important game, and the other part of me was concerned about what was going on. Both Vassy and Dimov were the type of guys who weren't likely to back down from anything. In Vassy's case, this was why I enjoyed watching him play against bigger opponents. In Dimov's case, this was why his mouth had gotten him into trouble with me before; he tended to act and speak before thinking.

As practice got underway, there was no sign of Dimov. I could sense that Menkov knew I was going to ask him about it, and he seemed to be avoiding making eye contact with me. With the game against Spanish lined up for tomorrow, though, I couldn't focus too much on who wasn't there. No matter what had happened, it was clear to me that we were going to play tomorrow's game without one of our starting guards, which would put us at a severe disadvantage. I looked at the players out on the floor and realized that my only other realistic option for that guard position was Pavel, whose version of handling the ball mostly relied on dishing out body blows to his opponent while he fumbled with the ball.

We were in the middle of a box-out drill and I was hammering home the point I'd been railing at for two years now: *we will win games if we play physically inside and box out*. I was accustomed to watching our deficiencies out on the floor: ball handling—except for Menkov and Dimov—decision-making on offense, and jump shooting. But we'd finally become a physical team, and our man-to-man defense and consistency in boxing out was causing headaches for Bulgarian teams who weren't used to this. Still, I was unwilling to let up on these key tenets of our success as a team.

That's why I became even more annoyed when several cell phones started going off in the middle of a box-out drill. My players knew their cell phones shouldn't even be turned on in the first place since there was no need for a cell phone during practice. I expected that when the cell phones went off, there would be some embarrassed looks from players on the floor, embarrassed and concerned that I might make them run for this. I definitely saw concern on the faces of my players, but it wasn't concern based on my reaction. They were legitimately concerned about why their cell phones were ringing in the first place. The box-out drill stopped, which further angered me, because I told them to ignore the phones; this was basketball practice.

Menkov now had the same pained look on his face that I'd seen from Vassy earlier in the day.

"Coach, I'm really sorry. I'm really sorry. But I have to go answer that," he half-asked and half-informed me.

Now I really had no idea what was going on, but tried to pretend like this didn't matter and continued with the drill. But as soon as Menkov ended his brief conversation, there was no denying the importance of what was going on. As Menkov hung up the phone, he nodded to Vassy who started making his way toward the revolving bubble door exit.

"Vassy, what the hell are you doing?" I barked. "Where are you going?"

He looked back at Menkov, who seemed ready to join him. Kosio and a couple other seniors also seemed to be on the brink of leaving, too, but were waiting to hear how anyone was going to explain this to me.

"Coach," Menkov said, and I sensed I might be getting the first semblance of complete honesty, "there's a fight. I think it's a big fight. And it's right outside the gate. We have to go. We have to go back up our friends."

As Menkov spoke to me, I saw that all eyes turned to me to see how I was going to react. Vassy was standing by the door, and Menkov and Kosio looked ready to run to the door. Pesho and Pavel didn't appear to know what was going on, but heard the word "fight" and both of their ears perked up. Sasho still appeared to be grinning, still lost in Holden Caulfield's world, presumably.

"You don't have to go anywhere," I stated, trying to sound as resolute as I could.

"But, Coach," Vassy pleaded with me, "I think there's big trouble this time."

"Then it's trouble you don't need to be involved in," I fired back.

"But, Coach," it was Menkov's turn to plead, "if we don't go, our friends are going to say we're cowards. This is a really big fight, and we need to be there for them. Dimov's already there."

I wanted to be sympathetic to the difficult situation they were in. Not only were these mostly 17-year-old males I was dealing with, whose testosterone was permanently raging, but this was Bulgaria, a place where your true status as a real man was determined by your willingness to fight. But I couldn't find sympathy with what was going on. Maybe that made me culturally insensitive, but getting in fights—whatever kind of fight this was—had nothing to do with our purpose as a basketball team. We were supposed to be practicing for the biggest game of our season so far, and leaving practice to go join a brawl was not even an option.

"If you really wanted to be there for your friends, then you would've told them not to get into a fight to begin with," I thundered away, realizing that I was preaching to a crowd that wouldn't agree with me. "Being a real man doesn't mean getting in fights. It means being strong enough to know that you shouldn't get in fights."

"Coach, that's not true," Vassy protested. "That's not the way it works here."

"Well, maybe that's not the way it works here in Bulgaria, but that's the way it works on this basketball team. If you want to walk out that door and go join the fight, you have that choice. But don't expect to be welcomed back to this basketball team."

The whole bubble went silent.

Players looked at me to try to see if I was really serious. Even Branch looked at me to see if I was serious. I remained stone-faced, trying to convince myself I actually was serious. I didn't doubt I was doing the right thing, but there was no way I could afford to lose this gamble. If Vassy, Kosio and Menkov left to go fight, we'd barely even have a team left.

The silence continued and no one moved. Vassy looked back at Menkov who still appeared to be in a pseudo-sprinter's stance, ready to run out the door.

Still, no one moved. No one said a word.

"Okay then," I broke the ice, well aware that things weren't okay, "let's get back to the box-out drill."

Vassy trotted back from the door as Menkov dejectedly made his way toward the hoop. For the moment, disaster had been averted, but that only concerned the disaster inside the gym. I had no control over the disaster that was occurring outside the gym.

What happened outside the gym, I'd learn later, was a fight that included at least 20 people. As a gang of 10 seniors—Dimov included—left school for the day, they were met by about 10 other guys, none of whom went to our school. The road down from the gate was long and narrow, and didn't offer any other options for turning away. There were fields littered with garbage and stray dogs on both sides.

Based on the fact that the group of ACS seniors left as a solid core of 10 people—one of whom was supposed to be at basketball practice—they were not surprised to be met just outside the gate. However this had been planned or arranged, they knew what to expect. They knew to expect a fight. The 10 ACS seniors were of all shapes and sizes, and half of them were in my 12th grade English class. I knew only a few of them were physically strong enough to actually belong in a fight, but that was no matter. This was Bulgaria, and to be a real man, you had to be in the fight regardless of your physical stature.

While I hammered away about the importance of boxing out, these 20 teenagers started hammering on each other. In the bubble, we could only hear the bouncing of basketballs and squeaking of shoes. About 200 meters away, though, just outside the gate to the school, I can imagine that the sounds of anguish and pain were far greater than those coming from the hard work of basketball practice.

The ACS boys in the fight, I was later told, assumed that this would be a fistfight. They'd made sure they had enough members of their crew to stack up with their opponents. They must've felt confident, at least in the sense that they'd be able to prove their manhood by taking part in this fight. As the aspiring prime minister and political hero of the country had said, *In my neighborhood if someone asks you to fight you either do it or you run away.* These boys were not going to run away.

As a result, they got pummeled.

It took several weeks before I was able to put together an entire picture of the fight. Like I'd experienced all throughout the process of trying to talk to my basketball players about what was going on, the responses I received were brief, uninformative and mostly interested in protecting those who were involved. There seemed to be great incentive to hide the truth about what was going on, and the only consistent response I could get from anyone associated with the fight was how proud he was to be associated with the fight. Their pride was alarming considering that the results of the fight had not been good for the ACS students, and particularly bad for one student in particular, Dimov.

The 10 involved in the fight were gathered in the foyer outside the auditorium the next morning, and they were about to be shuffled into the dean's office to sort through the entire mess. As I walked by their huddle, it was clear I was looking at a motley crew that had been roughed up. Two boys were wearing slings on their arms, indicating some kind of shoulder or collarbone injuries. One other boy had two black eyes to go with a white tape attached to what was clearly a broken nose. The final image of damage I saw was one that made my stomach turn. While most of the boys in the huddle outside the auditorium seemed to replaying the moments of the brawl from the day before, animatedly talking and gesturing, Dimov was hidden at the back of the huddle. And when my eyes finally connected with his, I barely recognized him.

His face was various shades of purple, black and yellow, and his left eye wasn't open. That's because it appeared to be protruding so far forward that it was too swollen to function. This matched the entire left side of his face, which now resembled a giant Easter egg, one that had been dyed sinister colors. There was dried blood that looked like it still hadn't been cleaned off his face, and to me, Dimov looked like an alien. I couldn't imagine what he'd been hit in the face with, but he clearly hadn't been hit by fists. It would take an awful lot of fists to do damage like that.

I froze in my tracks, staring at him, unable to comprehend what had happened. I'd spent the last two days alternating between concern and anger, knowing he was caught in something troubling. He'd been making bad decisions, decisions that were hurting our team, but I was no longer thinking about our team. I was only thinking about him, a 17-year-old kid, and how looking at his face—a face that looked harmed beyond repair—made me want to vomit.

Dimov caught my glance and quickly looked away. He said something to one of the members of his group, and then they all seemed to notice that I was staring at them. I felt helpless, unable to move, unable to even know what to say to them, and by the time I gathered my wits, they'd all marched away. Dimov ensured that he remained hidden behind his friends so our eyes wouldn't meet again.

He'd been hit across the left side of his face with a vodka bottle, I later learned. He needed stitches to sew his upper lip back together, but there was still a great deal of swelling and disfiguration wrecking the rest of his face. Until the swelling went down, there wasn't much that could be done. Along with vodka bottles, their opponents in the fight had also come with bricks that had been hurled at the ACS boys, causing the broken nose and various other injuries. While the ACS boys had showed up ready to fight, they showed up with their fists. They ended up getting beaten up with weapons. Of the 10 who were in the fight from our school, I could only count two who didn't have noticeable and serious injuries.

The school was outraged that something like this could happen, especially since it happened just outside the gate in front of a myriad of armed police academy cadets and guards. They had watched the entire fight—in fact, they basically had front row seats—and done nothing. This fight was a part of the culture, and they weren't about to step in to prevent someone from getting hurt. Several ACS boys had to be sent to the hospital, with Dimov's injuries being the most serious.

As the 10 of them headed into the dean's and president's offices, though, their most ardent concern had nothing to do with their collective injuries. They were adamant that the school let this matter drop, and several of the boys came armed with arguments about how the school could not get involved since the brawl occurred just outside the campus gates. To take it one step further, several parents of injured students had already called the school, demanding that the matter be dropped without any further investigation. This baffled school administrators, who were expecting these phone calls to be from parents demanding that justice be done. In a bizarre reversal of fate, these students and parents were begging the school not to pursue criminal charges against the opposing gang of young men who had beaten up their children with fists, bricks and glass bottles.

During my first period class, I asked some of my other seniors what this fight—which had apparently started much earlier than just Tuesday—was all about. "Oh, Mr. Jones, it was ... uh ... over a girl," was the standard response.

"All these people ended up in the hospital after a 20-person brawl over a girl? Are you serious? I find that hard to believe. There's no way this many people were fighting over one girl," I said to anyone who was listening.

With this, some heads went down, indicating that it wasn't the best cover story. Some of the males in the classroom, either eager to defend their friends or feeling left out because they weren't part of the brawl, continued with this same line.

"No, it was—it was definitely just about a girl," came the measured, though stuttered response. In the weeks that followed, more details about the entire brawl trickled out, and none of those details had anything to do with girls. The dispute between the two groups was based on unpaid gambling debts, and it appeared that the ACS boys had been up against a group that was much older than high school age. They'd been visiting underground blackjack and poker games, and, at some point, ran out of cash to pay for what they'd been betting. And when mugging Vassy and slashing Dimov's tires didn't send the message adequately, the brawl ensued.

Both students and parents didn't want the police involved because all the gambling that was taking place was illegal to begin with. There was more trouble to be had if the ACS students said anything more about the fight, other than it was "over a girl." This was trouble that the high school students—and even more so their parents—wanted to avoid. I started asking around about how much money was being gambled in these poker and blackjack games, and in hushed tones, I was told that a bad night for one of our students would meaning losing 400 *leva* in a night (more than 250 U.S. dollars). But considering the root of the violence, I was told that the fight stemmed from something much worse than just a bad night. There might've been more than 1000 *leva* at stake–about 700 dollars. This was no small sum in the poorest country in the European Union.

I didn't need an understanding of Bulgaria to know what happened when gambling debts went unpaid. There were universal actions taken in situations like these, and I didn't need to increase my cultural awareness to grasp what had happened this Tuesday afternoon while we were working on boxing out in practice. As the story slowly became more publicly understood, I learned that the gambling debt wasn't Dimov's, but it was his group of friends who were involved to begin with. He'd wanted to be involved, wanted to prove his merit as a tough guy, or "real man." His tires had been slashed because he was the only one of the group who had a car. His face had been bashed in because he happened to be in front of someone who had a vodka bottle that he was poised to strike with.

"Mr. Jones, I don't know if you'll ever understand," one of my students told me in the week following the brawl. "It was so great to be there for my friends, so important that I was a part of this fight. If I hadn't been there for the fight, I never would've been able to forgive myself."

"But Deyan," I told him, "look what happened to your friends. Look what happened to you. So many people got injured–some really seriously. How is that worth it? You were fighting over some kind of gambling debt, and look what happened."

"No, no, Mr. Jones," Deyan replied, wagging his finger in front of my nose, showing even further how I'd never understand. "This was a moment of glory for us. We were all there together. We fought together, bled together."

"I really hope you learn to see this differently, Deyan," I told him sympathetically. "People getting hurt like this is never worth it. I hope someday you'll see what I mean."

"No, Mr. Jones," he said with a smile. "I don't think I will. I don't think I want to."

As he walked out of my classroom, I knew my optimism about him changing his viewpoint was probably very naïve. I was teaching at the best school in Bulgaria, educating students who dreamed of going to the West for university and perhaps life after university. But their mentality was always going to be Bulgarian, and in Bulgaria, your honor is tested when you have a chance to fight–no matter how valid the reason behind the fight is.

We entered our Wednesday game against the Spanish school with a lot of momentum, at least in theory. We'd won four straight games, our best winning streak in two years, and now had a chance to prove our mettle against one of the highest-quality opponents the city of Sofia had to offer. But Wednesday had started with my seeing Dimov's mangled face, continued with gossip all day long about the brawl, and was supposed to end with the basketball game. As much as I wanted my players' focus after school to be on the basketball game and nothing else, I knew that was highly unlikely. I was still thinking about what had happened the day before, and I knew they were, too. To me that was certain. What was uncertain was how they viewed what happened, and even more specifically how the seniors who wanted to join the fight—Vassy, Menkov and Kosio—viewed the entire situation. I was either their coach who had saved them from getting their faces bashed in, or I was their coach who had prevented them from experiencing a moment of Bulgarian glory, a chance to fight and bleed together with their friends.

Most immediately, we were facing a problem of not having one of our two starting guards. I had no choice but to start Pavel at shooting guard, even though there was nothing remotely "shooting" or "guard" about Pavel. Before the game started, I talked about how we needed to focus on what was happening in front of us during this game, not what happened yesterday. I talked about how we needed to focus on who was here with us right now, not who wasn't. With each new line of advice I was giving my team, I realized that I was also trying just as hard to convince myself not to think about what had happened with Dimov.

The beauty of high school boys, though, was something that came to the fore almost immediately. While I was worried about the hangover from the previous day's fight, and the noticeable absence of one our best players, once the game started, it seemed like I was the only one who could remember this. Sixteen and 17-year-old males aren't known for their tendency to dwell on things or reflect on the past for very long. They're trained—for better or for worse—to focus on the next task at hand without looking forward or back. In our biggest game since we'd played 35th, we came out on fire. At the end of the first quarter, we had an eight-point lead. I looked over to the Spanish sideline to see Starter Jacket incredulous. He didn't speak English, but if he did, I could tell he was going to say to me, "Is this the same team you had last year?"

The momentum I thought we might've lost was well intact. In fact, where Pavel had deficiencies in handling the ball and shooting, he was more than making up for with his tenacious defense and rebounding. While the brawl outside the gates might've lost us one of our starting guards, all Pavel saw was a chance for him to become one of the starting guards. He'd scored six points in the first quarter, pulled down four rebounds and had a steal. When he approached the bench toward the end of the quarter, his face was scrunched up, angered that he'd missed a jump shot.

"I won't miss again, Coach. I won't miss again," he declared definitively.

I knew this wasn't true, but loved him all the more for saying it.

There was now an added burden on Menkov to handle the ball at all times, but this didn't seem to be bothering him. He was weaving and bobbing past a Spanish defense that quite honestly seemed surprised by everything we were doing well. They remembered last year's game, and knew they were one of the best teams in Sofia. They didn't see any reason to take us seriously. But at halftime, our lead remained eight points, and our team was as fired up as ever.

Spanish started their comeback as the third quarter started. I knew this was inevitable. As I looked out at the floor, they had a confident senior point guard who was a head taller than Menkov, and a much better shooter than Menkov as well. Their small forward could both shoot and take his man off the dribble, something that was making life difficult for both Ivan and Kosio. And their best player was a 6'3" power forward, goateed and 23-year-old-looking, who had smooth post moves and the ability to finish with both his right and left hand. Compared to all three of these players, we had no one on our team who was even close to them in terms of offensive ability. That's why it didn't surprise me when we were trailing 53-51 halfway through the third quarter.

This lead, though, seemed to relax the Spanish team. It was as if they were thinking that since they now were winning, this would be good enough and we would fold soon. But I sensed a different emotion from my team, and I harped on this during every huddle. We weren't playing this game to keep it close; we were playing to win.

Sasho finished consecutive put-backs to put us up two points. This was followed by a nifty left-handed finger roll at the other end, a silky shot by their power forward that led to an epiphany for the majority of our team: *Oh, so that's how you want us to use our left hand, Coach....*

Menkov would not be denied, though, and he raced to the other end and flipped in a runner. Spanish came back down the floor and re-tied the game, but we continued to be patient against their zone defense. Pavel found Pesho on the block and he tossed in an easy hook shot, not fading away, which left me elated.

At the beginning of the fourth quarter, the game was tied. I could tell we were confident. I could also tell that the Spanish school, with Starter Jacket sitting and tapping both of his feet nervously, was either anxious or annoyed. I gave a speech similar to those I'd given at the beginning of many previous fourth quarters: *We're in better shape, we practice harder for this moment, and we want it more.* In the past, even though all these things were true, they hadn't amounted to much success for us. But still, all these things were true.

And halfway through the fourth quarter, all these things were abundantly true. Menkov stole the ball at half court and made a layup at the end. Pavel pulled down a tough rebound and made an outlet pass to the runaway train that was Pesho, who took three dribbles past half court and pulled up for an off-balance 18-footer. It was a terrible shot. And it went in. Against the Spanish zone, we found Ivan twice in the short corner; once he drove the basket and finished high off the backboard, and the next time he tossed in a soft 10-foot jump shot. Following another Spanish turnover, they failed to get back on defense, and Menkov and Kosio converted a perfect 2-on-1 fast break for a layup.

We were up by 10 points. Starter Jacket had no choice but to call a timeout. His players—especially his top three—couldn't believe what was unfolding in front of them. They could grasp the notion of having a bad first half, but once they came back and took the lead, this wasn't how the script was supposed to be written. They were clearly the better team, and once they asserted their might in the third quarter, in Bulgaria, that was supposed to be the end of us. But it wasn't, and now they were in a huge hole with only four minutes to go.

But they had the talent—plenty of it—to come back from this deficit, and I knew it. I just hoped the celebration hadn't started too soon on our bench. Following the timeout, their point guard immediately hit a three to cut the lead to seven. As Sasho had his slow set shot blocked at the other end, Spanish found its best player on the break, and he finished with another smooth finger roll. Just like that, the lead was down to five. Spanish was intent on getting steals to get themselves back into the game, and this meant that most every possession was going to be all or nothing. As their shooting guard flew into the passing lane and barely missed intercepting a pass to Pavel, he was off, rumbling to the hoop. With a three-on-one break ahead of him, Pavel charged to the basket and finished at the rim, clearly remembering that he'd told me he wouldn't miss again.

At the other end, though, their power forward pulled down a long rebound, gave a head-fake and scored, plus a foul. The lead was down to four, and was then cut to two when they stole Ivan's inbounds pass and scored once again. With all the worries I'd had all week, I was now stewing on the sideline, half-terrified that once again, based on talent alone, we would lose to a team with more talent. We'd outplayed them the whole game, but now their burst of energy at the end, combined with superior talent, had them right back into it. There were less than two minutes left.

Menkov's runner didn't fall and Spanish came back down the floor with confidence. Dribbling between his legs—something I'd explicitly told my players to never try in a game—their point guard used a high screen to wriggle free from Menkov and pull up for three: nothing but the bottom of the net. We were losing by one point with just over a minute remaining.

Starter Jacket was frantically yelling for his team to stop applying pressure, sprint back and play defense, but his voice was heard by basically no one. Three of the Spanish players started pressuring us in the backcourt, and the other two lazily celebrated the three-pointer that had just splashed through the net. Once the ball had been inbounded, Menkov found Pavel cutting down the middle of the floor. Pavel raced to the other end, head down, full steam ahead. I was desperate for him to pass the ball to a wide-open Sasho under the basket, but convinced there was no way Pavel could see him: his head was down.

But then Pavel did the unthinkable: he passed the ball.

Sasho was all alone under the hoop and easily put the ball up off the backboard and through the hoop. We were leading by one point again.

Now the yelling was frantic on all ends of the floor. I was hollering to get back on defense, the Spanish coach was yelling to get the ball down the floor faster, and the crowd was just a loud amalgamation of Bulgarian cheers, directives and swear words. Their point guard brought the ball down the floor and tried to make a move on Menkov. As he'd done so many times in practice, Menkov slid his feet left, right and then back left again. The point guard couldn't get by him. The clock now showed 15 seconds remaining, and the point guard continued to pound the ball at the top of the key. On the right wing, their power forward now shot out to the three-point line to receive a pass.

I felt like I was watching him in slow motion as he feinted right and used a crossover dribble left to try to get by Pesho. When the possession started, Ivan had been guarding their power forward because Ivan normally did a much better job sliding his feet to get into position. Pesho, who loathed every defensive drill we ever ran in practice, wanted nothing to do with moving his feet. He just wanted to jump and block shots.

But Pesho had switched out to guard their power forward, and as he faked right and crossed over to his left, Pesho was in a defensive stance. He moved quickly each way their power forward dictated. Stopped on his path toward the lane by Pesho's big chest, he spun to the baseline to give himself room to shoot the ball. As he rose up to shoot the shot that would potentially win the game, I could see a look of surprise on his face: his series of moves hadn't resulted in an opening. Pesho was right there with him. He arched back a little bit farther and started to fade away—the same fadeaway I'd told Pesho so many times to stop attempting. The shot left his hand with perfect form and rotation, but it was clear there was something wrong the minute he let it go. The shot was well short.

Sasho grabbed the rebound out of the air and immediately flung the ball ahead to Menkov. As time expired, the last thing I saw was Menkov running frantically toward the other end, dribbling the clock out, and securing our biggest win in two years.

As I spoke to the team afterward, I felt pride based on their effort and achievement, but I also couldn't get the image of Dimov's bashed-in face out of my mind. From my Western perspective, the *real men* had just competed on the floor and earned an incredible victory against a team that had much more talent than them. They'd stood up to the challenge of this fight, and hadn't backed down. We had every right to be thrilled, and I thought I'd feel nothing but satisfaction bordering on elation. But there was another side to the definition of *real men* in Bulgaria, and that's why we were one player short on that Wednesday. That's why I couldn't get the horrifying vision of Dimov's disfigured face out of my mind. I told my players how proud I was of them, and how proud I'd continue to be of them if they played this hard, and continued to do things the right way. I tried to emphasize how great it was to be a part of this team, how great it was to stand up for each other the basketball floor, and how great it felt to have it all pay off with a victory like this.

I hoped that they would understand the parallels I was making to the previous day's fight, but I could never be sure. As I finished my postgame speech, several players high-fived me as they left the bubble. The last one out of the gym, I left with too many emotions swirling inside of me: pride, anger, satisfaction and sadness. When I reached the cold Bulgarian air outside I realized I was crying, and didn't even know if I could say exactly why.

.

Chapter XXI
Character Counts

"It's London, Mommy! London! It's London, Mommy!"

"No, sweetie," the British mother patiently responded as she looked out of the window of the plane, "that's not London."

"London! London! It's LONNNNDDDONNNN!"

"No, sweetie," the mother replied with a bit more urgency. "We left London. This isn't London. Now we're in Sofia."

"LONDON! LONNNDDDONNNN! LONNNDDD—"

"No!" came the final reprimand. "This isn't London. It's Bulgaria."

And for this little girl, sensing she shouldn't push her mother any further, this put an end to the London-Sofia conversation. It was a conversation that was occurring in front of me on a British Airways flight, and I couldn't help but laugh as I gazed down at Mt. Vitosha and one row house block building after another—certainly not reminiscent of London and most definitely not London-esque. Unofficially, I had to note that this was the first time in modern history that anyone had ever mistaken Sofia, Bulgaria for London, England. Considering the source—a four-year-old British girl—was important, but the moment was comical nonetheless. We were on a British Airways flight and I was returning from a weekend in the West where I had been taken aback by things like functionality and overt friendliness. Now that the London-Sofia connection had been made by the girl sitting one row in front of me, I had even more optimism about my return to Sofia. But then I found a taxi to drive me home and everything changed.

"You have lots of baggage," the taxi driver gruffly stated in Bulgarian as I started to put my suitcases into the trunk.

"Yes, I do," I responded, not seeing why this really mattered.

As he put the car in drive and headed out of the airport, he asked me where I was headed. When I told him, he then indicated how much it would cost.

"Twenty *leva*," he declared in Bulgarian.

"No," was my immediate response. "Please turn on the meter."

"No, it is 20 *leva* for this ride."

"This is an eight-*leva* taxi ride with the meter," I tried to respond calmly in Bulgarian.

"No, you have heavy bags. The cost is 20 *leva*," he retorted stubbornly.

"Then please stop the taxi and let me out. Please stop now. I'll take another taxi."

Sadly, these were lines I had rehearsed, since I'd had to use them before. But usually my last statement led to the taxi either being stopped or some compromise being reached. On this day, though, the taxi driver started driving faster.

"You speak English?" he fired away with a hostile tone. "Then we speak English! This cab 20 *leva*!"

"No, absolutely not," I responded in English this time. "Please stop and let me out."

"You," he said as he pointed at me, "you are not from here. You— you foreigner. The price 20 *leva*."

"Yes, I am a foreigner," I tried to reason with a man who clearly didn't want to be reasoned with. "But I live here. I have taken this cab ride many, many times. Every time I take this ride it is eight *leva*. I will give you 10 *leva* in total."

I thought this was plenty generous since most Bulgarians didn't tip taxi drivers.

"Ha! What you think I am? This 10 *leva* – it is five Euro. What you think I am? This is only five Euro for you."

"Well, if you don't want my money, then please stop the cab."

"Okay, okay," he conceded. "Fifteen *leva*."

"No," I answered defiantly. "I'll give you 10 *leva* or please let me get out of the cab."

He paused, weighing my words and his next words.

"You'll see," he said, and wagged his finger in my face. "You'll see how my country will change one day."

I had no idea what this meant.

So I told him I had no idea what this meant.

"Yes, you do. Yes, you do."

"No, I really don't."

"One glorious day," he delivered with a Dracula smile, "one glorious day Bulgaria will be for Bulgarians—not for you. And then you will see how wonderful my country will be."

I was dumbfounded. Somehow, our argument over a fair price for the taxi ride from the airport to my house had led to his theory about how foreigners were ruining his country. Foreigners who weren't willing to pay unfair taxi rates were ruining his country. Michael Bolton, clearly a foreigner himself, came on the car stereo, and my acrimonious driver started humming along.

As I turned to him, trying to formulate a response, he cut me off curtly.

"We no talk anymore. No talk. You have nice day."

I stared straight ahead. I certainly had no interest in talking to him anymore.

When I got out of the taxi at the gate to the school, he made a great effort to drop one of my suitcases hard onto the pavement. I grabbed the second one before he'd have an opportunity to do more of the same.

I gave him a 10-*leva* bill and walked toward the gate. All comparisons to London were forgotten.

I'd had this behavior explained to me numerous times before. When I'd return home perplexed by an encounter with a taxi driver like this one, astounded by the behavior of the coaches or referees at a basketball game, or puzzled by the surly tones I'd receive trying to pay a cell phone bill or buy pastries at the bakery, a Bulgarian colleague—or even some of my students or basketball players—would listen to my story and try to explain to me what was going on. They'd say that Bulgaria was in a period of transition. This was a country that didn't really know how to handle democracy and didn't know how it was supposed to behave in a free market. The only models Bulgaria had for success were in the West; that meant countries like Germany, France, England and the U.S. And the people in those countries—seemingly not so different from

311

Bulgarians—had so much. They looked so happy.

Bulgarians didn't have the things that Westerners had, and they didn't feel as happy. But they certainly wanted what they saw in the movies or magazines or on the internet. In the moment, so many were striving to attain that lifestyle, that happiness, but had no idea how that was supposed to happen in Bulgaria. As a result, in my interactions as a foreigner with some Bulgarians, I would encounter jealousy and bitterness—bitterness that to me seemed hard to comprehend.

In terms of life as a teacher at a Bulgarian school, I could also see the transition in process, and see how quickly my students wanted to transition out of Bulgaria, either by shedding this Bulgarian bitterness or by leaving Bulgaria all together. For some, this meant hard work and determination. This meant a dedication to their studies because high grades and a high SAT score was the ticket out of the country. But for others, this meant finding the quickest path possible to success through cheating. Democracy and a free market system seemed to include an awful lot of freedoms. I sat on the Faculty Council, a group of nine faculty members that heard all disciplinary cases for the school, and the litany of students paraded in front of the council echoed similar themes:

"I don't know how my answers on the test were identical to hers, even if she was sitting next to me. It must be coincidence," I'd hear one week from a student.

"Just because our essays are the same word-for-word doesn't mean we copied off each other," was the next most typical response.

"I don't know how you found an essay exactly like mine on the internet written by someone else. That's just not possible," also was commonplace.

The school was so determined to tackle the cheating problem head-on that it resorted to not allowing students to use their own pens on exams (they would sometimes wrap cheat-sheets around the pens). Exams also had to have four different versions to decrease the incidence of students copying off each other. Even with these different versions that students were cognizant of, it still wasn't uncommon for a student to fail an exam because he or she copied from a neighbor who had a different version of the test. In this case, the score would be so low—almost impossibly low—that it was unclear whether or not more punishment should be levied for cheating on top of the already dismal exam score. It was also clear that Bulgarian teachers were caught up in the questionable ethics as well. They knew that cheating was wrong, but many sympathized, or even empathized with the students. Most of the teachers had been raised during communism, and at this time, cheating the system was a way of life, the only way you could survive in many cases.

In another case at ACS during my first year there, students hacked into a teacher's email account and stole the semester exam a week before it was to take place. So many students knew about this—and had the exam—that a small group of students approached the teacher to let her know about it. They didn't think it was fair that so many of their classmates already had the exam and planned to cheat. They thought the exam should be conducted fairly for everyone. Without notifying the students, the teacher re-wrote the exam, and shocked a good portion of the class when they looked at it and realized it wasn't the copy they'd stolen. Some even had the audacity to express their anger to this teacher; how could she trick them like that? To them, she was the one who had been dishonest; her ethics were now in question because she'd changed the test.

Later in the year, during a faculty meeting where new technology software was being introduced to help with attendance and report cards, the American president of the college excitedly talked about how user-friendly and effective this system was. It would transform many aspects of teaching life at the college because grades and attendance would no longer have to be completed in archaic and gigantic Bulgarian notebooks, all by hand. His excitement for the new computerized system, though, was met with skepticism from Bulgarian teachers.

"Have you tried this system before?" the president was asked by a Bulgarian at the faculty meeting. "I mean, how do you know it's safe from hackers?"

"Oh yes, yes," the president responded swiftly and confidently. "In fact, at my last school in the States, we used this software for the past 15 years. In that time, there wasn't one single incident of hacking that occurred."

Another hand shot up quickly as Bulgarian murmurs rippled through the crowd.

"You tried this at your school in America. But has it ever been tried here in Bulgaria?"

Whether this was the intention or not, laughter rained down from all Bulgarian members of the audience. In the next question for the president, a teacher referred to our school, and Bulgaria in general, as "Hacker Central." It became clear that the general Bulgarian sentiment was that American experience with a software program for attendance and grading was deemed as irrelevant. This was Bulgaria, and the rules—if there were rules—were completely different. The president continued to tout the program, trying his best to spread optimism for change, and I felt for him. It was not easy to convince this crowd that change was going to work well in Bulgaria.

The fact that cheating was occurring was something I became accustomed to. The most difficult part of this equation was listening to the justifications afterwards. In the same way that Bulgarian basketball coaches expected everyone else to be cheating, the same thing applied with Bulgarian students. Their parents had lived in a world where they'd had to cheat to make ends meet—usually by selling things on the black market, or providing some service that wasn't reported to the state. Now that the shackles of communism had been lifted, Bulgarians liked the freedom of not being held down by draconian rules, but they exploited this as well. And when cheaters were caught, their reactions usually didn't include remorse. Their reactions ranged from, *So what?* to *That's not really cheating, is it?* to *Everybody else is doing it; why shouldn't I?*

Many classes I taught developed a teamwork mentality, which in theory was the same idea I was trying to get across to my basketball players. But this sense of teamwork within the classroom meant that everyone would do his or her share, and no one would have to carry too much of the burden. It was an ode to the communist past, without a doubt. This system called for Dobri to do the homework on Monday night and give it to the rest of the class to copy. Mitko would take notes in class on Tuesday so no one else would have to. And when it came time for the test, Iliana would make sure her answers were visible to as many people as possible so that others who weren't prepared could succeed. From my American point of view, this was cheating. To Bulgarian students, this wasn't cheating: "This is just how we help each other. We're all in this together," was a common refrain. In fact, I heard this so many times that I started to realize that students who didn't conform to this teamwork/cheating system were routinely ostracized. I could tell that Svetla, the model of integrity and honesty, had fewer friends because she insisted on doing her own work and not giving answers to others.

The longer I lived in Bulgaria, the longer my mental list grew of all the character-based infractions I was becoming accustomed to seeing on a regular basis. This convinced me that while it certainly wouldn't be easy,

I wanted to try to start a character-based education program to stem the tide of ethical transgressions. If nothing else, I thought a Character Counts Club would at least offer an alternative to those who might've felt that cheating wasn't the way to go. I was hoping to create different parameters for what honor really entailed, and I hoped there would be students who would be attracted to this new model for character.

I was able to lure in a flock of idealistic 9th graders and easily tabbed Svetla to be the unofficial leader of the club. Some of the bigger questions still seemed to stump them, such as: *Why is your character important?* That would be answered with, *Because I want to be an interesting person*, instead of something more integrity-based. Yet we still had momentum from the beginning to make campus a more character-driven place. We enacted simple activities like advertising for trash to be thrown away in garbage bins and giving candy away with character-based, anti-cheating quotes attached, and my group of character enthusiasts liked what they were doing. Every month we'd watch a different movie–from *American History X* to *Crash* to *Little Miss Sunshine*–and talk about what it was like to be different, and how much character you had to have in order to stand up against the rest. I did my best to conceal the fact that the copies of the films were bootlegged. It was difficult to find real DVDs in Bulgaria.

The club was small, and many of my older students scoffed at character education, probably because it represented such a drastic change. When I'd ask my students about what their life was like in public schools before they came to ACS, the answers were downright frightening.

"My computers teacher in 7th grade used to drink vodka out of the bottle all day long in class," one of my students told me. "Usually, he just drank it himself, but sometimes he'd give it to us, too. You know, he didn't really teach us anything, but some people definitely started becoming alcoholics after his class."

I was bewildered by comments like these from my students, and continued to remind myself that these were just isolated incidents re-told by young high school students. But then an exposé documentary from a Bulgarian journalist came out, detailing his life for one year as a public school teacher in a Bulgarian high school. Nikolai Georgiev, the journalist, wanted to see what life was really like, so he got a job teaching high school English. Though his English was only middle school level, he pointed out, he was hired right away. Snippets from his documentary provide haunting images of life in Bulgarian public schools. A *Sofia Echo* report on his video documentary revealed details about what was "normal" for Bulgarian public schools:

"From day one he was subjected to abuse and a hostile atmosphere generated by almost everyone in the class. There was complete disregard of his position, with students openly drinking alcohol, gambling, sexually groping one another, exposing themselves and using obscene language. Georgiev was repeatedly told to 'shut up' and to 'sod off.'"

It's safe to assume that Georgiev was not teaching at a school that was known for high achievement, but still, the descriptions of what was going on—and these would be supported by video he shot for his documentary—were staggering. When Georgiev tried to hold students accountable for their behavior and their work, things didn't get much better. On film, Georgiev is seen talking to his students about their homework. Here is the exchange that followed:

"'Where is your homework?' Georgiev asks a young student. 'Are you insane? Get out of here,' replies a child no more than 12 years of age. 'And where is your homework then?' he asks a female student. The girl replies: 'How about a threesome tonight, you, me and my boyfriend?'"

The article goes on to say that even though Georgiev is teaching English to students who have studied English for at least four or five years, many students "are incapable of saying a single world in English, apart from fuck and bastard."

Facing the unenviable and unbelievable task of educating these students in this system, Georgiev thought that perhaps grades would end up being the equalizer. The students who didn't do their work would not pass. But he soon learned that the system didn't quite work this way. He was reminded on a daily basis by students whose parents had money or influence that, "any day he can be bought off and told what to do."

Hearing stories from my students and reading articles like these made me glad I worked at the best school in Bulgaria. We were certainly facing ethical concerns at ACS, but it was nothing like this. So the Character Counts Club pushed forward and started a new initiative, a celebration of those who were "Caught in the Act" of doing something good. We'd found a space on the wall near the auditorium foyer where we were going to place a glass frame to highlight good deeds done by students on campus. This was hardly a new idea; I'd worked in schools before where this was done. But when I introduced it to the Character

Counts Club, they were elated and eager to start "catching" people doing good deeds like helping people pick up books that had fallen, picking up trash and throwing it away, returning a lost wallet or cell phone—anything that represented genuine kindness or goodness. I figured this idea couldn't go wrong, since nearly every academic institution in the world liked giving students' recognition for being good Samaritans. So I presented the idea to Americans and Bulgarians alike at a faculty meeting, asking them to help our club "catch" people in the act of doing good things. Once a student was "caught," we would take his or her picture and put it up in the glass frame with a description of what happened.

The initial response from Americans and Bulgarians in the crowd was positive, and many remarked to me after the meeting that they already had a student they'd like to nominate. I thought this represented positive first steps, and knew that Svetla and the Character Counts Club would be excited to expand on what we were already doing. But then I received an email shortly after the meeting from the Bulgarian assistant principal saying that we needed to discuss my plans for the Character Counts Club.

In most situations, an email from an assistant principal regarding the plans of a character and integrity-boosting club wouldn't result in much concern from its adviser receiving the email. But this assistant principal stood in contrast to any other administrator I'd ever worked with. She was in her late 40s, stocky and serious with dark Bulgarian features, and so stone-faced that even when she smiled or laughed, you couldn't be sure that her expression wouldn't turn to gloom and disappointment soon after. She chose her words carefully while speaking both English and Bulgarian, and gave off the impression that she was choosing them carefully so they'd have the most impact—or pain. One of the first conversations I'd had with her took place during my first month in Bulgaria after we'd both attended the concert of one of the Balkans' most famous singers, Tatiana Serbinksa. Within about two minutes of the concert starting, I could tell it wasn't going to be my kind of music. Serbinska's high-pitched wailings matched what I'd heard on Bulgarian radio, and while I was doing my best to appreciate Balkan music, I couldn't say that I actually enjoyed it.

But I knew the assistant principal really liked Balkan music, and when I saw her the next day in the staff break room, I decided I'd try to strike up a conversation and show that I was at least trying to appreciate her culture.

"I thought that was a really nice concert last night," I said enthusiastically. "I was so happy I had a chance to go."

I'd approached this conversation brightly and eagerly, but the minute I finished speaking, her face turned sour. It looked like she might spit on me.

"I do not know how you can say this," she said slowly, measuring her words with a thick Bulgarian accent. "This concert–her singing was terrible."

Her face started twitching as she gave off a disgusted snort, and she seemed to be in pain.

"Terrible, just *terrrrrible*," she finished.

I stood three feet away from her, feet firmly planted in the ground, not wanting to move, and completely unsure about what to say next. I thought I'd be complimenting her culture by showing my appreciation of last night's concert. I thought this would be seen as a good effort to make a cultural connection. But she didn't see it this way at all. She'd hated the concert. And honestly, I had, too. My mind was now racing: *should I admit that I hated the concert? Should I say that I liked the architecture of the theater? Should I pretend to know something about how the singer might've been good in the past, but wasn't any more?* My brain was stammering, sweat was rolling down the back of my neck and thankfully, she put me out of my misery. Before I could say anything, she stormed out of the room, still muttering under her breath.

I came to think of our assistant principal as a type of Nurse Ratched behind the Iron Curtain. Unable to emasculate the likes of McMurphy and Chief Bromden any more, she'd found a new frontier where oppression was still mighty popular: Bulgaria. So when she emailed saying that we needed to discuss my plans for the Character Counts Club, I wanted to look at this optimistically, but I was far too realistic for that.

"Welcome, Andy," she said, and her accent made this greeting sound like *Velllcome*, and therefore much more intimidating.

"I wanted to talk to you about what you are planning to do with this club of yours."

"Okay, sounds great," I responded amicably, not sure why I thought an amicable tone would make a difference with her.

"You see, I understand that you are trying to do good things. I understand you want to improve character in our school. I understand this."

I knew the "but" was coming, so I just bided my time and waited for it to happen.

"But you have to know we've seen this all before."

"Seen this all before? Oh, has someone else tried a club like this before?" I said innocently.

"Ha, ha," she bellowed, clearly pointing out my ignorance.

As I listened to her laugh, I felt, well, ignorant. I think that was probably her intention.

"*Someone else* has not tried this. It's not *someone else*. But we've seen *this* before. This picture frame idea–celebrate a good deed, I think you call it? We've seen this before."

"I'm not sure if I understand," I told her. "Have you seen it before and something went wrong?"

"No, Andy," she said calmly, and followed this with an uncomfortable pause for effect. I assumed the pause was entirely for her benefit and my detriment. "We have all lived through this–some of us for many, many years. And we've all seen the propaganda. We've seen the communist propaganda, the 'Heroes of the Motherland' up on our wall, celebrating those who served this country, served Mother Russia. Do you honestly think we're going to fall for your version of communist propaganda?"

Communist propaganda?

While I was stunned by the question, I could tell she wanted me to answer her question–a question I'd hoped was rhetorical.

"I don't intend to spread communist propaganda. This is just an exhibit to celebrate–"

"Andy, Andy. We are too smart for this. So many of us have lived through this. Do you think you can trick us?"

"I'm not intending this to be a trick. It's just a way to motivate stu—"

"This is communist propaganda, Andy," she reiterated, her voice gaining more steam. "You did not live in this country for 50 years of Soviet rule. You do not know what it was like to have propaganda all around you."

"No, I certainly don't. And I don't intend for this to be propaganda as much as a celebra—"

"No matter what your intention is, I know Bulgaria. I know Bulgarians. I know what they will see. They will see Mother Russia. They will see communist propaganda. This is nothing but communist propaganda."

At this point, she'd repeated the phrase *communist propaganda* so many times, that it was serving a propaganda-esque purpose in my brain. I couldn't get the phrase out of my head. The other part of my brain was trying to balance my responses between defending what we were doing, and not stepping on cultural sensitivities, which had clearly been activated at a high level. With the assistant principal plowing forward, I was getting the impression that it didn't matter what I said.

"All we'd like to do is encourage students to do the right thing. We'd just like them to think about their character, make good choices and do the right thing," was my next defense and explanation.

"The right thing," she scoffed. "The right thing *for the Motherland*?"

"I have no communist intentions," I admitted, becoming exasperated.

"I believe you, Andy," she agreed with me for the first time that day. "I believe you are not a communist, but we Bulgarians, we are used to this. We are too smart to fall for your tricks. The students, they will see right through this."

I'd never before been accused of trying to trick someone when, in my heart, I couldn't have been further from actually tricking anyone. I'd thought the "Caught in the Act" idea was about as wholesome—and even downright cheesy—and as genuine as it got. I had no ulterior motives, and if I had any intentions of brainwashing students, my only goal was to brainwash them to do good things, stop cheating and maybe not smash vodka bottles on each other's faces.

I left the assistant principal's office after a forced agreement that I would give up on my plans to create the "Caught in the Act" board. It was clearly communist propaganda, she continued to argue, and would not be tolerated at our school. Like so many public statements of guilt in the communist past, I was left with no choice but to indicate that I'd made a mistake in judgment with my idea for a "Caught in the Act" board.

When I'd entered her office for the meeting, I was intimidated, but halfway through, this feeling morphed into confusion and disbelief. Here I was, the Westerner, the American, the capitalist, in a land where I was trying to understand all of Bulgaria's history and culture, and perhaps most notably, the communist influence on the country for the second half of the twentieth century. But with all of this, I was now being accused of being the communist. To say I was baffled and shell-shocked would be an understatement.

I tried to bring up this issue with the president of the school, a

Westerner, an American, a capitalist, like myself. I explained to him what happened during my meeting with the Bulgarian assistant principal, and ended up laughing as I defended myself, explaining that I most definitely was not a communist trying to spread propaganda.

"Yeah, Andy, I think I feel pretty confident about that. I don't think you're a communist," he laughed as well.

"Well, then what I can I do?" I asked him. "Is there some way you can talk to her about the 'Caught in the Act' idea and convince her that it's not communist propaganda?"

The conversation had been light up to this point, but I'd now asked this question seriously, expecting him to come to my capitalist rescue. But he paused for an inordinate amount of time before he answered.

"You know, Andy," he replied slowly, "I'm not sure if there's anything I can do here."

"Really?" I was surprised.

"If, um, if she thinks it's communist propaganda," he said, and seemed to have a little trouble getting the words out, "then we might just have to let this whole issue drop."

I didn't respond right away, awed that he wasn't wholeheartedly debunking her point of view–a point of view I found to be absurd at best. As I left his office, I was dejected, as if there was no one I could turn to for help with this. I couldn't believe how arduous doing what I thought was the right thing was turning out to be. I was walking out of his office and closing the door when he stopped me before I could leave.

"Andy," he looked up at me, biting his lip a little bit, "I'm sorry about this."

There seemed to be a lot that he wasn't saying, but this apology with a dour look on his face gave me all the explanation I'd need: he couldn't support me on this because this wasn't the first time someone had been accused of spreading communist propaganda. The morose look on his face expressed both sadness and empathy. I got the impression that he knew exactly how I felt, and I could tell he was most likely flashing back to the past for one of his first visits to the Bulgarian assistant principal's office. He was probably sitting and reflecting on how he felt the first time she accused him of spreading communist propaganda.

I reported back to the Character Counts Club that we wouldn't be able to push forward with our "Caught in the Act" idea. Celebrating good deeds amounted to communist propaganda, and would not be allowed at our school. I had to repeat this several times to the club before they accepted that I was actually telling the truth and not being sarcastic.

"Wait a minute," one of my earnest 9th graders said, "you're from America. Why would you ever be the one spreading communist propaganda? That doesn't make any sense."

At least this exchange helped restore some of my sanity. Knowing that it didn't make sense to someone else was a very comforting feeling for me. But it still didn't change the fact that we had now found a roadblock for what we thought was the simplest of proposals. I had little doubt that the club was having a positive effect on its 15-or-so members, but the goal was to reach out to the student body of 700. Our first serious attempt to make a noticeable difference in character, though, had been squashed by the anti-communist fist of the assistant principal. In so many ways, though, her anti-communist directives seemed exactly the opposite: she came crashing down on our new idea just like communist authorities who had suppressed any kind of change for half a century in Bulgaria.

Some would say that my attempts at changing the character and integrity of a Bulgarian student body were too idealistic, that it would never work. But I still held out hopes that I could effect positive change with the kids who showed up for our regular club meetings—and for two years running, I'd made sure that character was a topic that was covered every day in basketball. No matter how much I covered broad issues like playing hard, playing together and doing things the right way, though, there was always a reminder on the other side of the court of how things could be done differently.

Propelled by five straight wins and a thrilling finish against the Spanish school, our next game pitted us against another quality opponent, and another opponent who had beaten us the year before. The next Wednesday we played against the French school, a team we'd competed with for three quarters the year before, and then completely collapsed in the fourth quarter. These were all things I pointed out to my team before the game was about to begin. There was no excuse for not competing with this team, and this time around, we had to finish what we started.

I was approaching all things cautiously at this point, knowing that we were still basically playing with a one-guard lineup, with Menkov as the only player who could consistently handle the basketball. Stefan was loving his life at a boarding school in the States, and to the best of my knowledge, Dimov had been in and out of the hospital getting different treatments for his facial wounds and scars. But he hadn't spoken to me since the brawl. In his place, Pavel would play as the second guard sometimes, but he really wasn't a guard, especially not on offense. Kosio would also play as the second guard sometimes, but he really wasn't a guard, especially not on defense. He had no interest in moving his feet to guard people on the perimeter. But against the Spanish school, our deficiencies at guard didn't hurt us too much, and that's because they—like nearly every Bulgarian team—relied on a relatively lazy 2-3 zone defense. Without our guards—or non-guards—being pressured on the perimeter, we could rely on Menkov being the sole ball handler.

As the game with the French team tipped off, I noticed the same thing was happening once again. They were playing a 2-3 zone, allowing us to relax and run a patient offense without much interruption. When I looked at our team, I figured beating us would be rather simple if opposing teams did one of two things: pressed full court or played pressure man-to-man defense. These were two things we did every game. But Bulgarian coaches, I'd learned early on in my first year in the country, were not ones who liked to make changes during games. They had a game plan and they stuck to it. (And in some cases, they didn't have a game plan at all.) Much like changes introduced by the Character Counts Club, the idea of switching defenses in the middle of the game must've seemed blasphemous.

Still unable to hit outside shots, we relied on our rebounding ability to take a two-point edge into halftime. Aside from allowing players to become complacent on defense, the other problem with playing zone defense is that it's more difficult to find a man and box out once a shot is taken. As a result, many teams enjoy offensive rebounding success against zone defenses. At halftime, we'd scored 29 points, and 14 of them had come from offensive rebounds. Pesho, Vassy and Sasho were dominating the boards, and Branch and I both knew this was our saving grace.

"Man, if we could ever make an outside shot, we'd be killing them," Branch said to me at halftime.

"I know," I chuckled in response, "but when is that going to happen? When are we going to start making outside shots?"

"Exactly," he grinned. "So tell 'em to keep running and crashing the boards. No matter how much we work on making our offense fluid and smooth, it just never seems to look that way."

"Yeah, I know. So we've got no choice but to out-hustle them and try to win ugly."

I hesitated to ever use this phrase with my team because I knew they wouldn't like it. They loved basketball, and the sense of camaraderie and excitement that had built up as we'd started winning games had us cresting on a wave that I didn't want to break. The previous year, the discovery that we weren't a very good basketball team hit my players hard. It caused bouts of what appeared to be team depression that lasted throughout the season. This season, I also noticed that they might be suffering from perception problems: since we were winning, that must mean we were a good basketball team. That must mean that we were doing things well on both ends of the floor. That's why I didn't want to tell them that we had to rely on winning ugly. Yes, we were winning games, but no, we were not winning games in a way that would make veteran basketball observers think we'd become a fluid, well-oiled machine of a basketball team.

In the second half against the French school, we continued to grind it out, and as was becoming the pattern, a team we'd beaten the year before started to get the deer-in-the-headlights look when they realized we weren't going to go away. The game seesawed back and forth with Menkov continuing to find seams in their 2-3 zone for runners, short floaters and layups. With each new basket that he scored, the two French guards at the top of the zone—neither of whom seemed particularly interested in guarding Menkov—started yelling at each other, immediately placing blame on the other for Menkov's latest basket. I could sense that the entire French team on the floor was bubbling over with frustration. They'd beaten us easily the year before; why wasn't that happening again?

We entered the fourth quarter with a one-point lead, and Menkov continued to drive hard to the basket. This time, his runner glanced off the rim into Vassy's hands, who scooped up the rebound and finished with his dominant left hand. Facing a three-point deficit, the French school brought the ball back down the floor. All game long, they'd seemed annoyed that we were playing man-to-man defense, a defense that forced them to move much more on offense. As the second half had evolved, they'd stopped moving much at all, and just turned to their reliance on one-on-one moves on the perimeter and in the post. The only reason this was working with a relatively decent success rate was because they had good individual talent.

324

But on this trip down the floor, the French point guard appeared to have had enough with trying to run any plays or serving his role as the point guard, the one who passes the ball to his teammates. With his head down, he barged toward the basket. Menkov was right on his hip as he dribbled out of control into the lane. He flipped up a desperate shot that was nowhere near the hoop. Pesho snatched the rebound out of the air and flipped the ball ahead to Ivan. Looking down the floor, we now had a 4-on-2 fast break headed the other way. With Menkov streaming down the floor trailing the play, he would soon make it a 5-on-2 advantage.

All signs pointed toward another basket for us, and an extension of our lead. I excitedly watched from the bench as Ivan crossed half court, surveying how he should lead this fast break. But then the whistle blew and stopped everything. From what I was watching in front of me, there was absolutely no reason for a whistle to blow. No infraction had occurred while Ivan was dribbling, and no contact had been made between any of the players in the frontcourt. But I had to turn to see where the whistle had come from, the entire other end of the floor.

Right after the whistle had blown, I saw the referee take his left hand and put his fingers together, straight up in the air. With his right hand, he brought his palm down smack on top of the tips of his fingers. His two hands formed an emphatic "T." The French point guard had just been given a technical foul.

And now I started to understand why the whistle had blown. The only time I could see the referee was when he'd signaled for the technical foul. Now, he was being dwarfed by an enraged Bulgarian high school athlete, who was spewing vitriol in his direction. His yelling at the referee was so loud that my players couldn't help but notice. I hoped they wouldn't be as intimidated by this as they had been by the Italian coach from several weeks ago.

I'd seen Bulgarian players pick up technical fouls before, so this was nothing new. But I hadn't seen a Bulgarian player as outraged as the French point guard was at this point. Ostensibly, the point guard was upset no foul was called on his last chaotic drive to the basket. But realistically, he had to be projecting his overall anger about the game onto the referee. Of course my point of view was biased, but it seemed to me that he'd received plenty of calls throughout the game. I figured that he was most angered because Menkov kept scoring on the other end of the floor.

As he continued to argue with the referee—a referee who'd already given him a technical foul—the French coach sent a sub into the game for him. This was the action that surprised me more than any. Most other Bulgarian coaches we'd played against had barely batted an eye when a player acted in an unsportsmanlike manner or received a technical foul. Now this coach was doing exactly what should be done—taking the offending player out of the game—and I was pleasantly shocked.

Menkov went to the free throw line to shoot the two free throws for the technical foul, but before he could release the first one, the French point guard unleashed a new maelstrom from the sidelines. With this, Menkov couldn't help but glance over at him as the decibel level of his hollering continued to increase. The referees seemed to have no choice but to take notice either, as the point guard matched his vociferous verbal attack with wild pointing and gesticulations.

Now the whistle blew again, and both of the referee's hands shot up toward the roof of the bubble. To my American eyes, this appeared to signal a touchdown, but I quickly gathered that this was no time for rejoicing; two hands straight up in the air meant the player had been ejected. Instead of rejoicing, both arms were equally extended in the air as if to say, "I've had enough."

But still, the French point guard hadn't had enough. The barrage of curse words continued to be flung in the direction of the referees, or at this point, simply anyone who was curious enough to listen. I'd been able to follow some of his more conventional Bulgarian epithets, but he was now using such a wide variety that I was having trouble translating. I turned to the bench and asked them exactly what he was saying to the referee.

"Well," Pavel answered, clearly trying to be as accurate as possible, "there was a saying about the referee's mother, and then there was another saying about a dog. And then," he stopped, a little confused, "well, I'm not really sure how to describe the last saying."

I didn't need too much more help with translation thankfully, as two of his teammates literally carried the French point guard out of the bubble. He had to be restrained the entire time, displaying his own sense of honor by telling the referees that they would pay for this. The only reason he wasn't coming after them right now was because he was being restrained by two of his teammates. As they grappled with him and tried to get him out of the gym, I sensed that it was possible this French point guard had admiration for life in the West, too: he looked just like a movie star in a clichéd bar fight, someone who had no business fighting, but could act like it while he was being held back by his buddies.

Once he was gone the bubble seemed noticeably quieter, the exception being the cheers from the bench and our crowd as Menkov made all four free throws. On the ensuing inbounds play, Pesho got open right underneath the basket for an easy layup. In a matter of seconds, we'd taken a close three-point game and extended our lead to nine points. The French team, now without one of its best–and mouthiest–players would never recover. Like the game we'd played against them the year before, it had been close for three quarters, and then one team fell apart. I was just glad that this time, it wasn't us who had fallen apart.

I was also glad that this time, it didn't seem like I needed to include mention in my post-game speech about the French point guard. It seemed our players understood exactly what had happened.

"Coach, he just lost his team the game," Sasho said thoughtfully. "I mean, it was a close game up to that point, and then he just completely blew it. I have no idea why he thought he should act that way."

With that, I felt like our team's character lesson had already been covered for the day. It was easy for them to finger the turning point in the game, and it had little to do with basketball skill or execution, and everything to do with character.

A few days after the French game, and in total, about two and a half weeks after the fight, Dimov finally came to speak to me in my classroom for the first time since the fight. I knew he'd been avoiding me, not wanting to be lectured, not wanting to feel any more pain than he already felt. I was relieved to see him because both time and doctors had done wonders to heal his face. His lip still looked too puffy to be normal, but the swelling was gone from the rest of his face. His left eye was open, and the purple and black had faded away. If I didn't know what had happened, from a distance, I might've thought there was nothing wrong. But up close, all I could think of was how lucky he was to have recovered. There were no permanent scars, it appeared.

"Coach, I just wanted to talk to you and say that I'm ready to come back to the team," Dimov said quietly, but proudly.

I was surprised by his opening salvo since I had expected some kind of apology as an opener. The whole reason his face was smashed by a vodka bottle was because he'd made bad decisions, and then skipped practice for two days to be involved in two different fights.

"My face is healing, and the doctor says it's okay for me to start playing sports again."

I knew this conversation was going to come at one point or another, and I'd played it over and over in my head numerous times. Branch and I had even practiced the conversation, just because I knew it wasn't going to be an easy one. I knew it wasn't going to be an easy one because I'd already determined that I was going to tell one of our best players he was no longer welcome on the team.

"It's great news that you're getting better, Dimov. And I can see that your face looks a lot better. I was really worried about you; I couldn't believe how bad it looked."

"I know, Coach," Dimov assented. "I got hurt real bad. I can't believe they hit me with that bottle. But it's all over now."

"Good, I'm glad," I said, hoping that 'all over' also included a new perspective on getting involved in these supposedly honor-based battles to begin with.

"So," Dimov continued, and with this I could tell he was a little nervous, "what time is practice today?"

And here's where I started to get a little nervous, too. As much as I'd rehearsed this before, I'd never kicked a senior off a basketball team. Our goal this year was to win the ACS Open, and I was about to tell one of our most important players that he was off the team. But I felt I had little choice in the matter. He'd skipped practice two straight days to be involved in what ended up being a gang beatdown, had since missed several handfuls of practices, two games, and during that time, had never come to talk to me. I spent so much time preaching character and doing the right thing to my players that there was no way I could take Dimov back on the team—even though having him would greatly increase the talent on the floor. It would send entirely the wrong message to every player on the team who was doing things the right way, every player who was making good decisions. I'd been over and over and over this in my mind. There was just no way.

"Dimov, practice is right after school today, but you're not invited to come to practice. I'm sorry."

"What? Coach, what do you mean? The doctor says my face is fine. He says I can play!"

"Dimov, I'm happy that your face is better. That's great news. But you abandoned the basketball team. You abandoned the basketball team so you could fight with your friends."

"But Coach," he pleaded, "it's not my fault! It's not my fault. It was one of those other guys who hit me with the bottle. There was no way I could've avoided it."

Continuing to explain this to him was causing me just as much pain as he was feeling.

"You definitely could've avoided it," I said firmly, and he looked at me dazed. "You shouldn't have ever been there in the first place. You should've been at basketball practice. That's how you could've avoided it."

With this, he started stammering.

"But, but, but—they hit me! Somebody else hit me! It wasn't my fault!"

"Dimov, when you put yourself in a bad situation like that, it becomes your fault. You never should've been there. You missed two practices for this fight. Then you got hurt and missed two more weeks of practices, and two games. The team had to move on without you."

"But Coach," he entreated, "the team will take me back. I know the team will take me back. I'll talk to the guys; they'll be okay with it."

"You're probably right, Dimov," I told him, knowing that probably half of the team would be shocked by my dismissing Dimov, one of our best players, from the team. This sort of thing, I knew they'd tell me, just didn't happen in Bulgaria. "But as the coach of this team, I can't take you back. You haven't been a good representative of our basketball team. You've made decisions that harmed yourself, harmed our basketball team, and made us look bad. You know how often I talk about doing the right thing and making good choices. You made a series of really bad choices, and unfortunately, there are consequences to those choices."

Now his head was down, and I sensed that he realized I wasn't going to change my mind no matter what he said. My decision was the last thing he'd expected, and somehow I knew this coming in. In the States, Branch and I had discussed, like many others, this decision would be a no-brainer. Dimov would never be allowed back on a team after the decisions he'd made. But in Bulgaria, I was doing more than going against the current with this decision. In Dimov's downtrodden eyes, I was creating an entirely new set of waves. The nature of this kind of decision in Bulgaria was completely unheard of.

Dimov stood before me with his head down, and he appeared to be considering one last attempt at an appeal, but something must've told him it wasn't going to work. He looked up at me one more time, and I thought he was going to start crying.

"I'm really sorry, Martin," I said to him, calling him by his first name for perhaps the first time ever. As I reached out to put my hand on his shoulder to try to comfort him, he abruptly turned and walked out before I could reach him.

Martin Dimov never spoke to me again.

Chapter XXII
A Bloody Mess

Martin Dimov wasn't the only young Bulgarian athlete to be involved in a massive and violent brawl. In fact, there was a precedent set by perhaps Bulgaria's most famous athlete of all time, Hristo Stoichkov. Stoichkov became famous during Bulgaria's surprising fourth-place finish in the 1994 World Cup, and then later attained heroic footballer status while playing for FC Barcelona. In his prime, Stoichkov was one of the best players in Europe, and one of the best players in the world. But his career almost didn't get off the ground because of a fight he started in a Bulgarian youth league game. Stoichkov was notorious for his hot temper and physical play that always bordered on dirty, so much so that author Franklin Foer, in his book *How Soccer Explains the World*, indicated that "his most innocuous movements look like wind-ups to a punch."

The brawl Stoichkov instigated when he was 17 years old was so over-the-top and brutal that it led to him receiving a lifetime ban from Bulgarian soccer. Reading about this, I thought that perhaps my dismissal of Dimov from the team would perhaps be understood. But as I read on, I saw that this wasn't the end of the story. Fans, upset they would be deprived of seeing the brightest young soccer star in the country, protested the lifetime ban. Officials eventually acquiesced and reduced Stoichkov's suspension to just one year. He would go on to have an illustrious career, if not one that was constantly controversial. In his four years playing for Barcelona, Stoichkov managed to get ejected a whopping 11 times. I could think of several players on opposing Sofia basketball teams who fit the Stoichkov mold, and might even be unwittingly emulating his demeanor.

It was the combination of Stoichkov's energetic play and volatile personality that led Foer to seek him out to help explain how exactly soccer explains the world. In his chapter about FC Barcelona and its worshipping followers, Foer thought Stoichkov would be able to help him understand the Barcelona mentality, and the ardent following the team has. FC Barcelona touts itself as more than just a soccer team, and while it doesn't officially state what the "more" actually is, it can be inferred from Barcelona's followers that the club can be a Catalan political party, a religion, or even a way of life. Foer saw Stoichkov as a representative of all of these things, and that's why he sought him out for an interview.

But when he met with Stoichkov, the interview didn't go as planned. In fact, the interview never even got off the ground. Before Foer could start asking his questions about Barcelona, Stoichkov started interviewing the author.

"How many copies will you sell?" Stoichkov asked, wondering how successful the book would be. "Sharing my thoughts, will that entitle me to earn some money out of this?"

Foer calmly explained that he didn't know how many copies he'd sell, but that he didn't pay for interviews. As a journalist, he didn't believe in compensating his interview subjects for their time. It just wasn't part of his ethical system.

"Well," Stoichkov responded defiantly, "it's part of my ethical system."

When Foer tried to explain that it was normal for journalists to interview people without paying them–this was generally accepted as how the world of journalism worked–Stoichkov would have none of it. He bristled at Foer's words and said he felt offended by the "solicitation of this bribe." With that, the interview ended, and Foer wasn't given any direct insight into Stoichkov's experience playing for Barcelona. But Stoichkov's contemptuous attitude probably gave Foer more than he could have been hoping for from the interview. Foer went on to describe how Stoichkov's attitude was representative of the Catalan region of Spain and the Barcelona mentality. Stoichkov was fiercely proud, a fighter unwilling to give an inch, and so loyal to his cause that he didn't feel the need to share anything with an outsider. Foer attributed all of these qualities of Stoichkov as personality traits he'd honed while living and playing in Barcelona.

But this didn't ring entirely true to me. I was fairly certain that Stoichkov fit right in with the spirit of Barcelona, and that's probably why he was so popular during his time with the club. But from his experiences as a brawler to his suspicion of an outsider to his refusal to cooperate if there wasn't anything in it for him, that description might've fit FC Barcelona, but it also fit with many things I'd observed in Bulgaria.

The rest of Foer's chapter provided an insightful look into the world of FC Barcelona and how it intermingles with the mentality of the people in the Catalan region of Spain. But well before Stoichkov ever became a part of Barcelona tradition and lore, he was, and always will be, a Bulgarian. To me, his paranoia about foreigners seemed to gel with the taxi driver who told me that his country will be great when it's only for Bulgarians. And just the fact that he wasn't willing to participate in an interview seemed extreme, but it was an extreme I'd witnessed before in Bulgaria. Because there wasn't something in it for him, this interview wasn't worth his time. Even though he was just being asked innocent questions by an author, a published and well-regarded author, he became suspicious, self-serving and was using words like "solicitation" and "bribe."

As my basketball team prepared for its next games, I found out that Stoichkov wasn't the only one who didn't feel like being generous or friendly just for the sake of being generous or friendly. I was elated about the international tournament we were competing in this year, the aptly-named Vampire Classic, a tournament hosted by the American International School of Bucharest. Having experienced the previous year's debacle in Greece, I felt better prepared to handle the international tournament experience as a whole. I felt much better that this was solely a basketball tournament, and we wouldn't be traveling with eight different sports teams. And this time, I made sure we would be playing against actual high school teams. This time around, I was ready for the deluge of Bulgarian paperwork that would allow my team to leave the country, and things seemed to be running much more smoothly. In fact, it was only at the very end that I ran into problems—problems I'd never expected.

"Okay, one last thing we need to do before we leave," I told my team after practice one day. "The school in Bucharest will be hosting you, and that means you'll be staying with families of players from the Romanian team. This should be really cool. You'll get a chance to meet some of the guys you're playing against and hang out with them."

Even though I'd already heard the ignorant remarks about Romania–it's the only country in Europe that's worse than Bulgaria, students and players would tell me–I'd been able to convince my players that going on an international trip to play basketball anywhere was cool. They seemed to finally see the light, and let up on their snide comments about Romania, a country that not a single player on my team had ever visited, but most were certain had to be a terrible place.

"But the school in Bucharest has a policy about hosting players from other schools. In order for them to host us, they want confirmation that we will be willing to host them in the future."

This seemed like a great policy to me, especially since it encouraged the forging of relationships between international schools, and the spreading of good deeds from one school to the next.

"So what I need each of you to do is sign this paper saying that we'll be happy to host Bucharest student-athletes in the future."

I thought this would probably take about a minute to get the 10 signatures I needed. But it ended up taking more than a minute just to quell the firestorm I'd caused by bringing this up in the first place.

"You're not serious, Coach. We don't really have to do this, do we?" Pesho asked.

"Yes, I'm serious. They're hosting you, feeding you and giving you a place to sleep, and in return, you should offer the same thing to them."

"Well, I don't want to host them," came a quick and indignant response from Kosio.

"What?" I was astonished. "How can you not want to host them? They're willing to host you."

"Well, I don't care. I just don't want to host them. I'm not gonna do it."

I could feel my ears start burning with choler.

"Coach, I can already tell you what my mom's going to say," Vassy chipped in seriously. "She's going to say 'We'll have nothing to do with this.'"

With this comment, conversation was started between several players, and it seemed they all shared the same opinions. Either they didn't want to host the Romanian players or their parents wouldn't allow it. No matter what, the answer to what I thought was a harmless and basic question was a resounding no.

"Coach, Coach," Pesho continued. "This–this is just not possible. Not possible. *Ne modje, ne modje.*"

Branch looked at me and from the bewilderment in his eyes, I saw he had no explanation or quick-fix solutions to this either. The Romanian school and the parents of our opponents were willing to host all of our players, sight unseen. This was ingrained in the Romanian international school culture. If you wanted to play sports, you had to agree to host players from other schools. There was no way I knew exactly how the Romanian school families felt about this, but I was operating under the assumption that they enjoyed hosting and being nice to foreign players. Clearly, this was not the case with my players.

When I expressed my disappointment at their attitudes–attitudes I explained to them sounded awfully self-serving–this was met with many shoulder shrugs. I was the crazy one here, according to them. They had no interest in inviting some stranger into their homes for the weekend and doing nice things for him. It was fine if the Romanians wanted to do that for us, but it wasn't a favor they were interested in returning. Practice ended with my holding an empty signature sheet, incredibly discouraged.

When Nikolai entered the gym a few minutes later to start practice for his girls, I asked him about this so that I could try to understand what was going on. Immediately from the look on his face, I could tell he'd had similar problems with this issue. Both boys and girls teams were taking the trip to Bucharest and both had the same signature sheet, indicating that we'd been willing to return the favor and host them in the future. None of the girls had been willing to sign the sheet either.

"It's not our mentality as Bulgarians," Nikolai told me after a pronounced sigh of frustration. "I would be happy to host any player to stay at my apartment–and we already have six people living there–but others don't feel the same way. I cannot explain it. It's just not our mentality as Bulgarians."

I wanted to pry further because I was truly baffled by this, but I could tell that Nikolai was more than baffled; this whole issue depressed him. He repeated the phrase "not our mentality" twice, and to both of us, it seemed we were contemplating the trouble our players were having with a mentality based on the Golden Rule.

I tried to rationalize that there was a legitimate and justifiable reason that my players would be unwilling to host players from another school: space in their apartment. It was possible, I thought, that some of our players' apartments were already overflowing with family members. Nikolai had just pointed out that he had six people living his small apartment. Whether there was space or not, some of my players might consider it embarrassing to host student-athletes from another country in their cramped row house apartments. This was probably the case for some players on my team, but this didn't explain all of their attitudes. The two loudest and most vocal opponents of hosting players from other teams were Pesho and Kosio—and these were perhaps the two players on the team whose families had the most money. These were the only two players on the team who routinely had new basketball shoes, basketball shorts and other practice gear. I knew they lived in nice homes, and yet they were the most adamant about not wanting to host the same players who'd be hosting them so eagerly in Romania.

In the end, I was able to garner some signatures, but only after explaining to the seniors on the team that since they were graduating after this year, they would never have to host Romanian players in the future. They wouldn't be in high school any more, and signing would never have a binding effect. They were calmed by this, though several reluctantly signed only after saying, "Coach, you promise me that even though I'm signing this, I'll still never actually have to host, right?" Deflated and discouraged, I said yes, got the signatures and tried to forget about how embarrassing this entire issue was. When I presented the signature sheet to the Romanian athletic director in Bucharest, he looked at me with a very confused look on his face. The signature sheet was a little more than half completed, and it was clear he'd never seen anything like it before. If I had an explanation for why our Bulgarian students weren't interested in returning a favor that was being done to them, I would've given it to him. But there wasn't a whole lot I could explain, so I just gave the athletic director the half-completed signature page and sheepishly said, "This was the best I could do." I didn't have any answers, justifications or explanations. Nikolai didn't either. I thought maybe Hristo Stoichkov could explain it, but odds were he wasn't interested in talking either—unless you were willing to pay him.

I hated to think that the "what's in it for me?" attitude was prevalent in Bulgaria, but I was starting to worry about the impression I got from time to time: compassion was a quality that seemed to be lacking. When I'd first arrived, I was reading Robert Kaplan's *Balkan Ghosts*, and he highlighted the importance of Georgi Markov's description of

Bulgaria. "While the citizen in the West is constantly striving to acquire more," he wrote in the 1970s, "our main instinct is to preserve what we have." It seemed that 'preserving what we have' included not wanting to branch out to help others for fear something could be lost in the meantime.

This mentality seemed to resonate in different aspects of Bulgarian society, most notably the collection of blood for hospitals. Bulgaria's hospitals were experiencing frightening blood shortages, so much so that relatives of people awaiting surgery had no choice but to hit the black market to purchase blood so the surgeries could be undertaken. Hospitals were short on blood supplies, and in some cases, would have to tell patients that they'd have to purchase their own blood for an operation to occur. Sometimes surgeries would have to be postponed for weeks because of the shortage of blood. As opposed to having a line outside the national blood clinic with people willing to donate, the clinic would routinely have men sitting outside smoking cigarettes, waiting for those who needed blood. These were black market blood dealers, and most people knew that if you needed blood for an operation or a transfusion, you'd find them outside the national blood clinic ready to supply whatever you needed—for a hefty price. It was not uncommon for desperate relatives to pay between 250-400 U.S. dollars for necessary blood supplies.

The entire operation seemed backwards and wrong to me. Here you have a national blood clinic, a place where people show up to donate blood that helps save lives, but if blood is really needed, you find people outside the blood clinic. There are so few donors that there wasn't blood available inside the clinic. This seemed to be a form of free market capitalism in play in Bulgaria. Why donate blood for free when you could sell it to the highest bidder just outside the clinic and make good money?

The American Association of Blood Banks indicates that the rate of voluntary blood donors in the United States is 53 people per one thousand. This average is also reflected in most EU nations. In Bulgaria, though, the rate stands at 23 people per one thousand, more than 50 percent below the United States and a good portion of Europe as well. In Europe, only Albania, Bosnia and Moldova have lower averages than Bulgaria. Stavri Toshkov, a Bulgarian expert in hematology, has referred to these rates, and the blood shortage in Bulgaria as a "crisis." His analysis of the situation includes a sad glimpse at life in Bulgaria: "Economic hardships have led to a deficit of such important values in society as solidarity, compassion and the willingness to help."

The players on my team didn't have the willingness to help in regards to hosting other student-athletes for a weekend, and this frustrated me to no end. But learning about Bulgarians' lack of willingness to voluntarily donate blood and save lives certainly trumped my concerns about weekend-hosting volunteers. In both cases, Bulgarians were enjoying the freedom of choice previously unavailable to them during years of Ottoman oppression and Soviet communist rule. I just wished that the freedoms they were now afforded would lead to a stronger desire to help others.

Another scandal relating to health care sent ripples through central Bulgaria, and it seemed to echo similar themes. The elderly in small villages near Devin, Bulgaria, a beautiful little hamlet nestled in southern Bulgaria in the Rhodope Mountains, were finding it more and more difficult to receive dental care. With no dentists in their small villages, if they wanted dental care to treat their problematic, infected and rotting teeth, they had no choice but to travel to Devin. It seemed, though, that Bulgarian dentists didn't have much interest in caring for elderly patients, especially since many of these patients were very poor and didn't have health insurance. One of the elderly villagers told a Bulgarian news source, "Everyone is corrupt in Devin; they want far too much money for dental services." For a tooth to be pulled, the going rate was 20 *leva* (about 13 U.S. dollars). But transportation from tiny villages to Devin to see a dentist would cost these villagers around 30 *leva* (around 20 U.S. dollars), making the total cost of a trip to the dentist prohibitive and unrealistic for these elderly patients. As a result, they turned to the only solution they could think of: they started pulling out their own teeth in their homes.

This practice caught the attention of an American dentist in Bulgaria who realized the health concerns—not to mention the extreme pain—associated with elderly Bulgarians pulling out their own teeth. He understood the dire need of dental care for these Bulgarians in remote locations, and also sensed that dentists in Devin weren't going to budge. While they undoubtedly had an interest in helping people, it seemed that making money was trumping their desire to help.

So the American dentist, a volunteer from the humanitarian organization JCBA, traveled to the Rhodope region and announced that he would be providing free dental service for a week for all patients who needed care. He stationed himself in the village of Selcha, a central location for many of the small villages in the area. In his week of free dental service, the villagers were quoted as being "very grateful and very happy" with the American dentist who finally gave them a better option than pulling out their own teeth.

The reaction to this free week of dental service, though, was not positive all around. The Bulgarian Dentist Association (BDA) was outraged by the arrival of this American dentist and his willingness to provide dental care for free. They felt he was poaching on their business and ruining their ability to make money as dentists. They went even further to threaten the mayor of the region with a fine for allowing an unauthorized dentist to enter their region and treat residents. They were determined to make someone suffer the consequences for what they perceived was an affront to their dignity—or wallets.

In the end, though, the villagers rallied in support of the American dentist. This was the first time they'd even been able to receive dental care in a long time, and they were thrilled to receive free treatment from this good Samaritan. A local schoolmaster had offered up rooms in the school for the American dentist to use to treat elderly patients, and he deemed that "the BDA were out of order, simply trying to strip the poor people of money they did not have in the first place." The mayor ended up avoiding the fine, and the issue calmed down when the American left after his week of free dental care. But the sour taste in many observers' mouths lingered, as it did not appear that the mindset in the Rhodopes had changed much. Human qualities such as "solidarity, compassion and the willingness to help," attributes the blood expert bemoaned the lack of, seemed to be missing from the vocabulary of the dentists in Devin as well.

When we arrived in Romania for the Vampire Classic, each of the members of the boys and girls teams were met warmly by their host families. Some of these host families were Romanian, and some were American, families of ex-pats living and working in Bucharest. It was clear to me that the members of our team had never had an experience like this before, and they were shocked by the overt and friendly welcome they received from people who had never even met them before. Throughout the weekend, our players would show up at the gym in the morning with different stories of how well they'd been fed, and how much they'd been made to feel at home by complete strangers in a strange land.

"My host mom told me," Ivan said to me on Saturday morning, "that she'd be thrilled to be my mother. I couldn't believe it," he shook his head in incredulity. "She's just *so nice, so nice.*"

Pavel showed up on Saturday morning with piles of Tupperware, one meal on top of another snack provided by his host mom for all of Saturday. He just couldn't believe it.

"Coach, look at this," he said to me, motioning to the feast he had laid out before him. "She made me so much food; it's incredible. I've never seen so much food," he hyperbolized. "I just can't believe my host mom. I can't believe she made all this food—all this food just for me. And she doesn't even know me."

I now wanted to ask Ivan, Pavel and several other members of our team if they would like to re-consider their decision not to sign, indicating their lack of willingness to host one of these families in the future. But in the back of my head, I could hear Nikolai repeating the phrase *it's not our mentality*, and I was scared to hear the answer to my question. So I didn't say anything and watched as my players munched on their smorgasbord of pre-game snacks.

Chapter XXIII
Bucharest Blues

Preparing for the trip to Romania, I was focused on how to prepare our team to play against different international schools, but I was also focused on avoiding the problems we'd encountered with the previous year's trip–most specifically the boozy bus driver. I'd pleaded with the athletic director to use a different bus company because I wasn't willing to put up with missing more games because of our driver's alcoholic leanings. I was told, though, that our school always used the same bus company for all its trips. When I talked to the athletic director about the bus situation, his initial response was certainly Bulgarian–*ne modje*–but when I indicated there were many bus companies in Sofia willing to take us to Romania, he softened up and was willing to do the highly unlikely: consider making a change and do something that bucked tradition. The athletic director impressed me by considering changing bus companies based on all of last year's problems, but in the end he decided he would just hire the same company again. There wasn't that great of a reason to change.

Our bus rolled onto campus in the dark of an early Friday February morning ready to take us to Romania, and I'd be lying if I said my fingers weren't crossed, wondering what this bus driver was going to be like. At least he was on time, which was a step in the right direction. Then as the middle-aged gray-haired bus driver stepped off the bus to welcome our team aboard, I noticed a distinct difference from our Greece trip: this driver didn't smell like booze. And as Nikolai got on the bus, the driver animatedly showed off the bus's new GPS system, which was going to help him navigate us north to Bucharest. This seemed to be a major improvement from last year where we got lost both days on our way from the hotel to the Greek school. I wondered if GPS was going to function as we traveled through rural Bulgaria and Romania, but I had confidence that GPS would at least help us when we were in the city of Bucharest.

We were leaving in the dark on Friday morning because we needed to make it to Bucharest in time for our first game on Friday, which had a 4:30 p.m. tip-off. Things were uncommonly smooth as we cruised along empty Bulgarian highways, headed for Bulgaria's neighbor to the north, Romania. I'd printed out a map the night before the trip to see where we'd be heading. Half of my motivation was simple geographical curiosity, and the other half was out of necessity: I figured it'd help if I knew where to go if and when we started to get lost.

The border between Bulgaria and Romania was established entirely by the mighty Danube River, which traveled the 470-kilometer distance between the two countries before finally depositing its water into the Black Sea. The path we'd be taking to Bucharest would lead us over the Danube, and I started scanning the map, trying to find out what our different options would be for the route to Bucharest. Looking at the map, though, it seemed that we didn't have much choice; all routes to Romania ran through Ruse, a Bulgarian city in the middle of the border between the two countries. It appeared that we would be crossing the Ruse Bridge of Friendship, whose name I determined seemed to be a bit of a misnomer. "Such is the friendship between Romania and Bulgaria," Kapka Kassabova wrote in her memoir, "that along a 470-kilometer-long border, this is the only bridge."

As we were about to approach Ruse and the bridge, I started feeling relieved. I looked at my watch and felt comfortable that we would arrive in Bucharest well ahead of our 4:30 tip-off. But then our sober and GPS-happy bus driver pulled the bus off to the side of the road in the middle of what appeared to be nowhere. I knew we were on the outskirts of Ruse, but looking at a few dilapidated houses, and one garage that had a beaten-up car miraculously resting on top of the garage, I felt this qualified as the middle of nowhere. Neither Branch nor I understood why we were stopping, so we leaned forward to ask

Nikolai what was going on.

"Ah," Nikolai said, "we have been driving for four hours. Now it is time to stop. This is the law; the bus must stop and take a break every four hours."

Branch and I looked at each other, each confirming that we'd never heard of any law like this.

"It is like this everywhere in Europe," Nikolai added calmly.

I bit my tongue instead of rattling off a list of buses I'd taken in Bulgaria and other European countries that certainly didn't follow this law that supposedly affected all of Europe. I was curious, though, how long we were going to stop for.

Nikolai leaned forward and asked the driver, and he responded in Bulgarian. I understood his response—45 minutes. I also asked Nikolai why we'd stopped in the middle of nowhere on the side of the road, instead of somewhere rational-sounding like a gas station.

"Well, it has been exactly four hours," Nikolai replied, sensing my frustration, "and he must be following the rule exactly. I asked him if it was possible for us to stop at a gas station or a restaurant, but he just kept pointing at his watch and saying 'Ne modje.'"

During his 45-minute break, I didn't see the bus driver do much more than what he'd been doing already. He just sat in his bus driver seat and looked straight ahead—but for the next 45 minutes, we didn't go anywhere.

When the bus mercifully started moving again, we crossed the Bridge of Friendship—a friendship with limits, clearly—and then proceeded to stop at numerous gas stations. We made it to five different Romanian gas stations within our first hour in the country. With each new stop, I looked at my watch, growing more and more nervous about our 4:30 p.m. game. The stops at the gas stations were necessary because the bus driver needed to purchase a vignette sticker that would allow him to legally drive his Bulgarian bus in Romania. Such is the friendship between Bulgaria and Romania that it's necessary to pay a fee just to have the right to drive on their friendly and neighborly roads.

At the second gas station—the first one didn't have vignette stickers—I leaned forward once again and questioned Nikolai about what was going on. Couldn't one of these stickers have been purchased by the bus company before we left Sofia? Yes, Nikolai told me gravely, and I could sense his annoyance was burgeoning, too.

The second gas station didn't have vignette stickers either, so we moved on to a third one. When the bus driver returned, he reported that he'd finally found a place that sold the vignette stickers. I understood what he said in Bulgarian, and my spirits rose. But then he started muttering in a much quieter tone. The Romanian gas station would not accept his Bulgarian *leva*; he couldn't buy the sticker.

Nikolai turned to translate this to me, but I waved him off. Unfortunately, I understood exactly what the bus driver had just relayed to us.

"Basically, Andy," Nikolai said, with his cheeks puffing out as a display of chagrin, "this bus driver is just not prepared to do his job."

I brought up the notion of using an ATM card at the machine in the gas station to extract Romanian *leu* to pay for the vignette, but Nikolai nixed this idea.

"Andy, he does not have an ATM card. Very few Bulgarians have ATM cards. You and Coach Branch are probably the only ones here who have ATM cards. We all brought Bulgarian *leva* to exchange."

I found this hard to believe, so I quickly turned to the back of the bus and asked our players who had an ATM card that he had brought with him. No hands were raised. Nikolai was right.

At the fifth gas station, the bus driver found vignette stickers, and a hospitable clerk who surprisingly would accept foreign currency. With that, I figured we would finally be on our way for good. Then we discovered that traffic in Bucharest was actually worse than traffic in Sofia. Branch and I discussed taking alternate routes, consulting the completely inadequate map I'd printed the night before.

"Do you think we could get off this road and try a different way?" I asked Nikolai. We were stopped on a two-lane highway next to a large flock of gulls that was hovering over a large Romanian landfill scouring for their lunch.

"I already asked him this twice," an exasperated Nikolai told me, "and he just keeps pointing to his GPS. He's not willing to do anything the GPS doesn't tell him to do."

As the clock ticked past 3:00 and we were still inhaling the odors of the landfill, I started giving our players instructions about how we needed to be mentally ready for our first game at 4:30. We were now riding a previously unheard of six-game winning streak, and this was something I'd forgotten about since I had spent the majority of the day in the front of the bus analyzing the behaviors of our Bulgarian bus driver. When I'd arrived in Bulgaria the year before, we had three strong candidates who could rotate our two guard positions: Menkov, Stefan, and Dimov. Now, for one good reason and one bad one, Menkov was our only guard. Yet we were still playing the best basketball we'd played at any time during my two years in Bulgaria, and we were doing it with a lineup of one guard and four forwards. I wondered what was about to happen in Bucharest. We were leaving the comforts of Bulgaria, where we could almost always expect that our opponents wouldn't play hard for an entire game–and would most likely get one or two technical fouls. And we were going to be playing two different international teams. We were scheduled to play against the host school from Bucharest and also an international school from London who would be flying in for the tournament. We'd get two games apiece against each of these teams. As we stalled in Friday afternoon Bucharest traffic, we were getting precipitously close to being late for our first game. This felt like Greece all over again.

Thankfully, once I started talking about game preparation and focusing on basketball-related topics, traffic relented and the bus magically started moving. Close to 4:00, we arrived at the Romanian school and hopped off the bus, ready to prepare for the game. Our players walked around the school, mouths agape as they toured this new and pristine campus. Gone were the sights of Bucharest landfills. And as we walked through each new hallway and courtyard, I was also seeing that our players were realizing that many of the prejudices they held toward Romania were untrue. This would be the nicest high school with the nicest high school gym we would visit in two years.

I was greeted by the Romanian coach, and this represented something new for me: he was an American. I relaxed, feeling that lots of things would be different in this tournament. I'd frequently been frustrated by the lack of sportsmanship from Bulgarian teams and the incredible number of outrageous incidents that would occur because the opposing coaches either weren't concerned with the behavior of their players–or they were the role models for bad behavior themselves. I talked to the Romanian school coach who hailed from Michigan originally and began to feel a sense of comfort and relaxation. But then he started talking about his star player.

"Yeah, we've had a lot of trouble with a few of our players. They aren't getting the job done in the classroom," he told me.

"Oh, really," I said, feeling fortunate that this was one problem we didn't have with our team.

"Yeah, you'll see our best player out there today–a really electric two-guard, a great scorer. But he's actually ineligible for our other international tournaments. He's failing too many classes. But since we're hosting this one, we get to make the rules."

With this, he smiled at me, indicating he was happy with this situation. The Romanian coach walked away and Branch pointed out that I hadn't said much after he had revealed he would be playing technically ineligible players.

"Did he really just admit to you that his star player is ineligible—and that he's going to play him anyway?" Branch asked, clearly stunned.

"Yep, that's what he said."

"Are you kidding me? What does he expect you to say to that? 'Congratulations, I'm happy your kid who is failing in the classroom will be playing against us today?'"

"Yeah, I have no idea," I told him glumly. "I think it was a mistake to think that because their coach was American, we'd be dealing with a whole different—and better—set of ethics. This is just more of the same."

As we warmed up for our first game, I fell into my old Bulgarian habit of watching the other team warm up to see what we'd be facing. And I quickly fell into my old Bulgarian habit of thinking, *Oh no, we're in big trouble.* The Romanian team was big, and appeared to be bigger and stronger than our team. But this wasn't what worried me the most. As I looked down to their end of the floor, I saw that their layup lines—both left and right—were fluid. And as they slapped fives jogging to the end of the lines, I could hear some of the things they were saying to each other to get ready for the game. It wasn't what they were saying, but the language they were speaking: these kids were all speaking English to each other. Some of them—like the aforementioned two-guard—were clearly Romanian. But at least half of them weren't Romanian; they were from the States. They spoke English, dribbled confidently, made their layups, and looked like they'd been playing basketball since they were little kids. This looked like a U.S. varsity basketball team.

During the course of our two seasons, players would intermittently talk to me about the States. Inevitably they would ask how much better basketball was in the States than it was in Bulgaria. I usually deflected these questions as often as possible after indicating that yes, basketball was played at a higher level in the States. I didn't want to go into too much detail. Once I was in my second year, however, I slowly began to forget about coaching basketball in the States. I was firmly entrenched as a basketball coach in Bulgaria. Watching the Romanian team warm-up brought me back to the States. And more importantly, it made me think we could be in for a rough ride this weekend.

We'd spent a long day on the bus, and even though we'd had enough time to warm up, I was worried about how we'd start the game. We were in a completely new environment and I knew this was a disadvantage for us. We had grown accustomed to playing games on our own court. My pre-game speech centered on coming out strong, not being nervous or intimidated, and playing with a purpose from the moment the ball was thrown in the air. Once the game started, it appeared all of those words had been in vain.

It was 8-0 before I could blink.

We'd had four possessions: three turnovers and a missed three-point desperation shot from far, far away from the hoop. I had no choice but to call a timeout to try to calm my team down. The Romanian team was running us up and down the floor. Unlike Bulgarian teams that were talented but still had holes and didn't work very hard, this team was talented, didn't have holes that I could see, and was out for blood like vampires right from the beginning.

Even after my timeout, the Romanians ran off seven more points before we got on the scoreboard. It was now 15-2. Our bench cheered when Pesho scored, but even their cheers were of the stunned variety. We were getting killed.

It was 21-4 when Menkov chucked up an impossible runner from 18-feet away. The ball clanked off the backboard and rim, and Romania grabbed the rebound and was headed down the right wing toward our basket. Even though our players were running back on defense, they had never seen a fast break like this—organized, efficient and *fast*. In short, it looked like a fast break you'd see in the U.S.

As their point guard sped across half court and took the ball to the middle of the floor, he expertly flung the ball to the right wing to a blond-haired American forward who caught it at the three-point line. He took one right-handed dribble, two steps and then exploded up toward the hoop. Pesho had hastily retreated to put himself in a position to challenge the shot. His ears were permanently ringing with two years of my yelling at him for not challenging shots and just letting guys have open layups, as he was wont to do when he didn't feel like jumping. As Pesho and the American both elevated together, their chests collided, bumping the American away from the hoop and forcing him to shoot off-balance. The ball trickled off the rim as the whistle blew, and the American forward would get two shots at the foul line.

But this wasn't what everyone was paying attention to. With Pesho standing over him, trying to help him up, the blond-haired American was yelping in pain. The gym had gone silent, and it seemed like the only noise you could hear was the plaintive cries of the American forward. Pesho made one more effort to help him up, but then turned aghast when he saw what the problem was. The American forward's foot wasn't in its right place; it was dangling precariously off to one side, as if his ankle was about to break off. He had dislocated his ankle.

The school needed a stretcher to take the American forward out of the gym and to the hospital. In the time it took for that to happen, Pesho came to the bench terrified, feeling guilty for what had happened. His defensive play warranted a foul, but it wasn't even remotely dirty. He'd gone up to try to block the shot, and ensuing ankle dislocation had little to do with him, and much more to do with bad luck. Off-balance when he shot the ball, the American forward had landed awkwardly, his body contorted and his ankle now dislocated. Pesho, the player on the team most likely to dress up like a mafia member for Halloween, was so shaken, though, that I had to take him out of the game, telling him over and over again that it wasn't his fault.

With the rest of the team, I wasn't sure where to begin. So many times they'd asked me what American basketball was like and I'd given them vague answers. Now they were receiving an answer with plenty of details. This was American basketball—in your face, take no prisoners—and we were getting crushed. To make matters worse, it now appeared like no one on our team wanted to commit a hard foul. They didn't want to dislocate anyone else's ankle.

The electric and ineligible two-guard that the Romanian coach had referred to was one of the best players on a Romanian team that was very good. But it didn't take long for me to understand how someone like him could be academically ineligible. A few minutes after the injury, he seemed to take it upon himself to get revenge for his teammate, and swung a wild elbow in Sasho's direction. It was blatant and threatening, but the referees either didn't see it, or chose not to see it. It missed Sasho's nose by a few inches, and as a result, he still didn't lose his customary goofy smile.

But the next time down the floor, their two-guard didn't miss. This time, his flying left elbow nailed Vassy in the collarbone as he was running down the floor on offense and sent him flying. The referees caught him this time, and he was assessed a technical foul—a technical foul that he vehemently protested while Menkov helped Vassy up off the floor. The look in Vassy's eyes said that he'd had enough. He'd spent two years suffering the brunt of cheap shots to his face and torso, and now it looked like he was through being a target. He yelled something to the Romanian hothead, and this led to both Vassy and the Romanian being restrained by teammates.

I summoned Kosio from the bench to go sub in for Vassy, and as Vassy came to the bench, he already knew what I was thinking.

"I know, I know, Coach," he admitted. "I know I'm not supposed to act that way. You don't want me to stoop to his level."

I looked him in the eye, indicating that I didn't need to say anything more.

"But that guy," he motioned toward the floor where the Romanian guard was still fuming, "he's a real asshole."

Vassy couldn't have been more correct, and he provided yet another reason why the Romanian shouldn't have been playing in the first place. As Menkov went to the foul line to shoot the two technical free throws, the Romanian coach calmly looked on from the sidelines. His star player still had steam coming out of his ears, and I got the impression that his first technical foul was simply that—just his first. Another one might be coming soon, and the next elbow might hit something easier to break than a collarbone.

"Coach," I hollered down the sideline to my Romanian counterpart, "are you serious? Are you seriously not going to take him out of the game?"

With this, I'd gotten the coach's attention, but he seemed surprised that I was talking to him.

"He's going to hurt someone. In fact, he's trying to hurt someone. You can't leave him in the game."

The American coach from Michigan considered my words for all of .4 seconds and then instinctively waved his hand in my direction. He wasn't interested in anything I had to say, and wasn't interested in sportsmanship any more than any Bulgarian coach we'd squared off against. On the next possession, the Romanian two-guard took the ball to the basket and intentionally thrust his airborne body into Pavel, again using his elbows to inflict more damage, and eventually sending him flying. This earned him a charging call, an offensive foul. Vassy immediately jumped up from the bench, infuriated by the dirty play.

"Coach, why do I have to sit out while he gets to stay in the game to do that?"

It was a fair point, but one I didn't have an answer for. I glared down at the Romanian coach who still seemed unaffected until his assistant tapped his shoulder to let him know this was the two-guard's third foul. For this reason—and not because he was causing harm for other players by playing dirty—the Romanian coach took him out of the game. He was muttering swear words and pointing at our bench as he sauntered off the floor.

"I think I understand why he's ineligible," Branch offered, a severe understatement.

There were only three minutes to go and we were trailing 41-12. We'd come out slow and groggy from a long bus ride, but that wasn't a good enough excuse to explain the scoreboard. We were just being completely outplayed in every aspect of basketball. All the things I'd tried to harp on in practice, but never gained much traction with, were now being exposed. On offense, we were running a motion offense that consisted of a whole lot of wasted motion, players running around aimlessly instead of setting screens or making hard cuts. On defense, we were caught off-guard against a team that passed the ball and screened well. We'd become inured to Bulgarian teams that didn't pass much and just played a one-on-one style of offense that wasn't that difficult to defend.

With not a whole lot to play for other than pride, it was nice to see Menkov dive for a loose ball and go flying out of bounds. He'd taken a bad shot—one of many we'd taken already—but followed it, deflected the rebound, and then dove to save it as it headed out of bounds. He flipped the ball behind his back as he went crashing onto the floor. It was a fantastic hustle play, but one that just resulted in starting a fast break the other way. His attempt to save the ball fell into the hands of a Romanian player. Once again, they quickly headed the other way.

Pavel was the first one back, sprinting back to the foul line as he'd been coached to do. Ivan was next behind him, also sprinting to take his place to try to defend. Sasho never moved particularly quickly, but he was putting his best effort in to getting back. And even Menkov, who had ended up out of bounds on the floor, quickly sprang to his feet and was near half court, hustling as if this was the most important possession of the game.

But there was one more player out on the floor—Kosio.

As I watched four of our five players scurry back down the floor on defense, doing the best they could even though we were trailing by 30 points, Kosio seemed to have no interest in any of this. He'd barely made it past half court, and had settled into a comfortable jog, which might have been an overstatement. He wasn't moving fast at all.

"Kosio, get back on defense! Hustle!" I hollered instinctively.

Nothing changed as a result of this decree. He loped back on defense, barely making it to the three-point line in time to watch the Romanian team miss their initial shot, but get the rebound and score.

At this point in the game, I knew we were going to lose. I'd actually known this for quite some time. So I'd already decided there was little point in getting upset at our players for the inevitable difficulties we were going to have executing, especially on offense. But I had no tolerance for not hustling back on defense; this had less to do with basketball and everything to do with character and pride. This wasn't the first time it had happened with Kosio either. He was the sure bet to be the one in practice to come up limping during sprints or claim he was too injured to run to begin with. But he never seemed injured when it came time to play offense, his favorite part of basketball.

His attitude and approach to basketball, I'd come to understand, was not unique in Bulgaria. He had offensive talent, and that was all that really mattered in basketball. Defense was secondary and therefore optional; he could choose to play defense, choose to run hard and help his teammates, or in some cases, like he did with me, choose to stick his leg out and trip his opponent instead of working hard. During our second season, we'd won numerous games because our opponents didn't all feel like hustling back on defense. Our victories didn't reflect an up-tick in strategy and skill as much as they were representative of simply playing hard for the entire game and never walking or jogging up and down the floor.

Even though it wasn't even halftime yet, it was clear that we'd be playing this game for little more than pride. With that in mind, there was no way I could keep Kosio on the floor if he wasn't going to be running hard. When he came to the bench, he didn't want any part of my lecture.

"You only yell at me! You only yell at me to run hard! Why don't you yell at anyone else to run hard?"

I was annoyed by his immediate displacing of blame, but figured maybe it was fitting. When things went wrong for Bulgaria with the EU, politicians often pointed to Romania and said that Romania was worse. Now that we were in Romania, it seemed Kosio had found solace in this strategy as well. The fact that he wasn't running hard wasn't in dispute; he just wanted me to find someone else to yell at.

"The others run hard and sprint back on defense," I told him calmly. "If you run hard on defense, I won't yell at you. But watch all your teammates; they always run hard. That's the way we play."

As he passed me, he muttered something in Bulgarian that I couldn't entirely decipher, but I was pretty sure it was derogatory and offensive–and directed at me. We were already getting annihilated in the game; the last thing I wanted to deal with was his attitude. But I was also aware that it was much easier for tempers to flare when the scoreboard looked like it did: Romania 49, ACS 16.

At halftime, Branch and I assessed the damage, and things didn't look good for us. It'd already been a long day, but this game seemed interminable. We still had a long weekend of basketball ahead of us, and getting off to this horrific start was not what either of us had in mind.

"The only way we can even make this remotely respectable is if we get back on defense and stop their fast break opportunities," Branch said.

"I know. That's why I can't let Kosio play if he's not going to run back on defense. It's embarrassing to the team to watch him jog and not care."

"I'll talk to him, and see if that makes a difference. As much trouble as we're having scoring the ball, it would help to have him back in the game."

The second half started, and my main focus at halftime had been that we needed to improve and had an entire half to get better in pretty much every aspect of basketball. The scoreboard didn't matter; we needed to play better and continue to play hard. There would be no acceptable excuses for giving up or giving in. At this point in our second season, looking at Pavel, Pesho and Menkov, I could see that this speech almost didn't need to be uttered. They hadn't forgotten the huge deficits we'd faced in the past, and they were accustomed to my attitude regarding how we'd finish the game. I knew they would continue to play hard because they knew they'd sit on the bench otherwise.

I wasn't sure what to do about Kosio because quite honestly, I didn't want to deal with any more conflict on this day. From the bus driver to the Romanian coach to Kosio's spat with me, I was wearing down. But halfway through the third quarter, I decided to give him another chance. He was still a temperamental high school kid, and one who could learn from his mistakes and make a change.

For the rest of the game, our deficit hovered in the range of 30 to 40 points. The Romanian coach seemed to be following Bulgarian tendencies. Even though the outcome of the game had entirely been decided, he had no intention of taking his starters out of the game. His hot-headed and academically-challenged two-guard wreaked havoc on our defense. Part of this came from his talent, and part of it stemmed from some of our players' fear that he would take a swing at them.

Toward the end of the third quarter, we put together our best offensive run of the game. Menkov made a floater in the lane, and then on the next possession, Pesho faced the basket from the free throw line and drove to his right. He was able to score on an athletic move, and get fouled. On the following possession, Kosio caught the ball at the three-point line, pump-faked, took two dribbles and banked home a 12-foot jump shot. He pumped his fist in celebration of making the shot, and once again started to drift back on defense. I tried not to focus solely on him, but it was becoming difficult. The other four players on the floor didn't waste any time getting back on defense. The Romanian team liked to run even on made baskets, and this placed even more importance on hustling.

"Do you see what I see?" Branch leaned over and said to me, as we watched Kosio amble back on defense.

"Yeah, I see it," I said bitterly. "I don't know how much more of this I can put up with. He just doesn't seem to get it."

"I don't know if he's ever gotten it," Branch replied. "It's just easier to hide this sort of thing when we're winning."

I bit my lip, resolved not to overreact and hoped for the best. Our next time down the floor, though, Kosio tried a similar move from the three-point line. He pump-faked and took two dribbles to his right. This time his defender still stayed with him so Kosio spun to his left. Picking up his dribble, he now appeared to have nowhere to go. His defender was right in front of him and now another defender had joined the mix. I could see Kosio was panicked by the extra attention, and he didn't notice that Menkov was calling for the ball, wide open on the left wing. Kosio started to lose his balance and tossed up a right-handed half-hook shot the caromed off the backboard without even hitting the rim.

As the Romanian center easily corralled the rebound, Kosio flung his hands up in the air and yelled at his teammates, blaming them for his bad decision and missed shot. And what happened next was then all too predictable.

The Romanian center made the outlet pass and the fast break was started. Menkov sprinted back to the foul line first, followed by Pavel soon after. Pesho tried to stop the ball-handler and at least slow down the fast break. Vassy also hustled back, desperately chasing his man who had a step on him. All the while, Kosio stood at the opposite foul line, miffed his shot hadn't gone in. A moment later, he started walking back on defense, and then finally picked his legs up and increased his walk to a light jog.

The rest of his teammates had quelled the Romanian fast break, but now they were playing 5-on-4 in half-court offense. Once Kosio realized the play was still continuing, he managed to run from half court to join the rest of his team on defense.

Branch didn't need to say anything to me, and I didn't need to say anything to him. We'd both seen enough. I tapped Ivan on the shoulder and told him to go replace Kosio in the game. Before the whistle blew and a substitution could be made, Kosio managed to score another basket, and in a similar fashion, act petulantly and not sprint back on defense. At this point, it appeared he was doing this more out of rebellion than a lack of energy or desire.

Finally, the whistle blew and Ivan motioned to Kosio that he was coming out of the game. Similar to what had occurred the last time he was subbed out, I wasn't the one who started talking first. Kosio was ready for his assault well before my lecture would ever arrive. He started yelling at me while he was still on the floor and not yet even near the bench.

"What do you want from me? What do you want from me?" he bellowed.

I could feel warmth rising up to my face; my pride was being insulted. I sensed this was just the beginning of the disrespect.

"Take someone else out of the game! Not me! I just scored! All you ever do is pick on me!"

The bench was quiet and so was Branch. No matter how this played out, everyone knew it wasn't going to be pretty. As Kosio came to greet me face-to-face, it struck me as incredible that I would have so many problems with a player like him, a person like him. Far and away, he spoke the best English on the team. And he probably had the most natural offensive basketball talent on the team. Heck, he could even make a jump shot, something Ivan–who just replaced him–had only done once or twice in two years. But so much of what we'd focused on the last two years had little to do with English-speaking ability or making jump shots. This was a team that only experienced success when it worked hard, hustled and played good defense. While I knew Kosio was intelligent enough to understand these concepts, I was left to interpret that he just didn't want to.

"Kosio!" I retorted, surprised that I had yelled in response. I had intended to keep my calm. "Nothing about my expectations has changed in two years. You have to run back on defense and play hard the entire time you're on the floor. You're not hustling and you're not playing hard, and that's why you're going to sit on the bench. I don't need you to yell at me; I need you to start sprinting back on defense."

As my rant was completed, he brushed past me and once again started grumbling in Bulgarian. I knew he thought I couldn't understand, but his displeasure and disrespect was evident regardless of whether or not I had the translation correct.

"Sit down, Kosio," I fired away. "Sit down and shut up."

I felt my eyes burning through his body as I watched him sulk to the bench. As I diverted my glance from his, I saw Sasho looking up at me terrified. This signaled to me how riled up I was. Sasho rarely expressed any emotion on his visage other than goofiness, and I could see he was intimidated by how upset I was.

Branch then put his hand on my shoulder expressing sympathy, and said something I had little trouble agreeing with: "There's no point in your talking to him anymore. Just let him sit there and don't put him back in the game."

This wasn't the first time I'd had a player pout on the bench, and certainly wasn't the first time a player was frustrated with me as a coach. But Kosio was taking the entire episode to new levels. What I was asking him to do wasn't something complicated like I had asked my American players to do in the past: execute an intricate offensive set play, run a designed secondary fast break, or hedge out against a screen-and-roll to stop a ball-handler. These were all complicated basketball skills that were the cornerstones of practices and games in the States. And an inability to do these things right usually reflected either a lack of effort in practice or a mental mistake. In these cases, I would take players out of the game and explain to them that they could only play if they were able to overcome these mental mistakes and execute properly.

But in the case of Kosio, I wasn't asking him to execute any specific play on offense or scheme on defense; I was just asking him to run hard. Even though this had been explained to him during pre-season running, practices and games for two years, it still seemed like a foreign concept to him. At the beginning of my Bulgarian tenure, other players also scoffed at my proclamations that running back on defense was paramount. This just wasn't something they were used to, they'd tell me. But quickly enough, they figured it out. If they didn't run back on defense, they sat on the bench. So they started hustling at all times because they didn't want to come out of the game. This system of consequences seemed to work across many cultures, even if it took some of my Bulgarian players longer to realize it.

With Kosio, it was difficult to understand why this concept hadn't set in. During less-heated moments, he always seemed to have the right answers, and they were always spoken in fluent English. But I wasn't interested in hearing him talk. And perhaps I wasn't interested in where he came from–his father was a *businessman* and his family had money. I couldn't figure out what the issue was, but nothing I'd done as a coach in two years had convinced Kosio that he needed to work hard. Maybe it was the new form of democracy in Bulgaria that influenced him to believe there was always a short cut. Maybe it was a sense of fatalism that he'd inherited from other people in his country: *we're not going to win anyway, so what's the point?* Or maybe this was just Kosio: he had a questionable work ethic and a sullen demeanor.

No matter what the answer was, when we entered the team huddle to begin the fourth quarter, I tried not to think about Kosio. With his legs lounging out as far as they could go, he leaned back in his seat on the bench and refused to join the huddle. I saw Branch motion to him that he should join us as part of the team, but he pretended like he didn't see his assistant coach.

"We can't pay attention to the scoreboard," I said to the team in the huddle. "We're playing this fourth quarter for pride, and we need to look at this as a great opportunity. We're playing a really good team, and this is a chance for us to get better. In this quarter, we have to play harder than them."

"We have to play harder than them," came a smurf-like, mocking voice from behind the huddle.

I paused for a second, not sure if I'd heard correctly, and certain I didn't understand.

"This fourth quarter is about pride and showing your character. How hard will you play when things aren't going well?"

"How hard will you play when things aren't going well?" came from the bench, in the same mimicked, third-grader tone.

This time, I had no doubt about what was going on, and had no choice but to stop what I was doing. Kosio was sitting on the bench outside the huddle with a smirk on his face, enjoying the proceedings while derisively imitating the speech I was giving.

"Are you kidding me?" I exploded. "I can't believe you! You have that little respect for what we're doing here?"

To this, Kosio's eyebrows raised as if to say, "Who? Me?"

"I don't want to hear another word out of you. And if you can't be quiet, then you should leave the bench. You're not a part of this team right now anyway. The only thing that matters to you is yourself."

The rest of my speech to the team was effectively nullified by my rapid increase in blood pressure. I tried to focus on the rest of the fourth quarter based on what was happening on the floor, but it was difficult for me to get past the disrespect I'd had to deal with from Kosio. I didn't have answers for where this was coming from, and that didn't really matter. By the time the game was over, we'd lost by 38 points. Our six-game winning streak came to a resounding halt, and any momentum we'd accrued over the last month was definitely gone.

"I don't think you should talk to Kosio," Branch advised me. "Do you want me to go talk to him?"

"Well," I looked at Branch, "do you want to talk to him?"

"No," Branch said immediately, "I have no desire to speak to him whatsoever."

"Then I think that makes two of us," I sadly concluded.

I summoned Menkov over to us before we were about to leave the gym, and told him that I needed him to be a leader and talk to Kosio. They were friends, and he was going to have to find out what was going on. And if Kosio planned to continue being on this team, things were going to have to change in a big way. As I was talking to Menkov, I noticed he had a pained expression on his face—not because I was asking him to be a leader and take charge, but I could sense that he didn't want to talk to Kosio either.

"I'll talk to him, Coach," Menkov told me, "but I don't know what in the world is going on."

Thankfully, our exit from the gym soon after that left many of the players feeling the same way. They were greeted by the families of some of the opposing players and immediately given snacks and drinks to help re-hydrate after the game. There wasn't much to say about the 38-point loss, so it was good that our players were all now being introduced to new families and new worlds. Some would spend the night playing video games with the opposing players. Others would go to the hospital to visit the forward with a dislocated ankle. And some others would tell me they ate more food for dinner than they'd ever had before. All these things helped me realize that showing up in

Romania, getting blown out by 38 points and having a blow-up occur on the bench might not be the most important parts of this trip.

Nikolai, Branch and I headed out of the gym and it was clear that we'd have plenty to talk about at our hotel that night. Of course, I had no idea how difficult it was going to be to get settled in our hotel. Even though darkness had already fallen in chilly Bucharest, the night was still very young.

Chapter XXIV
Second Class Citizens

The Romanian coach was certainly pleased with his team's victory, but I don't think he was very pleased with anything about the American College of Sofia. We'd brought a team to his tournament that was well below his team's level of play, and then I'd loudly questioned his ethics as he allowed his ineligible star player to flagrantly throw elbows all over the floor in an attempt to hurt people. He never vocally expressed his frustration or displeasure with either the shoddy product we'd just put out on the floor or my comments to him during the game. But he was able to provide us with enough condescension to make up for it. As the four of us–Nikolai, Branch, myself, and the bus driver who was now also included in our posse–waited in the school's reception area, we wondered where the shuttle bus was that was supposed to be picking us up. Our bus driver was more than happy to tool us around in his bus, but several employees of the Romanian school had cautioned against it.

"It's not easy to navigate the way from here to the hotel," we were told, "and once you get there, you're not going to have anywhere to park the bus. You're better off leaving the bus here and taking our shuttle to the hotel. That's what we have all of our visiting teams do. The shuttle will take you back and forth at the beginning and end of each day."

This was fine with me, and I sensed Branch and Nikolai were happy about it as well. We'd been stuck in enough traffic jams and jostled around on enough Romanian potholed roads for one day. Branch, Nikolai and I all agreed we'd be thrilled to get to our hotel and be able to relax for a little bit. But I could tell that the bus driver was not thrilled with this decision. Nikolai had translated our plans into Bulgarian for him, and now he was fidgeting with his hand-held GPS, seemingly lost without being inside the confines of his bus.

"Did he watch our games?" I leaned over and said quietly to Nikolai.

Nikolai looked inquisitively at the bus driver who was wandering around the school hallways, testing out his GPS, eyes fixated on it like it was either a treasure map or a Game Boy.

"No, I don't think he did," Nikolai responded. "He said he really enjoys being in his bus. So he just stayed in the bus."

Both Branch and I had to wait a moment to see if it was okay to laugh at this. Once Nikolai wasn't able to stifle his grin, we deemed it appropriate to laugh a little bit.

"Our bus driver," Nikolai seemed on the brink of a breakthrough, "he certainly is a different type. How do you say? How do you say in English...? Well, you know what, I don't even know how to describe him in Bulgarian."

With this, we laughed some more, and it felt good—like it was the first time we'd laughed in a week. The Romanian coach finally graced us with his presence, and we figured this meant our trip to the hotel would be imminent.

"Okay guys, here's the deal," he said to us, and the lack of optimism in his tone clearly indicated to me that there wasn't going to be any ride to the hotel. "The shuttle bus left a while ago with the London school, and we're not going to have it come back here and pick you guys up. Unfortunately, we'd hoped that you could get on that bus, but you were too late."

Too late? We'd been waiting in the school's reception foyer for the last 45 minutes—and that's exactly where we'd been from the moment our game ended.

"So what we're going to do is this: here are some subway tokens," he said as he dropped a coin in each of our hands. "The subway's only a few blocks away so that's no problem. And you're going to take the subway to this stop—" he handed me a piece of paper with the name written on it "—then walk two blocks east and you'll be at the hotel."

I looked up at him, wanting to add several editorial comments about how the school from London was sent in a private shuttle while the school from Bulgaria was told to take the subway, but I bit my tongue. Nikolai translated this to our roving GPS bus driver, and we picked up our bags and started walking. Not much was said until Nikolai broke the ice.

"Maybe I am reading this situation wrong," Nikolai wondered aloud, "but this treatment we are receiving—it seems, uh, it seems not entirely nice."

Branch gravitated toward this comment right away, and I could hear dogs barking—feral growling that reminded me of Sofia.

"No, Nikolai, it's not *nice* at all. There's no way—no way in hell—he'd make the big money school from London take the subway."

"I worry," Nikolai continued, "that he views us differently than the other school that got to take the shuttle. I don't want to be offended as a Bulgarian, but I don't like it when I feel like I'm being treated differently."

There wasn't a whole lot Branch or I could say. I thought that possibly it was my fault for mouthing off to the coach during the game, or maybe we were receiving second-class treatment because our students hadn't all signed the agreement to host their families in the future. Or this could be reflected in the fact that our boys team had just been defeated by 38 points; the coach felt we didn't deserve respect. But more likely than anything else, the lack of respect we were being shown probably had everything to do with money. The London school, the third team in the tournament, had flown in from London for the tournament. We'd taken a bus. The London school brought a fleet of coaches along with at least one parent of every one of their players. There were three of us, our perplexing bus driver, and no parents. The London school didn't chafe at staying at one of the most expensive hotels in Bucharest. When the athletic director had told me the cost of the rooms for coaches—nearly 400 dollars a night—I'd told him that our school couldn't afford this. The London school had already organized a dinner and reception at a fancy Bucharest restaurant, and the only reason I knew about this was we'd been told that the reception would be on Saturday night, but we wouldn't be invited.

For almost two full years, I'd been living in Bulgaria, but still looking at Bulgaria as an outsider who was living, experiencing and studying the country. When I was in Bulgaria, I felt like a foreigner, and sometimes I had trouble connecting Bulgarian culture and behavior to my life. There were times when I felt connected, but most of the time, I felt like the other, the outsider, the one who might understand, but still didn't entirely belong. I thought of Kassabova's memoir and how she felt that "the rest of Europe looks to Bulgaria with either indifference or condescension." This had always been a quote that made me think of what others thought about Bulgarians, but I didn't include myself in that category.

As I clutched to my subway token and we left the darkness of the Bucharest night to enter the subway stop, I no longer felt like an outsider. To the Americans running the Bucharest school, I was Bulgarian; we were all Bulgarian.

And we were taking the subway.

Nicolae Ceausescu was about as reviled a figure as you could find anywhere in Eastern Europe. Even in Russia, you could find those who support Stalin, a man who committed far more atrocities than Ceausescu did in Romania. Still, though, by the time his 24-year reign had ended, Romania was caught in a revolutionary fervor and a unified hate for both Ceausescu and his wife, Elena. Revolutionary spirit had taken hold in Romania in December of 1989 as bread lines grew longer and longer, and the communist leader seemed more and more oblivious to the impoverished conditions that were afflicting most Romanians. Ceausescu was able to bask in his luxurious home and enjoy the sight of the king-like presidential sceptre he'd had made for himself. His wife had acquired a grandiose taste for opulent furs and jewelry, and was reported to have a distaste for the unceasing wants and needs of the hungry Romanian people. In their mansion, she kept her riches along with a bag of Western currency just in case it would ever be needed. While cupboards were bare in many Romanian homes, Elena is reported to have commented about the people of Romania, referring to the general public as "worms": "The worms never get satisfied," she said, "regardless of how much food you give them."

While the country was slowly starving and finding it increasingly difficult to find food at grocery stores, Nicolae Ceausescu would appear on television in the late 1980s in front of aisles full of food, celebrating the greatness of life in Romania. To Romanians, some believed that Ceausescu simply had no idea how the country was suffering. This was the favorable and sympathetic view he received from some. But others weren't willing to give the tyrannical leader the benefit of the doubt; they'd had enough, and it was time for change.

The December revolution of 1989 initially started in Timisoara, a city in western Romania, as a rally in support of a Hungarian pastor who was about to be deported from the country. It didn't take long, though, for the rally to morph from its original intentions. Romanian students, infuriated by the lack of opportunity in the impoverished country, joined the rally, and soon it became a general anti-government rally. This led to military and Securitate—the Romanian secret police—to fire into crowds to quash the protests. Many people were wounded and killed, and Ceausescu expected this would be the end of any uprising. One thing he could count on, too, was that Romanians had no access to anti-government news. The only way Romanians even discovered what was happening in Timisoara was either by word of mouth, or by listening to Western radio stations, like Radio Free Europe.

Ceausescu might've thought the revolution had subsided once his troops stomped out the rebellion in Timisoara, but it's also highly likely that Ceausescu didn't even see this as a serious rebellion to begin with. Whether he was supremely arrogant, oblivious or delusional, Ceausescu couldn't fathom the notion of his people—his starving people—revolting against him. As a result, he scheduled a meeting where he would speak publicly to the masses in what is now known as Revolution Square in Bucharest. As he appeared in front of the masses, Ceausescu seemed genuinely baffled that the people were upset. He tried to convince himself that the crowds had gathered as a public showing of support for their communist leader, but he ended up being faced with a crowd that was anything but supportive. As he tried to give his speech about the glory of Romania, he was repeatedly shouted down by the crowd. Confused and terrified, Ceausescu and his wife retreated inside for shelter. Outside, the rally turned into a revolt, and unarmed Romanian citizens ended up fighting against armed Romanian military. Though the killed and wounded piled up from this unfair fight, this in effect was the seminal moment for the Romanian revolution.

Ceausescu attempted one more public speech, and this time the reception was even worse. Fearing for his safety—and rightfully so—Ceausescu and his wife boarded a helicopter and left Bucharest. During the course of his flight from Bucharest, Ceausescu lost control of the army, as they collectively wondered why they were fighting against the Romanian people who wanted the same things they did. The army forced Ceausescu's helicopter to land, and he was arrested soon after.

Things moved swiftly from there, and it's likely Ceausescu and his wife were still having trouble believing how quickly their world had been flipped upside down. On Christmas Day, a brief trial was held and the couple was both convicted on a whole host of charges related to the gathering of their excess wealth all the way up to charges of genocide. Once the guilty verdict was handed down, the couple was swiftly executed by a firing squad composed of elite paratroop soldiers. Perhaps the only thing that might've stalled this exceptionally speedy process was the fact that hundreds of others had volunteered to participate in the firing squad, clamoring to have their chance to put a bullet in Romania's despotic leader and his wife. After the execution, the video was released to the Romanian public who cheered loudly at the death of their tormentor. Christmas in 1989 came in a very different way to Romania.

We were discussing Romania's revolution during our subway ride, and I commented that it seemed interesting to me that Romania had reacted so angrily and bloodily to remove their communist dictator. The standard of living was low, people were hungry, and they were being ruled by a tyrant who seemed to have no idea or concern about what was going on in the lives of normal people. The same could be said about Bulgaria; Todor Zhivkov was at the helm for an even longer period of time than Ceausescu. But as the Berlin Wall fell and freedom started to spread in Eastern Europe, there was no violent revolt in Bulgaria. There was no cathartic—if not troubling—video of a tyrannical leader being executed by firing squad. There weren't bloody revolts either, but an election that followed where Bulgaria more or less elected the same figures who had been in charge throughout the last several decades. I asked Nikolai about this, uncertain as to why Bulgarians and Romanians approached the beginning of freedom in Eastern Europe so differently.

"I really don't know, Andy," he told me seriously. "As a people, I guess we are not like Romanians. I can't see us rising up and revolting. I just don't think it's our nature."

The famous dates of liberation in Bulgarian history always struck me as interesting because the important dates of liberation occurred when Russia liberated Bulgaria from the Ottoman Empire. Bulgarian blood had been shed throughout the process, but it was Russia who eventually liberated Bulgaria from its longest period of oppression. Maybe it was that sense of historical appreciation that led Bulgarians to ease their way into freedom from Russia, instead of revolting. But as Nikolai had taught me so much about the *nature of Bulgarians*, it seemed to me that he was always telling me what *wasn't* in their nature, not what *was in their nature*.

The iron grip that Ceausescu clutched Romania with clearly didn't sit well with Romania as the winter of 1989 rolled around. But during his reign, he certainly had a flair for the extravagant, and fashioned Romania as becoming much less like Bulgaria, and much more like a Western power. Romania already had a Triumphal Arc that was very similar to the Arc de Triomphe in Paris. Ceausescu intended to make Bucharest the "Paris of the East" by bulldozing an entire section of town to create wider streets modeled after the world-famous Champs-Elysees. All told, Ceausescu ended up demolishing one-sixth of the city, displacing 30,000 residents, and demolishing pretty much the entire historic center of Bucharest. Bucharest was left with a stray dog problem akin to Sofia from all the abandoned homes and dogs that now found themselves homeless. Ceausescu's demolition gave him the wider streets he wanted, and also gave him the Palace of the People, as he dubbed it, a monstrous structure befitting of his monstrous personality cult. The imposing Palace of the People—ironically used by very few people—now stands as the second-largest building in the world, only behind the Pentagon in Washington, DC. It is 12 stories high, has over one thousand rooms and it's impossible to look at without thinking aloud, "Oh my God, who would ever need a building that big?" Despite Ceausecsu's ostentatious designs to display glory, the Palace was never actually completed, and still stands unfinished today. The gargantuan structure appears to encompass an entire neighborhood, and there is very little motivation from anyone to actually finish it. There's probably much more of a push to knock the whole thing down, but it's so gigantic that the cost of demolishing the other-worldly structure would be just that, other-worldly.

The one thing Ceausescu did finish, though, was the subway. And since we'd spent enough time in Bucharest traffic, I didn't mind smoothly whooshing along underground. I'd heard that Bucharest's stray dogs were actually more severe in number and ferocity than Sofia's—and of course, a Bulgarian who had never been to Romania told me this—so I wasn't upset we were missing out on a brisk February drive through Bucharest. I sensed Branch and Nikolai felt the same way as we sat on the subway content that we didn't have to think about anything until we arrived at our stop.

Our bus driver, though, was anything but a picture of contentment. He was nervously fidgeting, his eyes darting left and right, his entire body seemingly incapable of sitting still on his subway seat. Every 30 seconds or so, he would unintentionally alert us to what the problem was: his GPS system didn't work underground.

The bus driver, as he twisted, turned and shook his hand-held GPS system like he was trying to get Super Mario to the next level, was clearly a man without his country. It was one thing for him to leave Bulgaria, but entirely a different thing for him to be lost in a GPS-less ocean. Again, Branch and I had to look at Nikolai to see if it was okay to laugh. We didn't want to be culturally insensitive with a Bulgarian who clearly had his own comfort zone, but we were once again being pushed to the brink. Sofia had a subway in the making—work had started on a subway in the 1970s—but it still hadn't been completed. It was likely that our bus driver who had told us he'd never been to Romania had also never been underground before.

So it was not surprising to us that he was the first one out of the subway when we came to our stop. He seemed downright giddy when we surfaced in the heart of Bucharest's downtown above ground. His GPS was once again functional, though I doubt he had any idea where we were going. The only thing that mattered was that the lights on his console started flashing again, spitting out street names. We found our way to our hotel, and I had to admit I was eager to find out exactly what this place was like. At 400 dollars a night, the last place I expected to be heading was Howard Johnson's. But as we crossed the street into the mammoth and luxurious lobby, I quickly took note that this was not the same HoJo's roadside motel that my parents always took us to some 20 years earlier on our cross-country road trips because they had the cheapest rooms with special rates for kids. Howard Johnson's had come to Romania to create a whole new image.

All of us were wowed as we walked into a lobby with sparkling chandeliers overhead. Branch and I were awestruck at the contrast between the Howard Johnson's of our youth in the States versus what was in front of us right now. Both Nikolai and the bus driver were just awestruck; they'd never stayed anywhere like this before. To prove this point directly, Nikolai was the first to speak.

"I've never stayed anywhere like this before," he said, his mouth agape.

When the receptionist greeted us in what appeared to be fluent English, I knew we were in a different world. I'd stayed in all different types of accommodations in Bulgaria, but couldn't recall ever being greeted in fluent English. This probably stemmed from the fact that while Ceausescu was reviled by his own people, he was considered a rare Eastern European ally by the United States. Because he'd broken with the Soviet Union–daring to publicly oppose the 1968 invasion of Czechoslovakia–and was determined to oppress his people without Mother Russia's help, Ceausescu's Romania received Most Favored Nation status from the United States. As a result, while Cold War Bulgarians were becoming fluent in Russian, many oppressed Romanians were learning English.

To complete our check-in, the receptionist pleasantly asked for a credit card to cover incidentals for each of the rooms. I didn't think much of this, and Branch couldn't have either. We both handed over our credit cards. But our transition to the high life did not match the adjustment being made by Nikolai and our bus driver.

"What is this? What is this?" Nikolai stammered. "I do not understand. We have already paid. Why do we need this?"

I could sense Nikolai's anxiety was reaching levels similar to those experienced by our bus driver when his GPS stopped working.

"Well," I explained to him, "this is just in case you want to use anything extra in the room. If you do, it gets charged to the credit card."

"What is this 'extra'?" Nikolai snapped right away. "What extra would we use?"

Without a doubt, during my two years in Bulgaria, Nikolai was the nicest Bulgarian I'd met. He was also the most organized, most patient and most responsible Bulgarian I'd met. He was perhaps the only Bulgarian I knew who I'd never seen yell at anyone. But in this moment, I worried he was going to start yelling at me, or the receptionist. Either way, the frazzled Nikolai in front of me was not the one I knew on a daily basis. He appeared to be losing his cool. The credit card issue was one he'd never encountered before.

In the meantime, Nikolai was hurriedly translating to the bus driver who didn't seem nearly as affected. His smile had returned, and he was rarely looking up in our direction. His GPS was working great, and he was enjoying walking in small circles in the lobby.

"Extra, Nikolai, means the extra things in the room," I told him calmly. "You don't need to worry about extra charges if you don't drink anything from the mini-bar, and don't order any movies on TV."

"There's a bar in the room?" Nikolai exclaimed incredulously. "And what kind of movies would I order?"

While he was clearly incredulous, it wasn't a "Wow, this is cool" kind of incredulous. All these new revelations seemed to be an uncomfortable affront to the way things were normally handled in

Nikolai's life, or the life of any Bulgarian. The reason that Nikolai was thrown off-guard to the point of borderline anger was that in general, credit cards in Bulgaria were the exception much more than the rule. As much as he was shocked at the manifestation of such foreign commodities as mini-bars and pay-per-view movies, he was more alarmed by the fact that a hotel would ask for a credit card. On the bus earlier that day, we'd already confirmed that no Bulgarians on the bus had ATM cards. I'd also known ever since I first set foot in Bulgaria that very few Bulgarians had credit cards. It was a cash-based society, and perhaps this was partially because few Bulgarians trusted anything but cash. In a society where corruption was rampant, there couldn't have been a lot of faith in a credit-based system where bills would be paid at a later date. In fact, when we were making the hotel reservation to begin with–and the Romanian school offered to pay half the room rates, the only way our school agreed to pay–the school's director of accounting was terrified to pay online with a credit card.

"Andy," she said with consternation oozing from her pores, "I do not trust this at all. I put this number in and then they will take our money. They might take all of our money. There is no way, no way. I cannot do this."

In the end, after I tried to assuage her fears unsuccessfully, we compromised: I'd use the school's credit card, and if the Howard Johnson's stole the school's money, she'd tell the president that I was the one who made the reservation. As a Westerner, I saw this as an easy compromise, but the Bulgarian accountant was shocked I'd be willing to take such a risk. As I stood in front of the Howard Johnson's reception desk, there was not an ounce of me that was concerned about them using the credit card information to steal money. But I was growing more and more concerned with Nikolai; nothing that either Branch or I was saying was alleviating his concerns.

"Andy," Nikolai said firmly, "things do not work like this in my country. I do not feel comfortable with us staying here. I do not understand why they are treating us this way."

"Nikolai," I pleaded, "this is just common practice. This is normal–"

"This is not normal in my country. Not–how do you say?–common practice for me."

With this, I realized that angle of persuasion was not working well. Even though Nikolai stood in contrast to so many Bulgarians that I knew, he was now faced with a completely new and different situation. Time and time again, I'd seen that Bulgarians just weren't accustomed to things changing. In this case, the credit card request was rocking Nikolai's post-communist world.

"Nikolai, you don't need to worry about this—"

"Yes, I do need to worry. I do not have a credit card!" he exclaimed. "We Bulgarians do not have these credit cards!"

"That's fine, Nikolai," I told him. "I already told the girl at the desk to put all the rooms on my credit card. You don't need to worry about it at all. I took care of it."

"Oh," Nikolai said, and seemingly relaxed a little bit, "so you gave her your credit card?"

"Yes, and everything will be fine."

"Okay," he eased out, "but I still don't like this. I still think maybe we should go stay somewhere else—somewhere where they don't have credit card rules like this."

I wanted to explain to Nikolai once again that the credit card rule was standard, that the school had paid for him to stay in one of the nicest hotels any of us would ever stay in, and that everything was going to work out fine, but I could see that he was going to be frazzled no matter what I said. So I just opted to ask him to translate to the bus driver the part about not drinking out of the mini-bar or ordering any pay-per-view movies.

When he was finally able to distract the driver's attention away from the GPS, Nikolai started explaining things to him. The first time Nikolai explained the situation with the mini-bar and the movies, the driver looked confused. He asked Nikolai to repeat what he'd just said. So Nikolai repeated himself. The driver remained puzzled. As much as I thought Nikolai was having difficulty with these concepts, this was nothing compared to the driver. A third time—and I knew Nikolai's frayed patience was being tested—he explained the situation to the bus driver, and a third time he was baffled.

"Just don't use anything in the room," Nikolai finally snapped off in a brisk Bulgarian.

To this, the bus driver started shaking his head, bobbing it side to side in assent. He still didn't understand what was happening, but he could grasp the last directive given to him by Nikolai. With this, we all grabbed our respective bags and headed for the elevator. It was only at this point that I noticed yet another oddity concerning the bus driver. While I'd been so focused on his extreme attachment to his GPS console, I failed to notice the "suitcase" he'd brought with him for the three-day trip: it was just a plastic grocery bag. There didn't appear to be any clothes in it either.

We rode the elevator up to our respective rooms, and Nikolai, Branch and I met moments later in the hallway, intent on touring Bucharest. Branch and I both noticed how large and immaculate our rooms were, and I knew this was going to make an impression on Nikolai.

"This room, this room," he stumbled, "I have never been in one like this before."

This time, I noticed his incredulity was heavily weighted with excitement. He was like a little kid who'd just gained enough confidence to take the training wheels off his bicycle.

"Do you think we should ask," Branch changed the subject, as we planned to go out and explore Bucharest, "the bus driver if he wants to join us tonight?"

I didn't respond, but looked at Nikolai.

"Well," he pondered, "I really don't know. But I can't imagine he's going to leave his room. He has his GPS, and maybe he won't enjoy coming with us."

I realized that Nikolai, still the nicest Bulgarian I knew, was trying his best to say that none of us would particularly enjoy having the bus driver out with us on Friday night.

That night, we wandered Bucharest, walking down streets that had been filled with revolution 20 years earlier. We found makeshift memorials to those who had lost their lives in the heart of Bucharest's downtown, and found the hotel where the international press watched the violence occur. We walked by the balcony where Ceausescu had been so shocked to find his beloved subjects shouting him down instead of roaring in approval. On this February Friday night, there were people out enjoying the evening, but it was a cold and brisk evening. While restaurants and bars were busy, outside it was quiet, giving me a chance to ponder how I was walking historic streets. Maybe this wasn't the Champs-Elysees, but it certainly was historic.

The events of the day—a day that started in darkness in early morning Bulgaria—all seemed to jumble together, and as a result, lose some of their individual significance. Recalling 45-minute breaks on the side of the road and five gas station stops for a vignette sticker, I finally let go of my frustrations with the bus driver. Considering a coach who played an ineligible player, and then that ineligible player throwing malicious elbows at our players, I realized there wasn't much I could do about either one of them. And I thought about Kosio, and how his blow-up on the bench, followed by his mimicking of my speech at the end of the third quarter, represented the single worst experience of disrespect from one of my players that I'd ever encountered as a coach. As much as I'd spent meaningful time agonizing over what happened and wondering why it had happened, I didn't have any answers. And I probably wasn't going to find any answers either. All the questions and answers that rattled on in my head about a crazy day seemed insignificant once I started thinking about a revolution that occurred on these very streets 20 years earlier.

Just past Revolution Square, we stumbled upon some green and red lights that seemed to advertise something Branch and I had yet to see anywhere in Europe: Mexican food. We couldn't believe our eyes, and each of our mouths started watering for the tacos, nachos, and burritos that had been staples of our past lives in the States. In Eastern Europe, though, the mention of Mexican food would just draw odd glances and confused stares. Mexican food, as far as we could tell, didn't exist in Eastern Europe. But Bucharest was telling us a different story.

Branch and I excitedly started telling Nikolai just exactly why we were so geeked up. I realized that this trip to a Mexican restaurant would represent yet another change in a day that had pushed us all outside our comfort zones, but I wasn't about to hold back. Some changes would have to be for the better, and introducing Nikolai to Mexican food was going to have to fall into this category. There would be no other option.

"Nikolai, you have to understand," Branch began, "that eating burritos is basically how we survived college. Maybe you had a burrito for lunch, or maybe you had one for dinner–but no matter what, when you came home from a party late at night, you never went home without eating a burrito. That's the way college in the States works."

Nikolai looked at me to see if I agreed, and I did. His eyes widened with interest.

"In fact, Nikolai, where I went to school, we'd only go to the burrito restaurant that had big burritos. They'd say the burritos were as big as your head."

"As big, as big," Nikolai stammered, trying to come to grips with this, "as big as your head?"

Branch and I both nodded and smiled, and we knew Nikolai understood what our American nods meant.

"Wow, this sounds incredible," Nikolai said reflectively.

At this point, I was trying to gauge if this was a good "incredible"–the rooms at Howard Johnson's–or a bad "incredible"–the credit card fiasco. But as the three of us stood outside the door, Nikolai answered this question quickly. He took the first step and opened the door. Grinning bigger than ever, Branch and I followed him inside.

"I cannot wait to try one of these," Nikolai beamed. "I think I'm really going to like it."

The three of us ordered, and Branch and I taught Nikolai how to load up his burrito with salsa and other toppings. With each new dollop of sour cream and salsa verde, Nikolai would look at us for approval, wanting to make sure he was dressing his burrito correctly. While Branch and I were paying attention to him, we were also both lost in the deliciousness of the first burrito we'd had in Eastern Europe. On a day that seemingly had a little bit of everything uncommon and out of place, it was ending on a glorious note. It was ending on what used to be a familiar note for us, but now was everything but.

As we licked our plates clean of every inch of spicy sauce and seasoning, the three of us sat there, feeling weighted down, but contented. We didn't talk about basketball, we didn't think about being told to take the subway, and we didn't talk about the culture of Bucharest of the Romanian revolution. We just basked in the glow of the burritos we'd scarfed down, and seemed to have lost all concern for what had happened that day, or what would happen tomorrow. Well, that was until Nikolai spoke up.

"These burritos are excellent. I wish we had them in Bulgaria,"

"We do, too," I answered for both of us.

"You know what," Nikolai said. "We need to come back here again tomorrow night."

In the morning, we met for breakfast early and I was surprised to see that the bus driver appeared to be joining us as we were about to board the shuttle–instead of the subway–to take us to the school for our Saturday slate of games. The driver, in effect, had the entire day off. While he was being paid to drive us wherever we needed to go on Saturday, we weren't going to need him to drive us anywhere. With the shuttle taking us to the school and players being driven by their host families, he had no responsibilities whatsoever. When Nikolai explained this to him, I expected to see his face light up with gratitude. But it didn't.

"I'd like to come with you to the school," he said plainly in

Bulgarian.

"But you have the whole day to enjoy the city and do whatever you please," Nikolai told him cheerfully.

"No, that's okay," his tone hadn't changed. "I'd rather go to the school with you."

Nikolai was puzzled, and had already had plenty of trouble explaining things to the driver before, so he didn't want to leave any stone unturned.

"You understand, though, that we're going to be here from 9 a.m. to 7 p.m. You won't be able to leave. It's going to be a long day."

"Yes, I know," he responded, as if this was all part of the plan.

As we walked to the bus, I was waiting to see if Nikolai had an explanation for this. Even as a Bulgarian sometimes intimidated by change in a foreign land, he had thoroughly enjoyed touring Bucharest the previous night with us. Clearly, though, this wasn't an opportunity the bus driver was going to jump at. He was dead set on coming to school with us. To make matters more curious, all three of us knew that the bus driver hadn't even watched our games on the previous day. So we wondered what exactly he planned to do for 10 hours at a basketball tournament on this day.

"Andy," Nikolai finally elaborated on the bus driver's predicament, "I think he's too scared to stay in his hotel room."

"Too scared?"

"Well, he didn't understand when I said not to use anything extra in the room, so now he's not using anything at all. He doesn't want to turn on the water, flush the toilet–anything. He's afraid he's going to get in trouble."

As Nikolai said this, I took a look at the bus driver, who was clearly wearing the same clothes as yesterday, and his hair was disheveled. He clearly hadn't showered.

"You've got to be kidding me, Nikolai?" I said, still in a bit of shock.

"No, I'm not," Nikolai said, while shaking his head in a nod to non-Bulgarian customs. "No matter how many times I explain to him that he just shouldn't use anything *extra*, he doesn't seem to understand. This is all such new territory for him."

"So what's he going to do all day?" Branch asked. "I mean, wouldn't he rather just have a free day in the city?"

"I have said this to him as well," Nikolai conceded, "but he is not interested in the city. He told me that if he spent his free day in the city that he would die of boredom."

Branch and I looked at each other with raised eyebrows, both trying to wrap our minds around how getting paid for wandering around a European capital city would lead to boredom.

"So he, so he," I stammered, "thinks he'll be less bored at a high school basketball tournament for an entire day?"

"Well, Andy," Nikolai spoke and shrugged his shoulders while doing so, "I don't think he's going to watch the basketball games. He says he'll be happy spending the day in his bus."

Neither Branch's nor my mouth moved from their completely-open poses.

"He says he has everything he could ever need in his bus."

As the shuttle zoomed off to take us to the school, Branch and I should've been thinking of our upcoming games, but instead both of us were mesmerized by our bus driver. We ended up keeping our minds busy, making mental lists of all things not related to his GPS console that were baffling us about him:

- He still had no Romanian money, even though he was spending three days in this country.
- He was not using the toilet, the sink, the shower or anything else in his room.
- He was now choosing to spend an entire day sitting in his bus–a bus that would not be moving anywhere. It would just be parked in the school parking lot.

I knew Bulgarians were hesitant to adapt to change. This character trait could've been caused by any number of historical factors. Bulgarians had lots of reasons to cling to what they had and not look to branch out. But what we were witnessing from our bus driver was not a hesitancy to change; it was a complete refusal. Change, in this case, was represented as having a free day of fun and relaxation–or at least that's how Branch and I saw it. The status quo was spending a day in a bus, something difficult for us–Nikolai included–to see as enjoyable. When Robert Kaplan referred to the Balkans as a region of "narrow visions," I was now wondering how narrow the bus driver's vision would be sitting in the driver's seat of his bus, not moving for an entire day.

On the flip side of this, I'd been so proud of my basketball team because of the changes they'd made, and because they'd rid themselves of the dangerous tag of being losers in order to build confidence and win games during this season. I knew this year would bring about an improved, if not great, version of basketball. We'd improved all throughout the previous year, but I'd been constantly worried that improvement wouldn't matter to them if we didn't start winning. And the previous year, we'd never started winning.

But this year, wins had been rolling in, and an entire culture change was occurring with our basketball team. Playing hard, playing together and having success had become the change we were living on a regular basis. The previous day's game had been reminiscent of too many games we'd had our first year when we were blown out of the game from the very beginning. But I'd even noticed a difference from the previous day: we'd been blown out, but blown out by a team that was far superior to us in all areas. In the past, when we'd been blown out by Bulgarian teams, these teams had more talent than us, but they weren't teams that worked hard. They weren't teams that played smart. Yesterday we'd been up against the perfect storm of all three—a talented team that played hard the entire game, and played smart basketball (with the exception of the flying elbows).

As the bus rolled up to the school on Saturday, I'd already decided that I could deal with losing games like this. Except for Kosio, we'd continued to play hard all throughout even though we were trailing by a wide margin. My biggest concern, though, was how we'd respond now that we'd been given a rude awakening to basketball outside of Bulgaria. I could handle these losses as good experiences that would help us win our biggest tournament of the year, the ACS Open. But would the players see it this way, too?

This question dominated our entire Saturday of basketball. The London school was different from the Romanian school, in that they didn't have any players from the native country. Their team was entirely American, and they had so much parental support with them for the tournament that looking up in the stands, it appeared there was a designated London school parent section. In my two years as a basketball coach, I had yet to see a Bulgarian parent come to one of our games, and this was a trend that would continue throughout the entirety of my time as a coach in Bulgaria. The London parental support, though, wasn't needed against us. This London team was superior to the Romanian team we'd played the day before; they executed plays on offense in a way that made me once again think about American teams I'd coached in the past. Their offense was a blur to our defenders who marveled at the patience of the London players to work for a good shot—a good shot they got nearly every time.

With more of an emphasis placed on half-court offense, the

London school didn't run nearly as much. As a result, while the scoreboard displayed a clear mismatch, we were trailing by less than we had been the day before. As halftime approached, we were down by 25.

The coach of the London school was an American, and I appreciated the fact that he was clearly trying to get his team to focus on execution on both ends of the floor even though they probably could've beaten us without execution. They continued to work on running set plays because the coach knew these would be necessary to beat better teams. Since my team was still not basketball-aware enough to run any kind of complicated set plays on offense, I had to continue to harp on the importance of defense and running the fast break, two things that had been easier for them to understand and put into practice. Our half-court offense against a man-to-man defense could be described as ugly at best, and most possessions left me feeling pity for Menkov as he dribbled around the top of the key, desperately looking for an opening to drive through, or a teammate to pass it to.

Like the previous day, we played with passion and energy, but this was not going to be enough against a team full of players who'd been playing basketball their entire lives. I could see the frustration on several players' faces, and they'd frequently look to the bench with expressions of, "How'd he do that? None of us can make a move like that."

With under 10 seconds to play in the half, the London school's lead stood at 26 points. After a missed shot, the rebound was batted around and eventually went off Pesho's fingers out of bounds. The clock now showed three seconds to play, and I was surprised when the London coach called a timeout at this point in the game. With three seconds left, the only reason a coach would call a timeout would be to run a set play. In a close game, something like this would be expected and lauded by any basketball observer. But in a game with a 26-point differential, this was unheard of. Even though it wasn't halftime yet, there was no doubt about the outcome of this game. Our biggest goal, though I would never tell my team this, was not to get embarrassed. And when we'd been on the other end of a score like this, I'd told my team over and over again that exact thing: under no circumstances will we show up or embarrass our opponents.

We'd seen this on a regular basis in Bulgaria, with coaches leaving starters in the game to run up the scores, and coaches leading teams in half court dances after the game. I always took more offense to this than the players did because, as they'd tell me, "Coach, this is Bulgaria.

We're used to this sort of thing." But well into our second year together, players were starting to come around to my way of thinking. They understood why I took a stance against embarrassing other teams, and they also knew when it was happening to them. In fact, just the day before, Vassy had continually commented on why the Romanian two-guard was left in the game to score as many points as possible when his team was up by more than 30. The fact that an American coach had made this decision infuriated me even more; I couldn't just throw my hands up in the air and say, "Well, this is Bulgaria."

Now, as my team trotted to the sidelines, I was left to wonder, once again, exactly what was going on. The London coach, an American, appeared to be calling a timeout in a 26-point game to try to run a play to extend his team's lead. This would mostly serve the purpose of deflating our team—a team that already had plenty of reasons to be deflated if they looked at the scoreboard.

"Is he really drawing up a play right now?" Branch approached me and asked.

I could feel myself starting to get angry, and didn't even muster a response. Losing was one thing—one thing I hated, but had no choice but to accept at the moment—but this was entirely different. Being in charge of teaching young men about character and dignity was always a top priority of mine, and I perhaps incorrectly assumed it was also a top priority of other coaches, especially American coaches. As we broke our huddle and headed back to the court, though, I was seeing just how incorrect this assumption was.

From underneath the basket, the London school ran a double-pick after a quick fake to the wing that caught Pesho off-guard. He wasn't sure if he should dash out to cover the shooter, or stay inside to protect the paint. As a result, he was stuck in no-man's-land. The play worked perfectly, as an overhead lob was thrown in front of the basket. The London center deftly grabbed the pass and finished a perfect alley-oop. With this, there were cheers from the London parents and the horn sounded just after the ball went through the net. Our players didn't want to look up at the scoreboard as they trudged back to the bench. I wasn't paying attention to them, though. I was incensed, and couldn't take my eyes off the London coach.

"Nice play, Coach, nice play!" I hollered sarcastically, determined in some way to exact revenge, a revenge I knew we couldn't achieve out on the floor.

"Thanks," he said in a surprised tone.

I continued glaring at him, and the fact that he didn't realize I was being sarcastic fit with the situation. He clearly saw nothing wrong with running up the score against an inferior team.

"Yeah, that's a really nice play to run when you've got a 26-point lead," I continued my sarcastic barrage, wondering when he was going to get it. "That's the sign of a really good team, one that runs alley-oop set plays with huge leads. That's the sign of great coaching."

At this point, there was no way he couldn't finally understand that my tone was sarcastic.

"Wait a minute, Coach. Wait a minute," he started pleading as he walked briskly toward half court to meet me. "That's just a play we've been working on. You know, we didn't mean anything by running it."

"*Didn't mean anything by running it*?" I repeated. "What do you think it means to my group of kids who are still learning the game of basketball? What do you think it means to them to have an alley-oop play set up to extend the lead to 28 points? You don't think that means anything to them?"

"No, no, no," he argued, and I could tell he didn't like the conflict that had been created. "That's just a play we've been working on—"

"To run when you've got a 26-point lead? That's how you teach your players about class and respect?"

I knew I was angry and letting my emotions get the best of me, but frustration on many levels was now spilling over, and perhaps the worst part of it was that I expected so much more from American coaches. When I saw things like this—and things worse than this—happen in Bulgaria, I could eventually console myself that this was a different place where people were raised differently. "In America," I'd tell myself, "this wouldn't happen." But now that I was seeing a lack of class from two different American coaches in two days, I felt like my world, and not just my Bulgarian world, was being forever shaken.

The rest of the conversation consisted of a series of rushed apologies from the London coach, and I was too indignant to even begin to understand if these were genuine or not. Mercifully for both of us, I suppose, the conversation ended once I'd heard enough apologies. That didn't mean I felt any better, but if I told my players they better not go down without a fight, I wanted to emulate that profile as well.

"It's okay, Coach," Pavel said as I walked back to the bench.

"No, it's not okay," I snapped.

"No, Coach, we don't need to worry about him. We just have to play better. It's our fault."

In the moment, I focused on what to say to my players at halftime and how to keep them motivated to work hard and improve in the second half. But when I had time to think about what Pavel said, it was that last three words that struck me as most decisive. *It's our fault*, Pavel said, and took responsibility and ownership for the 28-point drubbing we were now receiving. The statement was so simple, so obvious and so correct, but it's something Pavel never would've said the previous year. I'd been fighting a culture of blaming other people for so long that Pavel's admission of responsibility was a far greater victory than any actual victory we had little chance of earning in this tournament.

We played three games on Saturday and got blown out in each of them. The outcome was never in doubt as we battled on in futility. But, nevertheless, we battled on. The score of each game was closer than the one previous, a fact I continued to harp on during each timeout.

"We have to get better," I said to them over and over again. "We have to use these games as an opportunity to improve. By playing hard here we give ourselves a better chance to win the ACS Open. That's what you have to keep in mind. We want to win the ACS Open."

"Coach," Ivan said to me from the bench at one point, "there aren't any teams like this in the ACS Open."

"I know, Ivan," I responded, not sure if he understood how painstakingly obvious his comment was. "That's why we still have a chance to win the ACS Open."

After spending the first game on the bench without me looking at him once, Kosio decided that maybe he should talk to me between games. It wasn't difficult for him to see that I had no intention of putting him in the game. He approached me nervously, a rarity for someone who spoke confidently like he did, and apologized for not running hard in the games yesterday.

"Kosio," I said matter-of-factly, "you don't need to apologize to me for not running hard. You need to apologize to your teammates. They're the ones you let down by not running hard."

Kosio paused at this point, clearly reticent to apologize for anything else. But it was the other apologies that I was looking for. These weren't as easy for him to utter.

"I shouldn't have yelled at you when I came to the bench either," he said meekly. "I'm sorry about that."

I figured I'd take care of all concerns with one swoop, so I responded.

"And what about mocking me on the bench while I was talking to the team?"

"Oh no, Coach, I wasn't mocking you," he said, his eyes pervading a sense of *I really hope he believes me.*

"You weren't mocking me?"

"No, Coach, I was mocking someone else."

"Who?"

This question seemed to stump him.

"Just someone else—just someone else."

With Pavel leading the revolution to hold himself and his teammates accountable, I could see that I shouldn't jump to conclusions about the progress the entire team had made. Kosio had been able to man up and apologize for some of his transgressions, but not the most serious and ridiculous instances of disrespect, in my opinion. He was able to offer no good excuses, but was still trying to deflect blame or change the story, something I assumed had worked for him in the past. It was futile for me to argue with him over what he did or didn't do, so I just told him he wasn't going to play again this weekend, and if he ever planned to play for the rest of the season, his attitude had better change. As he eventually walked away from our conversation, I wondered if he understood the change I was really talking about. I started to think that no matter what I said or did, he'd be metaphorically sitting in the same bus with our bizarre and immutable bus driver.

As the first quarter of each of our Saturday games ended, there was little doubt that we were going to lose. That's why, at the beginning of each quarter, I gave the team a goal: win the next quarter.

"If you can win this next quarter," I'd tell them, "that's as good as winning the championship game of the ACS Open."

The first time I said it, I was met with confused looks from a tired and defeated group who were getting pounded by teams with much more experience, savvy and talent.

"Think about it," I explained. "There won't be a team like this in the ACS Open, not one that's even close. But if you can beat one of these great teams here—even just for a quarter—that's just as good, or even better than beating 35th."

Now, my message was starting to set in. In the huddle, I saw some nods and some head-shakes, all convoluted Bulgarian signs of understanding.

"Thirty-fifth has been the team we've had our eyes on for two years, and they're not as good as these teams," I went on.

"No, it's not even close," Menkov agreed.

"What I want to see you do is go out and win a quarter. We might not be able to win these games, but I think we can win a quarter. I think we're still improving out on the floor, and I think we can win the ACS Open. But to win the ACS Open, we've got to win a quarter here first."

I felt like I was grasping at straws for motivational tools, but I also believed in what I was saying. There was no way we could be entirely motivated to play in these games when we were getting so consistently drubbed. Even if we managed to win a quarter, we wouldn't win that quarter by much, and odds were we'd still be losing the overall game by somewhere in the neighborhood of 20 points anyway.

Against the London school, whether they ran alley-oop plays or not, we had a lot of trouble scoring. Their defense was disciplined, and continued to force us to shoot outside shots, something we did oh-so-poorly. Our only legitimate shooter was perched on the bench, still determined that he'd been mocking "someone else," not his coach. The closest we came to winning a quarter against the London school was a quarter we lost by seven points.

In our last game of the day, I still kept pumping our team full of as much hope as I could muster. The Romanian team was very good, but not as disciplined as the London team. When those two teams faced off, the London team was able to wear down the Romanians with their discipline, and frustrate their leading scorer, which honestly wasn't that difficult to do. We went into the fourth quarter of our last game only down 19, which represented the smallest fourth quarter deficit of the day. I knew our players were tired, and so were the Romanian players. Their two-guard seemed to have no interest in passing the ball, and our help defense was finally making a difference. Vassy, steeled in his animosity for the Romanian, insisted on guarding him each time down the floor.

"This is it," I said in the huddle. "Your last quarter—and we need to play this quarter like it's the championship of the ACS Open. This is your championship right now and the score is 0-0. You need to win this quarter."

In the fourth quarter, it was clear that my words mattered. The passion and hustle displayed out on the floor made me proud to coach my team—a team that was clearly outmatched but not giving up. When the Romanian lead ballooned to 22, the bench hollered out for more hustle, more intensity. When the Romanian lead dropped to 17, the players on the floor gritted their teeth, determined to win this final quarter. It'd been a long and exhausting two days in Bucharest, and I knew players and coaches alike were on their last legs. My voice was starting to fade into a sore-throated crackle as I pleaded and begged for one more defensive stop, and one more strong move to the basket.

The fourth quarter of our last game against the Romanian team was the best quarter we played all weekend. It was a testament to our resolve and willingness to get better, and also the team's willingness to believe that this weekend was no longer about what was happening in Bucharest, but what would happen when we returned to Bulgaria.

Scrapping and clawing, we hung with the Romanian team for the entire fourth quarter. The game ended as Pesho grabbed a defensive rebound and headed the other way, attempting his own version of a one-man fast break, something I'd advised against from the very first day I coached him. With the clock running down, Pesho crossed half court and made a head-down dribble move to his right. Just inside the three-point line he pulled up with two defenders chasing after him. He stopped, elevated, and released a wild, contorting jump shot just before the buzzer went off. His momentum carried him sideways and he ended up stumbling to the ground. The shot was much closer than it should've been, but it rattled in and out and fell harmlessly to the floor. Pesho was still down on the court, not injured, but exhausted. Pavel and I went over to him, trying to show our appreciation for his effort by helping him up off the floor.

"Sorry about that shot, Coach," Pesho said sheepishly. "I really thought I had it."

"It's okay, Pesho," I told him. "I'm proud of you for your effort. You played so hard."

That was the truth. As the weekend of basketball came to a close, Kosio's lack of effort was a blip on the radar. The other nine guys who'd played had given it everything they had, and then some.

"But Coach, but Coach," Pesho responded. "Did we win? Did we win?"

I looked at him puzzled, not sure if he was asking if we won the game, which we clearly had not. Then I realized he was referring to the fourth quarter score. I'd been so focused on encouraging them to keep playing hard, I'd forgotten about the fourth quarter score. Now, though, I looked up at the scoreboard:

Romania 53, ACS 33.

We lost by 20. That meant we lost the fourth quarter by one point.

"No, Pesho, we didn't," I said, sensing I was crushing him with this news. "We lost by one point. Almost, but we lost by one point."

"Dammit!" Pesho exclaimed, and looked like he wanted to sit back down on the floor again. "I really thought we would win that quarter."

Half-thrilled that it mattered that much to him, and half-depressed that we came so close to a goal but still couldn't get it, I put my arm around Pesho's sweaty shoulders and we walked over to the Romanian team together to shake hands. As the handshakes finished, Menkov ended up walking back to our bench with me.

"When you yell at us in practice, Coach," he said, "and tell us we need to improve, now I think I see why. You wish we could play like these teams."

On the one hand, the realization that Menkov had was a huge step in his maturity, and I was happy for that. But on the other hand, I was far too immersed in my team to think too long about how other teams were playing.

"You're right, Menkov," I replied, "but all I'm thinking about right now is how proud I am of how hard you played. I don't want you to be like anyone else."

"Thanks, Coach," Menkov smiled in defeat. "But we still lost the fourth quarter by one point."

"I know we did, but we're not going to lose the ACS Open–not if we play this hard."

"No, Coach, I think we're going to win the ACS Open."

The two days in Bucharest consisted of four straight losses–and all bad losses, too. But we'd set our sights on a different goal, a goal that was attainable, and a goal that really mattered to all the Bulgarians on my team: we were going to win the ACS Open. We were going to take what we'd learned in the last two years, and what we learned in the last weekend, and apply it to the tournament that meant the most to everyone on our team. That's why when we left Bucharest, none of us was too down. Unlike Greece where we'd had to forfeit games because we were late, in this tournament, we'd played a ton of basketball. And all the players loved the experience of staying with a host family—an experience that I thought might've even changed their opinions about hosting in the future. For Branch, Nikolai and me, by the time basketball was done for the day (Nikolai had coached a full slate of girls games), we didn't much feel like talking basketball anyway. We were much more content to explore Bucharest and focus on the finer things in life—things like burritos in Eastern Europe.

As we met in the reception area of the hotel to go out on Saturday night, we noticed the Romanian and London coaches and parents gathering for their evening soiree. They were dressed to the nines, and some managed to acknowledge us as they headed to their banquet dinner; others pretended like they didn't see us. We were coaches of a losing team from Bulgaria, all wearing jeans and sweaters.

"Something tells me," Branch quipped, "that your sideline outburst today didn't earn us an invitation to the banquet tonight."

I laughed, certain that he was right, but also not caring any more.

"I think we were uninvited to the banquet before we ever showed up," I responded. "But I probably didn't make any friends here either. I don't think either coach particularly liked having the lowly Bulgarian coach question his methods."

Nikolai joined us a few moments later, and just as we were about to head out on our own into the city, Branch put forth the same question he'd asked the day before.

"Do you think we should invite the bus driver to join us?"

We'd seen the bus driver in the morning as we took the shuttle to the school, and once we arrived there, he immediately headed straight for his bus. During our games, we never saw him in the stands. Between games, we never saw him in the school. We never saw him eat anything, and we never saw him as much as come inside and go to the bathroom. When we'd left the school at 7 p.m., he'd exited his non-moving bus and hopped on our shuttle bus.

"I already asked him if he wanted to join us," Nikolai answered. "But he said no right away. He said his back was very sore from sitting in his bus all day. He doesn't want to go anywhere tonight because he will need to do exercises to loosen up his back."

This time, Nikolai was laughing before he even finished telling us this. As we walked by the remainder of the banquet crowd, all three of us were laughing. Looking at the elegantly-dressed banquet-goers, it was clear we were headed in different directions. And that didn't bother us one bit.

The next morning when we all gathered on the bus to start the long drive back to Sofia, we didn't have to ask too many questions about the bus driver. His hotel routine had most likely been very consistent. He was still wearing the same clothes as Friday, and his hair was even greasier and more disheveled than it had been the day previous. When I'd checked out of the hotel, I felt confident he hadn't used anything extra in the hotel room. He'd stayed true to his word and hadn't used anything at all.

As the bus cruised over the Bridge of Friendship, it felt good to be heading back to Bulgaria. We were eager to get home, and even more eager to get off the bus. The driver's three-day body odor was starting to waft its way back toward us.

Chapter XXV
Change Matters

Back in Sofia, on Monday at lunch, I ordered my food from the school cafeteria and was given my standard Bulgarian plate of a stuffed red pepper with cream sauce–basically just milk–poured over the top of it. I'd learned my lesson early on that even though this dish was supposed to be served warm, and was served cold 75 percent of the time in the teachers' cafeteria, it was not a good idea to ask if it could be warmed up in the microwave. This apparently violated some kind of cafeteria worker code that roughly translated to something like, "Even though I cooked this food two hours ago, don't even think about asking for me to re-heat it during the lunchtime hour."

I headed to a lunch table that included a mix of Bulgarian and American teachers. As I sat down, an American colleague started talking to me about his upcoming fantasy baseball draft, a topic similar to burritos in that it brought me back to life in the States. It was also a topic that thoroughly confused the Bulgarians sitting at the table whose only sports knowledge was most likely Bulgarian and European soccer. This prompted me to quickly change the subject and turn to the Bulgarian teacher next to me and speak to her.

"Hi, how are you doing today?" I said to her, innocently enough.

I had a collegial relationship with this teacher, one that didn't afford me too much insight into her life. But we'd been friendly before, and I saw no reason that wouldn't continue now.

"*Theeees* is not a simple question," she enunciated carefully and unpleasantly while glaring at me from less than a foot away.

"Okay," I backed off–both literally and figuratively–in a conciliatory manner. "I was just trying to be polite, just trying to start conversation."

My comment must not have registered high on her polite-o-meter because her response to my innocuous explanation was to slam her fork down on the table, snatch up her cold stuffed red pepper plate and move to the adjacent table. Moments after she left the table, two other Bulgarian colleagues followed suit, each giving me a sour look and completing their exodus defiantly as if they were Kosovo seceding from Serbia. I sat there in shock, as did my American colleague, who seemed equally disturbed by what had happened.

"What the hell was that?" he said to me, once the secession was complete.

I had no idea.

So I told him I had no idea.

How could a simple question lead to a complete defection from the lunch table that included a demonstrative fork slamming? My American colleague offered some insight into the matter, but it still didn't help us gain a sense of clarity about what had happened–or what was happening with relative frequency in Bulgaria.

"You know, some Bulgarians just really don't like to be asked how they are doing," he mused.

"I know," I replied, and this was the truth. I knew that some Bulgarians didn't like to be asked how they were doing, but this didn't help me know what I should ask them. Saying, "Hi, how are you?" or some equivalent greeting, was firmly ingrained not just in American culture, but the culture of many places all around the world. In the past, I'd had a Bulgarian friend try to explain this to me, but her explanation–that came when she was upset because I'd asked her how she was doing–still didn't help me find solutions to the problem.

"You Americans," she told me, and it was clear that *Americans* did not have a positive connotation, "you always say 'how are you?' but you don't really care. You don't really mean it, so why do you ask the question anyways?"

In some cases, I thought her point was valid. It's true that many Americans start conversations with "How are you?" or "How's it going?" and that this was just a pleasantry intended to start conversations.

Commonly, the other person is supposed to respond to "How are you?" with "I'm fine," regardless of how he or she actually feels. In this regard, I could understand the criticism of this conversation opener. But in my case, I generally felt that I was sincere in asking the question, "How are you?" And I was especially sincere in the case of this lunchroom conversation since I didn't know the Bulgarian teacher sitting next to me very well. The way I saw it, I had very little other choice about how to start a conversation with her. I either could've hoped she'd jump into the conversation about Grady Sizemore's projected number of stolen bases for the upcoming season, or turned to her and asked her a question that related much more to her life. As I did this, and she, in turn, stormed off, I was left to believe that, once again, I was being painted as an American with a superficial concern in others' well-being. In truth, I was just an American grasping at cross-cultural straws for conversation starters.

That evening, when I went to the grocery store to allow for some variety to my cold stuffed red pepper diet, I greeted the cashier at the checkout line with the same ill-fated greeting I'd tried at lunch. This time, though, I said it in Bulgarian: *"Zdravete, kak ste?"* (Hello, how are you?)

As a high school and college student, I'd worked many customer service jobs, from making pizzas at Little Caesars to sandwiches at Subway to folding clothes and helping with shoe sizes at JC Penney. At each of these jobs, it became very easy to feel like nothing short of a minion sent to do others' bidding. I always remembered those who came in and treated me like I was more than just a pizza or sandwich maker, more than just a shoe-size fitter. When people approached me and asked how I was doing instead of just telling me what they wanted, I always appreciated it. As a result, I vowed I'd do the same when I was dealing with people in customer service-oriented jobs—jobs that, I knew, were easy to get frustrated and feel down about. Nearly all my experiences with cashiers and fast food workers ended up being positive as a result. Well, they were positive until I moved to Bulgaria.

"Rabota," came the gruff response from the 20-something cashier on this Monday evening.

I'd asked how she was doing, and she managed to grunt off her response: "Working," she'd said.

In Bulgaria, it seemed that 'working' qualified as a descriptor and an acceptable answer to how someone was doing. It was clear from her answer, as she rapidly rolled my groceries through the checkout aisle that 'working' did not translate to 'happy.' It seemed to translate into something much more obligatory, something that sounded like the communist party in the 1980s had appointed her to this job. She seemed to be saying, "I have to be here and I hate it, and you should've known that before you asked."

As I left without saying much else, I considered chastising myself for again failing miserably to strike up a conversation, but I was at odds with this issue. What exactly was I supposed to say to start a conversation? Or, was I not supposed to start a conversation at all? I felt like there might be a better chance if I turned to my colleague at lunch or to the cashier at the grocery store and plainly stated, "Work sucks, doesn't it?" Maybe this would be seen as an agreeable conversation starter. But I just couldn't see myself saying that–in either English or Bulgarian.

Making my way out of the grocery store, I had one more stop to make on my way home. I needed to visit a Bulgarian cell phone kiosk to pay my monthly cell phone bill. At the kiosk, I handed over my cell phone bill that indicated I owed 20 *leva* and 71 *stotinki*–Bulgarian for cents. After giving the clerk the bill–and not asking how he was doing–I handed him a 20-*leva* bill and a 2-*leva* bill. Immediately, he scrunched up his face to indicate his consternation.

"Do you have 71 *stotinki*?" he asked me in Bulgarian.

I didn't have 71 *stotinki*, and I immediately grasped that this was going to be a problem. He owed me a miniscule amount of change–1 *leva* and 29 *stotinki*–but I could already tell this was going to be a stumbling block.

"Then," he told me firmly in Bulgarian, "it is not possible. *Ne modje*."

He didn't have one leva and 29 *stotinki* change, or he did have it, but didn't want to give it to me. This was a cell phone kiosk that was visited frequently and he had been accepting payment for bills all day long. But now, for whatever reason, giving him 22 *leva* for a 20.71 bill made this situation impossible.

"Are you sure you don't have any change?" I asked him. "I'll accept just one *leva* if you have one *leva*."

"No," he said without looking at his change drawer. "I don't have any. It is not possible. You can come back tomorrow." With this, he thrust the 22 *leva* back in my face.

Exasperated, and not wanting to come back tomorrow, I did what I'd done in the past–just told him to keep the 22 *leva* and consider it even. I still had a strong suspicion that he had change inside the drawer but just didn't want to take it out. There was no way that a kiosk as popular as this one didn't have any change at all, but in this case, it was easier for him to respond *ne modje* than hunt for the change. Short 1 *leva* and 29 *stotinki*, I turned away from the cell phone kiosk wondering if maybe he would've been more amiable if I'd asked him how he was doing when I first arrived at his counter.

In the end, I was relieved that the bill had been paid. This wasn't the first time this had happened to me, and several times previously, I'd been shooed out of the store without even being allowed to pay the bill. "Come back tomorrow," I'd receive in a huffy retort, which was accompanied by the underlying threat, "And don't even think of coming back here without exact change."

Bulgaria, as I learned in more places than just a fancy Bucharest hotel, operated on a cash-based society where credit cards were rarely seen. In a cash-based society, I knew how important it was to have cash on you wherever you were going. But I was baffled as to how such a cash-based society could be so depleted of any kind of change. Several friends had espoused theories that shop owners, cashiers and clerks had the necessary change, but just loathed having to do the math associated with giving change. With few places having automated cash registers or computers, most shop clerks relied on doing math in their heads or using small calculators. This theory about clerks just not wanting to make change was widespread amongst Westerners I knew, but I had no idea whether or not it was actually true.

It became a regular habit for me to pay for whatever I was purchasing and immediately offer a Bulgarian apology for not having exact change. I deemed this was perhaps the only path to success in receiving change, and I estimated that I was apologizing on at least half of my purchases. Seeing how often the issue of not having change arose, I was surprised that shopkeepers and clerks didn't have signs displayed saying in Bulgarian, "We need fives" or "We need ones." This was a common practice that I was used to, and I'd made several of these signs while working at Little Caesars or Subway. And when we encountered a situation where we didn't have change for a customer, I was trained early on what to do: find some way, any way to get change for the customer. In Bulgaria, the onus was on the customer to provide the correct change, and I started to think that shop owners could be the most honest by putting signs on their counters that read, "We need exact change–or else."

More than once, I had been expecting change in return and been given candy or gum signifying the expression, "I'm not going to give you change, but I am going to give you things that have a little bit of value, even if you don't want them." This always left me in a helpless situation. I didn't want the candy or gum; I wanted my change. But the issue seemed non-negotiable so I usually tucked my tail between my legs and left the store. The only time I dared fight back against this bartering system of change giving was when I was handed two cigarettes instead of 50 stotinki. I could find some satisfaction from cheap Bulgarian candies even if I didn't want them, but as a non-smoker, I had to draw the line somewhere. I didn't want cigarettes. When I handed them back to the clerk, explaining that I didn't smoke, he looked at me confused, his facial expression saying, "But everyone in Bulgaria smokes." He then handed me three pieces of gum. I realized I probably should've taken the cigarettes. Two cigarettes were worth a whole lot more than three pieces of gum.

But still, all my change-related mini-crises paled in comparison to one experienced by my American colleague from lunch earlier that day, an American who generally focused on Cleveland Indians baseball far more than Bulgarian culture. Soon after arriving in Sofia, he made a quick trip to his neighborhood convenience store and put three-*leva*'s worth of snacks on the counter. When he gave the owner of the store a 10-*leva* bill to pay, the reaction from the owner was swift and decisive. He scoffed at the 10-*leva* bill he was being proffered, then swung the bag of snacks at my colleague, forcing him to step back to avoid being hit. He smacked the 10-*leva* bill down on the counter, indicating he would not accept it. My colleague was left stunned, not sure what to do, now that he had both the money and the snacks in his hand. But the owner clarified things very quickly by barking, "Get out! Get out now! And never come back to my store!"

We both laughed about this story and made the obvious connections to how it seemed that Seinfeld's Soup Nazi had come to Bulgaria. In reality, though, based on many of my customer service experiences, I began to believe that the Soup Nazi–and all of his relatives–was born in Bulgaria. His type just became more famous when he made it to New York.

I was coming to the end of my two-year run in Bulgaria, and while each individual instance of surliness could be met with surprise or frustration, I'd become inured to this just being the way things were here. As I would have done anywhere I lived, I'd learned to take the good with the bad. But in Bulgaria, "the good with the bad" could be taken to extremes that I wasn't always prepared for.

As we finished the basketball season, it was a similar kind of extreme that I was focused on the most. We'd just returned from a trip to Romania where we were summarily pounded in all of our games by teams with American players, teams that made basketball look like the fluid sport it was supposed to be. After two years of coaching this team, I'd given up on fluidity early on, and tried to create the scrappiest and hardest-working team we could be. In Romania, though, the outcome was not a result of our effort; we had plenty of effort all throughout—we were simply outmatched. I hoped in returning to Bulgaria and preparing for the ACS Open—now less than two weeks away—that I wouldn't encounter some of the same pessimistic extremes that I'd heard in the past. We needed to prepare for what I hoped would be a positive extreme—finishing our year with a championship in the tournament that mattered the most. I was pleased right off the bat hearing some of the things that our players were saying as practice was about to get underway our first day back from Romania.

"Coach, we can do this," Menkov said. "We can win the ACS Open. This past weekend was great practice, and I know we got better."

I marveled at Menkov's change from one year to the next. Last year, it seemed that each new loss came with an anvil that crashed down on his shoulders. Sometimes he'd recover slowly the next day, and sometimes it would be the next day or several days before I'd see his optimism return. I note this about Menkov because he, without a doubt, was the most positive and optimistic player on the team. The anvil that crashed down on the rest of the team seemed to have even longer-lasting effects. But this time around, with only two weeks left in the season, I sensed that the team had understood the way I'd framed our experience in Romania. We weren't going to be able to beat those teams, but competing with them would give us a chance to win the ACS Open.

"Coach, Coach," Pavel told me hurriedly, though it seemed he'd been thinking about this for a while, "we're going to win it all this year. I have the confidence. I know we can do it."

As comments like these rolled in, both Branch and I had to lift our eyebrows to one another. This kind of confidence was unheard of, and especially from my perspective as someone who'd made it my year-long goal the year before to be a cheerleader to build confidence. Even though we were coming off losses that last year would've seemed devastating, I sensed nothing but confidence from this group of players. Even though they'd spent the weekend being exposed as basketball players in the making—but far from finished products—they still felt optimistic about our chances.

"I just think," Vassy told me honestly and resolutely, "that it doesn't matter if 35th is bigger and better than us. We can beat 'em because we'll work harder than they do."

"Well," I told him, "I love your attitude, but let's make sure we get to 35th first. We're going to have to beat good teams to get to them."

"Oh, we'll beat them, Coach. We'll beat them."

Our last Wednesday tune-up was against the Sofia Math School, and it became apparent early on that this school's strengths lay within their study of parabolas far more than their ability to break a full-court press. Frustration hit high levels early on both from their coach on the sideline and their players on the court. They were utterly confused by the press, and our steals were leading to easy opportunities for us—baskets that came without our needing to run good half-court offense. And after facing disciplined man-to-man defense in Romania, we returned to Bulgaria to be comforted by the presence of a lazy 2-3 zone. Pesho and Sasho were wreaking havoc inside, flashing to find openings and attacking the basket. In the middle of the second quarter, Menkov jogged over to the bench asking me a question that made both of us happy.

"Should we stop the full-court press, Coach? We've got a big lead."

He knew I didn't want to embarrass the other team, and as I looked at the scoreboard, I could see we were on the brink of doing just that. With three minutes to go in the first half, we were up by 18 points.

"Good call, Menkov," I told him. "Let's just play half court man-to-man."

With the ACS Open coming up, I could sense that this game would be a tune-up, and a great opportunity to rebuild any confidence that might've been lost during the throttling we received in Romania. I subbed liberally, trying to get as many people into the game as possible. By the time the second half rolled around, I saw the benefits of having a big bench with lots of guys who were interested in playing basketball. We were able to continue rotating fresh guys into the game. Even though there wasn't always a lot of basketball talent on the floor, fresh legs meant a lot, as the other team struggled getting up and down the floor. The Math School had only come with six players, and now that they were down by 20, they were six mostly deflated players.

With four minutes to go in the game, the referee's whistle blew and one of the Math school's forwards was assessed his fifth foul. When Nikolai held up five fingers at the scorer's table, the referee indicated that the offending player needed to go to the bench. His game had ended; he'd fouled out.

As he made his way to the bench, though, the Math School coach turned to look at his bench to tell his one substitute to go into the game to replace the player who had fouled out. But the substitute was nowhere to be found. Turning to an empty bench, the coach called out the player's name, and this appeared to be a futile attempt since it was clear there was no one on the bench. He was bewildered, having no idea where his sixth player had vanished to.

"Did one of their players just take off?" Branch asked, amazed. "How is that even possible?"

I could hear some snickering from our bench, and though they knew I'd come down hard on them for embarrassing another team, I had to admit that right now the other team was embarrassing itself. How had one of their players disappeared in the middle of the game?

"Hey Coach," Ivan directed and started pointing, "I see him. He's over there."

We all looked across the court and found the Math School's sixth player. He was sitting in the third row of the bleachers, talking with two girls from our school. He seemed to be having a great time, and had no idea he was needed in the game. Or if he did know, he definitely wasn't too concerned. As the Math School coach continued his half-frantic, half-annoyed search for the missing player, Ivan stood up and pointed him out in the crowd on the other side of the floor. The visualization of his player in the stands garnered the ire of the Math School coach, and he hollered across the floor to his player who was enjoying life with the girls far more than life on the bench or on the court.

Once he heard his coach yell over to him, the Math School player took a look at his two female companions in the stands and waved his coach off.

"No, Coach, I'm happy here," he said nonchalantly in Bulgarian. "I don't really want to play in the game."

With this, more laughter erupted from our bench, and I had a hard time trying to subdue it. If I were in the place of this other coach, I thought, I'd probably blow a gasket right now. I'd potentially consider going over to the stands and yanking this deviant out of the stands and dragging him back to the bench. The Math coach looked annoyed, but he also looked powerless. He shrugged his shoulders to both the referees and me and said in Bulgarian, "I don't know what I can do. It is not possible to put him in the game."

Ne modje was striking again.

I couldn't believe this was his response to a situation that he was clearly in charge of, but now both the coach and referees turned to me to see if I had a solution to yet another unique Bulgarian mess. I saw no reason why I should be responsible for any of this, but all eyes appeared to be turning to me. I thought the matter was fairly simple; the Math School coach needed to keep his team under control, on the bench and ready to play. But looking over at him, he looked meeker than ever, hoping I'd have some kind of solution to maybe help him save face.

"I guess it's okay with me," I said in English, knowing that Nikolai would help translate, "if that player—" I pointed at the one who'd just fouled out "—stays in the game. It's okay if he plays with five fouls."

"Blagodariya, mnogo blagodariya," was the immediate response from the appreciative coach. Thank you, thank you very much.

The game finished with the fouled-out player remaining on the floor, and the Math School's sixth man enjoying his time in the stands with the girls. I figured this had to be yet another teachable moment for our players of what not to do, though I hoped it went without saying.

"I just want you to know," I said in the general direction of the bench where several starters were now relaxing, "that if any of you ever try something like that, I don't even—"

"We know, we know, Coach," Pesho interrupted me, and seemed exasperated. "You act like we haven't learned anything these last two years."

With this the members of the bench alternately nodded and shook their heads, all in their own form of Bulgarian agreement that I should stop trying to lecture them on how to behave.

"Okay, okay," I conceded, "maybe you have learned some things. But you still keep launching those ridiculous fadeaways and they never go in. So don't tell me you're done learning, Pesho."

With this, the laughter increased, and even Pesho found the joke directed at him humorous.

"Good joke, Coach," Pesho responded. "Good joke. I like this."

As I walked toward the other end of the bench, Branch whispered in my ear, "Does he realize you're not joking? Does he realize how terrible those jumpers are?"

"No, and he probably never will. But at least he hasn't defected from the bench to go hang out with girls in the stands."

As the final horn sounded and we gathered for our post-game wrap-up, I didn't think there was much that needed to be said about this game. We'd played against a weaker opponent and we'd beaten this weaker opponent just like we should've. Now it was time to look forward to the games that had been on all of our minds for the entire season.

"It's always great to get a victory, but I hope you know this was just a warm-up. This was just a warm-up for the real deal, and that's what next week is."

"The ACS Open," I heard Menkov say, as others around him all understood what I was talking about.

"We've worked so hard this year to improve – and we've improved a lot. And all year long we've talked about why it would be so great to have the ACS Open at the end of the year, to have it be the culmination of everything we've worked for. It's not just the culmination of everything we've worked toward this year, but these last two years. Most of you have been here these last two years, and you know how tough it was sometimes."

With this, again there were head shakes and nods, indicating clear understanding of what I was talking about.

"But now we have our chance. We have our chance to practice harder than we've ever practiced, and show up to games readier than we've ever been before. For some of you, when you show up at practice tomorrow, it will be the beginning of the end. For you seniors, it will be the last time you come to basketball practice, the last time you get to play and compete with some of your best friends. And when we start the tournament next week, there will be no reason to hold anything back. Everything we've worked for, every time you've hated me for making you run so much, or do extra defensive slide or box-out drills, it all comes down this: our road to an ACS Open Championship starts tomorrow at practice."

Looking at my team, their eyes were glued to mine. I meant every word of what I was saying, probably because I felt like a senior, too. The next practice would be the beginning of the end of my two years in Bulgaria, and there was no way I was going to hold anything back either. The team looked as amped and ready as I'd ever seen them. I almost wished I'd saved this speech for before a game, not after one.

"I hope you're excited," I told them. "Because I sure as hell am.

Now bring it in together. TEAM on three!"

As an excited bunch echoed "TEAM!" in unison, they slowly started to gather their belongings and head out of the bubble. I talked to a few players, congratulating them on the victory and some of their signs of improvement in this game. Before they'd cleared out, though, Menkov turned from a distance and called out to me.

"Coach, do you know the schedule of games? I mean, who will we be playing? What is our group?"

I paused for a second before answering.

"I think I know what you're asking, Menkov," I responded loudly, and now this got the attention of the majority of the team. "And both 35th and Spanish are in the other group."

"That means, that means—" he stumbled.

"That means that if we advance, we'll most likely see Spanish in the semifinals and 35th in the championship."

This prompted lots of chatter from nearly everyone on the team, and I could tell that the chatter was positive. They were excited about our prospects.

"Coach, this is going to be a lot of fun, a lot of fun," Pavel told me as he walked away grinning.

Nikolai had given me a reprieve this year, and said I didn't need to come to the ACS Open pre-tournament meeting, the meeting last year where I was so loudly introduced to Khrushchev, Starter Jacket and Yellow Teeth. When he told me I didn't need to come, I felt like responding, "Of course I don't need to come. How in the world could I help make that meeting any better?" But I didn't say this because I knew what Nikolai was really saying: *I don't want to put you through that again. It's okay if you stay home.* For that, I continued to think that Nikolai was the nicest Bulgarian I'd ever met.

When he reported back to me with the randomly-drawn groups, I couldn't believe it. The two best teams in the tournament—two of the best teams in Sofia—weren't in our group. We'd play two other teams in the group stage, teams that were decent, but certainly not talented like 35th or Spanish. I'd had nightmares about a tournament draw where we played 35th and Spanish like last year, and saw all of our hopes dashed by losing the first two games. But now that I looked at the draw, I knew we were pretty much guaranteed to win one of our first two games, and we stood a good chance to win them both. Thirty-fifth and Spanish could beat each other up on the other side, and we'd play them in the elimination rounds.

Branch and I walked out of the bubble together not talking too much about the game that just ended, but like everyone else, we were looking ahead to the following week's start of the ACS Open. There was no doubt that we'd received a favorable draw, but the story still remained the same: to win the tournament, we'd have to beat two of the best teams in Sofia, and most likely beat the team everyone indicated was the best team in Sofia, 35th.

"I know you might not want to hear me say this, Coach. I know we shouldn't be overly optimistic without reason," Branch said to me as we walked together on campus, "but we can win this tournament."

"I know we can win this tournament," I replied quickly.

"Well, then I should re-phrase that," he added. "I think we're going to win this tournament."

"You know what, Branch," I looked him square in the eye, not completely believing what I was about to say, "I think we're going to win this tournament, too."

We walked across campus together, a campus that was starting to warm up and turn slightly green as March was approaching, and felt the excitement of a new life, a new opportunity. It might've only existed for the two of us, but the added life of approaching spring left us each sensing a buzz was in the air. It felt like March Madness was coming to Bulgaria. And for the first time as a Bulgarian basketball coach, I would be going into a tournament thinking that my team was going to win.

I was still struggling with Bulgarian greetings and having people lash out at me when I said "How are you?" And I figured I never stood a chance of getting the correct change back on a consistent basis. These were Bulgarian breakthroughs I thought I'd never make. But that didn't matter. The one breakthrough that was most prominent and right in front of us was the one that mattered most: we were going to win the ACS Open.

Chapter XXVI
Taking Charge

Practices were well attended.

And they were fiercely competitive.

Some players who had barely shown up in the last month got the message that the ACS Open was a big deal and started coming to practice.

"They can't really think," Branch said, pointing to two 9th graders we hadn't seen in three weeks, "they're going to play in the ACS Open, can they?"

"Who knows what they think," I laughed, "but at least word is spreading about ACS basketball. Last year at the end of the year, I had to beg them to come to practice. Now this year, they're coming to practice begging to get a chance to play."

Menkov had come up to me earlier that day in my classroom to tell me how all of his friends wanted to come watch the ACS Open games. He was telling people to create excitement and try to get them to come to the games, but people already knew, he said. They were already planning to come, and already excited. As I watched him rattle off the names of different groups of people who were planning to come and cheer for us, I tried to take this all in slowly. What Menkov was doing was listing fans that we'd have at the game; but what he was really doing was thanking me for making basketball important.

"Last year," he said, "no one on campus cared about basketball. But now, people want to come to our games. This is going to be so cool."

I didn't say much in response to this because I didn't need to say much. Menkov's enthusiasm and eagerness said it all. As a coach, I should have no qualms whatsoever with seeing my players so fired up for the tournament. This is exactly what I'd wanted all along. Last year, we didn't even have enough uniforms for a full team, and I had to plead with some players on the team not to drink the night before morning games. Basketball as a priority? It was anything but. Now, excitement was through the roof, and this not only excited me, but it also warmed my heart. This is what I'd wanted these kids to experience all along. But there still was something that worried me.

"What if, what if," I started slowly, arduously working my thoughts out of my head as I talked to Branch, "what if we don't win the tournament?"

"What do you mean, 'what if we don't win the tournament?'" Branch responded. "We've *not won* a whole lot of tournaments; it won't be anything too new."

"But this one—this one's different," I told him, looking at him solemnly. "This is the one we've basically worked two years for, and we've built it up to be larger than life."

"I know, and I think that's what makes it so cool. These kids are so energized it's incredible."

"I agree, it is incredible. But what if we've built it up so big and we end up failing?"

With this, Branch needed more time to respond, clearly internalizing what I'd just said.

"I want them to be excited, and I want them to have this goal to win the tournament," I continued, "but it won't be easy for us to win. It's still highly possible we won't win the tournament."

With my latest pause, Branch still didn't say anything. I could tell his silence reflected worries burgeoning inside him.

"I guess I just remember how they reacted after we lost the first two games of this tournament last year. And now this year is different, but I'd just hate it if we lost and that ruined everything for these guys. I've tried so hard to make this not always about winning and losing, but playing together and playing hard. But now, what if we don't win? Will they think none of it was worth it?"

"Well," Branch finally broke his silence, "I don't know how they'll react if we don't win. I just know how badly all of them want to win right now."

Now it was my turn to be silent.

"So we better go out and win the damn tournament," Branch finished.

I smiled, and he smiled. These were both smiles that showed our own version of enthusiasm—enthusiasm that we could win the tournament. But deep down, we were both nervous. What would happen if we didn't win?

Thankfully, none of these nerves was apparent in our first group game. With three teams in each group, and the top two teams advancing, the pressure was on, but there was still room for error. The majority of the errors, though, were being committed by our opponent. Once again, our full-court press was wreaking havoc on a team that kept looking at each other wondering why we weren't playing a lax 2-3 zone. Every other team in Sofia did; why did we insist on pressuring them all the time? With the added presence of fans—many who I'd never seen at a game before—the bubble rocked and echoed a little louder with each new steal and transition basket we'd convert.

Menkov was playing like a man possessed, like a senior who knew he was close to the end, but wasn't going to give in one inch. He was darting into the passing lanes, deflecting passes and flying to the other end of the floor. When I took him out early in the second quarter, he looked at me bewildered and said, "Coach, what are you doing? I don't need a break. I'm not tired at all."

Normally, I believed in always giving players a rest even if they said they didn't need it, but I knew Menkov well enough at this point. He'd been at all the pre-season running for two years, and never missed practice. He definitely wasn't tired. And I knew basketball was his escape. Desperate to go to university outside of Bulgaria, he still hadn't heard back from schools, and knew he'd have to earn a great deal of scholarship money to be able to afford a good school. He didn't like to talk about it, but when he did, he displayed an unease and nervousness that I rarely saw on the basketball floor. Basketball was his outlet and his escape. I knew he wanted to be nowhere else but out on the court. So I put my hand on his shoulder and sent him back into the game.

In the second quarter, we held a solid 14-point lead, but I still felt it could and should be more. The team we were playing looked dazed by our defensive pressure, and I got the impression they didn't feel like playing a game with this high level of intensity any more. I urged my team to hammer home the nails in their coffin. I told them to extend the lead so that by halftime our opponents wouldn't even want to come back for the second half.

That's exactly what happened.

Pesho used his pogo-stick legs to snare a rebound, hoisted a shot back up at the rim, missed it, then used his pogo-stick legs to go get it again. He scored on the second attempt. Sasho had become the opposite of Pesho, relying on fundamental post moves that we'd worked on day after day in practice. He'd catch the ball in the post, spin left, pump-fake, and then finish with his right hand, getting fouled in the process. Pavel still couldn't score to save his life, but his defense at the front of the press was instigating many easy basket opportunities. After his two years of offensive struggles, I got the impression he might've finally figured out that his best move on offense was to pass the ball and crash the boards.

Kosio and I hadn't spoken much since his Romanian outburst and subsequent evasion of responsibility, but I'd made one thing very clear to him: either he ran hard or he didn't play. It was that simple. I was ready to yank him the minute he let up, but it wasn't happening.

"It looks to me like he doesn't want to sit on the bench anymore," Branch said midway through the second quarter. "I've never seen him run this hard before."

At halftime, our lead was 23 points. Our opponents clearly hadn't prepared for any of this. They looked frustrated and spent, and I knew they weren't coming back. In the first game of the much-anticipated ACS Open, we rolled our opponents, cruising to an easy victory.

"This is just one game," I told the team after the game, "and I think you know this. We're going to need to win three more to win this tournament, and they're only going to get tougher. Don't think this win is good enough. We've got three more to go."

After our game ended, Branch and I sat in the stands to watch the first game of the other group, and this one was a battle of the titans: 35th vs. Spanish. Even though we'd managed to beat Spanish during the year by one point, I knew they didn't take that game as seriously as they would a game in the tournament. As we shook hands when that game ended, I sensed a collective look in their eyes, and it seemed to say, *We're going to see you again in the tournament, and next time it will be different.*

I still considered the Spanish school to be the second best team in Sofia, behind 35th. Beating them once had given us the confidence that we belonged, but I knew beating them twice would be even tougher. But as Branch and I watched the first round game between the two favorites to win the tournament, we were shocked by how easily 35th was beating the Spanish school. Certainly, they had the talent to beat any good team, but at the end of the first quarter, they were ahead 20-4. It already appeared like the Spanish school wasn't even trying. Their point guard, who had routinely shredded our defense for the last two years was content to stand at the top of the key and pass the ball. He had no interest in exerting enough effort to drive to the basket. Their power forward, who was a match-up nightmare for any team, didn't dictate play on the inside at all. He just lingered around the perimeter shooting threes, probably the only part of his offensive game that wasn't excellent.

"Can you imagine this?" Branch said to me. "Can you imagine showing up to a big tournament game like this and barely even trying?"

That's exactly what was happening, though. The Spanish school clearly had come into the game, content to lose, knowing that they would only need one win to advance to the elimination round. Apparently they'd decided that getting the win against 35th wasn't important.

"Coach, I talked to some of the Spanish guys before the game," Vassy leaned over from his seat in the bleachers and said, "and they said they already decided they didn't want to play hard. They don't want to exert themselves in this game. They want to save their energy for later."

To both Branch and me, what Vassy was saying was ridiculous to two coaches who prided themselves on hard work. What we were watching was disgusting. The notion that a high school team would show up for a game content to not try seemed incredibly foreign and wrong to us. But it was also entirely correct. While Khrushchev was boisterously celebrating on his sideline, Starter Jacket seemed completely at ease on his sideline. The score was now 32-6. Spanish turned the ball over again, and several of their players didn't even bother running back on defense. It was an embarrassing display from a talented team—a talented team who had decided that this game didn't matter. They had no interest in playing hard for the sake of pride or anything the else. They'd given up before the game even started.

From the other end of the bleachers, a group of 35th students were enjoying the rout, and now had started chanting *"ISKAME RAKIA! ISKAME RAKIA! ISKAME RAKIA!"* We want *rakia*! We want *rakia*! We want *rakia*! the crowd chanted over and over. What I'd thought was going to be a good basketball game was anything but, and it was clear the 35th fans saw only one way they could be enjoying this—with Bulgarian grape brandy liquor.

Branch and I had hoped to watch the game in order to scout both teams, and make some decisions about how we would approach strategy for our upcoming games in the following days, but there was no way to scout this. One team was trying, and the other team wasn't at all.

"Well, if Spanish plays like this when we play them," Branch said, trying to find some amusement in this embarrassing display, "then I think we're going to do just fine."

"Yeah," I chuckled, "but I know they're not going to do this when we play them."

As the horn sounded to end the game, Khrushchev joined his team in a gratuitous dance at half court, much to the delight of the 35th fans who were now more eager to get drunk on *rakia* than ever. They'd won the game by 44 points.

We had one day to practice in between games, and I was noticing how little pleading I was doing in practice. Defensive-slide drills that were usually met with groans were completed without complaint. Box-out drills that Pesho had spent two years protesting were now a necessary part of the routine, and Branch and I were thrilled with the intensity we saw. And fast-break drills—always the most preferred drills—were led with even more speed, and perhaps even more understanding that we'd have to outrun teams in order to win.

Our second game in the tournament was on Friday night. We knew that winning meant we'd win our group, and play the second place team from the other group in the semifinals. That meant we'd most likely play the Spanish school, and that was preferred over playing 35th, a team that solidified its status as the best in Sofia with their trouncing against a half-trying Spanish team in the first game. I pointed out how important it was to win this game and win our group, and wasn't sure how aware our players were of the implications of playing Spanish or 35th in our next game.

Once the game started, though, I put all these concerns to rest. We came out running, and we started out the game dominant. Against a team that I knew would've given us some trouble the year before, we weren't having any problems. Part of this stemmed from our hard work to improve, and that went right along with a significant increase in confidence. We jumped out to a double-digit lead using our full-court press once again to stymie a team that was happier being able to walk the ball up the floor. I was rotating different guys in and out of the lineup, always leaving Menkov in, but knowing that he could lead any number of different lineups to success.

The only hiccup came in the second quarter when Sasho once again gave a great shot fake to create space for him to score at the rim. When he gave the shot fake, though, his defender came flying at him with arms and elbows raised. Sasho attempted to make the move we'd worked on so much–the up-and-under–but he couldn't escape from the elbow that came crashing down on his head. It was a direct blow, and immediately blood started flowing down the left side of his face. Our bench reacted immediately, seeing the blood and knowing this was a serious hit. Of course Sasho reacted like he reacted to everything, smiling in a goofy manner, seeming slightly confused that blood was now pouring down his face.

He started walking over to the bench, as the school's doctor hopped up from his half-sleeping position. I was hoping and praying that he wouldn't try to fix this injury with a frozen bottle of *rakia*. As far as I could tell, *rakia* did not have healing powers that included closing up gashes and stopping blood flow.

"Coach, Coach," Sasho's red face told me, "I am okay. This is no big deal. I can keep playing."

I looked at the doctor, who didn't speak English, but seemed to understand Sasho's desire to keep playing. The doctor started gravely nodding his head, and I knew this head-nod was the Bulgarian version; the cut above his eye didn't look good. The bleeding was slowly subsiding, but he'd been hit in an area where there isn't much skin, and the cut looked deep.

"Sasho, I think you're going to need stitches," I told him.

He seemed shocked by this, and then turned to the doctor and asked him the same question in Bulgarian. The doctor bobbed his head from side-to-side indicating that stitches were necessary.

"But, but," Sasho stammered, looking at the clock, "do you think I can get the stitches in time to come back before the game is over?"

With this, several members of the bench started laughing, and while Sasho was seriously injured, I had to laugh, too. His attitude–*I'm not coming out of the game no matter what*—was exactly what I'd want out of a basketball player, though his savvy and pragmatism were a little bit off.

"Sasho, we're going to be fine in this game without you," I said, noting that the scoreboard showed that we had a 17-point lead. "The most important thing is for you to get stitches and get better. We need you for next week."

"Okay, Coach," Sasho resigned himself to say. "But I really don't want to go."

Once Sasho finally left for the hospital, the rout continued. It appeared to me that the biggest thing we'd learned from the Romania trip was what it meant to actually play hard for an entire game without letting up. As much as I'd encouraged and demanded this in every game, it was difficult to make this a reality in games in Bulgaria. There was a guarantee that the other team would either not play hard to begin with, or at least take extended breaks during the game. As a result, this became a difficult mentality to break for our team, just because it wasn't necessary to really play hard *the entire game*. We could still get away without doing this.

But the first two games presented us with an entirely different reality: two blowout wins, thorough and convincing in every way. Menkov was leading the charge and others were filling in their roles nicely. Ivan continued to improve to the point where he was consistently making 12-foot jump shots, and mixing this in with a dribble-drive move to the basket as well. As he stood at the free throw line in the fourth quarter and made two free throws, he was 7-for-7 at the foul line in this game. I couldn't help but think back to the ACS Open a year before when he was 2-for-10 at the free throw line, and three of his misses didn't even hit the rim. What a difference a year had made.

The game finished with high-fives, fist-pumps and general happiness. We'd won our group, had made it to the semifinals, and I'd never seen my team look more confident. I had to caution them about over-confidence after the game, and reinforced the importance of Monday and Tuesday's practices before our semifinal game against Spanish, who had advanced by actually playing hard and beating the lesser opponent in their group. As the team broke the huddle and headed off for the weekend, Branch and I felt good about our chances moving forward. There was no way we couldn't feel good based on how we were playing.

"Spanish has no idea what's going to hit them on Wednesday,"

Branch, always the more brash of the two of us, said. "They have no idea how confident we are and how hard we're playing."

A few hours after the game, I called Sasho to see how everything went at the hospital. He said he was given five stitches, but that he was okay. He didn't want to talk about the hospital, but only wanted to talk about the game.

"I just talked to some of the guys," he said excitedly, "and they all said how great we played. They said it was a great team win."

"Yeah, Sasho, it really was. It was a great win today. And it's great news that you're okay, too," I told him.

"Coach, I can't believe you called," he said, sounding genuinely surprised. "I mean, it's just so—it's just so nice that you called."

"Well Sasho, I wanted to make sure you were okay," I responded.

"It's just so nice, so nice," Sasho continued, and I got the impression that no teacher or coach had ever called him on the phone before. "And you know what Coach? You know what? Wednesday's game—it's going to be even *nicer*."

Monday's practice continued the trend of intense practices with focused players. This was now becoming the rule, when for the majority of our first year, and even some of the second year, this was the exception. On this day, the only thing that seemed different was Pesho. While I was used to him selectively listening to my coaching instructions and generally disregarding every post move I'd tried to teach him, he had no problem relying on his springy legs and unparalleled athleticism to just try to jump over everyone. The reason he hated box-out drills so much was because he saw jumping over people as a much more efficient way to rebound. But on this day, Pesho wasn't jumping. He wasn't rebounding, and he wasn't even fading away to take horrible shots that he loved as much as I detested. Perhaps most telling, Pesho hadn't made any comment about the "beast in the wild," or tried to talk to me about the beauty of Bulgarian women.

Branch and I both noticed something was wrong, and this was not a good time for something to be wrong. In two days, we'd be playing against Spanish in the semifinals of the ACS Open. This was the biggest game we'd ever had, and I'd touted these practices as the most important we'd ever have as well. I'd asked Pesho several times if he was okay, and several times he'd said he was fine, but I knew this wasn't true. So I went to Pavel, his closest friend on the team.

"Pavel," I said quietly, "what's going on with Pesho? Something's wrong."

He looked like he didn't want to respond, but I knew he would.

"Today's just a tough day for him," he said softly.

"I can see that. What's up?"

"The divorce became official today," Pavel cringed. "His dad moved out over the weekend. I don't think he wants to talk about it, though."

I looked across the court to where Pesho was shooting free throws, and instead of joking with his teammates and attempting fadeaway free throws, he stood morosely at the line, hoisting up each free throw as if weights had been strapped to his shoulders. It was hard for me to watch. For two years, Pesho had been a character, a character who would end up defining so much of my Bulgarian experience. He was a six-foot-four giant with a shaved head who laughed garrulously. He'd infuriated me with his stubbornness and unwillingness to adapt his game the way I wanted him to. But he'd electrified both the team and me with his athletic play and undying motor in games. He'd fought me—usually with a smile—on every box-out drill, and grinned every time I yelled at him to move his feet on defense instead of trying to steal the ball and block every shot. He'd led horribly misguided one-man fast breaks that surprisingly worked far more frequently than they should've. And he'd even been outrageously sincere in offering to buy me a prostitute as a Christmas present. There were so many different descriptions that I could apply to Pesho because he'd become an integral and entertaining part of nearly every day I'd had in Bulgaria for two years. I came to practice waiting to see what Pesho had in store for me, and even looking forward to how we'd spar over what I wanted him to do, and what he was determined to resist doing.

But now I looked at Pesho and all those descriptions faded away. As he launched a feeble free throw toward the basket at the other end, he was simply a 16-year-old kid. He was a 16-year-old kid who was hurting because his dad had moved out.

At the end of practice—a spirited practice for everyone other than Pesho—I called him over to me as players were exiting the gym.

"What's up, Coach?" he said with a little less zing than usual.

"Pesho, you know if you ever need to talk," I said carefully, "if you ever need someone to listen, I'll be here."

Pesho watched me as I was speaking, and then immediately started looking down. I could tell he was trying to follow his usual pattern—by making a joke out of this—but he couldn't.

"I know you're hurting, Pesho, and it's okay. I'm here for you.

We're here for you."

Finally, Pesho looked up, and I could see that the six-foot-four giant was fighting back tears.

"Coach, I'm okay. Everything's fine," he said, semi-proudly.

I looked him in the eye and smiled, knowing that he didn't want to talk about this, and knowing that it wasn't in his persona to let loose and be emotional. In fact, not only was it not in his persona to show emotion, it didn't fit the Bulgarian male persona either. As a rule, Bulgarian men kept their emotions to themselves and rarely let their sadness show. In that moment, I decided I didn't want to make Pesho break the mold by continuing to talk about this.

"Pesho, I know you're going to be fine," I said as I clapped him on the shoulder, "but if you're not, that's okay, too."

"Come on, Coach," he responded, regaining some of his panache, "you know me. I'm Pesho, I'm always fine. Let's just worry about beating Spanish on Wednesday."

Pesho smiled at me, a not entirely convincing smile, but a smile nonetheless, and then he turned and trotted out of the bubble. I was worried about how he was doing, but he was also right. I needed to worry about how we were going to beat Spanish on Wednesday.

"They killed us off the dribble last game," Branch said to me on Tuesday morning as we sat in my classroom, trying to devise the best plan for our last practice before the game. "Their point guard and power forward attacked us off the dribble at will. If we let them do that again, we're going to be in big trouble."

"You're right," I replied. "They're the two best players on the floor, better than anybody we've got. If we can stop them, we'll win the game."

We'd been going back and forth on who would guard Spanish's point guard. Menkov was the obvious choice because he was the quickest player on our team, but he also was the player who we relied on to handle the ball almost exclusively on offense. Having him guard one of their best players ran the risk of exhausting him. The only other feasible choice we saw was Pavel, whose offense was not nearly as important to us. But Pavel's best asset on defense was his strength, not necessarily his quickness. Between the two, we weren't able to come to a solid decision, and this was still left up in the air. The other big decision was who should guard their power forward. While Sasho had the size, he was just too slow. While Pesho was athletic enough, we had no idea what to expect from him. Vassy was too small, but guaranteed to battle him. And Ivan probably wasn't strong enough. It was clear that no matter what we did, there was going to be a mismatch.

"We have to step in and take charges," Branch said. "That's the only way to neutralize them. They will continue to drive to the basket every time, and unless we start taking charges, they won't think twice about doing it."

I knew Branch was right, but I also knew that taking a charge—getting in position and basically allowing yourself to be run over by your opponent—was not a big part of Bulgarian basketball. There was always great potential to draw offensive fouls like this, but almost all Bulgarian players—those on our team and others—shied away from this kind of contact. Like soccer players who learned how to dive and flop at an early age, our basketball players had no trouble flopping, but they didn't want to actually take the hit first. That's why charges were so rarely called by referees; it was rare that a Bulgarian basketball player would be willing to stand there and take the hit.

"Branch, we've been telling them to take charges all year—hell, I've been doing it for two years—but it still hasn't made a difference. Do you really think we can change that in time for tomorrow?"

"Well, it's worth a shot, isn't it?"

He was right; it was worth a shot.

As Tuesday's practice began, I talked about the importance of defense in Wednesday's game. This was a speech topic that Menkov, Ivan, Pavel, Sasho, Pesho, Kosio, and Vassy had heard like a broken record for two years. But I didn't think it could be overstated enough. Branch and I both talked about their two best players, and how we would have to pay attention to them at all times, and be ready to rotate our defense to help against them. That led me to talking about the importance of drawing offensive fouls, moving our feet to get in front of them and then being ready to take the hit. This, too, was nothing new, but this was something unpleasant that was never received with enthusiasm.

When I lined the team up for our designed *take-a-charge* drill, I could sense the apprehension in the air. The drill worked by having every member of the team stand at various points all around the three-point line. There would be one player in the middle standing at the free throw line and he would be waiting for me to throw the ball to one of the players on the perimeter. When that player got the ball, his instructions were to drive to the basket as hard as he could. It was the defender's job to move his feet and get into position, and then absorb the full force of the offensive player who was dribbling to the basket. The players knew this drill well, and they disliked it more than any other drill we ran.

Pavel volunteered to go first, a testament to his puffed-out chest and fearless attitude. As I passed the ball to Ivan, he started dribbling to the basket, heading Pavel's way. As the play unfolded, though, it was difficult to place the blame on solely Pavel or Ivan. What both of them were doing was problematic. Pavel had readied himself in decent position, but he was ready to fall down, already slowly tipping, well before Ivan ever hit him. And Ivan, well, he had no interest in actually hitting Pavel. He slowed down his dribble and jumped to the side, anxious to avoid contact. All around, this looked terrible.

I pointed out the flaws with this, and most of the flaws stemmed from our fear of contact. When I threw the ball to the other side of the floor and Vassy drove into Pavel, it didn't get any better. Unfortunately, this was exactly what I'd expected when Branch had suggested this drill. No matter how many times we indicated how this should work, there was a great consistency in how it wouldn't work. Our players were afraid of this kind of contact. It just wasn't part of the Bulgarian version of basketball.

"Okay, I've had enough of this," Branch hollered, and I was shocked to hear him raise his voice, something he rarely did in practice. I was just about to say the same thing, but he did it for me. Now I was wondering exactly what he was going to do.

"Coach," he directed to me as he flipped me the ball, "take this ball and come hit me."

As he said this, Branch stormed to the middle of the lane and put himself in the ready position. I was left holding the ball, a bit apprehensive myself, near the three-point line. In theory, I had no problem with demonstrating what taking a charge really meant, but I did have a problem with running over my assistant coach. My problem didn't originate from the fact that he was my assistant coach; I had an entirely different concern. Branch had a torn ACL. He couldn't walk without a slight limp, and he couldn't run at all. The torn ACL had been diagnosed in the winter, and he was opting to wait to have surgery in the States in the summer. But in the meantime, I felt for him as he hobbled around during most facets of his life. He was clearly injured. I knew it, and every member of the team knew it, too. But now he was standing at the foul line, fire coming out of his eyes, telling me to run him over.

"Coach, I'm not sure that's such a good idea," I cautioned him. "Your knee–I just don't think it's a good idea."

"Screw that," Branch fired back quickly, and I could tell he was serious. "Hit me. Come on, hit me."

Even in the moment, I don't think the absurdity of the situation was lost on me. I was 29. He was 32. We were two middle-aged men, well past any semblance of fleeting basketball glory we'd ever come close to experiencing, standing in a bubble-domed gym, preparing to show 16 and 17-year-olds what being physical really meant. In normal circumstances, it worked the other way around. Young boys with no fear showed middle-aged men what it meant to be tough and physical. But now the two of us stood 12 feet away from each other, wondering if there was any way our players could learn how to take a charge unless I took the ball, put my head down and completely obliterated my assistant coach. I knew there was a good chance this would further wreck his knee, and I didn't know how I was going to reconcile hitting him with the blunt force of my body. In fact, I wasn't even sure how I was going to dribble at him at full speed without thinking of his torn ACL. But then he kept calling me out.

"Hit me. Come on, dammit. Hit me."

With his last salvo, though, I felt I had no choice.

I was off.

I took the ball in my right hand and pushed the dribble out just to the right of where he was positioned. I saw him slide on his gimpy knee to get in front of me as I dribbled the ball one more time. The ball soared back up to my right hand and I gathered it in, knowing that the moment of impact was upon us. I could see Branch's body firm and straight, not willing to lean or give an inch until I hit him. And when I did hit him, our collarbones smacked, and we could each feel the crunch of our ribs as they ricocheted off one another. Branch absorbed the full weight of my body and fell backwards. I absorbed the momentum from the collision and my body went shooting off to the right. Both of us ended up in various forms of disarray on the floor. The ball went shooting wildly out of bounds. From the crowd gathered behind us, I heard several exclamations of dismay in the form of Bulgarian swear words.

Before I could ask Branch if he was okay–and based on the force of the collision, I had serious doubts he was okay–he sprung up to his feet, using the last fragments of knee cartilage he had left.

"Now that," he declared, "is how you take a charge."

I got back on my feet slower than Branch, and started assessing the shocked looks on several players' faces. They weren't sure what they'd just witnessed. As different as basketball had been for them with two American coaches, and as many times as they thought our methods were crazy, this exceeded all of those previous limits.

"Do you understand," Branch bellowed, "how you're supposed to take a charge now?"

Some of the players gathered around the three-point line bobbed their heads back and forth. Some nodded. And Pavel, who had always been eager to take a charge, was the first one to speak.

"Yes, Coach!" he howled.

With that, I flipped the ball to Pesho who took the ball, seemed to think about it for a moment, and then barreled full-speed at his best friend. Pavel slid to the left and got his body in perfect position. As Pesho was about to hit him, he didn't let up. And as Pavel was about to get annihilated by his much larger best friend, he didn't start to back out of the way. The collision was thunderous, and this was soon followed by thunderous approval from both Branch and me. Pesho got up first and extended his hand to Pavel. They both smiled.

From that point on, one player after another understood exactly what was being expected of him. The player with the ball was the freight train and the defender was in charge of getting run over by it. One after another, players lined up, with the memory of their assistant coach and his torn ACL getting obliterated fresh in their mind. The drill was run with more intensity, passion and physical contact than any we'd run in two years.

Amidst the carnage—carnage that our players soon found they really liked—I meandered over to Branch, hoping to hear that his knee was okay.

"How's your knee feeling?" I asked. "You okay?"

"It feels like hell," he grinned, "but that doesn't matter."

With that, he hobbled away from me, emphatically congratulating Vassy for taking three consecutive solid hits. As I turned the other way, Sasho continued to be the only problem with this drill. With the stitches still freshly sewn above his left eye, he was begging me to let him be in the middle and get run over. For the fourth time, I told him no. But I smiled as I said it, knowing that the problem he was causing was one I was gladly willing to deal with.

Chapter XXVII
The Spanish Showdown

On game day, neither Branch nor I could think of anything we'd left uncovered in practice. Our game plan was clear, and now that we'd finally cured our fear of contact, we felt like we were in the best shape we could possibly be going into the semifinal game. I didn't worry much about the mentality of the team either, as to a man, I could tell that they were treating this game exactly like I was: it was the biggest game of the year, maybe even the biggest of a career. We waited for the first game to end, and it was clear that Khrushchev and 35th were going to win easily, cruising to the championship game without even being tested.

"Playing them would be so wonderful," Branch said as they took a double-digit lead into the fourth quarter, "because they're so arrogant. They assume they've won every game before it even starts. I'd just love to beat them."

"Me, too," I agreed. "But we've got to beat Spanish first."

I gathered our team right outside the bubble in the blossoming, warming weather of early March in Bulgaria. So many times I'd looked up at the dilapidated row house that hovered over the bubble and saw it as an ominous augury, but with the sun about to set, I swore I could even find beauty in the light bouncing off the decaying cement. That's how eager I was for this game.

"We've prepared for an ACS Open semifinal not just this week in practice, not just in our games here in the last couple weeks, and not just in our games in Romania. We've been preparing for this all year, and for the last two years. And I know you're ready. I know you're ready to play hard, to play together, and go out there and play the best game you've ever played."

There was silence in the team huddle, but I sensed it was a silence of understanding.

"I'm not going to be worried about the scoreboard tonight," I said, and though this was an obvious lie, I thought I was playing it off well. "And I don't want you to worry about the scoreboard either. If you are willing to go out there tonight and leave everything on the floor, play hard and play without regrets, the scoreboard won't matter. The scoreboard will take care of itself. The best *team* will win–and you know that we're the best team."

With this, the silence was broken by shouts of approval and excitement. They had just heard the horn inside the bubble signifying the end of the previous game, and the beginning of our warm-ups. As our team hit the floor and began its warm-up, there wasn't much that Branch and I had to say to each other. I don't know that either of us had much left to say. We'd talked and talked and talked this game to death, and now all that was left was for it to actually be played. Looking to the wooden bleachers across the way, I saw students and teachers I'd never seen before at a basketball game. It was clear that I wasn't the only one who thought this was a big game. I walked down the sidelines and shook hands with Starter Jacket, wishing him good luck in Bulgarian. From his demeanor, I couldn't tell if he was nervous about the game or completely unconcerned. I guessed it was more the latter than the former. As I turned back toward our bench, I saw Khrushchev laughing with a few parents from 35th, and it appeared that he was leaving. He didn't see it as necessary to stick around and scout our game to see who won. Finally, my glance swerved back to the court to see my team warming up. After two years, our warm-up routine was rehearsed, fluid and confident-looking. Menkov was jogging up and down the layup lines, shouting words of encouragement and slapping high-fives to his teammates. I looked at Branch and couldn't think of too many insightful things to say. I thought about why we hadn't said much to each other during warm-ups, and then suddenly it hit me: I was more nervous than I'd ever been as a coach in Bulgaria, perhaps more nervous than any game I'd ever coached in my life.

"Goddammit, I hope we win this game," I said to him.

"We will," he responded confidently. "We will."

Spanish won the opening tip, and even though we'd played nothing but man-to-man defense for the entirety of the last two years, they immediately looked annoyed they wouldn't be facing a zone. With Menkov practically attached to their point guard's shorts, he wanted nothing to do with handling the ball. He flipped it to a teammate, who looked equally as apprehensive about handling the ball against Pavel's pressure. So he lobbed the ball into the post to their best player, their athletic power forward who finished well with both his left and right hands. But on this occasion, he wouldn't finish with either. Ivan jumped around the high side and deflected the pass with his right hand. The ball bounced to the corner where Pesho picked it up. They'd turned the ball over on their first possession and we were headed the other way.

In contrast to their apprehension on offense, we looked very comfortable against a 2-3 zone. I sensed this on the first possession, and knew it should be the case. We'd done nothing in practice but work on our zone offense, and we were executing it in practice with ease and fluidity. On our first possession, the ball swung from Menkov to Pavel to Ivan. Ivan pitched the ball to the elbow to Pesho who caught the ball and faced the basket. Just as he caught the ball, Menkov deftly cut to the basket, surprising nearly everyone on the Spanish team. Pesho hit him with a perfect pass, and Menkov extended his right arm to toss in an easy right-handed runner from four feet away. We'd taken our first lead of the game. And now it was time to press.

The press seemed to annoy Spanish nearly as much as the man-to-man defense in the half court. Again, I saw no reason why they should be either annoyed or unprepared. While what we were doing was rare and out of the ordinary for a Bulgarian team, it was what we'd been doing for the entirety of the last two years. It was what we'd done when we'd beaten Spanish by one point about five weeks previous. But still, they looked flustered by the full-court press, and once again, their point guard didn't appear to want the ball. He flung it across court, where Pesho stepped in and stole the pass. He sprinted toward the hoop, a man on a mission, but mostly an out-of-control mission. His layup careened off the backboard, but Ivan hustled to grab it and score on the rebound.

I let loose my first fist-pump of the day from the sideline, elated by most possibly the best start we could've had. It was 4-0 and Spanish hadn't even taken a shot. We had two steals, two baskets and already one offensive rebound. This was everything we'd practiced for, and everything I'd predicted as a best-case scenario as I'd played this game out in my head.

But I also knew that Spanish was too good to be completely stifled by either our press or our man-to-man defense. They had the two most talented players on the floor, and two others who at least came to the level of our best players. The next time down the floor, they broke the press without difficulty and their point guard beat Menkov, pulling up for a jump shot and draining it from 16-feet away. No matter what, this was an advantage they were always going to have over us. I'd explicitly told our players to not even take shots like that because the odds of our making them were so low. For the Spanish point guard, this was a normal shot in his repertoire.

Despite our shooting deficiencies, though, we were more than able to make up for it by attacking the offensive boards and going after rebounds. After Menkov missed his second floater, Pesho pogo-sticked and deflected the ball to Sasho who grabbed it, kept the ball high and finished high off the backboard. This seemed to establish a trend. Spanish would come down and shoot a jump shot with varying levels of success, but would not get a second shot on a miss. We'd come down, settle in against their 2-3 zone, pass the ball around, get one shot inside, and then usually a second or a third. Pesho and Sasho were dominating down low, if only because they were working hard to fight for position. Ivan was giving us a third player unafraid to play physically down low, and when I subbed Vassy in for Sasho, he immediately scored two baskets as a result of scramble situations where he grabbed the ball quicker than anyone else.

As the first quarter was drawing to a close, Menkov stole the ball from their point guard and started streaking toward the other end. The Spanish point guard didn't bother chasing him, and neither did anyone else on his team. I watched triumphantly as Menkov laid the ball into the basket, with Pavel and Pesho following close behind him. The first quarter ended and we had a 16-7 lead. The huddle at the end of the quarter was jubilant, but I tried to keep them focused.

"Guys, that's just one quarter," I warned sternly. "The second quarter needs to be even better than the first. Come on, you have to play even harder. And I still worry that they're getting by us too easily on the dribble. Don't be afraid to move your feet and take a charge."

On the first play of the second quarter, Menkov clearly showed that he'd been listening to me. As their point guard crossed over from right to left and started barreling toward the basket, Menkov was right in step with him. The point guard lowered his shoulder in an attempt to create space and cleared out Menkov, sending him flying down the lane on his butt. It was an obvious offensive foul, and I was thrilled; this was exactly what we'd worked on the previous day in practice.

The referee blew his whistle and signaled a blocking foul on Menkov.

"Are you kidding me?" Branch started yelling before I could.

That was mostly because I jumped two feet in the air when I saw the call, not believing it could be a blocking foul. "That's a charge! A charge! That's terrible!"

Even though the referee didn't understand English, he certainly understood Branch's tone. He waved his finger in Branch's direction, and then the other referee came over to me and told me in Bulgarian that I needed to keep my bench under control. The general rule in basketball anywhere was that the head coach was allowed to do the yelling, but not the assistant coach. Still, there was no way I could blame Branch.

"Coach," Pavel said from the bench, "that's exactly what you taught us in practice yesterday and now they call the foul on Menkov."

I wasn't sure if this was a statement or a question, but Pavel's incredulity matched mine.

"These refs—they hate us, they hate us," Pavel quipped.

"I don't care about the refs," I firmly responded to Pavel, and knew that couldn't be further from the truth. "The refs can call whatever they want, but we have to keep playing hard."

While admonishing Pavel for criticizing the referees, my mind was centered on the horrible call that had just occurred. Maybe I'd never focused too much on taking charges because I knew this would happen; we'd never get the calls anyway. Branch tapped me on the shoulder to bring me back to the reality of the game.

"Coach, Menkov's got two fouls," he told me.

I started to think about what to do, but already knew I couldn't take him out of the game. He was our best player, our smartest player and our leader. We couldn't win this game with him on the bench.

"Menkov," I shouted out to the floor with two fingers raised, "you've got two fouls. You have to be careful."

"I know, I know, Coach," he fired back immediately, complete with a *don't-take-me-out-of-the- game* look on his face.

Forcing Spanish into another jump shot, Sasho cleared the rebound and passed the ball to Menkov who led the fast break. He had Ivan running on his left and Kosio running on his right. The sensible decision– the one I was hoping he'd make–was a pass to Ivan on the left who was already headed toward the basket. Kosio was fading to the three-point line. Menkov jump-stopped at the free throw line just like he'd been taught, but he swung the ball backwards to his right. Kosio launched a three-pointer.

It banked in off the backboard.

Again, I found myself fist-pumping on the sideline. It was the absolute wrong pass to make and a low-percentage shot, but it went in. And in this game, I was willing to take any points we could get.

Immediately following the three-pointer, we were back into our press, and it was clear our aggression had surprised Spanish and thrown them out of their comfort zone. As their point guard once again made a cross-court pass, eager to get rid of the ball, Menkov came charging toward the ball. But he also went charging toward a member of the other team. They both arrived at the same time and the whistle blew. This time it was the correct call, and now Menkov had three fouls.

With this, Menkov's hands ran up to his face and through his hair. I'd just warned him to be careful, and he'd just done everything but. The majority of the second quarter still remained and our best and most indispensable player had three fouls. He started jogging toward the bench before I'd even called him, and I grabbed Pavel to send him into the game.

"I'm sorry, Coach," Menkov said glumly. "I screwed up."

As he took a step toward the bench, I grabbed him.

"I know you screwed up," I told him, "but you're not going to let it happen again. I'm not taking you out of the game."

Menkov looked at me, surprise etched all over his face. I could imagine Branch's face must've looked the same way, too. Pavel certainly looked surprised from the scorer's table.

"Pavel, take Vassy out of the game. You're going into the game, and you guard their point guard."

Menkov was still stunned, but not unhappy.

"The only way we win this game is if you're in it," I told him firmly. "You have to play smart. We have to have you in this game."

Menkov nodded his head vigorously, jump-turned and sprinted back into the game.

As Branch came over to me, I had to wave him off before he even expressed doubt about the decision.

"I know this might be really stupid, but is there any way you see us winning this game without him in it?"

"No," Branch said, and he didn't need to hesitate. "There's no way at all."

Pavel relished the challenge of guarding their point guard, and while he didn't provide us much on offense, the trade-off was worth it. Their point guard had started to become more assertive, but was having trouble maneuvering around Pavel's broad shoulders and chest. He was hoisting up off-balance jump shots, and again we were cleaning up the boards. The one player we had trouble finding an answer to was their power forward who, when he was allowed to catch the ball in the post, was a safe bet to either score or get fouled. I continued to plead with Pesho, Ivan and Vassy not to allow him to catch the ball in the post to begin with. This was our best path to success, and we'd already garnered numerous steals as a result of denying him the ball.

Menkov seemed even more rejuvenated on offense since I'd told him he had to take it easy on defense. When the rebounds were cleared, he was demanding the ball on the wing and shooting us up the floor. When the fast break opportunities were there, we were capitalizing. And when they settled into their trademark 2-3 zone, we were finding seams inside. Once Kosio hit another three, the inside was opening up even more. Ivan was making nice moves on the baseline and hitting short shots in the paint. I couldn't believe how efficient our offense was, and I almost forgot how worried I was about Menkov's three fouls.

As halftime rolled around, we were in complete control of the game. The score was 32-21. And perhaps more importantly, Menkov had not picked up another foul. When I asked Branch what we needed to talk about at halftime, or what adjustments we had to make, he gave me a very honest and accurate assessment of what was happening out on the floor.

"Spanish is playing a lot harder than last time, and they're not playing that poorly," he commented. "It's just that—well, honestly, this is the best we've ever played. I don't think you should change a thing. Just tell them to keep playing hard. We've never looked this good as a team."

Branch just voiced exactly what I was thinking. It's rare in any sport to have a team perform at its absolute highest level when it matters the most. In theory, this should always happen, but it rarely does. Right now, I was approaching the halftime huddle of a team that was doing everything they'd been coached to do and then some. We didn't need to change the game plan, but stick to it, and prepare for their comeback.

"Don't think we've won this game," I told them. "You're playing against a very good team—and one that's going to mount a comeback. That's why the beginning of the quarter is so important. You have to stomp on them right from the beginning. Don't feel bad for them and don't let them back into this game."

As the second half started, I felt jitters on the bench that might've been worse than the first half. I'd meant exactly what I'd said at halftime, and fully expected the Spanish comeback to start immediately as the clock started ticking in the second half. Bulgarian teams had a habit of folding when things weren't going well, but I knew this game would be different. It was the semifinals of a tournament—a tournament that mattered greatly for both teams. Squatting nervously on the sideline as the second half started, I braced myself for the third quarter comeback.

But it didn't happen.

While I'd hoped our players were also braced for the comeback, they'd gone one step further: they were attacking more than ever before. Spanish missed their first shot of the second half, and Pesho cleared the rebound. He made the outlet pass to Menkov who started speeding the other way. He reached the middle of the floor and now had players on either wing waiting for him to pass it to them. But even though there were two Spanish defenders back on defense, I could tell he wasn't going to pass the ball. Menkov charged into the seam between the two defenders and hung in the air until he'd cleared both of them. With his right hand, he scooped the ball up off the backboard, and we all watched it softly bounce into the basket. It was a remarkable move, one that not only showed Menkov's ability, but his resolve. Watching him make that move, I thought that he personally was determined to make sure we'd win this game.

Following his lead, the third quarter resembled the first two quarters, but was even better. While Spanish was making a more concerted effort to get the ball inside for higher percentage shots, Pesho was keeping both his hands straight up and not fouling, making life difficult for their big men. Menkov, still with three fouls, had no choice but to back off their point guard and force him to shoot from the outside, but his shots weren't falling. And without a doubt, our rebounding was proving to be the unstoppable force driving our performance. Spanish wasn't getting any second shots, and on our offensive end, we were shooting our relatively normal, mediocre-at-best percentage. But we were getting more and more extra opportunities against their zone defense that seemed allergic to boxing out. When Vassy replaced Sasho, we lost a significant amount of size, but replaced it with even more energy and heart. He continued to soar much higher than his six-foot frame should've allowed him, in order to grab rebounds over and around Spanish players who were much bigger.

With each new basket we scored—and there were many in the third quarter scored by Pesho who just kept jumping and jumping on the inside—my fist-pumps garnered more intensity. These fiery exclamations on the outside were matched by a welling of pride on the inside. We'd never played this well at any point during this season or last, and I was so proud of what was occurring out on the floor. As the lead swelled to 14 points toward the end of the third quarter, Spanish looked thoroughly frustrated, and we looked ultimately confident. I allowed myself to think briefly about the championship game against 35th. I didn't know if we could win that game, but if we played like we were playing right now, I certainly wouldn't bet against us.

The horn for the third quarter sounded and both teams headed toward their respective benches. The scoreboard displayed our triumph up to this point: ACS 49, Spanish 33.

"Now there's one quarter to go," I spoke to a rapt audience as we huddled near our bench. "And this is no different than any other fourth quarter we've played all year. I don't care what the score is right now, but we need to win this fourth quarter. Go into this quarter thinking about all the sprints, all the pre-season running and all the hard work you've put into this season. You should realize that you're not tired. You should realize that you're the better team. And you should know that now is the time to finish them off. Now is the time to go out and win this game!"

Excited arms were quickly thrust into the middle, and the huddle broke with a powerfully echoed "TEAM!" As I watched the five players head out onto the floor, I saw that they were talking to each other, conferring on different elements of strategy. As I looked to the bench, several players were tapping their feet, and I sensed they were nervous for a different reason: they couldn't believe we'd almost made it to the championship game. We were one quarter away, and we had a 16-point lead.

On our first possession, Menkov found Pesho on the right block, and he put up a short hook shot. It glanced off the rim, but Ivan swooped in to grab the rebound. He let loose an eight-foot jumper that hit both the front and back rim, but bounced out. With each new shot, I could hear both the crowd and the bench get worked up, only to be let down. But we weren't done yet. Pesho grabbed yet another rebound and attempted our third shot. This, too, missed the target, and Spanish finally cleared the rebound.

"Great effort, great effort!" I clapped loudly from the sidelines. "Great effort! Do that every time, and don't worry about a thing!"

I knew that if we continued to work that hard to get extra shots, we couldn't possibly miss that many in-close attempts for the rest of the quarter. Our effort was so superior that it would have to be rewarded.

And in the next moment, I got more evidence of our superior effort. As Spanish brought the ball up the floor, the point guard passed the ball to the wing, and the wing player flipped a nonchalant pass right back to the point guard. Against a 2-3 zone, this pass would be fine. But against an aggressive man-to-man defense, it wasn't. Menkov darted into the passing lane and deflected the pass back toward half court. He shot after the ball and started dribbling, all alone toward our basket. Several members of our bench were already standing up, waiting to applaud his effort and celebrate two more points for our team. With plenty of time and no one posing any kind of threat to him, Menkov went up for the right-handed layup. I watched in anticipation as the ball glanced off the backboard just a little bit too hard, hit the rim, and fell to the left side of the hoop. He had missed a wide-open layup.

If I could have wagered on which player I'd want to shoot any kind of shot at any time, it would've always been Menkov. He wasn't necessarily the best shooter on the team, but he lived for the moment, and he had a scorer's mentality. As he approached the rim for this layup, I would've bet any amount of money on him making it, and felt completely confident in doing so.

But he didn't make it. The ball rolled off to the left side of the hoop, and while he lunged over to grab the rebound, a retreating Spanish player corralled it before Menkov could recover. Running back down the floor, he looked dismayed, and inside my stomach, I didn't want to admit what I was thinking. I didn't want to admit what I could've sworn I'd just seen on his face: he was nervous.

Once he'd made the steal and realized he was all alone, he slowed down to make sure he didn't make a mistake. But while that may have been prudent, it wasn't something Menkov normally would've done. As a rule, he never slowed down. But once he slowed down—even if it was only a slight alteration to his normal routine—it gave him a chance to think about what was happening. And when he thought about it, he missed the layup.

From the sideline, I didn't want to look at Branch, didn't want to confer with him on anything, and didn't want to acknowledge the uneasiness I now had rumbling around in my gut. We were still up by 16 points, but we'd just missed four easy shots in a row, the last one being the easiest of them all. There wasn't anything I could say from the sideline other than to encourage my team, but deep down, I wondered how they'd react to a missed layup from our best player, something I know had to be unsettling to them all.

Coming back down the floor, Spanish was the team to react first. Using a high pick and roll between the point guard and power forward, the point guard pulled up for a contested three-point shot, a shot he'd already tried several times. But this time it went in. I saw him pump his fist in approval, and couldn't help but notice the contrast. We'd missed a wide-open layup, and they'd come back down and hit a guarded three-pointer.

On the other end of the floor, Spanish did something that shocked me more than any shot they could've made: they switched out of their zone—a zone that had been highly ineffective all game long—and started playing man-to-man defense. Though I started calling this out immediately from the bench, our players didn't react well, and still stood in their normal zone offense positions. Without any movement, and far too little recognition of the defense, Kosio threw an errant pass that was stolen. The 2-on-1 fast break the other way resulted in a Spanish layup. The lead was quickly cut to 11. I called a timeout immediately.

"Just relax, just relax," I said right away, talking to my team but also talking to myself. "So they made a couple shots and we missed a couple shots—so what? That's gonna happen, and it's not a big deal. Now they're playing man-to-man defense, so we need to run our motion offense. Let's get the ball inside and get a good look this time down the floor, and remember, we're going to win this game with our defense."

Based on our most recent performances on offense, I knew that defense might be the only thing we could count on. But after breaking the huddle, the quick breather seemed to have made a difference. With cutting and moving on offense, a hole opened up for Ivan to dribble to the basket and finish with a layup. The crowd, the bench, Branch and I all cheered in unison. We were back on track. Things were going to be all right.

On the other end, though, Spanish found their power forward quickly on the baseline. With a right-hand dribble, he powered toward the baseline, sensing he had a mismatch against Vassy. But while Vassy was smaller, he was quick. As the power forward attempted to get around him on the baseline, Vassy slammed his foot down on the line and prepared to absorb the blow. The power forward had committed to this move, and had no choice. He bowled over Vassy. I was already prepared for my next fist-pump, thrilled Vassy had drawn a textbook offensive foul. Even the Spanish power forward seemed to expect this, as he slowed down almost to a halt after Vassy crashed to the floor.

But there was no whistle.

The Spanish power forward looked at Vassy lying beneath him, deftly stepped around him, and laid the ball in the basket. Branch and I were aghast at the no-call. How could one player be completely knocked to the ground and the referee not call anything? The referee from the baseline started wagging his finger in our direction before either of us had uttered a complete or intelligible thought.

"Dammit!" Branch yelled, probably more to me than anyone else, "How can they not call that? It's so obvious."

At the other end, it seemed that our offense might've been dazed by the lack of call as well. With little movement in our motion offense, Menkov resorted to shooting an ill-advised three-pointer that wasn't even close to the rim. In a move that signified, *Let me show you how it's done*, their point guard raced the other way, pulled up behind the three-point line and swished his three-pointer. The score was now 51-43. Our lead had shrunk to eight. This was a blowout no longer.

At the other end of the floor, Pesho did what Pesho did best—he played volleyball with several rebounds and missed shots. The culmination was worth it, though. He grabbed the final rebound and scored. But as Spanish was coming back the other way, it seemed like I was watching a video replay of what had happened only a minute ago. Unable to find space for another three-pointer, the point guard fanned his dribble to the wing and started heading for the baseline. Once again, though, we were the first to the baseline and Menkov established position. He was run over by the out-of-control Spanish point guard. The whistle blew. Menkov was called for the blocking foul.

"I told you, Coach," Pavel quipped from the bench. "I told you these refs hate us."

Menkov first looked at me as if to say, "What am I supposed to do?" and then I looked at the referees with the same look of amazement. These were easy charging calls, and I couldn't believe they were missing them time after time.

"How am I supposed to teach taking a charge," I yelled in English with plenty of futility to the referees, knowing it wouldn't be understood, "if you refuse to call it?"

Menkov now had four fouls, and I opted to go the same route I had before. I sent Pavel in for Vassy, and told him to guard the Spanish point guard. On the next possession it didn't matter, though, because Spanish inbounded the ball down low and scored on an athletic, twisting shot. Our lead was down to six. Our problems were compounded when we came down the floor on offense, and Kosio immediately threw the ball out of bounds.

"Calm down, just calm down," I pleaded. "Just focus on your defense and we'll be fine."

I felt I had little choice but to say this because if we started thinking about how bad our offense was right now, we'd be in big trouble.

Thankfully, the focus did return to defense, though, and for the next two minutes, Spanish did not score. Unable to get a charge called if our lives depended on it, we still moved our feet and stayed in front of their best players, forcing them into difficult shots. They didn't make any of them. At the other end, though, the problem wasn't our shooting. We actually didn't take any shots. That's because we seemed to have forgotten how to pass and catch the ball. Pesho threw a pass at Pavel's feet that went between his legs and out of bounds. Menkov simply dropped a pass from Ivan that went out of bounds. And once again, Kosio threw a pass to no one in particular that harmlessly trickled out of bounds.

"We're panicking, we're really panicking," Branch whispered in my ear.

But as he said it, our defensive intensity continued to be ratcheted up. Menkov deflected another pass and garnered another steal—at least his fifth of the game—and led a fast break the other way. It was a 3-on-1 break and he made a bounce pass to Pavel for what appeared to be a wide-open layup. Pavel hesitated, though, and allowed the defender to recover to him. By the time he attempted the layup, he was fouled by the Spanish defender. Going to the free throw line, he badly missed the first, wide left and off the backboard. Thankfully, he found some gumption and accuracy at the right time, and precariously rolled the second one in. The scoreboard read 52-45 with three and a half minutes to play.

Knowing that defense would win us this game, I pounded on the floor, encouraging our team to stay in position and be disciplined. This time, though, that discipline fell apart. Running the same high pick-and-roll, neither Pavel nor Pesho communicated and this resulted in them both staying with the power forward who had set the pick. This left the point guard wide open at the top of the key. He hesitated, shocked he was so open, and then lifted up for another three-pointer. I'd hoped that his hesitation, like Menkov's earlier, would cause him to think too much and alter his rhythm. But that didn't happen. He drained the three-pointer, and put both of his arms up in the air. The lead was down to four.

Before I could even yell, "It's okay. Just be patient on offense," Kosio took the ball on the wing and dribbled the ball off his foot out of bounds. Two decisions were now staring me in the face and both were obvious: with Kosio's third turnover in the last three minutes he had to come out of the game, and I had to call a timeout to try to settle our team down.

I thought about all the times I'd told them to relax, just play and have fun, but it seemed to me that none of that was working. The scoreboard read 52-48. That meant we'd been outscored 15-3 already in the fourth quarter. Our defense hadn't been bad, but offensively, we looked terrified. We looked jittery, nervous and afraid–and this was the worst possible time for this to happen. So many times already during this quarter I'd indicated that calming down was the key, but this clearly wasn't happening. As the team approached me in the huddle where I was squatted down, I sensed far too much defeat in their drooping eyes and worried brows.

"We're going to win this game," I declared with vigor.

There wasn't much response, either audible or from body language.

"Did you hear me? Did you hear me?"

This time, there was a mix of subdued head-shakes and nods.

"We're going to win this game," I shouted, pounding my clipboard with my marker for emphasis. "I don't want to draw anything up for you on this clipboard; I want you to believe what I'm saying. We're going to win this game! We're going to win this *fucking* game!"

With this added swear word—one I rarely ever used—I saw Pesho crack a smile, something I was hoping would happen.

"Stop worrying about losing the damn game and play it like you're going to win it!"

Branch patted me on the back as the team headed back out to the floor.

"I liked that," he said. "I think they needed that."

"I don't know what we need," I replied honestly, "but I feel like I'm trying everything to find it."

On Spanish's next possession, our defense returned to its aggressive form, but their power forward dropped in a nifty left-handed hook. The lead was down to two. But Menkov took the ball the other way, and finally looked like the man who wouldn't be denied once again. He scored in the lane to re-establish our lead. The score was 54-50. At the other end, it seemed like the same thing was happening once again, as the power forward made a beautiful move but was still forced into a difficult shot. The shot still looked perfect but bounced in and trickled out. Pesho yanked the rebound out of mid-air and started running the other way. Dribbling amidst my continued shouts of "Get it to Menkov! Get it to Menkov!" Pesho was oblivious and recklessly dribbled the ball into the lane. Fortunate for us, though, the Spanish defenders were startled by Pesho's desperate charge to the hoop, and bailed him out by slapping him across the arms as he went up for a ridiculous fadeaway jumper. He made one of two at the line, and our lead was five again.

Then their point guard hit another three. There wasn't much I could do or say about this. Menkov had switched over to guard him and had a hand right in his face, but in this fourth quarter, it didn't seem to matter. Determined not to let him have the spotlight alone in the fourth quarter, Menkov got the ball from Ivan at the other end, and tossed in a floater that banked off the backboard at a perfect angle. 57-53. There were only two minutes left to play.

Forced to pay even more attention to their point guard on the high pick-and-roll, the power forward was the recipient of a nice pass that led him in for a layup. When the shot went up, I couldn't believe it. He'd missed the easiest shot he'd taken all game. But then, the one thing that had rarely happened all day occurred: we didn't get the rebound. The power forward slid to the other side of the hoop and finished with his right hand.

At the other end, Pesho was determined to make up for this, but unwisely dribbled into a crowd and lost the ball–probably our 10th turnover of the fourth quarter. Coming back the other way, the crowd was loud on both sides. It was a two-point game with under a minute to play. This time, when the power forward got the ball on the wing, he faked the baseline drive, but was then content to loft a 15-foot jump shot over Pesho that hit nothing but net. The game was now tied.

Feeling like I was more emotionally exhausted than the players were physically exhausted, I called a timeout with 41 seconds left to play and the scoreboard showing a score of 57-57. The last time the score was tied, it was 0-0. There was no point, though, I'd decided, in talking about the 16-point lead we'd squandered. All that mattered now was what happened in these last 41 seconds.

"You can't think about what's happened up to this point. You just have to think about what's going to happen now. We've got 41 seconds left to win this game. Don't freak out, and don't worry. We're not losing; it's just tied. And we've got the ball and we're going to score. Here's how we're going to do it."

I drew a rough sketch of the play we wanted to run, and knowing that our lack of basketball intelligence always created hiccups along the way, I included two or three alternate options for the play. When we headed back out onto the floor, I hoped the team couldn't sense that my confidence was shaken. It felt like just a few moments ago we had a 16-point lead and now suddenly this game looked like it was all over. Now the game was tied.

Menkov brought the ball up slowly, and Pesho stepped out to set a high screen for him. As I'd expected, Spanish focused all their attention on Menkov, double-teaming him immediately. This left Pesho open, rolling to the basket exactly as I'd told him to do. As I watched the play unravel in the slow motion, I couldn't help but think that Pesho picked the best time ever to actually listen to what I wanted him to do. He caught the pass from Menkov at the elbow, took one power dribble and elevated for his shot. Everything about this play was perfect.

But Pesho missed the shot.

It caromed hard off the backboard and was soon lost in a scrum of outstretched hands. No sooner was I lamenting Pesho's miss, though, than I saw Vassy miraculously wrestle the ball out of the crowd. He leaned back toward the hoop and let loose a left-handed baby hook shot.

This shot missed, too.

Then it was back to the mad scramble in the lane for the next rebound. The crowd was vibrating, yelling and pleading with each new opportunity, and I felt like I could just listen to them to find out what happened. If we scored, I knew there'd be a roar. If we didn't, I wasn't sure I even wanted to hear the groan.

But we weren't done yet. Pavel had sneaked in from his guard position to fight for the rebound. Seeing him in the middle of the floor made me realize that he'd better get the rebound or else we were screwed. Menkov was the only other player capable of getting back on defense quickly. But I knew Pavel had strength and courage unlike any other player on the floor. He grabbed the loose ball off the floor and hoisted up a shot of his own.

He missed.

The crowd groaned.

For a third time the rebound was loose, and for the third time, our players would not give up. The ball ended up back where it started. Pesho ripped the rebound off the backboard and elevated to try to finish this once and for all. A Spanish player came down on his arm, and I heard the whistle blow. We all watched as the ball trickled toward the basket and just rolled off.

Pesho had missed again, but this time, he'd been fouled.

The entire crazy sequence—four missed shots and three offensive rebounds—left everyone in the gym gasping for air. There were now 18 seconds left, the game was tied, and Pesho stood at the free throw line.

I knew this was an opportunity for us to take the lead, and also knew that Pesho was actually one of our better free throw shooters. But as he stood at the line, pretending to be loose and unaffected by the pressure, I didn't look at him as a freakishly athletic 6'4" Bulgarian wild man. I looked at him as a boy whose parents had just been divorced. He was a boy who was having one of the roughest weeks of his life. Pesho was already dealing with so much—and so much that he would never admit was bothering him—and now there was this added pressure, too.

Please, oh please, make the first free throw.

The first free throw clanged off the rim and bounced away harmlessly.

There were cheers from Spanish bench that I knew would turn into taunts if he missed another one. I kept calling out to Pesho, wanting to let him know that he was okay, he was going to make this one, but he never turned to look at me. I wondered if he didn't want me to see the nervous look on his face. Quite honestly, I didn't want to see the nervous look on his face either.

As he rose up for the second free throw, time, motion and sound were all suspended. All that mattered was the fate of the fluttering orange ball as it rotated its way toward the hoop. The noise that followed was all anyone needed in order to know what happened: loud cheering.

He made the second free throw.

The entire gym simultaneously snapped out of the free throw daze, realizing that Spanish now had the ball, down by one point, and was heading the other way. They didn't have any timeouts remaining and neither did we. The clock ticked down under 15 seconds as their point guard crossed half court. Menkov was determined to move his feet, stay in a stance and keep the point guard in front of him. Just in case he wasn't, I barked this over and over again, urging him like I'd done for two years of practices and games.

The Spanish point guard seemed content to take his time, and let the clock run down to 10 seconds. I expected the power forward to come out and set a high pick-and-roll, and was instructing Pesho on how to defend it. But the power forward seemed glued to his place in the corner.

Then the point guard made his move. Faking to the right, he crossed over to the left and made his way inside the three-point line. Menkov was right on his hip, but a quarter step behind because of the good crossover move. Pavel stuck his hand in to distract the point guard, but it didn't seem to make much of a difference. Menkov continued to slide his feet as the point guard neared the left block. Pesho sagged in from his man and put both his hands straight up in the air. As the point guard left the floor to attempt his final shot, I knew we were in trouble. He'd gained just enough leverage on both Menkov and Pesho that he would have a clear shot at the basket from about four feet away. This was exactly what happened.

As he floated the ball up toward the basket, I watched in amazement as I realized right away that he'd missed the shot short. It hit the backboard first, and then quickly clanked off the iron. The ball bounded to his left, and Pesho grabbed it immediately.

And that's when the whistle blew.

The whistle blew after he'd taken the shot, and just as everyone on our sideline was about to celebrate a defensive stop and a rebound. The whistle blew just as all of us thought we had won the game. The whistle blew and the referee pointed at Menkov, and indicated he'd fouled the point guard.

The ensuing reaction was swift and incredulous from a variety of sources. Menkov yelled first, then Branch, then me. But all the yelling in the world didn't seem to matter. It was a late call, it was a bad call, it was a call that could outrageously decide the game, but it was the call that was made.

The Spanish point guard looked over at our bench and released a sly grin, indicating he knew he'd gotten away with one. First off, he missed a very makeable shot—one of the easiest he'd had the whole game—and now he was being bailed out by an exceptionally late whistle for a phantom foul.

I tried to keep my nerves in check and looked at the clock. There were six seconds remaining, and I immediately tried to tell myself that the odds of him making both free throws weren't necessarily great. Under less pressure, Pesho had just made one of two. Now there was much more pressure, and their point guard would have to make both free throws to win the game.

Before I could wonder and predict what would happen with the free throws, though, I had another pressing issue: the foul was Menkov's fifth. He'd played the entire game in foul trouble, and played one of his greatest games in the process, but now with six seconds left and our season on the line, he had to come out.

"Coach, I'm sorry," he said as he stumbled his way to the bench for the final time.

I didn't know if he was sorry for fouling out or sorry for yelling at the referees after he'd fouled out, but either way, the last thing in the world I ever wanted him to feel was sorry.

"Don't ever apologize for this game, Menkov. Don't ever apologize for the effort you put into it," I told him.

Looking out at the floor, we now had no one who could confidently and quickly dribble the ball, and no one who I'd call highly capable of getting us a good last shot in a hurry. Kosio was the only player on the bench with any semblance of offensive talent, so I sent him in the game. Seeing the lineup we had in the game—Kosio, Pavel, Ivan, Vassy and Pesho—I knew I needed to think about what to do if he hit both free throws, but I started praying he'd miss at least one.

He made the first free throw.

With this, I started instructing the players on the floor, blatantly yelling in English because I knew the Spanish players most likely wouldn't understand my English directions anyway. On a made shot, I yelled, Pesho needed to get down to the opposite three-point line to receive a pass. He was the only player on the floor who had the ability to create his own shot and would be able to shoot it over defenders—even if he ended up fading away. Pesho understood what I was saying, and now I just told all of them to box out. We'd done so many box-out drills in two years, I hoped like crazy that we'd have one last chance to box out and grab the missed free throw, and save our season.

But we didn't. The Spanish point guard swished home the second free throw, and jubilation broke out on their sideline.

Pesho took off for the other end, and Ivan grabbed the ball out of the net and threw it in to Kosio. I screamed for him to fire the ball down the floor to Pesho, but the minute he started dribbling his head was down. He never saw Pesho.

Kosio crossed half court, spun left and found a defender waiting for him. Then he spun right—right into another defender. With time about to run out, he had no choice but to launch a 30-foot prayer over four arms raised to defend against him.

For a brief moment, the optimist in me thought this would be the most remarkable finish to our biggest game, and I watched the ball soar toward the hoop dreaming it would go in.

But that was just optimism.

Only in my dreams would the shot go in.

The ball ricocheted hard off the backboard and never even hit the rim. The horn sounded. The game was over.

With six seconds left to go in the semifinal game, Spanish took their first lead of the game, 59-58. It was the only lead they'd ever need.

The ball and the horn came crashing down at the same time, and players spilled all over the floor. The Spanish players were dancing and celebrating, and ours were falling to their knees, devastated. I looked on in shock, each one of my different emotions about to spiral down from a precipice. I decided anger might be the most appropriate emotion because I couldn't grasp how any of this seemed fair.

I wanted to do all the things I'd seen in the last two years at the end of Bulgarian basketball games. I wanted to kick water bottles onto the floor, throw our bench out there, too, swear at the referees and storm out of the gym so that everyone would see.

But I knew none of this would make a difference. My knees felt weak, and I just wobbled on the sideline, slowly coming to the realization that in the biggest game in the lives of my players—and what I now knew was the biggest game of my life—we'd lost.

By one point.

Chapter XXVIII
Lachoni's

"Coach, they're ready for you. You can go talk to them if you want."

Branch was pointing over to the bleachers that the fans had vacated, and where our team was sitting glumly, dutifully waiting for the post-game speech. I understood what Branch was saying, but I didn't know if I was capable of talking right now. I'd just been pacing back and forth, picking players up off the ground and trying to ignore the Spanish celebration. For the first time in my two years as a Bulgarian coach, I had no idea if our players had shaken the hands of our opponents. I had little idea about anything other than the fact that we'd lost.

I didn't want to face the team, didn't want to see their disappointment or anger, and more than anything, I didn't want it to be all over. I had no idea how the team would react to something like this because, quite honestly, it wasn't supposed to end this way. It wasn't supposed to end with three quarters of our best basketball in two years followed by an utter collapse in the fourth quarter. The effort had been there from the opening tip to the final horn, and had never wavered. I had little doubt that each player out on the floor had put forth the greatest basketball effort of his life, which was exactly what I'd asked for. But when it had mattered most, while our effort didn't falter, we tightened up and got nervous. When it mattered most, we missed layups and forgot how to pass the basketball, throwing passes at ankles, and others straight out of bounds. And as the coach who had told them this would be the year we won the ACS Open, I felt like it was all my fault. Whether there was any basis for this feeling or not, I felt I had let them down. I walked slowly over to the bleachers, trying to compose myself, and trying to think of what to say. When I picked my head up and looked at my team, most of their heads were down, and this sprung me into action.

"Please lift your heads up and look at me," I said firmly. "You have nothing to be ashamed of, and I won't let you hang your heads over this."

Heads started slowly rising, and I saw the reason that so many heads were down. They were committing the ultimate taboo for Bulgarian men: some of them were crying. This didn't help me maintain my composure.

"Sometimes in life—sometimes in life," I faltered as I tried to get going, "you do everything you can, you try as hard as you absolutely can..."

I felt my throat scratching and the tears starting to well, and tried to slow down.

"You do everything in the world you possibly can—and you still lose."

I had to pause again to fight back tears.

"And when that happens, it's one of the worst feelings you can ever have. Because when you put everything you have into something, you don't expect to lose. You expect to win."

Now I realized my speech was coming out stammered, and tears were streaming down my face.

"Tonight, you made me so proud. You played so hard, and you played—you played so well."

There were a few fresh tears dripping to the bleachers, and many of the heads that I'd asked to be held up had already drooped down again.

"I'm so, so proud of you. And I'm so, so sorry. I thought you deserved to win, and I thought you would win—and we didn't."

I wanted to continue talking and explain how basketball related to life, and how all of our effort still meant something even if we didn't win, but I couldn't. I couldn't stop thinking about the fact that we lost. When Branch put his hand on my shoulder, I realized I'd been silent—

except for choking on my own tears—for several moments.

"Thank you guys so much for this. I'm so proud of you for how hard you played, and how you played as a team—and, and I'm so sorry you didn't win."

I couldn't speak any more if I tried. My head went down to try to cover some of my own tears. I'd never felt like this after a basketball game in my entire life.

The rest of that Wednesday night was a blur. In the literal sense, my vision was foggy as a permanent mist settled over my eyes, and in the figurative sense, nothing else seemed to matter anymore. Once the players left the bubble, I slowly made my way out as well. On this night, I didn't notice how the moonlight was reflecting on the ominous row house overhead, and while I'm sure the stray dogs were yelping all through the night, I didn't hear them. I walked home in my own version of tortured silence.

We'd come so close.

That night, the next day, and for years to come, I'd replay the game in my head. So many times I'd want to think about the first three quarters—the best three quarters we'd ever played—but my mind couldn't fool itself to move away from what happened in the last quarter. The barrage of threes from the Spanish point guard, Menkov's missed layup, Kosio's errant passes, Pesho's missed free throw, the last phantom foul call—those images reverberated over and over. I tried to put the game in perspective, and keep in mind that it was just a basketball game. In the bigger picture of life, I'd experienced so much more in Bulgaria that was so far beyond basketball—from learning about Bulgarian Roma to surviving the Russian heat crisis—but still, this moment, this one game seemed to trump all of that. I had no perspective on anything other than the basketball game.

Looking back, I was certain that I'd probably coached games of a larger magnitude in the past, and I was fairly certain I'd coach even bigger games in the future. But without a doubt in my mind, I knew I'd never coached a game that mattered more—and never would in the future either. Whether I was coaching in the States or in Bulgaria, I'd experienced plenty of losing, and plenty of times I'd taken those losses personally. But somehow this game was different. The loss didn't hurt me personally because I had lost the game. It didn't matter that much to me for my own personal sense of satisfaction. But how the players felt meant everything to me.

I'd spent two years preaching about the values of hard work and teamwork. I'd spent two years telling them that even if we had bad games, even if we got dunked on, even if we had neo-Nazi elbows bloody our noses, even if we endured classless half-court celebrations, it would all be worth it in the end. In the end, our hard work, our dignity, our class and our teamwork would prove to be the most important things of all. And I truly believed that all of that would lead to us winning our final tournament. It would have been vindication for all the struggles, and proof that there was a different way of doing things in Bulgaria. We could break the mold, and create more meaning and pride than any of us ever thought possible.

But in the end, we'd lost by one point.

I didn't want to focus on the loss because I still thought all these other values, and everything we'd accomplished for two years should matter much more than the final scoreboard. I'd even told my team that I didn't care what the score was at the end of the game as long as they'd played their hearts out. I learned the minute the horn sounded that while I didn't know it at the time, I was lying. I wanted us to win more than anything.

I wanted us to win more than anything because I was so worried about how our entire basketball experience would be viewed if we didn't win. I'd entered Bulgaria with my basketball players telling me that they were expected to lose, and I never wanted them to have that attitude. I'd dealt with the pessimistic and fatalistic reactions after losses, and these were so much more crushing than the losses themselves. They lived in the ultimate underdog country—one of the smallest and poorest in Europe, and one that had few historical examples of glorious victories. Losing seemed to be imbedded in the culture. I'd been reminded time and time again that *Coach, this is Bulgaria. We are used to this sort of thing.* I'd spent two years trying to ensure we weren't used to losing. I'd spent two years trying to convince an entire team that regardless of the outcomes of the games, we could still be winners. I believed fervently in everything I'd been teaching them, but I also knew it was a hard sell. My players wanted results; they wanted to win. I knew we'd made progress in ability and attitude all throughout my two years, but now in one ghastly fourth quarter, I wondered how much damage was done. I didn't think I could stomach Menkov telling me that he felt like a loser, or Pavel saying that even though he'd learned a lot, it still didn't make a difference. We still lost and that was what mattered most.

440

Branch and I tried to re-hash the fourth quarter and figure out where things went wrong, but we soon came to the conclusion that there was little reason to try to pinpoint our exact downfall. There was one blanket statement that would cover the entire fourth quarter, and Branch indicated it.

"We got scared," he said simply. "We'd spent so much time focused on this goal, and then when we had it right in our grasp, we got scared to actually achieve it."

"And all this time," I continued, "I'd been so scared about us accepting losing as the way things were. It turns out we were more scared of winning."

The Spanish school had more talent than we did, and in the fourth quarter, this proved to be deadly. But even with the superior basketball talent resting in the hands our opponent, this shouldn't have been what did us in. And it wasn't. We were outscored 26-9 in the fourth quarter, and any number of the easy shots we missed would've put us through to the championship game. But instead, our season was over.

Our season was over, but we had one last gathering as a team. Branch and I had scheduled a team dinner for the night after the semifinals, which was also the night before the championship game—a game we thought we'd be playing in. Two weeks previous, we'd explained the idea of the team dinner to celebrate our season to the players, and they responded agreeably to the idea of having this celebration. When I'd told them what night we'd be having the dinner, I also told them we'd be having one last meal together to prepare for the next night's championship game. Branch and I had both agreed that we needed to have the dinner before the season was over for one very important reason: if the dinner was after the season—as would be tradition with every other team we'd been associated with in the past— we weren't sure the players would show up. But if it was part of the season, we felt much more confident that everyone would be there.

But now the season was over, and I already began to dread the dinner. I didn't want to wonder if they'd show up, and if they did, I didn't want to face the players' disappointment, their glum looks, their fatalism, or even their anger. When I'd told them they had no reason to hang their heads because they'd tried their hardest, I'd meant it. They had no reason to hang their heads, but I feared that they would. Spanish had whooped it up in the middle of the floor, and they wouldn't remember the first three quarters of the game. As much as I tried to remember the glory of the first three quarters of the game, I was having trouble doing this, too.

At school that day, none of the players came to see me in my classroom. I didn't know if this was a good sign or a bad sign, but it was probably for the best. Like me, they were probably sorting through all of their emotions in the same way I was.

"Do you think they're going to come to the dinner tonight?" I asked Branch after school.

"I don't know," he said shakily. "It's hard to tell. I mean, I hope they all come. They should come."

As much as I knew I was going to have difficulty talking to them about our last game, I hoped they would come, too. There were things I didn't want to talk about, but knew that we should anyway. Just after the subject of our total collapse in the semifinal game was covered, I had to deliver the next bombshell: I needed to tell them that I wouldn't be returning next year.

I had signed a two-year contract before first arriving in Bulgaria, and was offered the chance to stay at least another year if I wanted to. When I'd left the States, one of the most difficult parts of leaving was wondering how much I would miss being an American basketball coach. And when I decided in early winter that I was going to leave Bulgaria–to attempt a new adventure in Ecuador–I was shocked by how I felt like I was in the same situation I had been in two years ago. I thought about Pavel, Pesho, Ivan and Sasho–all juniors with one more year to play–and didn't even want to think about how much I'd miss being a Bulgarian basketball coach.

But I didn't let any of my players know I'd be leaving. They were used to being at an international school where teachers came and went at two, three, and four-year intervals. They were even relatively accustomed to teachers who freaked out in Bulgaria and didn't make it to Thanksgiving of their first year. Whenever they asked me, though, about my future, I told them I didn't know. I'd decided I didn't want it to be a distraction, and I never wanted the focus to be on me anyway. But now at our last team dinner, the last time we'd be together, I knew I now had to tell them I was leaving.

Branch and I were the first to arrive at Lachoni's, our favorite neighborhood restaurant that was famous to us for its drippy cheese pizzas and delicious Bulgarian *shopska* salads. Lachoni's was just a good stone's throw from the school's gate and a popular hangout for anyone who lived in the neighborhood, or anyone who went to ACS. It had an outdoor patio that uniquely functioned all year round, with intense heat lamps gushing out warm air in the winter, with industrial strength cellophane providing protection from the wind. Lachoni's was the first restaurant I ever went to in Bulgaria, and had been the site of some of my most memorable nights with friends–both American and Bulgarian. I first learned about the Bulgarian head-shake for yes at Lachoni's and would argue that Lachoni's waitresses had perfected the art of the bobblehead version of this consenting head-shake.

Lachoni's had even been the site of an American colleague's rendezvous with his Bulgarian landlord after he'd moved out of his apartment one month early, certain that if he moved out on time, he'd never see his security deposit–one month's rent–again. He'd asked three of us to join him at Lachoni's, concerned that when his landlord showed up to pick up the keys to the now-vacated apartment, he'd bring some of his friends–some muscle, as my colleague referred to it– to make him suffer for daring to try to keep the security deposit from the apartment he'd left in perfect condition.

"I just have a really bad feeling about this," he had told me, "and I would feel a lot better about it if you guys were there."

"So you're saying," I replied, looking at my scrawny arms, and realizing that I was bigger than the two other guys he had asked to join him, "that you want us to be there just in case something goes wrong– horribly wrong?"

"Yeah, basically that's it."

That night, I joined my colleague on what I felt was a doomsday mission. Our purpose was to be there out of friendship, and none of us hesitated to say that we'd go–but we all also knew that the only reason we were there was in case something went wrong. And when something went wrong in a situation like this in Bulgaria, that meant there was going to be a fight.

On that doomsday occasion, my colleague's landlord did show up with other people–or muscle–as my colleague had predicted. But as the four of us braced ourselves for the worst, his landlord showed up with just one person–his wife. After the exchange of keys, we all dug into our pizzas and enjoyed a good laugh over the whole affair.

As Branch and I sat at a long table in the outdoor patio, the clear plastic hanging over the patio was blustering in the March breeze, and I felt like I was bracing myself once again. There wasn't going to be a fight this time, but on a night that I'd intended to be a special and meaningful capper to our season, I wasn't sure if any of the players were going to show up. I didn't know if this would be my actual doomsday mission to Lachoni's.

But it turned out that my concerns were unfounded. Menkov and Kosio emerged through the doorway first, and this started an avalanche of players appearing in twos and threes for the dinner. Much to my surprise–delighted surprise–there were smiles on their faces. Pesho, whose smile had been elusive for a while now, seemed to be his normal self as he punched Pavel in the shoulder and dared him to strike back. Vassy, so often the one with a chip on his shoulder, the one who was eager to defend his pride, didn't look affected by last night's game at all. He joked with Kosio as they both predicted how much Sasho would eat at the dinner. Sasho, to his credit, stood up for himself and indicated that he'd eat far more than either of them predicted.

As I scanned the funky outdoor-but-not-quite-outdoor patio, I started to feel pressure release from my shoulders and neck. Not only had everyone showed up, but they seemed to be in good spirits, too.

"You know what," Branch leaned over and said to me, "it's really good we did this. It's really good that we had this dinner."

Looking out at the smiling faces, I definitely agreed with him.

"I just don't think," Branch kept going, "I just don't think they've had a team dinner like this to celebrate a season–any kind of season."

"Especially not," I laughed in response, "after we just lost our biggest game."

Somehow saying it and having it accompanied by a laugh was wonderfully therapeutic–and not just for me, but for Branch, too. But still, I wondered, was a convivial dinner going to be therapy enough for our players?

After everyone had ordered various versions of pizza–and varying amounts that made me yearn for the carefree, enormous appetite I had as a teenager–I started the official portion of the dinner by handing out awards for our season. We'd had the players vote on several different awards, and created laminated certificates to honor those who won. Sasho won Most Improved Player, Pavel won Best Hustle, and in a landslide, Menkov won MVP. With each new award that was handed out, my enthusiasm started to pick up. Even if we'd lost the night before, there were a whole host of winners–award-winners–currently scarfing down pizza, smiling and laughing.

I'd told the seniors that they'd have a chance to speak at this final dinner if they wanted to say something to the rest of their teammates.

I'd hoped they would jump at this opportunity, but also knew that the odds weren't necessarily high that anyone would want to speak, especially since they'd be speaking in English. And considering that their careers had just ended with a defeat that could only be understated as crushing, I didn't know what to expect. But as he'd done for two years without fail, Menkov stood up first.

"It's kind of hard to talk right now, thinking that it's all over," he said to everyone in English.

His words matched exactly how I'd felt for 24 hours, and how I feared I'd feel for many, many more hours after that.

"Last night was a great game, but last night we lost."

He was speaking slowly, trying to make sure he said exactly what he wanted to say. The way he accentuated *we lost* represented the sum of all my fears. No matter how great the game was, or no matter how great the season was, we lost. This was the final result. And now I was scared of what he was going to say next

But I shouldn't have been. Because what he said after that–and after that, and after that—showed me that all my greatest fears were unfounded. All the doubts I'd ever had about what we were doing as a team should've been shelved long ago. Menkov's speech was so much better than any speech I could've given, and while I'd cried the night before out of pain, the tears welling up in my eyes at Lachoni's had nothing to do with pain, and everything to do with pride. I became proud of Menkov, and proud of our team all over again.

"Last night, we lost, but that really doesn't matter. I'd love to be playing in the championship game tomorrow night, but that doesn't matter that much either. Because last night we played as a team. Last night, and all season long, all of us played so hard. We played together, and we had fun. And when the game ended last night, I was devastated because we lost. But when I got home, I started to think about why I was so depressed. And the truth is, I'd rather lose by one point in the semifinal game than play for any other team. I'd rather not play in the championship game if it means that I got to play with all of you, and that we were a team."

He paused here, and a fork dropping from a faraway table sounded clear as day.

"I love playing basketball, and I always used to think that I loved playing basketball because I wanted to win so badly. But what I learned was that it doesn't always matter if you win or lose. What matters is that I'm going to look back at my time as an ACS basketball player–and especially these last two years—and I'm going to have so many wonderful memories. I'm going to miss you guys so much."

In a culture where I knew males rarely expressed emotions outwardly like this, Menkov's speech was an anomaly. It was an anomaly that had captured everyone's undivided attention. Even Sasho had stopped eating pizza for this.

"Coach, thanks so much for these two years. I know that we learned so much, and I know we all wanted to win last night. I know you wanted to win, too. But I also know that what we all learned and shared together was so much more important than winning last night's game."

I was swallowing rapidly, trying not to cry. As a result, I felt unable to express any emotion with my face, and my lips became glued together in an attempt to hold in my own emotions.

"Thanks, Menkov," I said earnestly, "that was great."

I got up and gave him a hug.

Other seniors were clearly motivated by Menkov's speech, and I could see that they each wanted a turn to speak. The only time they mentioned the game from the night before—that dreaded game—was to say that that wasn't what they would remember from our season. They'd remember everything else—everything they learned together, every time they ached together, and every time we'd laughed together.

With one player to the next standing up and speaking about how much basketball had meant to him, and how much he enjoyed working hard and working together, I stopped feeling stunned. I stopped worrying that they'd been crushed by defeat. And I sat back and enjoyed how each of them had matured, and enjoyed thinking about how incredible our experience together had been these last two years. I'd always thought that I'd be able to convince them that all of their hard work, all those grueling practices and tough losses would be worth it once we finally won. But in those two years, we never really won anything. And on this night together at Lachoni's, I was being given reason after reason of why that didn't matter. Thoughts started shooting across my mind that would've been blasphemous a mere half-hour before: *Maybe it was okay that we lost the game. Maybe if we'd won I never would've heard speeches like this. Maybe if we'd won, the only lesson learned would've been that winning is great. Maybe if we'd won, the whole point of everything we'd done for two years would've been lost. Maybe we needed to lose to make this experience the most valuable.*

As speech after speech talked about the importance of the

experience, and how good it felt to know you played as hard as you could, and how much it mattered to be a part of the team, I couldn't believe how far we'd come in two years. I couldn't believe these were the same players who looked and sounded like they wanted to quit basketball because we'd lost two games in the ACS Open the year before. I tried to estimate just how far we'd come to get to this moment, but we'd come from too far for me to even quantify. So I had no choice but to just enjoy this moment.

Once the players were done speaking, I knew it was my turn to speak, and knew there was nothing I could say that would be more powerful than what had already been said by a steady stream of players, a steady stream of teammates. But I knew I couldn't avoid saying what I'd known all along: this was my last chance, my only chance to thank them, and tell them I was leaving. As I started speaking, I was alarmed by how nervous I was.

"This has meant so much to me for all the reasons you guys have just shared," I told them, "but even more because you welcomed me into your culture and were willing to believe in what we were all trying to do together.

"Last night after the game, I was really emotional," I said, realizing that I shouldn't use the past tense; I was still emotional. "I was emotional because I wanted for us—all of us—to win so badly. I wanted each of you to feel like all your hard work was worth it—that it paid off because we were going to be playing in the championship game against 35th. But I've told you many times that you'll be winners if you leave everything out on the court, and put every ounce of effort into the game. What I saw last night was a team that did exactly that. What I saw last night was a team full of winners.

"But I have to be honest, and being honest, I really wanted us to win last night because I wanted the season to end on a victory. I wanted the season to end on a victory because I won't be your coach next year."

Now the silence wasn't accompanied by forks dropping, but startled gasps instead.

"It's very difficult for me to leave you—each and every one of you—but I want you to know how much of an impact you've made on my life. And I want to thank you because I loved being your coach. No matter where I go in my career as a basketball coach, you will always be my team, and I will never forget what we've shared these last two years."

447

I felt like I could hear my own words and struggled to find any way to see them as not clichéd. Every word I was speaking was sincere, and I was even shocked by the levels that sincerity carried me. I was shocked that an experience—being a Bulgarian basketball coach—that could drive me up a wall and push me to my furthest limits of patience and understanding, could also be something that meant so much, and was so rewarding. I was shocked that there had been some days when I'd come home after practices or games thinking that it was too difficult, too challenging, that I wanted to quit, and now I was realizing that all other experiences as a basketball coach paled in comparison to this one. There was no easy way to say goodbye in this situation, and no matter what culture I was dealing with, I had no idea if any of my words were coming out right.

I could tell that my words, though, were making a difference. When I finished speaking, the team sat awkwardly and clapped, but I sensed many of them weren't sure what they were clapping for. They didn't seem to want to clap to celebrate my departure. I underestimated them in many ways, and that night, I learned that I never should've underestimated them in any way.

I didn't expect their speeches to get to the heart of the message I'd been driving at for two years—and then some. I didn't expect player after player to talk about the importance of hard work and teamwork. I didn't expect any of them to say they'd rather lose and be on this team than win and be on another. And I didn't expect they'd be that affected by the announcement that I was leaving. Teachers and coaches at international schools leave, and they knew that perhaps better than anyone. But as I looked halfway down the long table, Pesho's face was becoming permanently etched into my memory.

He'd entered the restaurant punching Pavel in the shoulder, then engaged in a pizza-eating contest with Sasho, and I fully expected that if he wanted to thank me for coaching him, he would come through on his promise to buy me a Bulgarian prostitute. This was Pesho, and I'd dealt with his antics for two years. But as I said that I wouldn't be coming back to coach them next year, his shoulders sagged. He stopped eating pizza. He stopped making jokes. He stared down aimlessly at the table in front of him.

As the dinner wrapped up and players slowly matriculated out into the March Bulgarian rain, Pesho's sullen and defeated expression hadn't changed. His father had just moved out of the house and his basketball coach was leaving him for good.

I went up to Pesho and put my arm around his neck.

"Pesho, thank you so much. You have to know that working with you these two years has meant so much to me," I told him.

"Yeah, yeah, yeah, Coach, I know. For me, too."

Once again, when it came to matters of the heart, I could tell Pesho didn't want to discuss matters of the heart. He was a proud Bulgarian male, and these types of conversations were still off-limits. I kept talking to him, trying to reassure him that he was going to be fine, and that I was sorry that I was leaving. I knew my words sounded hollow to a 16-year-old kid, but I didn't know what else to do. He finally responded in a nature fitting to Pesho, and I at least knew he'd reverted to his old self, at least a little bit.

"Coach you know me, I'm tough. I'm tough, Coach. I'll be fine."

With the light shining off his buzzed head, and his broad shoulders perking up to display this toughness, I couldn't help but think how every aspect of Pesho's hulking Eastern European physical nature would've scared the living daylights out of me before I moved to Bulgaria. But as I looked at Pesho, who was now determined to smile, and gave him a hug, there wasn't an ounce of intimidation included in our affection for each other.

"This has been one helluva night," Branch said as we both stepped back for a moment.

"It's been one helluva season," I replied.

"Yeah, you know, you just can't compare a season coaching Bulgarian basketball to anything else, can you?"

"No," I beamed reflectively. "You certainly can't."

The Lachoni's patio was now nearly empty, but I could see Pavel was hanging back, saying goodbye to teammates, but still not leaving. As he said goodbye to Vassy and Kosio, he then turned and walked up to me. Unlike Pesho—and unlike most of his teammates—Pavel bucked the Bulgarian trend, and had no trouble expressing his emotions. That's how I knew when he walked up to me that he was going to give me a hug before even saying anything.

"Coach, I don't know if you remember," Pavel said slowly after we released from our embrace, "but on your very first day as coach—our first day of open gym—I was the first one to come up to you to talk to you. I was the first one you met. Do you remember that?"

Though the two years had been filled with more stories than I ever thought I could remember, I remembered Pavel coming up to me at the first open gym like it happened yesterday.

"Of course I remember, Pavel. You were the first one–and maybe the only one–who wanted to talk to me."

Pavel grinned broadly, thrilled I'd acknowledged the importance of this memory for both of us.

"I left open gym that day," he continued, "so excited for basketball. I just couldn't wait for the season to start. I couldn't wait for you to be our coach."

"Thanks, Pavel. It was so wonderful to be your coach."

"I just remember that moment–I just remember that moment because something told me right there that we were going to start something special."

"Well, Pavel," I said with a smile, "how'd we do?"

Pavel's smile in return was even bigger.

"We did great, Coach. We did great."

When I walked home alone from Lachoni's, I didn't mind the rain. I'd made this same walk in the rain during basketball season so many times that it almost would've seemed wrong for it not to be raining. I walked slowly, absorbing the light rain and soaking in everything that had happened that night. I soon realized I was doing even more than just that: I was trying to soak in everything that had happened in two years. There was no way, I thought, that I could ever walk slow enough for that.

I'd arrived in Bulgaria on a sunny August afternoon, riding in a van that crossed through a gate with armed guards, as stray dogs chased after its spinning wheels. I'd been introduced to my new home, a school campus with wildly-growing grass, dwarfed by giant concrete slab row houses on its perimeter. My first impression of Bulgaria was nothing short of amazement.

I was now working on my last impressions, from Menkov's speech to Pesho's toughness to Pavel's hug. I thought about a fascinating and bizarre country, but mostly about a group of kids I was so proud to call my team. I approached the bubble, and as Mama Dog came hustling up to me, I knew a pack of stray dogs wouldn't be too far behind her. I reached down to pet her as she panted, and we strolled along in the darkness together, not particularly worried about anything. Even after nearly two years, Bulgaria still hadn't ceased to amaze me, and I figured it'd be a long time before it ever would.

EPILOGUE

"The cost for this ride will be 15 *leva*," the cab driver declared in English.

"I'd like you to turn on the meter, please," I responded.

"I will turn on meter if you like, but if I turn on meter, I will drive in circles until meter reaches 15 *leva*," the cab driver shot back without hesitation.

I laughed, not sure what else to do. If this had happened to me when I'd first arrived in Bulgaria, I would've been angry, and determined to come up with some futile attempt to show him how corrupt he was. But I only had two weeks left in Bulgaria, and I was in a taxi headed to the Varna train station after enjoying a sun-splashed weekend on Black Sea beaches. Not interested in driving around in circles, I gave in and decided to be agreeable, if not pathetic.

"Okay, then, I guess I'll be paying 15 *leva*."

"Good," he said cheerfully, and turned to face me as we were stopped at a red light. "So, how you like my country?"

There were many things that came to mind at that moment, and most of them centered on corruption, dishonesty and cheating. I'd just read the morning newspaper where a new poll announced that 20 percent of eligible voters indicated they'd be willing to sell their vote in the upcoming EU parliamentary election. The 20 percent figure seemed high to begin with, but then I realized that the 20 percent that was reported was only the 20 percent of the people who were willing to admit this. The percentage of those who would do it but weren't willing to admit it publicly had to be even higher. Amidst all of this—and most pressing at the moment was this ridiculous cab driver—I reminded myself that I had two weeks left in Bulgaria, and I'd just spent the weekend sipping delicious Bulgarian *Mavrud* wine. I didn't really want to focus on the negatives.

"Bulgaria is wonderful," I finally replied. "Beautiful mountains, beautiful beaches."

"Yes, yes," the driver was satisfied, "this so true, so true."

I was more content drifting off into reflection, and, thankfully the cab driver was content with my answer and the fact that he was ripping me off for the cab ride. We didn't need to speak any more. I knew I was being ripped off, but I just sat back and smiled, intrigued once again by the wonder of Bulgaria. Just after announcing that he was going to gouge me and take my money one way or another, the cab driver was eager to know what I thought of his country. He didn't seem even slightly concerned that his actions could be a reflection of his country. It hadn't entered his consciousness that I would be irked by the raw deal I was receiving as a foreigner in this taxi. He fully expected me to say great things about his country even though I was in the middle of an exchange that symbolized what was wrong with his country.

I'd told him Bulgaria was wonderful, though, and I wasn't lying. Despite—or maybe even because of—bizarre situations like this, Bulgaria really was wonderful. The beaches and mountains were beautiful. And every day seemed to present a new paradox, a new opportunity to learn and, on the good days, new ways to appreciate the differences.

Life after basketball season had given me a chance to enjoy Bulgaria in more conventional ways by being a tourist on the weekends. I was able to visit some of Bulgaria's most treasured spots from the Black Sea beaches, to the one-of-a-kind Rila Monastery to the tiny historic town of Koprivshtitsa, to the Shipka Pass, where Bulgaria first earned its freedom from the Ottoman Empire. But as much as I was enjoying the freedom to enjoy Bulgaria, eating *shopska* salads and drinking *Mavrud* wine without the responsibility of a basketball team weighing down on me, I realized that no Bulgarian experience could ever compete with being a basketball coach. No matter how much beauty and intrigue I found in the country as a tourist, it couldn't hold a candle to what I'd found as a basketball coach.

In May, Menkov, Vassy and Kosio graduated and all started focusing on how their lives would change immensely with a complete change of scenery at a university in another country. Menkov was headed to Italy while Vassy and Kosio were headed to England. Dimov was the other senior on the team who was graduating and taking the leap to leave the country, but he never spoke to me again after I kicked him off the team. I never found out where he went to university.

In July, Boyko Borisov, in tough-guy fashion, trounced the incumbent Sergei Stanishev to become the new prime minister of Bulgaria. He promised sweeping changes and an end to the corruption that had plagued Bulgaria for so long. I couldn't help but wonder if he'd have a chat with my taxi driver in Varna, or if I would've had to bribe the customs' officers to receive my Christmas presents under Boyko's watch.

Soon after Borisov's election, Svetla survived her first airplane ride, and didn't find European or American airports too daunting. She earned a full scholarship to an elite New England liberal arts college and declared a double major of psychology and Russian. Other than having to endure the snowy tribulations of winter in New England, Svetla would update me on how much she was enjoying life in the States, saying her only real nemesis was her Russian professor who insisted on referring to Bulgarian as a "peasant language." I still receive Christmas wishes from her mother's fifth grade class every year–although of course, they're now older.

The Character Counts Club dissolved after I left, much to the delight of the Bulgarian assistant principal, who was so concerned that ACS was going to be inundated with communist propaganda. At the same time, the Bulgarian national soccer team would continue their cycle of hiring new coaches, hoping to find the magic of 1994 once again. When a new coach was hired, he would inevitably promise to convince Dimitar Berbatov to re-join the national team, and this would inevitably end in failure. Berbatov would not return.

When I left Bulgaria for good, I knew I was leaving the basketball team in good hands. I knew Branch would approach the next season with just as much, or more, vigor than that with which I had tackled the last two years. While the loss of Menkov in particular was going to be difficult to deal with, he still had a solid core of players. Pavel, Pesho, Ivan and Sasho would all be back for their senior season, and all had gained valuable experience as sophomores and juniors. Thinking of all of them had made it so difficult for me to decide to leave.

To add to the mix, Stefan returned from his year studying in the

States and would be able to anchor the point guard position, perhaps filling Menkov's shoes. Stefan raved about his time in the States, saying he couldn't believe how academically and athletically driven his school was. This wasn't a complaint, though; he enjoyed the intensity. In fact, the only complaint I heard from Stefan when he returned to Bulgaria in June was about the one thing he loved the most, basketball. He'd been cut from the JV team and didn't get a chance to play competitive basketball in America. He had emailed me regularly throughout the school year to tell me about life in the States, and always wanted to hear about the results of our games. The only break in emailing we had was right around the time of basketball tryouts, when I assumed he couldn't stomach writing about getting cut, and getting his heart broken in the process.

For their senior year, there were possibly even more highs than we'd had the year previous, and Branch would keep me updated via email about how things were going. My heart leapt out of my chest the following February when he emailed me to report the final score from their game against the same Romanian school that had crushed us the year before. In a stunning upset—to probably everyone's surprise except for members of the ACS team—the final score was ACS 49, Romania 47. Pesho made two free throws with 30 seconds left to win the game. The same Romanian coach was furious this had happened and demanded a rematch be played on Sunday, the following day. But the bus back to Bulgaria was leaving early in the morning and the players had a long ride home to savor the victory.

ACS hosted an international tournament, and the Romania experience had certainly had a positive effect on all those who had been so stubborn or hesitant to host the year before. Pesho, Pavel and Ivan— among several others—each hosted student athletes from Macedonia to ensure that ACS could host an international tournament.

In a Sofia tournament hosted by the other American school, ACS advanced to the championship game against a team that only had five players. The other team asked Branch if he had extra players on the bench who wouldn't mind switching teams to get a chance to play a little bit more. Branch didn't see the harm in it, and gave the opposing coach two players who indicated they'd be eager to play since they hadn't played much in the tournament. The ACS team still figured this would be an easy victory, and didn't take the game seriously. As a result, they fell behind early and could never catch up. In the end, they lost this championship because of a lack of hustle and desire, but the fingers immediately pointed at the two players who'd been willing to play for the other team. Branch continued to point out that the only place the blame should lie is on the players who assumed victory was a given, and that anger shouldn't be projected onto two players who had little to do with the outcome anyway. It had been a year of many successes, but he still had no choice but to comment on the challenge he was facing: "So, we took a step forward with the hosting in the international tournament in the weeks before," he wrote to me, "but then that Bulgaria monster reared its ugly head with how they acted after this loss."

Then in the ACS Open, this time 35th and Spanish were paired up against each other in the semifinals, and ACS advanced to the finals relatively easily for the long-awaited match-up with 35th. After a furious comeback from an 11-point deficit, ACS tied the game at 62 with 10 seconds left. But then ACS inbounded the ball to Sasho who was called for a traveling violation. When 35th got their last chance, they fed the ball inside to one of their post players. He made a move to the basket, missed a shot close in—a shot he should've made—and the whistle blew late. The clock showed only two seconds to go in the game. Once again in the waning moments, the foul was called on ACS. The 35th big man made one of two free throws and the game was over. Yet again, ACS had lost by one point. Branch's email to me was entitled "Heartbreak," and he wrote words that I could completely empathize with: "I really thought we were going to pull it off.... Toughest loss ever."

Branch's tenure in Bulgaria ended up lasting one year longer than mine; he stayed a third year before moving on to Shanghai, China to see what basketball was like in that part of the world. His graduating seniors from 2010 also moved on to places all over the world. Stefan earned a scholarship to an Ivy League school, where he took his basketball skills and his long distance running talents and turned himself into a club volleyball player. When I emailed him to ask him about some of his reflections about playing basketball at ACS, he wrote back with five pages of Microsoft Word text, 10-pt. font. Because of the challenges he learned to love facing in basketball, he wrote, he is "not afraid to sign up for the most challenging classes if I know they will help me with my future endeavors, because through hard work, I believe I can achieve any goal. (It might take running a few hundred suicides, though....)"

I also received three pages of writing from Menkov in Italy. In each email he'd send me, the first or second line would include the phrase, "I really miss basketball at ACS." In one of his responses, he would go on to talk about how often he'd reflect on his time as a basketball player in high school: "Nowadays that basketball does not take such a big part in my life I clearly see what it gave me."

Sasho also earned a scholarship, and his was also to a college in Italy. In his first year on his university basketball team, Sasho's team moved into first place toward the end of the season. He emailed me to say that he'd been interviewed by a local journalist who asked when he started playing basketball. He told them he'd never really played before his sophomore year at ACS, but he's loved it ever since. Pavel headed off to a Western European university to study hospitality management, while Pesho and Ivan were off to different universities in England.

From Ecuador to China to the U.S. to England to Italy, it was clear that life was carving out different paths for everyone involved in this story. But no matter where each of us ended up, it was also clear that we would all carry memories with us of something that was at times frustrating, at times astounding, at times confusing, and at times exhilarating, but ultimately an incredibly momentous experience. After all, we'd been a part of something truly Bulgarian.

Works Cited

Print Sources

Crampton, R.J. *Oxford History of Modern Europe: Bulgaria*. Oxford: Oxford University Press, 2009. Print.

Foer, Franklin. *How Soccer Explains the World: An Unlikely Theory of Globalization*. New York: Harper Perennial, 2005. Print.

Kaplan, Robert D. *Balkan Ghosts: A Journey Through History*. New York: Vintage Departures, 1994. Print

Kassabova, Kapka. *Street Without a Name: Childhood and Other Misadventures in Bulgaria*. New York: Skyhorse Publishing, 2009. Print.

Reid, Robert, and Pettersen, Leif. *Lonely Planet Romania and Moldova*. London: Lonely Planet, 2007. Print.

Watkins, Richard, and Deliso, Chris. *Lonely Planet Bulgaria*. London: Lonely Planet, 2008. Print.

Online Sources

"1989: Romania's 'first couple' executed." *BBC On This Day*. BBC, n.d. Web. 11 June 2011.

"All Gone: Entire Bulgarian weightlifting team removed after doping cases." *CNNSI.com*. CNN Sports Illustrated, 09 November, 2000. Web. 17 September 2010.

Andric, Gordana. "City of the Tsars." *Belgrade Insight*. Balkan Insight, 10 April 2011. Web. 17 April 2011.

Archer, Michael. "David Cerny's EU artwork might be a hoax, but it's still art." *Guardian.co.uk.* The Guardian. 14 January 2009. Web. 01 June 2011.

Associated Press. "Romania: Death of a Dictator." *Los Angeles Times*. Los Angeles Times, 26 December 1989. Web. 07 June 2011.

"Balkan Blushes: The European Union softens its criticisms of Bulgaria and Romania." *The Economist*. The Economist, 24 July 2008. Web. 19 December 2010.

"Berbatov at the centre of kidnapping plot." *Soccer Portal: Live Football Blog*. 01 December 2009. Web. 07 November 2010.

Bilefsky, Dan. "Memo From Sofia: Without Gas, Bulgarians Turn Icy to Old Ally." *New York Times*. New York Times, 12 January 2009. Web. 12 January 2009.

Bivol, Alex. "EU ready to ostracise Bulgaria–report." *The Sofia Echo*. Sofia Echo Media, 10 May 2008. Web. 10 May 2008.

"Bulgaria." *New York Times World*. New York Times, 6 July 2009. Web. 17 November 2010.

Brunwasser, Matthew. "A Book Peels Back Some Layers of a Cold War Mystery." *The New York Times*. The New York Times, 10 September 2008. Web. 10 September 2008.

Carvajal, Doreen, and Castle, Stephen. "Mob Muscles Its Way Into Politics in Bulgaria." *The New York Times*. The New York Times, 16 October 2008. Web. 16 October 2008.

Drakulic, Slavenka. "Grand coup de toilette." *Guardian.co.uk.* The Guardian, 18 January 2009. Web. 01 June 2011.

Gardner, David. "British woman mauled to death by wild street dogs in Bulgaria died in husband's arms." *Mail Online*. The Daily Mail, 29 November 2007. Web. 25 May 2011.

Hershman, Gabriel. "Efforts at truth." *The Sofia Echo.* Sofia Echo Media, 22 October 2010. Web. 22 October 2010.

Hershman, Gabriel. "Socialist Romanticism." *The Sofia Echo.* Sofia Echo Media, 20 August 2010. Web. 07 September 2010.

Iliev, Nick. "Adolf Hitler billboards briefly go up Sofia." *The Sofia Echo.* Sofia Echo Media, 08 April 2009. Web. 08 April 2009.

Iliev, Nick. "Bulgarian dental association up in arms against JCBA dentists." *The Sofia Echo.* Sofia Echo Media, 18 April 2011. Web. 18 April 2011.

Iliev, Nick. "Shocking reality of Sofia schools–Europe's worst." *The Sofia Echo.* Sofia Echo Media, 06 October 2008. Web. 08 October 2008.

Iliev, Nick. "Two-thirds of Bulgarians say life is unbearable." *The Sofia Echo.* Sofia Echo Media, 28 May 2010. Web. 10 October 2010.

Jones, Tim. "Bulgaria: It's Europe's Wild East." *Chicago Tribune.* Chicago Tribune, 22 June 2008. Web 22 June 2008.

Kimmelman, Michael. "Abroad: Take my Bulgarian Joke Book. Please." *The New York Times.* The New York Times, 31 October 2010. Web. 01 November 2010.

Kostadinov, Petar. "Bulgaria goes down in Transparency International's corruption index." *The Sofia Echo.* Sofia Echo Media, 23 September 2008. Web. 23 September 2008.

Kostadinov, Petar. "Eleven Bulgarian weightlifters to miss Beijing Olympics." *The Sofia Echo.* Sofia Echo Media, 27 June 2008. Web. 07 November 2010.

Kostadinov, Petar. "End of kidnapping drama." *The Sofia Echo.* Sofia Echo Media, 30 July 2008. Web. 07 November 2010.

Kostadinov, Petar. "EU anti-fraud experts ripped off by a Bulgarian taxi driver." *The Sofia Echo*. Sofia Echo Media, 03 April 2009. Web. 03 April 2009.

Kostadinov, Petar. "Kidnapping insurance makes debut in Bulgaria." *The Sofia Echo*. Sofia Echo Media, 13 May 2009. Web. 13 May 2009.

Kostadinov, Petar. "Sofia mayor calls the Prime Minister a coward." *The Sofia Echo*. Sofia Echo Media, 23 March 2009. Web. 23 March 2009.

Kostadinov, Petar. "The deadly game." *The Sofia Echo*. Sofia Echo Media, 31 October 2008. Web. 07 November 2010.

Kostadinov, Petar. "Two-time world champion ice skater Maxim Staviski will not go to jail." *The Sofia Echo*. Sofia Echo Media, 12 May 2009. Web. 17 September 2010.

Kubosova, Lucia. "EU faces big Roma question after 2007 enlargement." *EUobserver.com*. EUobserver.com, 29 June 2006. Web. 23 June 2011.

Lebor, Adam. "Bucharest: Paris of the East looks westward." *The Independent*. The Independent, 29 January 1999. Web. 11 June 2011.

Leviev-Sawyer, Clive. "Totalitarianism and Todor: Bulgaria grapples with communist legacy." *The Sofia Echo*. Sofia Echo Media, 19 November 2010. Web. 22 June 2011.

"Remembering the Prague Spring." *BBC News*. BBC Online Network, 21 August 1998. Web. 21 September 2010.

Smith, Nicola. "A local Le Pen in race for President." *Times Online*. The Times, 1 October 2006. Web. 22 November 2010.

Sofia News Agency. "Bulgaria Bows to Stefan Stambolov: Founder of the Modern State." *Novinite.com*, Sofia News Agency, 30 January

2010. Web. 17 November 2011.

Sofia News Agency. "Police Want Unknown 'Vandal' Decorator of Sofia Soviet Army Monument." *Novinite.com*, Sofia News Agency, 18 June 2011. Web. 18 June 2011.

"The American College of Sofia History." The American College of Sofia Website. n.d. Web. 17 November 2010.

The International Committee for Bulgarian Holocaust-Era Truth. "End Bulgaria's whitewashing of Holocaust Truth." *The Sofia Echo*. Sofia Echo Media, 18 February 2011. Web. 18 February 2011.

"The People's Palace Bucharest." *Bucharest-Life.com*. Romania Travel Guide, n.d. Web. 11 June 2011.

"The rich, the poor, and Bulgaria: Money really can buy you happiness." *The Economist*. The Economist, 16 December 2010. Web. 18 December 2010.

The Sofia Echo Staff. "Bulgaria geared for demographic collapse by 2060." *The Sofia Echo*. Sofia Echo Media, 09 June 2011. Web. 09 June 2011.

The Sofia Echo Staff. "Bulgarian population shrank by 582,000 in a decade." *The Sofia Echo*. Sofia Echo Media, 05 April 2011. Web. 05 April 2011.

The Sofia Echo Staff. "Bulgarian population shrinks by about 600,000." *The Sofia Echo*. Sofia Echo Media, 01 March 2011. Web. 01 March 2011.

The Sofia Echo Staff. "CSKA on the rocks." *The Sofia Echo*. Sofia Echo Media, 29 October 2010. Web. 04 November 2010.

The Sofia Echo Staff. "Dimitar Berbatov quit Bulgarian team because of insults." *The Sofia Echo*. Sofia Echo Media, 29 September 2010. Web. 04 October 2010.

The Sofia Echo Staff. "Former interior minister: 'Scum' like James Warlick will be leaving soon. *The Sofia Echo*. Sofia Echo Media, 16 May 2011. Web. 16 May 2011.

The Sofia Echo Staff. "More trouble with stray dogs." *The Sofia Echo*. Sofia Echo Media, 14 February 2011. Web. 22 June 2011.

The Sofia Echo Staff. "Official: Bulgarian traffic police get more than 100,000 bribes a year." *The Sofia Echo*. Sofia Echo Media, 16 November 2010. Web. 22 June 2011.

The Sofia Echo Staff. "Romania declares war on stray dogs–report." *The Sofia Echo*. Sofia Echo Media, 07 April 2011. Web. 23 June 2011.

The Sofia Echo Staff. "State of affairs." *The Sofia Echo*. Sofia Echo Media, 04 December 2009. Web. 06 December 2009.

Toshkov, Veselin. "Bulgaria's Black Market in Blood is Flourishing." *HuffPost World*. The Huffington Post. 23 May 2011. Web. 24 May 2011.

16388129R00254

Made in the USA
Charleston, SC
17 December 2012